GIL HODGES

GIL HODGES

THE BROOKLYN BUMS, THE MIRACLE METS, AND THE EXTRAORDINARY LIFE OF A BASEBALL LEGEND

TOM CLAVIN
and
DANNY PEARY

NEW AMERICAN LIBRARY

New American Library
Published by the Penguin Group
Penguin Group (USA) Inc., 375 Hudson Street,
New York, New York 10014, USA

USA | Canada | UK | Ireland | Australia | New Zealand | India | South Africa | China

Penguin Books Ltd., Registered Offices: 80 Strand, London WC2R 0RL, England
For more information about the Penguin Group visit penguin.com.

Published by New American Library, a division of Penguin Group (USA) Inc.
Previously published in a New American Library hardcover edition.

First New American Library Trade Paperback Printing, August 2013

 REGISTERED TRADEMARK—MARCA REGISTRADA

NEW AMERICAN LIBRARY TRADE PAPERBACK ISBN: 978-0-451-23994-5

THE LIBRARY OF CONGRESS CATALOGED THE HARDCOVER EDITION OF THIS TITLE AS FOLLOWS:
Clavin, Thomas
Gil Hodges:the Brooklyn bums, the miracle Mets, and the extraordinary
life of a baseball legend/Tom Clavin and Danny Peary.
p. cm.
ISBN 978-0-451-23586-2 (hardback)
1. Hodges, Gil, 1924–1972. 2. Baseball players—United States—Biography.
I. Peary, Danny, 1949– II. Title.
GV865.H57C53   2012   796.357092—dc23
[B]

Set in Adobe Caslon Pro
Designed by Elke Sigal

ALWAYS LEARNING   PEARSON

146119709

To Leslie, and her Midwood High friends
T.C.

To Suzanne, our daughter Zoe, and
granddaughter Julianna . . . and everybody else who knows
Gil Hodges deserves to be in the Hall of Fame
D.P.

GIL HODGES

PRELUDE

Gil Hodges smiled, which was a big deal. The New York Mets manager had been stoic for 8⅔ innings of the fifth game of the 1969 World Series, just as he'd been for every game for the entire season as his team attempted to perform a miracle. Now, on October 16, at precisely 3:07 p.m., with his team one out away from a decisive fourth victory against the heavily favored Baltimore Orioles, he smiled slightly, because the biggest play, the greatest moment in Mets history, was unfurling before his eyes and he saw there was nothing to worry about. It wasn't the 1951 playoff, he wasn't a Brooklyn Dodger, and the Giants' Bobby Thomson hadn't just taken a mighty swing in the Polo Grounds.

The noise from the cheering, clapping, and stomping of the 57,375 deliriously happy fans that cool Thursday afternoon at Shea Stadium was so deafening that it's unlikely Hodges heard the crack of the bat as Orioles second baseman Davey Johnson put good wood on Jerry Koosman's fastball. But the forty-five-year-old had been playing and managing major-league baseball for twenty-two years and didn't need sound enhancement. He could tell how far the ball would go better than the delighted Johnson, who thought he'd never hit a ball so hard in his life, or the panicked Koosman, who thought it might clear the left-field fence for a game-tying two-run homer when he heard the crowd simultaneously roar and gasp.

Fortunately, Mets left fielder Cleon Jones also judged the flight of the ball correctly. Not realizing that the security guards had failed to unlock the bullpen gate he planned to use to escape the fans who were already storming the field, Jones tranquilly camped under the ball in front of the warning track. He thought to himself, *Come on down, baby, come on down; it's all over.* It came down, he squeezed it, and it was all over. Mets 5, Orioles 3. The New York Mets were the world champions of baseball.

As the ecstatic Mets players soared into the air, thousands of fans hurdled the railings and proceeded to rip apart the field and claw up home plate, and security guards escorted Mets' wives and family members through special doors and gates to safety. Gil Hodges calmly offered and accepted congratulatory handshakes in the dugout and then made his way into the clubhouse. His smile was broader now, yet still not as expansive as when he marched into the clubhouse after the Brooklyn Dodgers won their only championship in 1955. Was he being this reserved—while his fans were partying outside and his players around him were pouring champagne on one another's heads— because this victory wasn't as meaningful?

Minutes later, as he praised the organization, his coaches, and his team's unity and work ethic to the media, he was cheerful but not much more enthusiastic than a poker player who'd won a small pot. But what no one saw, his brother-in-law Louis Lombardi recalls, "was that Gil was shaking so badly from his emotions when he came into the clubhouse that Joe Pignatano, his coach and close friend, whisked him into another room and shut the door until he calmed down and was able to talk to the press." Ever the professional, Hodges didn't want anyone to see beneath the surface.

In truth, winning the 1969 title was Hodges' crowning achievement. His shocking death on Easter Sunday in 1972 would be devastating to his family, friends, and fans who loved him, but there was comfort in knowing that he had accomplished the ultimate in his career. He'd had many meaningful moments since he was an All-Star first baseman for the fabled Brooklyn Dodgers when they battled the New York Giants and New York Yankees for championships and the hearts and minds of the city's rabid fans in the late forties and fifties. But this was extraordinary. A Mets team that no one would compare to those great Dodgers teams, that had barely eluded last place in Hodges' previous year as its manager, and that was generously tabbed one-hundred-to-one underdogs to win it all at the beginning of his second season was going to be fitted for World Series rings.

Since Hodges was too modest to praise himself, it would be left to his star players, including Koosman, Jones, center fielder Tommie Agee, Cy Young winner Tom Seaver, and others to state that the primary reason the Mets were champions was their manager. Yet he definitely felt tremendous pride and fulfillment in their accomplishment, because he had given his players his complete energy, effort, and knowledge to ensure their success. He had taken every moment he observed and experienced as a player from 1947 to early 1963. He had taken everything he absorbed from teammates, coaches, and managers Leo Durocher, Burt Shotton, Charlie Dressen, Walter Alston, and Casey Stengel. He had taken what he learned in his years as a young manager with the Washington Senators and then the Mets. Finally, he had taken his belief in what was the *right way* to conduct oneself in work, sports, and life. All this he instilled in his young men, having to force-feed the ones who weren't immediately receptive. The '69 Mets understood that they didn't win because of talent alone. Hodges had helped them build character, which was his strong suit, a product of his upbringing.

Hodges lived in Brooklyn for nearly twenty-five years, and was associated chiefly with the Dodgers and Mets, yet, as his wife, Joan Hodges, a native of the borough, points out, "Indiana was his home."

There are two towns in the southwest corner of the Hoosier state that claim Gil Hodges. Princeton and Petersburg are about twenty-five miles and—due to morning fogs, starless nights, and a high speed limit on twisting country roads—an often harrowing thirty-five-minute drive apart. Petersburg, which was founded in 1817, a year after Indiana was admitted to the union, is the seat of Pike County and is on eastern standard time. Incorporated in 1818, the larger Princeton, to the southwest, is the seat of Gibson County and is on central standard time. There has never been more than a placid rivalry between the two towns, but if they have been a bit competitive in honoring Hodges, it's understandable. After all, the revered Hoosier spent the first eight years of his life in Princeton and the rest of his youth in Petersburg.

"We in Princeton recognize that Gil Hodges considered Petersburg his hometown and that he became a star athlete there," says retired youth coach Tim Nonte, a member of the Indiana High School Baseball Hall of Fame.

"But we'd like some recognition because he was born here and played his final year of Legion ball here. If Princeton wants to claim part of him, it's because there was nobody with finer character than Gil Hodges."

In almost every instance, character is molded during one's formative years and continues to develop and be modified as the individual enters adulthood and matures. But in the rare case of Gil Hodges, his fine character, which would rub off on all the young Mets, was a fait accompli before he finished high school. Hodges became wiser with age and experience and increasingly exhibited a *gravitas* that he thought befitted his adult responsibilities—surely to the detriment of his health, because he exhibited no emotions while the pressures built inside him—yet the man he became had the identical character as the youngster he had been. He could very well have been father to that boy. Growing up in the Midwest, in two mining towns in Indiana, this congenial and kind, witty but quiet, annoyingly stubborn, deeply moral Catholic boy firmly believed he found the *right way* to lead his life, and he *never* deviated from that very straight and very narrow path. Residents of both Petersburg and Princeton tend to boast that "Gil Hodges never forgot *where* he came from," but of equal significance is that he never forgot *who* he was.

PART I

From Princeton to the Pacific

CHAPTER ONE

If you were a red-blooded American boy growing up in the 1920s and 1930s, chances are you thrilled to the exploits of young Frank Merriwell in Burt L. Standish's numerous books and short stories that had been published since the 1890s; in a popular comic strip, on radio, and even in a movie serial. Even in southwest Indiana. Gil Hodges' major influences on how to conduct his life were surely his parents, Charlie and Irene, and his coaches, teachers, and priests in Princeton and Petersburg, but perhaps he drew some inspiration from the all-American boy because they were similar.

Class aside, Gil and his one-year-older brother, Bob, were very much the human counterparts for the fictional half brothers Frank and Dick Merriwell. They too were young gentlemen who were paragons of virtue, never swayed from their ideals, believed in God and country, never questioned authority, and did what was expected of them without complaining, bragging, or seeking praise. They also were too honorable to accept a tainted victory and, significantly, overcame obstacles to smash game-winning home runs, convert buzzer-beating baskets, and score go-ahead touchdowns as time expired.

Both Gil and Bob were born in Princeton, adding to the population of about 7,200. Their father, Charlie, grandfather Charles Hodges, and great-grandfather David Hodges also were born in this town that was thirty miles north of Evansville and surrounded by rich farmlands and productive coal mines. In 1898, thirty-two-year-old Charles married the boys' grandmother, thirty-three-year-old Mary Ella Manns. From a previous marriage, she had four children—Carrie, Agnes, Arvil, and Ed. She doubled that total with her second husband, giving birth to Ada in 1899, Charlie—who was called by his middle name, Piram—on January 3, 1901, Lottie in 1904, and Paul in 1906.

According to the 1910 census, Mary Hodges worked as a laundress at home, at 812 South Hart Street, and Charles and youngsters Arvil and Ed were laborers who did "odd jobs." When Ed got a bit older, Mary often sent Piram to coax him home from illegal poker games. In 1914, Ed was shot and killed after accusing a young cardplayer of cheating. The incident sparked a public outcry to make arrests and shut down gambling establishments. Two years later, fifteen-year-old Piram received a permit to work in one of the deep-vein coal mines near Princeton.

Charles, who found financial security working for the Greer-Wilkinson Lumber Company, succumbed to the same influenza epidemic that took the life of Princeton's popular mayor, Ernest E. Noble, in 1919. Mary had stomach cancer for three years and died a few months after her husband. She was buried next to Charles in the Oak Hill Cemetery in Patoka, outside Princeton.

His siblings moved away, but Charlie, as the eighteen-year-old Piram now called himself, remained in Princeton. Tall, slim, and handsome, he resembled the young and beardless Abe Lincoln, except that Charlie was a Democrat because of that party's advocacy of unions and miners' rights. As tough as bedrock and already with several years' experience, he couldn't imagine another line of work but mining. A photograph taken of Charlie and the rest of his crew at the mouth of the deep Princeton Mine in the aftermath of a cave-in that spared them all appeared in the *Princeton Daily Clarion* in 1922, the same year he married.

Irene Horstmeyer was born on July 20, 1904, in Winslow, about twenty-five miles southeast of Princeton. Like Charlie, she was Irish-German and a Catholic. Her father, Arthur, was born in Washington, north of Petersburg, in 1869. Seven years later Irene's mother, Ellen, was born in Kentucky to Bart and Bridget McCarthy Stinson. Red-haired Ellen, who people said looked distinctly Irish, was seventeen when she married Arthur in 1893. She bore him four children before the turn of the century, three of whom survived. Irene was her first daughter. When Irene met Charlie she was attending Winslow High, an excellent student with college potential. She was a little over five feet tall and of medium build, with brown eyes and red hair that she always curled above her shoulders.

Irene's father might have introduced her to Charlie. Arthur was the boss at a coal mine, and most of the miners in the area knew one another. Also their paths might have crossed on Sundays, because the baseball-obsessed Charlie played semipro ball for his employer's team against other mine-company teams. He had the reputation in Gibson and Pike counties for being a solid hitter and good first baseman. "I guess I was, too," he told sportswriter Harold Rosenthal in 1951, "before I got butchered in the mines."

Charlie, twenty-one, and Irene, eighteen, married when she graduated from high school. They rented a small house at 229 South Gibson Street in Princeton, and were living there on January 27, 1923, when they became parents for the first time. They named their child Charles, but his middle name was Robert, and he'd always go by Bob or Bobby.

Gil Ray Hodges was delivered by the same doctor thirteen months later, at 4:05 a.m. on April 4, 1924. The Hodges family lived at 521 East Broadway, two blocks from the town square, but relocated to 230 North Ford Street, perhaps because of the Great Tri-State Tornado of 1925, which damaged or destroyed half the town and killed more than thirty-five citizens. By the time Marjorie was born on April 11, 1929, the Hodges family had changed residences again to 866 North Hart Street.

Marjorie, who was listed as Margery Ellen when baptized, was Charlie and Irene's last child. On her birth certificate, it states that she was Irene's fourth child and third living child. "We always heard that there was a little boy born between Uncle Gil and Aunt Marge," says Ann Hodges, one of Bob's daughters, "but nobody knew what happened to him." What happened is that Kenneth was born on July 2, 1926, but died that October 22 after a two-week bout with whooping cough. Infant mortality was so high that there was a special row of graves for Catholic children at the St. Joseph Cemetery. (In 2011, Ann and her brother John purchased a headstone for their uncle's unmarked grave.)

A few years later, Bob almost died as well, from pneumonia, and was bedridden for some time. "That's why he and Uncle Gil ended up in the same class at school," explains Ann Hodges, "although Dad was one year older."

Gil, who was baptized in 1927, and Bob attended St. Joseph's School and St. Joseph's Church on South Race Street, where they went to Mass every Sunday without fail and heard sermons against wanton behavior. The mannerly brothers' lone indiscretion, always a secret, came on Halloween, when they turned over an outhouse and slipped a running garden hose through the principal's basement window.

The brown-haired, blue-eyed boys, who looked almost like twins when they were very young, were best friends and did everything together, including their religious training and learning sports. "We grew up playing all games, and especially baseball," Gil Hodges said in 1960. "Dad would take the neighborhood kids out on the street and coach us. He never played favorites among us, or compared us to other kids, saying, 'Why don't you do as well as them?'"

As Charlie taught his sons baseball, he was pleased that they both revealed talent, Bob in particular. Maybe they could follow in the footsteps of the area's biggest sports idol, Oakland City's Edd Roush, who in 1931 concluded his eighteen-year major-league career, mostly as an outfielder with the Cincinnati Reds, with a robust .323 lifetime average.

It was while playing baseball that Gil first exhibited that he was heeding the lessons about honesty, responsibility, and good citizenship that were being taught at church, school, and home. In 1969, Mabel Sisson, the widow of Gil's 1941 American Legion coach Eldon Sisson, wrote in the *Princeton Daily Clarion* of the boy's George Washington cherry-tree moment: "Gil and my son Darwin Sisson formed a baseball team of the neighborhood kids. We had rather a large side yard so my husband told them to play there since it was safer than in the street, but if any windows were broken the boys must replace them. They all agreed. There were some pretty rowdy games at times and when I heard the crash I knew it was our neighbor's window. Gil and Darwin were the only boys to be found when I went to inspect the damage. They knew there would be no more games until the windowpane was replaced. It wasn't long until each boy came back and I remember Gil saying: 'Team! We made a promise, we need practice, so bring your money if you want to play.'"

Princeton had been experiencing a period of growth, but like so many towns in the area, it was decimated by the 1929 stock market crash. "There was no money in Princeton, period," recalls Bud Howe, who would play ball with the Hodges brothers in the 1930s. "Bean sandwiches, peanut butter, and applesauce were pretty good foods back in those days. I'd go shoot rabbits in the ditch by the school building, eat some and sell the others. Even when we were hungry, we played ball to pass the time. There was no money to replace a baseball when its cover got ripped, so we'd just tape it up. When we broke a bat, we'd tape that up too."

Several mines in the county shut down, adding to the escalating unemployment. Charlie was more fortunate than most because he had a steady job as a loading operator at the Francisco Mine, which was halfway between Princeton and Oakland City, sixteen miles east. But working in the mines wreaked havoc on his health—his loud, violent, and persistent cough was his reward for inhaling coal dust for more than fifteen years—and was fraught with peril. Charlie wore glasses with one black lens after losing his right eye in a mining accident. Twice his back was broken, twice his legs. Then one night in January 1931, a machine he was moving slipped and crushed his foot. When the ambulance arrived, they found him balanced on an elbow, smoking a cigarette, and calmly telling other miners how to free him. He was whisked to the Methodist hospital in Princeton, where his father had died. The *Princeton Daily Democrat* reported the next day that the "second and third toes of the right foot were badly mashed, necessitating amputation." Another toe was mutilated as well. Charlie returned to work after a few weeks of convalescence. He was resigned to a career in the mines, but his mantra was, "Charlie Hodges' boys will never work the shafts."

"He was the most injured coal miner of all time," Gil Hodges told Tom Fox of the *Sporting News* in 1963. What made the biggest impression on Charlie's son was that "through all his misfortune, he never complained." Gil and Bob Hodges made certain to emulate their father in this regard throughout their lives, never expressing emotions of any kind when experiencing bad times.

"My dad was not a great man in the sense you would consider a man great," Hodges told Fox. "He was just a simple coal miner; he wasn't rich and he wasn't book smart. But he knew everything about two things—baseball and coal mines. No, he wasn't a great man. He just lived greatness, if you know what I mean. He was quiet and reserved but he had more moral courage than any man I've ever known."

Charlie recalled a significant event in 1951 to Harold Rosenthal for an article about Gil in the *Saturday Evening Post*: "The mine was having all kinds of bad luck, and there ain't nothing you can do when things just go against you in this business. We had cave-ins and all sorts of trouble. One morning I was in the wash house changing my clothes, getting ready to go down. They'd taken two loads down when suddenly I hear this sort of explosion. I turned to the next fellow and said, 'There ain't no use your changing your clothes. That durned operator has run his elevator right up through the tipple.' Then I look out the door and there are flames shooting a hundred feet in the air. We lose thirty-seven men in that one, and right after that they give up and no one has worked the mine since."

Suddenly out of work and with a family to feed, Charlie, now thirty, packed up everyone and made the short trip to Pike County, where eventually more than a third of the land would be excavated for coal. He had the sterling reputation in southwest Indiana for being accomplished at his job and getting along with his fellow workers, so he didn't have long to wait before the Ingle Coal Corporation hired him to work a mine in Ayrshire. It was only a fifteen-minute drive from the large hospitable town of Petersburg, so that was where he moved his family.

CHAPTER TWO

When Pike County was hit by the Depression, Petersburg experienced rough times, but its small, tight-knit community was resilient and resourceful, and a sense of normalcy was maintained. The nearly three thousand citizens, exhibiting no self-pity (a trait the Hodges family shared), tightened their belts and counted pennies and simply carried on, never acknowledging the wolf at their doors. According to Randy Harris, the mayor of Petersburg from 1992 to 2004 and a local historian, the primary reason the town didn't go into panic mode was because "it was poor, Depression or not. It wasn't impacted by the stock market crash like New York and other big cities were. Petersburg still had vegetable gardens and the rest of America still needed coal."

Money was in short supply, but the classrooms at school were still full; people still went to church *en masse* every Sunday; most shops remained open on Main Street; men still made regular visits to barbershops and women to beauty parlors; toe-tapping teenagers gathered around jukeboxes and deposited the nickels and dimes they had earned mowing lawns, chopping wood, shining shoes, packing groceries, and sweeping stockrooms; and everyone still went to the picture show, summer band concerts, and high school sports events. In sandlots, pastures, driveways, and the town's countless alleys, kids were still playing ball. For Bob and Gil, or "Bud," as everyone called him, Petersburg was a marvelous town in which to grow up.

Charlie rented a small house on an embankment by the railroad tracks, between North Fourth and Fifth streets on Cherry Street, "off of Prides

Creek, at the bottom of 'Goose Hill,' as the old-timers called it," says Harris. The only running water they had was the cold water in the sink. They had an outhouse, but after a few years they built a bathroom with a shower.

The house on Cherry Street was just two blocks from Main Street, and six more blocks to the Saints Peter and Paul Catholic Church, where Bob and Gil would be altar boys. Their school was one block south of Main on Walnut. There was no parochial school in the small town, just this large public school for every child who lived in Petersburg proper and on farms on the outskirts of town. First-grade through eighth-grade classes were held on the first floor of the large building. Petersburg High, ninth grade through twelfth grade, was on the second floor, and its 300 to 350 students were about one-tenth of the town's entire population.

"I was in the same class as Bud and Bob when they came to town, third or fourth grade," recalls Mary Malotte-Markham, "and we'd be in classes together until we graduated from high school. Many kids thought their last name was Hodge, which was a family nickname I think, but I knew them as Hodges. Bud was always very quiet and never got into trouble. He was never the type to talk in the back of the class, although Bob probably did that. I don't remember if Bud ever raised his hand to answer a question, but he had no problem going up to the blackboard if called upon. I don't know what grades he got, but he was very intelligent, and that really came out when he played sports and understood more than anybody else."

Like his father, Bob was gregarious in social situations and, as his son Mike contends, "never met a stranger," so he had no trouble making friends at his new school and in the neighborhood. Gil was much more reserved. The only surefire way to befriend him was to play ball with him.

"Bud, Bob, and I walked back from school together and played some games for the rest of the afternoon," recalls Arthur Beck. "They were good at everything, but they were young and Bud wasn't big yet, so I couldn't tell that they were going to be anything special as athletes. Bud really liked basketball and we played with kids from the neighborhood on the side of a garage on South Sixth Street. I thought his last name was Hodge. He wanted to be called Bud, and later we called him Moon because he had a big, round face."

Malotte-Markham, who lived on Vincennes Avenue, about two blocks from the Hodges' house, says, "The Hodges were good neighbors, and Irene was a sweet woman who was always kind to us kids. Her boys were both really nice, but it was easier to tell with Bob, because he'd stop and talk to you while Bud would just wave and walk by. That never changed. Bud was always off to play something. That's how I first got to know him. There was a big field by our house, Jimmy Higgins' Pasture, where the neighborhood kids played pickup games. Bud would come over to play football. We were not even ten and Bud wasn't any bigger than the rest of us, but I can say I played football with Gil Hodges."

New acquaintances were immediately struck by the brothers' opposite demeanors. "Bob was an extrovert and Gil was not," their sister, Marjorie, told Randy Harris in 1991 when he was the news director of WFPC Radio in Petersburg. "That's true personality-wise. Gil was much like Mother, and Bob was a lot like Dad." Ironically, at Winslow High, Irene, whom everyone characterized as being quiet and demure, had twice been president of her class and the athletic association, sang with the glee club and choir, performed in the senior play *Star Bright,* and was one of the best players on the girls' basketball team.

"I heard Grandma singing around the house sometimes," remembers Ann Hodges, who became very close to her as a young girl in the 1960s, "but she never said she did all that in school." Of her grandmother's reputation for being unwaveringly sweet, she says, "Yes, but she was tougher than people think. We grandkids knew that you did what she told you and didn't ask why." Unlike her husband, though, Irene didn't possess the lethal stop-what-you're-doing-right-now glare that would be passed along to Gil and Bob.

As sports increasingly became the focal point of Gil's and Bob's lives, their parents were unfailingly supportive. Charlie was never too tired after work to play catch with his boys or to drive them to the park so they could participate in pickup games. Unfortunately, circumstances would prevent him from seeing his kids play much organized baseball as they got older, because soon after his arrival in Petersburg, Ingle decided to make him a foreman at the Ditney Hill Mine.

"It was a fair-sized mine with a good vein of coal," recalls ninety-year-old sculptor Donald Ingle, whose father and brother ran the Evansville-based family coal business. "You could stand upright in it without hitting the ceiling. There were about a hundred and eighty miners working three shifts."

Charlie was delighted to be offered a promotion with a hike in salary, but the hitch was that the mine was in Elberfeld, which was about three times farther south than Ayrshire. He didn't want to uproot the family again or take his kids out of a school they liked so much, so his magnanimous solution was to make a slow ninety-mile round trip six days a week. Although Charlie wasn't often on the sidelines, he encouraged his athletic boys to play sports as much as possible. Bob was an all-around athlete but always favored baseball. Basketball was Gil's favorite sport, ahead of football. For much of his youth, baseball was a distant third at best, maybe behind even Ping-Pong and pool. He wasn't always eager to play, but Bob and their father could be persuasive. "Bob was a left-handed pitcher," Gil told Arnold Hano for *Sport* in 1960, "and Dad wanted to have us as a battery, so I'd catch."

Ann Hodges thinks that is the explanation for why her uncle Gil didn't share Bob's enthusiasm for baseball: "After Dad passed away, a gentleman from Petersburg said, 'Ann, your uncle Gil did not want to play baseball. Your dad would literally drag him to the field and make him play so they'd have enough players.' I asked, 'Why didn't he want to play?' He said, 'Because your dad always made him catch while he pitched. Your dad would throw his fastball and Gil would cry out, 'Stop throwing it so hard! I'm going to go home if you don't stop that!'"

The only time Gil really enjoyed playing catch was with his father. "Bud and Bob were close brothers and would do a lot together," recalls Tom O'Rourke, a neighbor of the Hodges and a future five-time mayor of Petersburg, "but on Cherry Street, Gil was always tossing a ball around with Charlie, out on the sidewalk or in their backyard."

When Bob joined in, it wasn't so pleasurable for Gil. "Gil told me that when he was just a kid, his father tried to cure him of his fear of a curveball," recalls George Harris, whose father was also a foreman at the Ditney Hill

Mine. "Charlie told him to stand up and he marked Gil's feet, putting some stakes beside him and tying his ankles to the stakes. Then he told Bob to throw at him."

In his 1969 book, *The Game of Baseball*, Gil wrote that Charlie sent his boys out to play baseball in the same casual way he would have sent them to school or the grocery. More likely Charlie had two serious intertwining motives for encouraging Bob and Gil to play as much as possible. First, he thought that they might consider baseball as a career—particularly Bob, who by his early teens had the makings of an imposing hurler, brandishing, said Gil, "a live fastball and good curve." Second, he didn't want Bob and Gil to be like the many boys in town who dutifully joined their fathers in the mines.

More than once, Charlie escorted his growing sons to the mine so they'd gain an appreciation for how hard miners worked under trying conditions. He also hoped to discourage them from pursuing a career in which their lives would be at risk every day and they'd develop chronic breathing problems like his own. "He never bossed us or tried to make us do the things he did," wrote Gil in the nonsectarian magazine *Guideposts* in 1960. "My father never let us forget that he was working in the mines so we wouldn't have to."

In 1937, Gil and Bob were among the nearly hundred students to enter Petersburg High. That winter, they eagerly joined the freshman basketball team. In the team photo, they were the boys on Doc Weathers' team with the biggest grins. They were placed in the first row, in front of the tall players. Gil, a stocky boy with thick thighs and swept-back brown hair, would benefit from having a delayed growth spurt. To compete against the bigger kids, he developed a deadly long-range, two-hand set shot and learned to dribble with both hands and employ nimble footwork to drive to the hoop. Once he became tall and brawny, he'd smoothly combine these little-man skills with his new big-man skills to be a complete player.

In the photograph of the freshman basketball team, Gil and Bob were virtually the same height. In photos of the varsity team taken two and three years later, Gil was three or four inches taller. By then he was about six-one, making him one of the tallest boys in school, hard-as-a-rock muscular, and manly-looking. Now, "the girls thought Bud was very handsome," remembers Rosemary Franklin Weathers, who was one year behind Gil in school, "and we would turn our heads when he walked by."

His hands had become so massive that they regularly drew oohs and ahhs from other kids. His coach Frank Conrad was impressed that his young player could palm the ball with either hand. "What I remember about Gil's hands," says Wayne Malotte, the brother of Mary Markham, "is that one day at Jimmy Higgins' Pasture, when we were playing baseball, he told the younger kids that he could catch them barehanded. They threw it as hard as they could and he caught every one."

"Gil became a big kid with hands like you wouldn't believe," recalls Ralph Thompson, who lived on the corner of Walnut and Fourteenth, where the Hodges family would eventually move. "One day a bunch of us kids were standing on the corner by my house. One of the boys had a pair of boxing gloves and tried to get someone to box with him. Nobody would do it. About that time Gil and Bob walked by, coming home from a movie. The kid said, 'Bud, put on the gloves with me.' He said, 'No, I don't want to fight.' The boy said, 'Aw, you're chicken. Put on the gloves.' He kept taunting him. Finally Gil put them on. I'm not sure he got those hands all the way in. This boy crouched down and put one glove in front of the other and was bobbing up and down. All of a sudden, Gil threw a punch that hit the front glove and drove it into the second glove and that glove was driven into the boy's nose. The blood just spurted and that boy dropped his gloves and turned around and walked home."

Those hands were also gentle, befitting the boy who Malotte-Markham says "wouldn't hurt a flea." O'Rourke recalls, "We didn't have school buses and all the kids had to walk quite a ways up to school, and Gil would grab the little fellows' hands and lead them." This can be seen as an early example of Gil taking on responsibilities without being asked and without expecting any commendation, a theme of his entire life.

"Saying that he was 'taking on responsibilities' is a way to define it retrospectively," says Gil Hodges Jr., "but in that moment my father was doing what was natural. His parents did a great job giving guidelines, but it was my dad who acted on his own."

Gil believed in setting a good example for younger kids, so he never lost his temper in public or cursed. But only on occasion did he take it upon himself to give advice. "I was five years younger than Gil, and just idolized him, as did all the other kids in town," says Howard Briscoe, a future coach. "When I was in junior high, a bunch of kids my age were playing basketball outside and we were swearing a little bit. Gil was walking up Eighth Street and heard us. He veered off and came up to us and said quietly, 'Boys, you don't need to talk like that.' He didn't yell at us, and that's all he said. But that had a profound effect on us, and I don't think any of us talked like that again."

There was no baseball team at Petersburg High, so Gil played sandlot, park-league, and eventually American Legion ball. Again he profited from having been short when he was younger—coaches saw that he was agile and quick and made him their shortstop, which at the time was not a tall man's position. Not only did his defensive skills—specifically his range and throwing—improve as he became taller and stronger in his late teens, but also he surpassed Bob as a hitter.

"Both Hodges boys were well-known in the area for their ball playing," says Roger Emmert. "I played a few games with them on a Princeton team run by V. M. Ferguson, who had a big grocery store in Baldwin Heights. I batted third and Gil batted fourth because he had some power, and I played shortstop and he played third. He never bragged and never said a word to umpires. Bob, who was a hell of a pitcher, was ready to argue with umpires every other pitch. The only thing Gil did wrong was sneaking a cigarette once in a while."

"Bob had a good left arm, but Bud was just a natural athlete and was better than anyone at everything," recalled Bill Thomas, a member of Petersburg's volunteer fire department for fifty years before his death in 2011. "Out at Higgins' Pasture, we'd pick sides, and Bud was picked first over Bob. They could be competitive playing against each other and really got into it once. They put on boxing gloves and it was settled and over. Who won? Well, Bud was bigger."

"Everybody thought Bobby would be the baseball player in our family and so did Dad," Gil said years later. Gil viewed Bob as a potential major leaguer, maybe the next Bob Feller, the eighteen-year-old flamethrower from Iowa who went directly to the Cleveland Indians in 1936. Gil viewed himself as a potential high school coach.

This attitude was likely the reason he continued to show a lack of passion for playing baseball. "When he played third base on the Legion team," remembers Wayne Malotte, "if the ball came down his way and he felt like getting it, he would. If he didn't, he'd just let it go."

"Lonnie Spade, the Petersburg Legion coach, kicked Bud off the team for loafing his sophomore or junior year," Arthur Beck recalls. "Bud wasn't even upset by it. He just went and played for someone else."

As a major leaguer, Gil Hodges was known to play ball with maximum effort and commitment and almost never to miss a game, yet it would take a while before the teenage Gil gave baseball the same respect he gave everything else in his life.

In 1938, the Hodges moved into 1401 North Main Street, a quaint two-story corner house on a small hill with a large front porch. Downstairs, there was a large living room, dining room, kitchen, and Charlie and Irene's bedroom, which was behind a staircase that faced the front door. Upstairs were Gil and Bob's shared bedroom with twin beds, Marjorie's bedroom, what was later a small dressing room, and a bath. The three kids would graduate from high school while living there, and Charlie and Irene would never move again.

Bill Harris, a retired minister and the brother of Bob Harris, a funeral director in Petersburg, recalls:

> I was about ten years old when the Hodges family moved in next door. They were a very warmhearted, dignified, traditional family who were always friendly and kept the property nice. They were among the few Catholic families in Petersburg, where the largest congregations were the Methodists, Presbyterians, and Baptists. The Ku Klux Klan started in Indiana, and there had been a KKK element in town until about 1930, but the Hodges arrived after that, and I don't think they were ever discriminated against. They were very pious and dressed up every Sunday and marched down to their church, and I think some of their pride was because within the community, they might have felt apart.

Marjorie was in my class. She was an attractive, smart, impressive girl, who was strong-willed and had strong opinions, and talked a mile a minute. She was also very caring of other people, particularly her parents and brothers.

My younger brother Bob and I walked with the Hodges boys and other kids the two blocks to school each morning. Bob was a bit rough, even frisky, while Gil was almost genteel and polished. They'd throw the ball back and forth in their side yard, and occasionally they'd call me over to play. What I remember even more is when Charlie came home from the mine and while Irene was making supper, he and Gil and sometimes Bob would play catch in the twilight, without really talking. I saw this every night, in the spring, summer, and fall.

"They were a close-knit, happy family," says Bob Harris, "and the boys were easy to get along with. When I was little, Gil would ride me on his bicycle. They had one bicycle, and Gil and Bob would argue over who got to ride it."

Petersburg was showing strong signs of economic recovery. While it would take the advent of World War II for it and other towns and cities in Indiana to experience an economic boom, it had benefited since the WPA began operations in the state in July 1935 and put tens of thousands of Hoosiers back to work, mostly at rebuilding infrastructure. In Petersburg there was the sense of revival, remembers Franklin-Weathers, the widow of high school coach "Doc" Weathers: "In the late thirties, when it was coming out of the Depression and the coal mines were going and everybody was working, it really was a lively town. We had several clothing stores, shoe stores, three bakeries, a few bars, beauty shops, four or five barbers, two hotels, everything. On Saturday night, the miners and farmers would come into town and it was three or four deep on Main Street. You'd have to weave through the crowds to go to the movies."

One of the most popular hangouts was the Blue Room on Main Street, where kids danced the jitterbug to big-band music on the jukebox. "The owner was Jimmy Sandage, and the Blue Room was at the back of his place," recalls Franklin-Weathers. "He sat by the door and it cost you a dime to get in and it cost the same to get a hamburger or sandwich or Coke. He and his wife ran a tight ship and wouldn't allow any hanky-panky."

A more exotic destination, River Nook, was on a riverbank in Jasper, about three miles outside Petersburg toward Washington. It was reserved for weekend nights, and only if someone could borrow his parents' automobile. "You didn't have to pay to get in," remembers Malotte-Markham. "They had a big dance floor, and you could get sandwiches and a Coke, no alcohol. It was mainly teenagers from different areas around Petersburg and Washington. A bunch of us would sing around a campfire."

Both boys went to River Nook on occasion, especially after they got their driver's licenses and could borrow their father's car. Bob probably made a beeline to the pretty girls on the dance floor, while Gil headed to another room to play Ping-Pong. "Bud seemed to care only about sports," says Malotte-Markham. "Bob loved sports but he liked girls too, and was always talking to them. He was a pistol. I can't remember Bud dating any girl."

Barbara Jane Vance was the girl Gil *wanted* to date, but it didn't work out. "Gil was a classmate of my mom's," says Vance Hays, whose mother passed away in 2010. "I think Gil asked her to go to a show, and her father told her that if she went out with him it had to be with other friends. He wouldn't allow her to date Catholics. So the only times they went out [were] as part of a group. They still spent a lot of time together. And when I was a kid in the late 1950s my parents took me to the ballpark in St. Louis to meet Gil and take pictures with him."

Other than Barbara Vance, it's not clear whether Gil was interested in any of his female classmates. "I dated both Bud and Bob at different times," says Patty Manhart Culley, the principal's daughter, who lived next door to the Hodges house on Main Street. "They didn't get jealous, because it was all in fun. We'd maybe go to the movies in Vincennes or to Catt's Café, where they made good, greasy hamburgers and you'd come home smelling like the place."

Catt's Café on Main Street was a hangout for kids of all ages, including Marjorie and her friend Norma Smith, who married Bill Thomas after graduation. "After a game we'd go there," recalls Smith Thomas. "It was a little place, but Marge and I didn't have any trouble getting seats, because everyone knew Bud and Bob, who were popular athletes, were going to pick us up and drive us home. One time they picked us up and Bob was driving a little too fast and had to slam on the brakes. It threw Marge and me forward, and Bud said, 'Stop this car right now!' Bob protested but Bud got out and took the keys and drove. They were always nice to us, not treating us like pests. I could see why Marge liked her brothers so much."

"I was the youngest and spoiled by my family, and my brothers were so wonderful to me when I was growing up," Marjorie told Randy Harris. "I was the little sister and they gave me special treatment."

For gas money and other expenses, the Hodges boys always found work. Summers they toiled at the Ditney Hill Mine, in the toolsheds and supply rooms up top. The hardest job Gil ever undertook at the mine was during the summer of 1940, when he worked not with Bob but with George Harris. Charlie and George's father, who was a maintenance and electrician foreman at the mine, got them the job of digging a twenty-by-twenty-by-twenty-foot hole in the ground for a cistern, to gather water. They made fifty cents an hour.

During the school year, Bud and Bob found less intensive work. Gil made some pocket change *at* school. Gil got by in math, science, history, and even Latin, but there was one class other than gym where he excelled: typing. Principal Manhart didn't think Gil should take typing as an elective because his hands were too big for the keyboard, but Gil typed accurately and quickly. "In that class," recalls Smith Thomas, "the kids were expected to type a high number of copies of various business letters and other letters. Gil typed extra copies and kids bought them for four or five cents so they wouldn't have to do all that typing. He was an entrepreneur."

Outside of school, Bud had two jobs. "My dad and uncle worked as ushers in the Lincoln movie theater," says Tony Hodges, Bob's oldest child. "Then they both worked at Johnny V's, which was both a grocery and bus stop."

Howard Briscoe remembers, "When Bud told you to sit down and be quiet in the theater, you knew better than to mess around with him."

The Hodges brothers delighted in the free movies and savory popcorn, but jobs at the groceries run by the Voyles family—the Home Grocery on Sixth and Main and the newer JV Store on Main between Eighth and Ninth—were coveted by every kid in town. They were particularly envious of Gil, who as an afternoon delivery boy got to drive around town in a Chevy van with HOME GROCERY emblazoned on its side.

When he drove the van and it was baseball season, "He'd rush through his deliveries," remembers Wayne Malotte, a fellow employee at the Home Grocery. "He'd drive fast so he could get out to the Legion field and play ball."

"He'd be in such a hurry to deliver the groceries," recalls Manhart-Culley, "that he'd sometimes show up at the ball field wearing his apron."

It is easy with hindsight to assume that working long hours for meager wages made Gil appreciate playing sports more than before. More significant is that he now had a heightened sense of responsibility and felt obligated to make the same effort when participating in sports as he did when he worked. He no longer took anything for granted but viewed every sport seriously, including, finally, baseball.

Despite there being no baseball at Petersburg High, Gil accumulated seven letters by participating in basketball, track, and six-man football, a popular sport for smaller high schools in the area. The Indians drew fair-size crowds to their Saturday-afternoon football games against other teams in the Pocket Athletic Conference. Gil was a backup end as a junior, but as a senior in the fall of 1940, he and Bob started in the same backfield. They were excited to play for head coach Lorel "Coke" Coleman and assistant coach Frank Conrad, who had graduated from Charlie's favorite sports college, Notre Dame. They were multisport coaches who had a lasting influence on both boys because they stressed sportsmanship, teamwork, and work ethic.

Bill Tislow, a sure-handed receiver, recalls, "The field was forty yards wide and eighty yards long, and it was four downs to make fifteen yards for a first down. It was tackle football, and we had thin shoulder pads, and no face guards or teeth protectors, so we had a lot of broken noses and chipped teeth. What usually happened that year was that our quarterback would snap a lateral back to Bud, and then he'd pass. He could throw a football almost the length of the field! I caught many a pass from Bud. Bob was good too. He was a vicious tackler."

"Between games, we had full scrimmages, running offense and defense," recalls Arthur Beck. "We tackled in practice and Bud was hard to bring down. One time he straight-armed me and put that big mitt in my face and I went rolling and saw stars for a while after that. He was the best player on the team that year." The Indians had a fine season, with a 5–1 record. They won four games by a combined score of 218–49, nipped Tell City 20–18, and then lost by that score to Mount Vernon in a battle of the unbeatens that determined the PAC title.

High school basketball was a vital part of Indiana's landscape, and in Petersburg it was the biggest attraction. Nobody missed the Friday-night games, including Charlie, Irene, and Marjorie, and the players were heroes all over town. While Gil always got more playing time than the shorter Bob, it wasn't until well into his junior year that he became something more than just a strong rebounder, and not until his senior year did he establish himself as a bona fide star.

Petersburg defeated archrival Winslow twice in Gil and Bob's junior year, including in the first round of the Pike County tournament, which the Indians, despite a 7–6 record, won the next day by defeating Otwell. The Indians upended Otwell again, 34–30, in the first round of the season-ending sectionals, but in the semifinals against Ireland, they had tough going until a new star emerged at the very end. The *Petersburg Press*:

> As the 1 minute light flashed on, the score was 17-14 in favor of the Spuds and the Indians had only scored one field goal in the last quarter. [Gil] Hodges suddenly intercepted the ball and broke loose to score from under the basket. Ireland stalled by passing the ball around but Hodges got the ball again and broke loose again to score. Petersburg was in the lead by 1 point. The Spuds came down the floor and Schnaus, desperate, tried a long shot which was good. Ireland then led by one point. Hodges again got the ball and passed under the basket to White who scored as the gun was fired, ending the game with a score of 20-19 in favor of the Indians.

During the 1940–41 year, Gil led his team in scoring in the majority of games, often achieving double digits. What made him difficult to defend was that he could both bring the ball up like a guard and then post up inside like a forward or center. "He was a good player, a good rebounder, and he could score," said his teammate Morris Klipsch in 1997. "He . . . seldom showed any anger, but if opponents did get under his skin, he could sure move bodies around under the basket."

Praise for Petersburg's new star was even coming from the press outside of Petersburg. Prior to a game against the local team, the sports editor of the *Tell City News* raved, "Petersburg possesses one of the great players of the present cage campaign. He is G. Hodges, ace forward. Hodges is a fine passer, excellent shot and guides his team with poise not generally found in a high school athlete." Bob, too, had a good senior season as the Indians went 11–7, their best record in the Hodges brothers' high school careers. That included another two wins over Winslow, one in the first round of the Pike County tournament, 40–27. The next day the Indians defeated Spurgeon in a low-scoring game, 25–18, to win the county title. Gil led the team in scoring in both games. Unfortunately, a month later Petersburg lost in the first round of the sectionals to Jasper, 34–21. Gil and Bob each scored a meager three points in their final game at Petersburg, but the younger brother still made the all-sectional team.

When seasons changed, Gil simply moved on to the next sport. Track had a strong tradition in the area, and in April of his senior year, he joined the track team. Gil occasionally competed in sprints and relay races on the school's cinder track, but being the strongest boy in the school made him the obvious choice to be its shot-putter. Against stiff, more experienced competition, the shot-putting neophyte didn't always win but invariably gave impressive performances. In May, he putted 47'1" as the Indians defeated visiting Princeton, 63½–51½. The shot turned out to be a few ounces light, so the new school record he set was declared to be "unofficial."

Having excelled at football, basketball, and track, Gil received the American Legion Athletic Award as Petersburg High School's top athlete, becoming the first person to win that award twice. Bob was acknowledged in the papers too, for having never missed a day or been tardy in his four years of high school.

In early May, Gil, Bob, and seventy-one other students proudly received their diplomas. "I can't remember what boy I walked with at commencement," Midge Hisgen Benjamin said nostalgically a few months before her death in 2011. "If it was Bob or Bud, I'd remember. High school and that whole time were exciting up until that very moment. And then it was the end of an era."

CHAPTER THREE

For Gil, the era didn't end after graduation. He needed the extra time to mull over an important decision involving his immediate future. St. Joseph's College in Rensselaer had offered both him and Bob athletic scholarships. Going to college there would enable him to pursue his dream of becoming a coach, and he could compete in basketball, baseball, football, and track. However, Gil was curious whether he had what it took to be offered a professional baseball contract. Scouts were making overtures to Bob, and he wanted their attention as well. He had a few more months of baseball ahead of him, and he was determined to give it his all and then make an assessment about his future.

Petersburg didn't field an American Legion team that summer, so Gil played for Princeton's Legion Post 25 team, which his childhood neighbor Eldon Sisson had managed since 1930. Sisson batted Hodges fourth and played him at shortstop as the V-8 Juniors marched to the district title. On defense, Hodges had impressive range and a strong arm, but he made headlines with his bat. After belting a couple of long home runs in key victories against Vincennes and Tell City, the *Clarion-News* called the outsider "Gilbert Hodges, Petersburg sensation."

The V-8 Juniors' hopes of winning a state title went up in flames in the first round of the regionals in Indianapolis. What made their 11–4 thrashing by East Chicago hard to swallow was that they scored all their runs in the first inning but managed only 2 more hits, for a total of 5. According to the papers, there was only one bright spot: "Again it was Gilbert Hodges who sparked the local attack, collecting two hits, one a double, in three trips, and turned in a masterful fielding job in and around the shortstop acreage."

Gil (not Gilbert) found time to attend a few tryouts for professional teams, which were fairly common in Indiana and neighboring states at the time. The St. Louis Browns conducted one in Princeton, at Lafayette Park. Gil, Bob, and their friends Princeton standout Jim Pegram, and Winslow basketball star Red Robert Smith were among the hundred or so local boys who showed up for the multiday tryout. "For the tryouts," Smith recalls, "they had two or three guys watching you take swings. They evaluated you on how you reacted to pitches and if you followed through on your swing. We got only about ten swings and they moved on to the next guy. Gil knocked one out of the park over by some maple trees."

"They kept about seven or eight of us till the last day," remembers Jim Beane, a left-hander who had just graduated from high school in Evansville. "Then they got down to about five, including me and the Hodges boys. But they didn't sign me or them, but the other two guys [Pegram and Smith]. As we were getting ready to leave, the Hodges brothers and I got to talking a little bit. I told them, 'I'm going up to St. Joseph's College in Rensselaer in the fall.' And they said, 'You've got to be kidding. So are we!'"

Based on his Legion play, a man in a fedora showed up at the Hodges home to persuade Gil to play D ball in the Detroit Tigers chain. But he talked it over with his father and decided to go with the better offer of an athletic scholarship to a fine Catholic institution. Still undervaluing his talents, he decided he had a far better chance to make a living as a high school coach than as a professional baseball player. A deciding factor was that he would be going to college with Bob. "They were inseparable," Marjorie said.

Rensselaer, Indiana, located two hundred miles north of Petersburg, had a population of about five thousand, of which one-fifth were the young men who attended St. Joseph's College. Founded in 1889 by the Catholic order Missionaries of the Precious Blood to be a secondary school for Native Americans, this small private institution had over five decades established the reputation for being a strict, staid liberal arts school where sports were an afterthought. But in the late thirties, the administration decided that the best way to attract new students was not by opening its doors to women but by quickly developing a strong athletics program. Sports scholarships were tendered to top athletes of all denominations throughout the Midwest, and the Hodges brothers were among the beneficiaries. Many years later, a still grateful Gil said, "We both got scholarships. Without it I don't think I'd ever have made college."

Enjoying their first taste of independence, Gil and Bob moved into a dormitory, explored the town and campus (including the Romanesque-style chapel that over time would get the reputation for being haunted), attended classes—St. Joseph's still put the emphasis on academics and required even physical education majors to take a heavy class load—and became acquainted with their new coach. Joe Dienhart had been a star football and basketball player at Notre Dame in the twenties before guiding Indianapolis Cathedral High to five state Catholic basketball titles and a national Catholic championship in 1933. That fall he coached the first Indianapolis NFL team, the Indians, before they disbanded after only three games. Dienhart was hired by St. Joseph's in 1938 for the express purpose of producing championship teams, and he did that in the early forties, thanks to being allocated a large number of scholarships.

"Even with scholarships it wasn't easy recruiting, because there was the feeling that any day we might become part of the war," recalls Frank Staucet, who was a five-foot-eight freshman shortstop from Hammond, Indiana. "But he got guys from everywhere for the sports he coached."

Dienhart earned the title "a coach for all seasons" as his football, basketball, and baseball teams achieved unprecedented success. Gil joined his freshman football team immediately upon arriving at school. Having no trouble adjusting to the eleven-man game, he was a bruising fullback on a Pumas juggernaut that went 7–0–1. Football didn't receive much coverage in the local papers, but he was singled out for praise on several occasions, including after "two thrilling touchdown runs" in a 31–0 thrashing of Valparaiso. "He was just an outstanding athlete with a terrific dedication to excel," Dienhart remarked a few years later about his former recruit.

As freshmen, Gil and Bob weren't allowed to participate on the varsity basketball team, although playing varsity baseball would be permitted in the spring. Without daily practices, they had more time to study, which was necessary because of the school's difficult curriculum, and to return to Petersburg on weekends and holidays. Pearl Harbor had been attacked on December 7 and America was at war, so there was a pall over the family's Christmas that year, as there had been on campus. Already some of Petersburg's young men were enlisting, and that number would jump upon graduation in May; the draft would take many more. Irene was noticeably worried about the uncertain futures of her eighteen- and seventeen-year-old sons.

When the brothers returned to Rensselaer in January, they were comforted to know that while Charlie was at work and Marjorie was in school, Irene's mother, Ellen, was keeping their mother company. Their grandfather Arthur Horstmeyer had died on May 2, and the widowed Ellen was now living in an apartment in Petersburg not far from the Hodges house. "Irene and Ellen were very social," says Bill Harris. "They would host teas and luncheons for their church group. They would also look after the altar at their church."

Back at school, Bob and Gil were kept abreast about what was happening in Petersburg. When the miners went out on strike, they were concerned the people in town were upset with their father. "After Pearl Harbor, FDR wanted coal," recalls Harris, "but John L. Lewis started calling for strikes to get concessions he wouldn't have gotten if there wasn't a war. Some people in town, particularly the Republicans who didn't like unions, felt that the striking miners were selfish, even treasonous. The miners were embarrassed to strike, but they were ordered to do it. I feel somewhat guilty, because we kids teased Marjorie and other kids whose parents were miners, saying they were supporting the enemy by going on strike. Poor Marge was only in the seventh grade and she would stand up for the union. Roosevelt gave in to labor in order to get the coal, so the miners did well. After the mine settlement, the ugliness died down."

At St. Joseph's, things were different from before the holiday. Staucet recalls, "You could tell right away there was a problem in that there was a diminishing return of students. Many didn't come back after the holiday break, because they had gone into the service. The draft wasn't in effect yet, so we were able to keep going to school, but we knew that after that first year it was *qué será será*."

Bob and Gil, who joined the Marines ROTC, fully expected to be in the service before long. Meanwhile they grew impatient for baseball practice to begin. They studied, went to Mass, and looked for ways to kill time.

"There was a small saloon in town that students would patronize," remembers Staucet. "It wasn't too far from the college, and you could walk there. Gil wasn't especially outgoing, but he was a really good guy and would join in. He liked playing pool in his spare time and was very good at it, so we'd shoot some pool and have the occasional beer. None of us were wild kids in that regard."

"Occasional beer" might be an overstatement. "There was *no* drinking," says Beane. "If you drank a beer on campus you were kicked out, no ifs, ands, or buts. But late one night, me and the Hodges boys slipped into Rensselaer, and somehow we got a six-pack. There's a little stream under a bridge that you went over when leaving campus, and we went down on the bank and we were drinking that beer. Suddenly Gil said, 'You know, we could get kicked out for this,' and I said, 'Let's not talk about it.' So we didn't."

Indiana winters are harsh and long, and when the baseball team eventually assembled for practices it was indoors. It wouldn't be until mid-March, a couple of weeks before the season opener, that the team vacated the field house and trained outside on the damp diamond. The team immediately impressed a sportswriter for the *Jackson County Democrat*, who declared Puma fans were full of optimism because the "1942 Team Shows Exceptional Strength in All Departments." The Hodges brothers and Beane and Staucet were singled out for praise.

Staucet, who one reporter raved "covers more ground than the morning dew," reserved his praise for Gil, saying, "He could hit the ball a long way. He also had a strong arm. I think of the word *strength* when I think of him. He was strong physically and had a strong character. I also liked him a lot because he was a team player. Bobby was also very popular and a good pitcher, but I thought Gil had better potential because of his size and power."

Gil's power was often on display during the season. "Our first diamond, before we moved out to a cow pasture, was close to campus buildings," recalls Beane, "and Gil hit one on top of the administration building." Another gargantuan blast broke a window in the science building.

There had been baseball at St. Joseph's since 1935, but there had never been a team as powerful as the 1942 squad. "We were a steamroller as a small college," says Beane. "I think nine or ten of us signed professionally," says Staucet.

The Pumas finished the season with a 12–1 record, losing only their finale, 3–2, to Illinois-Wesleyan. When Beane and Bob won a doubleheader from Butler, 10–2 and 7–0, allowing only six hits, St. Joseph's captured the Indiana Conference's baseball title.

Gil and Bob intended to return to Petersburg for the summer to work at the Ditney Hill Mine and play independent baseball, but their plans changed. Rensselaer was only one hundred miles west of Indianapolis, and factories were known to send scouts to watch St. Joseph's baseball games. Their task was to find summer employees who would play for the factory teams in the hotly contested Indianapolis Amateur Baseball Association. That summer, Gil and Bob lived with their father's relatives in Indianapolis and made some money working in a factory for P. R. Mallory, which produced dry cell batteries and electrical components. They also played in about twenty-five games on Saturday and Sunday afternoons for Schwitzer-Cummins, a company that produced automotive cooling systems.

According to Bob Hildebrand, who from 1942 to 1944 played for the meat-processing plant Kingan, Bob Hodges was one of the league's pitchers who "threw ninety-mile-an-hour fastballs and sliders, which at that time were called 'in-shoots' and 'out-shoots.' Gil handled the shortstop position well. He had a good arm and was mobile; he could charge a bunt or topped ball or go into the hole and make the long throw. He was a gentle, nice guy who never mouthed off to umpires."

Schwitzer-Cummins won its first eleven games and coasted into the tournament at Victory Field, where the Triple A Indianapolis Indians played. But they were knocked out in the second round by Kingan. In the big game, Bob held Hildebrand's team scoreless, fanning five, until the Reliables lived up their name with a rally in the sixth inning, scoring all their runs. A Schwitzer-Cummins rally fell short, and the season was over.

Gil never gave an explanation for why he didn't play varsity football at St. Joseph's when he returned to school in the fall of 1942. But in his 1969 book, *The Game of Baseball*, he advised young kids who hoped to be major leaguers to not risk serious injuries by playing football. Instead he made a case that playing basketball in the off-season would help them with baseball, particularly in regard to mobility, flexibility, anticipation, and hand-eye co-ordination.

After a lack of athletic activity in the fall, Gil was eager to play on Dienhart's basketball squad beginning in December. Dienhart had a strong front court in big Jim Huysman at center and his high-scoring captain Bernie Hoffman and Knobby Walsh at the forward spots, but he wanted Gil in the starting lineup. His solution was to put him in the backcourt with Don Schrenk and instruct him to take outside shots but also use his outstanding ball-handling skills to penetrate and to rip down rebounds when under the basket. Gil had a slow start but came on strong as the Pumas went 9–9. "Gil was a very good basketball player," says Staucet. "He was big and rawboned and was great on defense and at rebounding. He also handled the ball very well with those big hands."

The baseball team suffered an opening-day loss at Indiana but came back to win their second game at Ball State, defeating the Cardinals 7–6 in ten innings. They might have won earlier, but Gil, making one of the few bonehead plays of his amateur and professional careers, failed to touch second base on a ball that cleared the fence. The Pumas had only a so-so season as the last team Dienhart coached before becoming the assistant athletic director at Purdue University. At times the distracted Gil and his teammates seemed to be going through the motions, as several key players had dropped out and entered the military.

At Christmas, Beane had joined the Navy rather than waiting to be drafted and put in the army. Staucet, who would spend three years in the South Pacific before becoming a Double A all-star with the Albany Senators, also became a midshipman.

Bob had left too. On March 30, 1943, a few days before the Pumas played their first game, Charles Robert Hodges enlisted in the U.S. Army at Fort Benjamin Harrison in Lawrence, Indiana, and was sent to basic training at Camp Davis in North Carolina. It was the first time the Hodges brothers had been separated, and Gil had a hard time adjusting to Bob's absence.

Gil wanted to join Bob in the armed forces as soon as possible, but the U.S. Marines scheduled him for a fall induction date. He was able to finish his second year at St. Joseph's and had thoughts of returning after the war to finish his degree. "It was a great little college," he'd often tell reporters, "a fine place to study and play ball. I have a lot of happy memories of there."

Rather than return to Petersburg to wait out his time as a civilian, Gil went back to Indianapolis to again swing his big bat and play shortstop in the amateur city league. As he had the summer before, he worked for P. R. Mallory, operating a milling machine, drill press, and hand mill, and played ball for another factory—Allison, a division of General Motors that produced aircraft engines during World War II.

With a record of 17–14, Allison was the runner-up in the Manufacturers League during the regular season, but stormed into the city tournament on the strength of a solid offense led by Hodges, whose long homers awed everyone. However, when Allison captured its first city title by defeating defending champion Gold Medal Beer at Victory Field, its power-hitting shortstop was not in the lineup.

Gil Hodges was in New York.

CHAPTER FOUR

ortune had smiled on the nineteen-year-old. After a game in which his long blast had beaten Schwitzer-Cummins, he was approached by Stan Feezle, who was representing the Brooklyn Dodgers. Feezle was well-known in Indianapolis because he ran a wholesale sporting goods store with Donie Bush, who had managed the Pittsburgh Pirates to a pennant in 1927 over the Branch Rickey–run St. Louis Cardinals. Feezle, who later signed future major-league pitching stars Carl Erskine of Anderson and Bob Friend of Lafayette, was, according to Erskine, "a businessman who also officiated in the Big Ten, and though he wasn't a bird dog, he carried a scout card." Feezle had been watching Hodges in Indianapolis and at St. Joseph's and urged him to drop out of the summer league and rush to Olean, New York, where the Dodgers were about to hold a huge tryout under the auspices of their farm director, Branch Rickey Jr.

In later years, Hodges claimed he was thrilled by this development. However, some accounts say he reacted to Feezle's interest with ambivalence, because he was going to enter the Marines a month later and might not return for years, if ever. And there was another reason. "Gil told me he was very surprised that he was approached to become a professional *baseball* player," says Joan Hodges. "Basketball was his sport. Gil thought he was going to play professional basketball and then coach basketball."

Gil and his father knew Feezle was serious because the Dodgers were paying all Gil's expenses to go to the camp. With the excited Charlie's blessing, Gil immediately caught a bus from Indianapolis to Buffalo, and then

another one to Olean. When he arrived he met Jake Pitler, who had managed the Class-D Olean Oilers to consecutive PONY League titles in
1939 and 1940. Pitler was considered one of the shrewdest baseball minds
in the organization, and was helping Rickey Jr. make player evaluations at
the tryout.

The twenty-nine-year-old Rickey Jr., who, oddly, had been appointed
the Dodgers' farm director by Rickey Sr.'s predecessor Larry MacPhail, at
first kept his distance from Hodges. Writing in a 1951 issue of *Baseball Digest*, "the Twig" remembered the first time he set eyes on him: "Well, I see
this big kid throw from the outfield, and while it is a throw with distance,
it is a high throw and not an impressive one. And then this big kid comes to
bat and the first time he hits one it reaches the cinder track beyond the
outfield. The second time he hits it over the track and the third time the ball
lands in the same place. Well, in these tryout camps you see a lot of kids who
can run like the dickens and who can throw hard, but it's a rare thing to see
a kid who can shillelagh a ball. He just beat the ball to death. I saw him and
I said: 'Hornsby or Foxx.'"

For three days, Rickey Jr. and Pitler took a good look at the several
hundred teenagers and young men trying out at Bradner Stadium, but, as
Pitler said in 1952, "we couldn't get enough of this boy Hodges." They
moved him to every position so they could determine where he was best
suited. As always he looked calm, but his stomach was churning, and he
made several wild throws and bad bobbles. They were all forgotten each
time he hit a pitch into the stratosphere. "I went overboard on Hodges after
I had seen him hit a few a country mile," recalled Rickey Jr. "I didn't know
whether he was an infielder, an outfielder, or what he was. I just knew he
could hit that ball to helangon."

What Rickey Jr. also liked about Hodges was his quiet manner, his
willingness to listen and do what he was asked without complaint or attitude, and his absolute modesty when he did anything special with the bat.
The young executive who had graduated from Ohio Wesleyan (as had his
father) would form a lasting bond with the young man from Indiana.

At the end of Hodges' grueling tryout, Pitler told Rickey Jr. something
he already knew: "He's one in a million, that big kid. Don't let him get
away."

In fact, Pitler and his team's owner didn't want him to get away from them either, and made an effort to sign Hodges to play at Olean. They were rejected. Rickey Jr. didn't want to let this prospect out of his sight, so he decided to personally escort Hodges by train to Brooklyn, where his father, the best judge of young talent in baseball, could make the final decision on whether to offer him a contract.

Hodges found himself on a train heading for New York City, soon to meet the famous Mahatma, as people called Rickey with either respect or derision. (He was also called "El Cheapo" because of the low wages he paid to his players and underlings.) "I was overcome," Hodges told Arnold Spano of *Sport* in 1960. "I couldn't believe it." He knew all about the man who made the Cardinals, his favorite team, into champions.

As a major-league catcher with the St. Louis Browns and New York Highlanders early in the century, and manager of the Browns and Cardinals, Rickey had had only sporadic success, but as a general manager and executive, Rickey's brilliance was never in question. With the Cardinals, he built a huge farm system and supplied a revolving door of managers and a colorful array of talented, down-and-dirty but fundamentally sound players needed to draw crowds and win pennants. During his watch, they won the National League flag in 1928, 1930, 1931, 1934, and 1942, when rookie Stan Musial had the first of sixteen consecutive .300 seasons. They lost to the Yankees and A's in their first two World Series, but defeated the A's, Tigers (with Dizzy Dean throwing a shutout in Game 7), and Yankees in their last three appearances, the final one coming just before Rickey's move to the Dodgers.

Rickey, a devout Methodist who didn't smoke, drink, curse, or go to the ballpark on Sunday, was brought to Brooklyn to run the club as a general manager and 25 percent owner after Larry MacPhail resigned as team president to accept a commission in the U.S. Army. Joining Rickey in a restructured ownership group, and also receiving 25 percent, were John Smith of Pfizer and Company, the pharmaceutical firm that had operated in the borough for nearly a century; movie executive Jim Mulvey, whose late father-in-law, Stephen McKeever, and uncle had been co-owners of the team with Charles Ebbets dating back to 1912; and the partner with whom Rickey would feud, Walter O'Malley, an attorney with the Brooklyn Trust Company, which was the mortgage holder on Ebbets Field. O'Malley also went to church, but he smoked, was a big social drinker, and had the ego and lust for power to match Rickey's and, as time progressed, make him a formidable foe.

Rickey believed that scouting was the lifeblood of an organization and wanted to stock the Dodgers' huge farm system with young recruits for his postwar roster. So with unrestrained rapaciousness, he held a number of tryout camps that year for walk-ons and those like Hodges, who were recommended by his scouts. Among the future Dodgers stars who were discovered were pitchers Ralph Branca and Carl Erskine; Edwin "Duke" Snider, a cocky but sensitive slugger from California; and Gil Hodges.

Hodges wrote in *Guideposts* in 1960 that he told his father, "Rickey Jr., he's the boss' son, took me down to New York to a big hotel, and told me how I was to take the subway the next day to get to his office in Brooklyn. Being a country boy I was ashamed to ask directions, and I got lost—why, it took me half a day to get to Brooklyn."

Hodges finally arrived at Ebbets Field, and was taken with the beauty, charm, and character of the stadium that had opened in 1913 on a site that included a garbage dump called Pigtown and was bounded by Bedford Avenue, Sullivan Place, McKeever Place, and Montgomery Street. He walked through the striking marble rotunda and found his way to the Dodgers clubhouse under the right-field stands. He saw that each player had a cubicle that was about a yard wide and was separated from the next cubicle by a chain-link fence that stretched from the ceiling to the floor. In front of each locker was a plain stool. In the middle of the room were a few tin lockers, and other lockers were around the perimeter of the room. He left the clubhouse and walked through a tunnel to get to the dugout and onto the field, immediately spotting the scoreboard, the Schaefer beer sign. He was struck by "the reddish brown diamond, the impossibly green grass" that historian Doris Kearns Goodwin wrote about in her memoir *Wait Till Next Year*, the short distance from home plate to the fence in left field, the scores of angles in the outfield, the giant signs, and the stands that were so close that the fans could hear the players chatter and vice versa.

Both Rickeys were waiting for Hodges on the field. Hodges was awed to meet Rickey Sr., and that made him even quieter than usual. Rickey Jr.

remembered, "And after a short interview Dad signed him to a Brooklyn contract."

The "short interview" consisted of three more long days of trying out for Rickey Sr. and, at times, a familiar figure with the number 2 on his back, Dodgers manager Leo Durocher, the onetime shortstop of the Cardinals' Gas House Gang. Both men were struck by Hodges' power, but they thought he was too slow to play short and worried there was no other place for him to play on the field. Then Rickey told him, "You're going to be a catcher." Having been a catcher himself, Rickey felt the young prospect could handle what he considered the most important position on the field.

Years later a bemused Feezle told *Brooklyn Eagle* sportswriter Tommy Holmes, "I thought I had bagged the greatest kid shortstop I've ever seen and that's the one position they never gave him a chance to play."

In future years, Hodges told various reporters that his signing bonus was for $1,500, $1,250, or $1,000. Because Rickey merited his reputation for being the most penurious executive in baseball, the last figure seems the likeliest. And it came "with a clause," Hodges said. "I got only half of it. If I came back from military service I'd get the other $500. I would say that Mr. Rickey was not taking any chances."

Rickey called Charlie Hodges because Gil wanted his approval before signing the contract. Charlie was thrilled that his son would be staying with the parent club for the rest of year and be on the same wartime roster as his favorite player, Paul Waner, the longtime Pirates star, as well as other future Hall of Famers Billy Herman (who led the team with a .330 average), Arky Vaughan (who was playing short with Pee Wee Reese in the service), and former Gas House Gang star Ducky Medwick. Charlie gave his consent, but as Gil stated years later, "Dad said it was my decision to make. I signed."

Always at the top of a handful of Hodges' treasured memories was the first time he put on the blue-and-white Dodgers uniform as a member of the team. He had no disappointment that the number on the back was 4, not the 14 that he'd be wearing in his Dodger glory years. His uniform was in place, his shoes were polished, his cap perfectly straight.

Hodges realized he wasn't ready to play in the majors, so he was content to spend the final month of the 1943 season catching batting practice or in the bullpen. He eagerly learned his new position from Mickey Owen, who was a fine catcher despite the infamous passed ball in the '41 World Series that led to his team's demise. He also got to experience Ebbets Field and its passionate and often vitriolic fans. Brooklyn had a population of about three million, but Hodges liked its small-town ambience and identified with the prideful people who were routinely treated like a national joke by comedians and Hollywood. Having grown up in rural Petersburg, he surely recognized that the Brooklyn people felt pride in themselves and their *otherness*. Rather than desiring to change because they felt inferior, they instead wanted the uppity Yankee and Giants fans and Hollywood hacks to recognize their specialness and treat them with deserved respect.

"We were Brooklyn, 'the other place,' and we were made to feel inferior," says author and television interviewer Larry King. "We weren't part of the city. If we went to see the Rangers or Knicks, we were going *into* the city. On occasion I'd see a game at the Polo Grounds. It was always so dark there. At Yankee Stadium, I felt like I had to wear a tie. But Ebbets Field, which I got to by taking two subways and walking from the Prospect Park station through the botanical garden—well, *that* was baseball. Our inferiority was only in regard to baseball and not winning a World Series."

The people of Brooklyn believed that the surest way for them and their borough to have an image upgrade was for their Dodgers to be champions. Under MacPhail and now Rickey, the "Bums"—their representatives on the field—were making significant progress.

As a spectator with the best seat in the stadium, Hodges took advantage of the marvelous opportunity to study the game at the major-league level. He also got to observe Durocher, arguably baseball's best manager, on and off the field. He saw the dapper man-about-town, the backroom gambler, and the brilliant but often bratty field general who heckled opposing batters, viciously argued with and kicked dirt on umpires, called for knockdown pitches ("Stick it in his ear!"), and employed clever strategies to disrupt the orderliness of the game and the logical thinking of the opposition. "Durocher had an effect on me, I'm sure," Hodges wrote in his 1969 book. "Leo was a daring manager. He'd take chances, and sometimes they'd work, and sometimes, they wouldn't. But, more than any manager I ever knew, Leo was the guy that other managers managed against. I've seen managers who'd ignore Leo's team, trying to stay one jump ahead of Leo. It didn't work."

Durocher pulled out all stops, but the Dodgers still ended the season 23½ games behind St. Louis (their biggest rival other than the Giants), whose record was 105–49. Their respectable third-place finish and 81–72 record were of little comfort.

The Dodgers' final game of the season, on October 3, was in Cincinnati against the second-place Reds. Hodges expected to watch the game, but in the second inning Durocher, whom Rickey had taken off the active-player roster four days before, decided to pull his battery of Whit Wyatt and Mickey Owen and several other starters. The manager informed Hodges that he was finally going to play in a major-league game. Hodges thought he was going to replace Owen behind the plate, but Durocher wanted the seasoned receiver Bobby Bragan, who had been playing third base, to catch his young reliever Chris Haughey. So after spending a month learning how to catch, Hodges trotted on wobbly legs to third base. (He would not play there again until 1957.)

The only thing the reporters in the press box at Crosley Field knew about the new third baseman was that he was a tall, strong kid whom Rickey Jr. "was a little nuts about." On the plus side, Hodges walked and stole a base in his debut. But he made two errors and was overmatched by veteran Johnny Vander Meer, the league's strikeout king. After whiffing for the second time against the lefty who had achieved baseball immortality by throwing back-to-back no-hitters in 1938, Hodges asked Durocher what pitch got him out. The annoyed manager replied, "Son, that was just his fastball." When Hodges admitted that he hadn't even seen it and got no pat on the back, he realized he had said too much.

The Dodgers went down quietly, 6–1. Hodges was disappointed in his performance in his first game, but when he returned to Petersburg he got needed encouragement from his father. "I didn't think I had a chance to make the Dodgers," said Hodges years later, "but my dad said, 'Who are you to say?' He never gave a thought that I might not make the grade with the Dodgers."

Following the suggestion of both Rickey Jr. and his father, Hodges took a catcher's mitt with him when he entered the Marines. He had no way of knowing that he wouldn't use it again in a professional game for three long years.

CHAPTER FIVE

On September 27, 1943, Gil Hodges, nineteen years, five months, and twenty-three days old, traveled to Indianapolis on a Dodgers off day and, as documents state, "executed the oath of enlistment as a private in the United States Marine Corps Reserve." He wasn't ordered to report for another three weeks, so after finishing the baseball season he returned home. As the only major leaguer ever to come from Petersburg, he received a hero's welcome, particularly from children. Gil was grateful, but felt that the real heroes of Petersburg weren't there to welcome him, but in the service. Foremost among them was Bob, who was stationed in Europe.

After the attack on Pearl Harbor, four hundred thousand Hoosiers enlisted or were drafted into the U.S. armed forces—about one-eighth of the state's population. There would be nearly twelve thousand fatalities and seventeen thousand injuries. A monument erected in Petersburg's courthouse square after the war by the Gold Star Mothers Association would pay tribute to sixty-two young men from that one town who were killed in action.

"If you were eighteen you were eligible for the draft," remembers Bill Harris. "Some kids dropped out of high school and enlisted once they became of age. Others waited for graduation day and then lined up, marched to the courthouse, and were sworn in. Within a month or two they climbed into big trucks and were hauled away to Camp Atterbury or Camp Breckenridge."

"There weren't many young men left in the town, because so many were in the service," recalls Ralph Thompson, who was one of the Boy Scouts the air warden sent around town on bicycles during blackout drills to tell people to turn off their lights. "Women went to work all over the country, and this area was no exception. Some women from Petersburg went to Vincennes and Evansville and took jobs in the factories."

Gil was ready to do his part. In the September 1960 issue of *Guideposts*, he wrote, "The war was on, I was 19 and left for the Marine Corps. My father said: 'There will be more baseball for you.' It didn't occur to him that I might get hurt, or I might not come back. He just believed I would, and prayed that I would. And that helped."

Gil Hodges reported for duty with the Marine Corps on October 14, 1943. After receiving a traditional USMC high-and-tight haircut, he was assigned to the 4th Recruit Battalion at the Marine Corps base in San Diego. When asked what job he wanted most in the Marines, he wrote down, "military police." He completed basic training, passing tests for marksmanship and swimming and showing he was capable of driving a large truck. He was promoted to private first class on December 21. Then he was assigned as a rifleman to Company A, Infantry Battalion, Training Center at Camp Elliot, where he successfully completed an eight-week course. On February 19, 1944, he qualified as a marksman with the Browning automatic rifle.

As part of the 44th Replacement Battalion, Fleet Marine Force, he shipped out aboard the USS *Santa Monica* to hook up with the 5th Amphibious Corps in the Pacific. On March 11, he landed at Pearl Harbor, which had been rebuilt and reborn and was serving as headquarters of all Pacific war operations. Two months later, Gil left Oahu for Kauai to join the 16th Antiaircraft Artillery Battalion.

The 16th Defense Battalion had been formed in November 1942 by Lieutenant Colonel Richard P. Ross Jr. by combining units from the 1st Defense Battalion that was stationed about 750 nautical miles west-southwest of Hawaii on Johnston Island. The battalion manned three-inch antiaircraft artillery guns positioned around the island, and despite there being few Japanese aerial attacks, that role didn't change after Ross was succeeded by Lieutenant Colonel Bruce T. Hemphill in July 1943. On April 19, 1944, the unit was redesignated the 16th Antiaircraft Artillery Battalion and became part of Fleet Marine Force, Pacific. By the time Hodges joined the battalion on Kauai, in May 1944, it had yet another commander, Lieutenant August F. Penzold Jr.

When he was not on duty, Gil kept in shape by playing in softball games as a third baseman or catcher. He realized that Kauai was just a way station for most of the Marines there and spent six anxious months waiting to be shipped out to where life was not as peaceful.

In Petersburg, whatever information had passed through censorship was published in a weekly newspaper column about the troops. An item that had appeared in an edition of the *Petersburg Press* in early 1944 reported: "Cpl. Bob Hodges is now in Germany with the Ninth Army, his parents, Mr. and Mrs. Charles Hodges, have been informed by a letter from Bob. A brother, Cpl. Bud Hodges, is in the U.S. Marines and is now stationed in the South Pacific." The local newspaper reporters didn't know that Gil was about to head into a precarious situation. And they had no way of knowing that Bob had neglected to mention in his letters home that he had almost lost his life.

"Dad never talked about it," states Ann Hodges. "The only reason my brother John and I found out was that sometime in the 1960s, Dad was doing something and his shirt came up and we could see a purple scar right above his hip. One of us asked what it was, and Uncle Delmas, who was at the house, said it was his scar from when Dad was blown out of a jeep during the war! Dad told him to shut up and that was the end of it."

By working long hours in the mines, perhaps Charlie Hodges was too distracted to spend entire days worrying about his sons overseas. But other than her volunteer work at the church, Irene had no such distractions. For her, the days were especially long.

"I was six or seven and I'd go over and sit with Mrs. Hodges," says Bob Harris. "She was a prince of a lady, a sweet person. She'd offer tea and cookies and we just talked. I could tell she was worried about her boys off at war. I'd see her eyes and that she was wringing her hands. Every day, military convoys from Indianapolis would roll through town, and sometimes they'd leave bodies behind in Petersburg for burial and she would see that."

In December 1944, the 16th Antiaircraft Artillery Battalion finally received orders to board ships. It sailed west for Tinian. During the journey, on the last day of the year, Hodges was promoted to corporal and assigned to the battalion's operations and intelligence division.

Although only ten and a half miles long and five miles wide, Tinian had played a pivotal role in the Mariana Islands campaign that was a turning point for America in the Pacific Theater. The U.S. Navy and the Marine Corps had devised a successful strategy, "island hopping," that called for American forces to work their way west across the Pacific, attacking and taking some islands, while leaving some Japanese strongholds isolated and withering. The Marianas campaign, also known as Operation Forager, lasted from June through November 1944 and set up the invasion of the Philippines.

On July 24, 1944, after a forty-three-day bombardment by the U.S. Navy, the 2nd and 4th Marine Divisions had landed on Tinian. Japanese resistance was stubborn, as they retreated during the day and launched fearsome attacks at night. The Tinian battle had the dubious distinction of being the first time that napalm, which was invented that year at the Eglin Air Force Base outside of Fort Walton Beach, Florida, was used as a weapon in war. During the Tinian ordeal, 147 "firebombs" were dropped from P-47 planes that probably had been built in Evansville. On July 31, the Japanese launched a last desperate suicide attack but were beaten back by the Marines. After only nine days, the island was declared secured at the cost of 8,000 Japanese and 328 American lives. By the time the 16th arrived in January, the fighting on Tinian was essentially over, but several hundred Japanese troops still held out in dense jungle areas. (Murata Susumu was not secured until 1953.) Though operations were ostensibly only of the cleanup variety, there were still occasional skirmishes and sniper fire, and thirty-eight Marines died and 125 were wounded over the next five months.

Tinian continued to play an important role in the island-hopping strategy, so camps to house fifty thousand troops were quickly built. Thanks to the construction efforts of fifteen thousand Seabees, the Tinian airfield became the most active one in the Pacific. Six runways provided takeoffs and landings for the B-29 Superfortress bombers that relentlessly attacked the Philippines, the Ryukyu Islands, and the mainland of Japan.

Riley Marietta, from Mansfield, Ohio, was typical of the young men like Gil Hodges who found themselves fighting on the other side of the world. At basic training near San Diego he was schooled to be a machine gunner, but he was shipped to the 16th and now drove one of the trucks that pulled the big guns into position to protect the advances made by the infantry. He met Hodges at pickup softball games played by Marines on downtime. "He was not well-known then and never acted or talked like any kind of star," Marietta says. "He was just a regular guy who got along fine with the other men. He was a pretty good-sized man and moved like a ballplayer and could wallop the ball. If I was on his team that was a good thing."

"My father was James Herndon from Mackinaw, Illinois," says Teri Kennedy, who resides today on Long Island. "He was seventeen when he got his mom to let him go into the Marine Corps, and he became a machine gunner. He told me that he played ball with Gil Hodges on Tinian. Apparently Gil had quite a presence. While he wasn't a big celebrity yet, my father and all these young guys knew he was special. Here's this guy who just outperformed everybody to the point that it was almost an embarrassment to be playing with him. Where did this guy come from, the one who hits the ball to the other side of the island?"

The 16th Antiaircraft Artillery Battalion was on Tinian for only two months. In March, Hodges and the other troops boarded LSTs and were taken to Saipan. There the unit joined the rest of the assembled assault force: the 2nd, 5th, 8th, and 16th antiaircraft battalions formed the 1st Provisional Antiaircraft Artillery Group under the operational control of the Tenth Army's 53rd Antiaircraft Artillery Brigade. On March 26, the united forces embarked for the Ryukyu Islands. The largest amphibious invasion of the Pacific campaign was planned for one island in particular—Okinawa. Irene Hodges was better off not knowing that the bloodiest battle yet between U.S. and Japanese forces was about to be fought, and her youngest son was going to be part of it.

Okinawa was located 400 miles south of Japan. Even before the attack on Pearl Harbor, the Japanese had fortified the 480-square-mile island as their front line in the defense of their country, and it served as the headquarters of the 32nd Japanese Imperial Army as well as other divisions. In March 1945, it was estimated that between 85,000 and 100,000 Japanese soldiers were entrenched there, supported by almost all the ships and planes Japan had left. Capturing the island would allow the Allies to deal a fatal blow to Japan's sea lines of communication and sources of raw materials. Should the invasion of Japan be necessary, as many in the U.S. military expected, Okinawa's airfields and harbors would serve as launching points.

Operation Iceberg was the name given to the invasion, which was scheduled for April 1, 1945. Two weeks earlier, the greatest naval armada ever assembled was off Okinawa—forty aircraft carriers, eighteen battleships, two hundred destroyers, and a hundred support ships, comprising the Fifth Fleet under the command of Admiral Raymond Spruance. In the twenty-four hours before the invasion began, the ships of the Fifth Fleet fired 3,800 shells in order to weaken the resistance. Okinawa civilians called the bombardment *"tetsu no bow"*: a storm of steel. Approximately 60,000 men landed on the island's beaches the first day, with thousands more to follow.

Gil Hodges, far from the ballfields of Indiana and Brooklyn, was right in the middle of the action, landing with the assault echelon near Hagushi Beach. After he returned home, Hodges never talked about the invasion, but Riley Marietta did in a 2008 interview in the Mansfield, Ohio, *News Journal*: "When I drove off the ship, the water was over my floorboards. I recall watching the Japanese planes come in at us with all guns firing. All you could do was hide and hope until our planes took care of them."

Nick Romagnoli and Rich Koenig, who became friends at boot camp on Parris Island, South Carolina, were also with the 16th Antiaircraft Battalion when it landed on Okinawa's rough beaches. "We were the tenth wave to hit the island," remembers Koenig.

"We had to bring in the heavy stuff, and antiaircraft equipment," adds Romagnoli. "It was foggy and stormy, a terrible day."

According to Koenig, the main purpose of the 16th after the beaches were secured was to set up positions around the airfield and erect netting to hide the guns. "We also went in to support the infantry and tanks when they went out into the field," he says.

After the invasion, Hodges was classified as a clerk who, according to a citation he received months later, "was entrusted with the safeguarding and stenographic preparation of highly classified documents" through "extensive periods of enemy aerial alerts and extensive bombing attacks." Comprehensive diaries were kept to detail the battalion's activities from March 1 to July

31, 1945, the five months when the fighting on Okinawa was at its most intense. Many were prepared by Corporal Hodges in the field. His commanding officer cited him for "his outstanding professional attainments and tireless devotion to duty . . . he diligently collected data and prepared vital combat missions." Maybe he wasn't the ballplayer who supposedly "ran through the jungles and killed the [enemy] with his bare hands," as his future Dodgers teammate Don Hoak and many others heard tales about, but his commander praised him for "contributing materially to the successful accomplishment of the battalion's mission."

The Japanese realized that an Allied invasion of their country was inevitable if they lost Okinawa, so as their ground forces were being pushed back across the island, they tried to support them by increasing the number and ferocity of their aerial attacks. Most vulnerable was the Fifth Fleet, as waves of suicidal pilots dived into ships, attempting to exchange their single lives for hundreds of Americans'. Even on land Hodges and the others in the 16th faced danger, because the kamikazes were also targeting the American airfields and munitions dumps that were protected by the big guns.

"The pilots and crews were bombing Japan, and they would come back almost without fuel and pretty knocked out from their experiences," remembers Romagnoli, who was a gun station operator controlling the lights. "While the planes were on the ground, we had to protect them against the kamikazes, mostly at night. Those crazy kamikazes—they would just dive at you and you had to shoot them and try to blow them up before they landed. It was a one-way trip for them no matter what. Sometimes they came in the daytime. They would dive at you with the sun behind them. You couldn't see them because they were low-flying targets; you couldn't pick them up until they were real close. At night, we didn't have radar down low, but we had good searchlights. We'd spot them and light them up and our aircraft and guns would attack them. When they got over our heads, we'd shut the lights out, turn the guns a hundred and eighty degrees, turn on the lights again, and fire on them from behind. It was all fast action. I had one of those big helmets on and earphones. By the time each night was over, I really had a stiff neck."

"The Japanese would come in and start to bomb us and the sky would just light up with red tracers," says Bob Stark, a Minnesota native who had to decline a tryout invitation from the Dodgers in 1943 because he was in basic training with the Marines. "The kamikazes would dive in from out of the sky. Our planes would show up and there would be dogfights. I remember wondering how I was going to get through this."

According to the official war diaries, over the course of the eighty-two-day campaign, the Japanese launched more than two thousand air attacks, and the 16th Antiaircraft Artillery Battalion fought off 108 air raids. On May 4, 1945, alone, the unit was subjected to fifteen such attacks. Men died at their guns.

Perhaps the closest Hodges came to suffering physical harm was on May 12, four days after V-E Day officially ended the war in Europe. The night before, enemy paratroopers had dropped behind the American lines. At dawn, they attacked the 16th's position. The adage of "every Marine a rifleman" was never truer than during that fight, as members of the battalion grappled with the Japanese using rifles, bayonets, knives, and their fists. Most of the paratroopers were killed or captured. Maps discovered on the Japanese dead revealed that among the targets of the attack was the 16th's radar equipment.

There was a great deal of activity between the B-29s taking off and returning from missions, and the Japanese mounting attacks. Between air raids, members of the battalion fell into a routine. While keeping a wary eye on the skies, they cleaned and repaired guns and vehicles, played cards or an occasional baseball game, slept, ate what they cooked in their little mess tents, gazed at their pinups, and reread the letters from home that took a couple of weeks to reach them. And "when it was time for Mass on Sundays," recalls Bob Stark, "Gil was one of the guys who'd organize it."

Baseball between battles, as disorganized as the games Hodges once played in Jimmy Higgins' Pasture when there was no real equipment and cowpies were used as bases, offered the Marines respite from the chaos. It was especially welcomed by Hodges because he'd never gone so long without participating in sports. Stark, who would be inducted into the Minnesota State High School Baseball Coaches Association Hall of Fame in 2010, was one of those who shared the makeshift diamond with Hodges. He remembers that Hodges was a catcher, "though he did pitch one game. We knew he had played some professional baseball, but he never put on any airs. He did do a little instructing when we were up at the plate—'cut down on your swing, Bob' and that sort of thing—but otherwise he was just a nice, regular guy who didn't say much. We had some players with professional potential and had some pretty good games. When we got everything under control, we got to play baseball every day."

Finally the fighting on Okinawa ceased. Mostly due to kamikazes, 34 allied ships and crafts of various types were sunk and 368 were damaged. There were 763 fleet aircraft lost. Over 12,000 soldiers and sailors died, with 36,000 wounded—one in five Marines was killed or wounded. The Japanese losses were even more staggering: 107,000 military personnel and as many as 100,000 Okinawan civilians had perished, and another 11,000 were taken prisoner. Also, 7,800 aircraft and 16 combat ships were lost.

If Hodges had remained on Tinian, he might have witnessed the take-off of the *Enola Gay*. The B-29 left the island on August 6 and headed for Hiroshima, where it dropped an atomic bomb. Three days later another B-29 took off from Tinian carrying another atomic bomb toward Nagasaki. The two cities were decimated and the Japanese surrendered, with the formal cessation of hostilities coming on August 15.

On September 26, Hodges was promoted to sergeant. Less than a month later, on October 22, he packed his clothes and catcher's mitt, because his unit had orders to sail back to America. It was a little over two years since he had entered the Marine Corps, and finally he was heading east instead of west. After a brief stay at Pearl Harbor, he boarded the *SS Meriwether,* which took him back to the States. He arrived in California on November 8, put his feet back on American soil, and spent a month at Camp Pendleton. The following month he found himself at the Marine Corps Separation Center in Great Lakes, Illinois, where he was detached from the 16th Antiaircraft Battalion.

Hodges' discharge was still six weeks away, but he was given a furlough and returned to Petersburg for the first time in two years. The Hodges family had a joyous reunion, one that included Bob, home in one piece from Europe. Gil probably sported only a faint tan after a month in the Midwest in the dead of winter, but he must have been an impressive sight in his uniform. After twenty-six months away, he had matured physically and mentally. He looked like he had muscles from head to toe, exhibited poise that belied his twenty-one years, and had an air of confidence that told the world he could handle anything. He was now a man.

Clearly, Gil could have arrived back home in Petersburg exhibiting his medals and ribbons and justifiably expecting to be treated as a war hero. But he didn't want any attention or to be asked questions about an experience he wanted to forget. The only thing he'd volunteer about the war was that it was in the foxholes that he became a chain-smoker like his father. He made no mention of his Commendation Ribbon, Combat Action Ribbon, Asiatic-Pacific Campaign Medal, Navy Occupation Service Medal with Asia Clasp, or Victory Medal.

It probably was unhealthy for Gil to keep his war memories inside, festering, his secret from the world. For years, family and friends sensed that something was troubling him, whether it be the deaths of friends, his own actions during combat, or guilt that he'd survived while so many died around him. But his reticence was understandable, even if damaging. It also was not uncommon in Pike County.

"A lot of the soldiers who came back would change the subject if you asked about the war," says Tom O'Rourke, who had gone to gunnery school.

June King, the wife of Gil's close friend Bob King, says, "Bob and I were married for fifty-three years before he died, and not once did he mention the war to me. He didn't want anything more to do with it. He didn't even sign up for a pension."

"We never talked about being in the service," says George Harris, "even when we were with other veterans. It was in the past. We just came back home and went to work."

Retired Marine Corps gunnery sergeant Chris Randazzo explains, "Marines who have been in intense combat tend not to talk about their experiences. The talk brings back horrific memories of friends being killed or grievously wounded."

"There's a revealing story about Hodges that I read many years ago," says Indiana sports historian Pete Cava. "It was told by a guy who went to see a war film with Gil. The guy said that every time a soldier got killed, Hodges quietly said, 'Amen.'"

During his furlough, Hodges reunited with high school friends. He and Bob went hunting with Bob King near Bowman. In town, Gil met up with

Bob and other friends at a new hangout, Dosch's Café, formerly Jimmy Sandage's place. The Hodges brothers also probably played some basketball, the sport Gil missed dearly in the service. Gil was relieved that his skills were intact.

Gil also wanted to enjoy some social life, and the most popular story about his furlough took place right after he got back. "The first night I was home, there was a dance in Jasper, Indiana, about thirty miles from Petersburg," Hodges told a reporter years later. Most likely he was speaking of River Nook.

"I had never gone out with Gil when we were in high school," recalls Pauline Wilson-Orbin, "but he was home on leave and we went to Jasper to where the kids danced and hung out. I don't remember him dancing while we were there."

"On the way home, somebody piled into me and I couldn't open the door on the driver's side," said Hodges to the reporter. "I went home and waited until Dad got up at 4:30 in the morning. I told him what had happened. He just laughed and got into the car on the other side and drove off to the mine."

"Well, the next night, Sunday night, Gil borrowed his father's car again," says Wilson-Orbin, "and drove me back to my apartment in Evansville, where I worked after leaving Petersburg that year. Another car hit us. My door was loose and I fell out on the street. Fortunately I didn't get hurt and the car wasn't particularly damaged and he was able to drive me home. I don't know what he said to his father!"

"I went home and waited for Dad to get up at 4:30 again," said Hodges. "I told him the story, almost the same story I had brought home the night before. He was a little mad this time, because he had to crawl through the window to get in the car. The next day he bought a new car. Not another word about the accident was ever mentioned."

When Gil's furlough ended, he returned briefly to Great Lakes, Illinois. On February 3, 1946, he received his honorable discharge. A month later he headed east to try to salvage his professional baseball career. He considered himself very fortunate.

PART II

A Brooklyn Dodger

CHAPTER SIX

Gil Hodges, once a laid-back, carefree kid, was known to be a worrier as an adult, and as he traveled by rail from Indianapolis to Florida, he fretted that his first spring training would be his last, and that he should have bought a return-trip ticket. After twenty-eight months in the military he possessed enough self-assurance to take on the world, but professional baseball was something else entirely. He might not have even climbed aboard if he hadn't had a talk with his father before he left home. In 1960 he wrote in *Guideposts*, "I told my father about my doubts. They were deep. 'God is giving you the opportunity,' he said. 'Who are you to walk away from it?' It wasn't a scolding, it wasn't preaching. He said it wondering why I should even question it."

The Dodgers' official spring training facility in 1946 was in Daytona Beach at City Island Park, but Branch Rickey decided to have an earlier, special camp thirty-five miles southwest in rural Sanford, Florida's celery capital. It had opened a couple of weeks before Hodges' arrival. He took one look at the hundreds of former GIs engaged in various physical activities and told another player, "This is just like the Marines." At Sanford, Rickey brought together veteran players returning from war, players who had filled roster slots in 1945, and young players like Hodges who had been signed just prior to or during the war years. His purpose was to weed out the players who couldn't cut it and assemble a talented *young* team that would battle for pennants for years to come.

Under Rickey's aegis, the Dodgers finished third in 1943, seventh in

1944, and third in 1945. He was well aware that it hadn't been him but the flamboyant, innovative MacPhail who, after leaving the Cincinnati Reds in 1938, made the savvy moves that resulted in the Dodgers' last pennant in 1941, their first since 1920. He also was responsible for helping what had been a financially strapped organization go over a million in attendance every season by installing lights, hiring Gladys Gooding to play the organ at the ballpark (including "Three Blind Mice" when the umps made questionable calls against the home team), and pilfering elegant radio broadcaster Red Barber from Cincinnati. Rickey wanted to put together his own championship team in Brooklyn and do MacPhail, who was now presiding over the Yankees, one better by bringing the much-maligned borough its first World Series title after losses in 1916, 1920, and 1941.

Naturally, he would keep his best player, classy shortstop Pee Wee Reese, whom he could see as a Dodger for another dozen years; the immensely talented but injury-prone center fielder Pete Reiser and dependable, fine-hitting right fielder Dixie "People's Cherce" Walker; and pitchers Hugh Casey and Kirby Higbe (whom the heavy-gambling Leo Durocher wanted to keep around to ravage at gin rummy). But he expected to phase out Billy Herman, third baseman Cookie Lavagetto, and others whose time had passed. Indeed, in 1945, Durocher had replaced Herman as his starting second baseman with scrappy overachiever Eddie Stanky and placed nineteen-year-old right-hander Ralph Branca in the rotation. But the manager and owner were willing to wait for the other players who had been signed to blossom and fill the holes on the roster. Those signees weren't just young white players like Hodges, Duke Snider, and Carl Erskine, but experienced Negro Leagues players as well.

In October 23, 1945, Rickey had shaken the foundation of not only sports but America itself by signing African-American Jackie Roosevelt Robinson of the Kansas City Monarchs to a contract to play for the Montreal Royals, the Dodgers' affiliate in the International League. Robinson was only one league away from being the first black since Moses Fleetwood Walker in 1884 to play in the major leagues. Major League Baseball's first commissioner, the despotic Kenesaw Mountain Landis, who had blocked all attempts to integrate the sport, passed away in 1944, and Rickey believed there was a good chance that his successor, Happy Chandler, would allow Robinson to take that final step into history.

Robinson, a four-sport athlete at UCLA and someone who had battled and triumphed over racism in the military, had agreed to Rickey's condition to turn the other cheek when he was targeted by hecklers in the stands or the opposing bench, spiked by baserunners, or thrown at by pitchers. Still, Rickey felt that it was best for Robinson to spend a year in the minors, in a friendly environment, before jumping into the fire, particularly since the Southerners on the Dodgers were not ready to accept a black teammate. Robinson would play in Canada the entire 1946 season. Rickey's other significant Negro Leagues signees, also scouted by Clyde Sukeforth, were veteran catcher Roy Campanella and young pitcher Don Newcombe. They would play for manager Walter Alston and general manager Buzzie Bavasi in Nashua, New Hampshire, a small town with a large French-Canadian population that had no problem rooting for black ballplayers.

"The Dodgers were signing blacks and then using a stair-step procedure for getting them to the majors," said Don Newcombe when interviewed for the 1994 oral history *We Played the Game*. "They hoped that the animosity would be swept away by 1949 or 1950. So Jackie was going to be the first, pitcher Dan Bankhead was going to be second, Roy was going to be third. Whoever came after them would be determined by talent."

Rickey took the heat and the credit for the signings of black players. But he undoubtedly had to consult his co-owners before taking such bold action. "I think he had at least tacit approval from Walter O'Malley for signing my dad, Robinson, and Newcombe," says Roy Campanella II. "O'Malley saw that it'd be good for baseball both in terms of social context and business. But I'm sure he was just a little worried that by bringing in another ethnic group, there could be potential problems."

Among those present at Sanford was a promising rookie outfielder from Reading, Pennyslvania, who had—as those who made up nicknames noticed—a rifle for an arm. He had just spent thirty-eight months in the service. "I went by train to Sanford, Florida, where the Dodgers had what they called advanced training for all ballplayers in the service," Carl Furillo recalled in Peter Golenbock's 1984 oral history of the Brooklyn Dodgers,

Bums. "Durocher had the best coaches there; I'll say that much for him. I was signed to a minor-league contract, and they wanted me to sign a Brooklyn contract, but they didn't want to give me any money. I went to see Leo, and he showed me a contract for $3,750. I said, 'I can't survive on that.' He said to me, 'Take it or leave it.' I hated Durocher's guts from that day on." Despite his troubles with Durocher, Furillo became one of the players Rickey built his team around.

Rickey also had his eye on Hodges. He told him to do as much catching as possible at Sanford. He caught batting practice, rookie games, and squad games during the day. Then in the evening, according to John Devaney's slim 1973 bio, *Gil Hodges, Baseball's Miracle Man*, "Dodger minor-league instructors showed him how to place his body to block low throws, how to position himself when there were runners on base, how to come out of his crouch and throw low and hard to second base to catch a base stealer."

Still, Rickey and Durocher decided to go with rookie catchers Bruce Edwards and twenty-eight-year-old Ferrell Anderson, and Hodges was assigned to Newport News. He understood that you can't teach experience, so he didn't second-guess them. Questioning men in authority, be they employers or umpires, was not in his makeup even before he was a Marine. He was going to a Class-B team, but Hodges took the positive attitude that he was being demoted as far down as Brooklyn could send a major leaguer who had been in the service because it was an ideal place for him. He was assured that he could learn the skills that would enable him to reach the major leagues from player-manager John Fitzpatrick, who had been a good catcher in his prime.

Newport News, Virginia, a historic town located on the James River, was known for its shipbuilding industry, primarily for the war vessels built there since Theodore Roosevelt's presidency. During World War II, it had served as a primary port of deployment for American sailors, and housed two POW camps for German soldiers. Of less interest to the population was the arrival of a minor-league baseball team in 1944. Managed by Jake Pitler, the Newport News Dodgers had a dismal 61–78 record in their premier season and landed in the cellar of the Piedmont League, but in 1945 they finished 69–69 before being knocked out of the playoffs in the first round. Fitzpatrick was optimistic about putting together a contender in 1946 and filling a lot of the seats that had been empty at old Shipbuilder's Park.

"Newport News was a sea town and there just wasn't much to do," recalls Bill Hardy, an infielder on the team who had played college ball against Hodges and also had been signed by Stan Feezle.

"Nobody went to bars, nobody drank beer, nobody played pool or bowled," recalls Norman Ozark, a second baseman. "We spent our free time going to movies. Gil and the rest of us were all together as a group, two or three guys going out together but never as a clique."

Unlike Hardy and the other married players who found separate lodging in town, Ozark and Hodges were among the single players who stayed in barracks. "The barracks were over what looked like a navy shipyard," Ozark says. "We had rooms but had to go to restaurants to eat. We got enough meal money for breakfast, and if we didn't go hog wild, we could pay for lunch and dinner, too. All of us hoped to reach the majors, so we weren't only there to learn how to play—we competed hard because we wanted to win."

Ozark—whose brother Danny would later manage the Phillies to three straight division titles in the 1970s—Hardy, pitcher Turk Lown, and outfielder Clarence Groat were among those who befriended Hodges. "He was a real nice, quiet guy," says Ozark, "real pleasant, the kind of person you liked to hang out with."

"He was always very good to me," Hardy remembers. "He knew I was trying to make it and would tell me what pitch was coming, and that helped me get a couple of hits. He was a soft-spoken, giant gentleman who never said a harsh word to or about anybody. I can't say how much I respected him."

"Because I had elbow surgery, I arrived at Newport News a bit late, and Gil came up and introduced himself and wished me luck," recalls Omar "Turk" Lown, a future major-league pitcher who took some shrapnel in his leg in Germany during World War II. "What I remember most about him as a teammate—and when I pitched against him on the Brooklyn and Los Angeles Dodgers—is that he was one of the nicest guys in baseball."

Groat was probably Hodges' closest friend on the team. A full-blooded Mohawk who, like Ozark, was from Buffalo, "Soddy" Groat had been an infantryman in the European campaigns during World War II and had received the Silver Star, Bronze Star, and Purple Heart. He was so fond of Hodges that he would name his son Gil.

Hodges thought it fortuitous to receive the tutelage of the forty-two-year-old Fitzpatrick, who played twenty-one seasons in the minors and still donned the tools of ignorance on occasion. "Jack would always sit with Gil in the dugout before games and they would talk," recalls Hardy. "He'd be giving Gil some instructions, including on how to call a game and how to throw to second without the ball sailing."

"It took some getting used to," said Hodges, "but I finally got to the point where I liked catching. It's harder work, maybe, but it's also more interesting."

Fitzpatrick was impressed by his young pupil's eagerness to learn and his quick improvement as both a receiver and hitter. After three weeks he inserted Hodges into his starting lineup.

At the plate, it was obvious to everyone that he was a dead fastball hitter but had trouble with the curve, particularly on the outside corner. It was a problem that would drive him batty for his entire career. It was the minors, and young pitchers struggled with their control, so Gil began to lay off that pitch because it was almost always called a ball. He also took first pitches, because more often than not, a young pitcher was unable to find the strike zone and the count would be 1–0. That Hodges was able to harness his aggressiveness served him well as a hitter at Newport News. However, it can be argued that he developed a pattern that didn't serve him well in the big leagues, where pitchers had the control to fire a first-pitch fastball over the middle of the plate and hit the outside corner with a two-strike breaking ball. His high number of strikeouts in the majors wasn't surprising, What was impressive is how well he did, considering that pitchers had such a big advantage.

In the '46 season Hodges suffered a dislocated right thumb and was spiked so badly on a play at the plate that, recalls Lown, "one of our teammates and I had to carry him off the field." But he talked his way back into the lineup without missing much time and tried not to let either injury hamper his development. Among the league's catchers, he was considered the best at throwing out base stealers, and his .278 average, 27 doubles,

7 triples, 8 homers, 64 RBIs, and 12 stolen bases were notable as well. He placed in the league's top ten in homers and was third on his team. "He was big and all muscle and could have hit more homers, but he wasn't pulling the ball then, but hitting to all fields, wherever the ball was pitched," says Hardy.

The Dodger who hit the most homers on the team and in the league, 17, was Kevin "Chuck" Connors, a six-foot-five left-handed first baseman who wanted to be an actor. He also would be the starting center that winter for the new Boston Celtics of the Basketball Association of America. Connors, Hodges, several other strong hitters, and a solid staff led by Wayne Johnson (16–7, 2.26 ERA), Pete Mondorff (12–9, 3.41), Harry Grundy (9–7, 3.41), and Frank Wilson (9–8, 3.78) led the Dodgers to a 76–64 record and a third-place finish behind the Roanoke Red Sox and Portsmouth Cubs. In the first round of the playoffs the Dodgers stunned the Cubs by sweeping four straight games. They then lost the first two games of the championship series to the Red Sox, but came back to win the next two. They evened the series when Lown got the key victory with relief help from Mondorff. After a 3–3 fourteen-inning tie, they went up in the series 3–2 with a 5–1 victory in Game 5, as Hodges had 2 doubles and 2 RBIs. Wilson, in relief of Grundy, then pitched the Dodgers to a Piedmont title in Game 6.

The conclusion of the Brooklyn Dodgers' 1946 season was much more disappointing. In the first playoff series in National League history, the Dodgers were beaten in back-to-back games by the Cardinals. (St. Louis star Stan Musial was particularly thrilled beating a team managed by Durocher, the only person, according to Musial biographer George Vecsey, whom he ever cursed on the baseball diamond.) Years before "Wait Until Next Year" became the heartbroken Dodgers fans' October mantra, the nationally syndicated Newspaper Enterprise Association used this headline on October 21, 1946, for an article by Harry Grayson: "Wait Until 1947 Is New Cry of Dodgers' Backers." Grayson wrote: "The Brooklyn club now has 300 players in its 22-club farm system, the bulk of them hand-picked youngsters. No other outfit has such a plethora of promising talent. Among the names more prominently mentioned as Brooks of the future are those of Jackie Robinson, Duke Snider and Gil Hodges, the latter pair perhaps a year away as the baseball man says."

The twenty-two-year-old Hodges, whose nickname at Newport News was "The Body," returned to Petersburg after the season, wondering whether Grayson was correct and the Dodgers saw him in their plans. He knew he had taken tremendous strides under Fitzpatrick, and it didn't hurt that he had been the catcher on a championship team, but he was never impressed by his own performances.

Back home, Gil played independent baseball for the first time since he'd gone off to war. Bob had been pitching in the semipro Indiana-Kentucky League, making a final effort to catch the attention of scouts. He still threw a curve that would tumble off a table, but his fastball was his calling card. "I don't know how many times older guys would talk to me about how hard my dad threw," says John Hodges. "One old gentleman told me, 'Your father threw so hard that the ball grazed a guy's head and took off part of his ear.' That's sure a source of pride."

Naturally, everyone in the area wanted to see Gil play ball after establishing himself as a professional. Roger Emmert, who played youth ball with Gil, recalled fifty-five years later: "I saw Gil catch a game in Princeton when he got back. Gil had the strongest hands I ever saw, and he'd do something I never saw anyone else do: He'd catch the ball in his mitt and instead of reaching in for the ball, he'd just squeeze the mitt and it would pop into his throwing hand!"

Also memorable was a game of softball Hodges played as a favor to some kids. "It was in Washington," remembers Norma Avanell Thomas. "These boys asked him to play in their softball game because they thought he was so good, and Gil couldn't turn down kids. But something happened, maybe he missed the ball, and he cost them the game. And it pained his soul. He kept saying, 'I lost that ball game for those kids! I lost that ball game for those kids!'"

Gil Hodges, who never showed emotion as a professional even after the most dreadful defeat, was visibly distraught after letting down children in a meaningless softball game. As an ex-Marine, being the weak link in the chain was unacceptable, and he was never more disappointed in himself than when he failed to live up to expectations. It was one bad and *revealing* moment in what was otherwise a tremendous year after the war.

CHAPTER SEVEN

In late February, Hodges again traveled to Florida for spring training, but this time he flew another ninety miles. Because the Dodgers didn't want Jackie Robinson to be subjected to the same harassment he endured in Florida in 1946, and since the facility they were building for themselves in Vero Beach wouldn't be ready until 1948, Rickey accepted a lucrative offer to hold spring training in '47 in Havana, Cuba. "Call the choice of Havana a decision made on behalf of Jackie and economics both," explained Buzzie Bavasi, a Dodgers jack-of-all-trades before he became the general manager in 1951.

Hodges knew there was a lot of young talent in camp, including his left-handed slugging counterpart, Duke Snider, and Robinson. He worried that he'd be lost in the sea of ballplayers. He was surprised when Dick Young, who started covering the Dodgers for the *New York Daily News* in 1946 and already had a huge readership, knew who he was and came up to him at Gran Stadium with his small hand extended. "Before I heard of Hodges, I heard of his hands," wrote the diminutive Young. "'We have a kid,' Branch Rickey Jr. said one day, 'who has hands like hamhocks. I want you to meet him. He's gonna be something.' When the time came, I stuck out my hand, flinching inwardly. 'Watch this big hick try to show me how strong he is,' I thought. It was like sticking my hand into a bin of feathers. The big hands were gentle."

Following long days of workouts and instruction, Hodges palled around with other young players, including Snider, Spider Jorgensen, who would be the Dodgers starting third baseman as a rookie in 1947, and pitcher Ralph Branca, who at twenty-one already had two years in the majors. Even these athletes were struck by Hodges' physical attributes.

"He was the only ballplayer I ever saw with a ripped stomach," Branca recalls. "In those days you didn't do weights; you did sit-ups, and he came out of the service with muscles in his stomach. Gil was a regular, likable guy. He was basically quiet, but if you got him to talk you'd discover that he had a great sense of humor, a dry wit, and, if you got to know him, he'd bust you a little. He was a rookie, but he was an ex-Marine and didn't need me or anyone else to take him under his wing."

Hodges hoped for a quiet camp at which he could concentrate on impressing Leo Durocher and making his twenty-five-man roster. A distraction, however, was that the manager was under scrutiny for his relationship with actor George Raft, who not only made gangster movies but also had ties with figures in the underworld. There were accusations that the two had bilked a chump out of $12,000 with some crooked dice back in 1945. Durocher's image took another hit when J. Ray Hendricks, a neighbor of Durocher's who ran the Santa Monica Airport, accused him publicly of being a "love pirate" for carrying on an affair with his wife, actress Laraine Day. That January, she had gotten a Mexican divorce from Hendricks and one day later became Durocher's third wife. The story made headlines not only in scandal sheets, but also in mainstream papers across the country. The Catholic Church came down hard on Durocher for carrying on an adulterous affair, and in February, the Catholic Youth Organization, boasting a membership of over fifty thousand youngsters, of whom a full third belonged to the Dodger Knot Hole Gang club, threatened to defect to the Giants and Yankees. Rickey was very concerned about losing a large part of the fan base and didn't make his usual defense of Durocher to his three troubled partners.

In the media, Durocher and Day's sinful romance was a bigger story than what also took place that January at the baseball winter meetings at the Waldorf Astoria in New York City. Fifteen owners wearing expensive suits and pained expressions declared a need to continue the "gentleman's agreement" that for sixty-two years had denied blacks equal opportunity to play in the majors. Yankees owner Larry MacPhail delivered an impassioned speech about why the Dodgers shouldn't be allowed to sign Jackie Robinson to a major-league contract for the coming season. Only Rickey spoke in favor of integrating baseball. The vote was 15–1 against.

It was now up to commissioner Happy Chandler to make the final decision, knowing that if he let Robinson into the majors he wouldn't be reelected by the owners when his contract expired in 1951. The former governor and senator from Kentucky, wanting to "face my maker with a clear conscience," boldly opened the door for Robinson, suddenly placing Major League Baseball at the forefront of social change in the country.

Neither Rickey nor Durocher appreciated MacPhail's stance against Robinson. And Durocher had another ax to grind with his former employer. He claimed that during the off-season, he turned down MacPhail's offer to manage the Yankees, and MacPhail's spiteful response was to swipe a couple of his coaches, Charlie Dressen and John Corriden. His March 3 "Durocher Says" column in the *Brooklyn Eagle*—which was ghosted by Dodgers beat writer Harold Parrott—stated, "This is a declaration of war. I want to beat the Yankees as badly as I do any team in the National League. And that is certainly saying plenty. I want to wallop them Yanks because of MacPhail and Dressen."

It's little wonder that when Hodges blasted a homer to topple the Yankees in extra innings in one hard-fought game in Caracas, the delighted Durocher rewarded his hero with more work. The young man probably didn't know what to make of the controversy surrounding Durocher, but he was appreciative of his manager for letting him catch more batting practices and more games as the season drew closer. Meanwhile, Durocher had to deal with a threatened revolt by players who didn't want blacks as teammates.

Robinson was glad not to be training in Florida again, but he and the other African-Americans in Havana, Roy Campanella, Don Newcombe, and Roy Partow, endured indignities there as well, including being denied an invitation to a party for players at Ernest Hemingway's bungalow and being relegated to a downtown hotel while the other Dodgers and Montreal Royals enjoyed fancy accommodations. "Training in Cuba was typical of the meticulous planning that Branch Rickey did in support of the black players," recalls Rachel Robinson. "But Havana wasn't what Jackie and the others hoped for. They were surprised when they got there and felt almost betrayed because they were kept separate."

For exhibition games, the black players were in the lineups of minor-league teams. Still under contract with Montreal although his signing with the big-league club was imminent, Robinson played seven exhibition games for the Royals against the Dodgers. Rickey wanted the Dodgers who were resistant to playing with a black to see what a tremendous player he was and realize he could help them reach the World Series and make extra money.

Robinson was magnificent against Dodgers pitching, but he didn't sway anyone opposing him. While the team was in Panama to play several exhibition games, Dixie Walker of Alabama circulated a petition to collect names of players who refused to play with Robinson. Among those who signed were Higbe, Casey, Lavagetto, Stanky, Bragan, and probably Furillo. But Pee Wee Reese of Louisville, Kentucky, hadn't forgotten the contributions of black soldiers during the war and refused to add his name, leading to a wave of rejections. Snider, who idolized Robinson when he was a multisport star at UCLA, didn't sign. "Hodges refused to sign the petition," says Roger Kahn, the author of 1971's celebrated *The Boys of Summer*, which immortalized the Brooklyn Dodgers of 1947–57. "Reese was a more important player at the time, but Hodges said no, too. Furillo said sure. He later recanted but still got unfairly portrayed as a racist when he wasn't. With Gil there was no black and white. If you were a teammate who played hard to win, no one was more loyal than Gil Hodges."

Durocher's finest hour was calling a meeting of players in the middle of the night and reading the malcontents the riot act. He told them what they could do with the petition and said that whoever didn't want to play with Robinson should quit. For those who wanted to play elsewhere, including Walker, he promised Rickey would make it happen.

The insurrection was squelched, but Durocher had other problems. He and MacPhail attacked each other in the media, each accusing the other of consorting with shady gamblers. Chandler's strange solution was to punish both men: He fined his friend MacPhail a few hundred bucks and suspended Durocher for a full year for "conduct detrimental to baseball."

The new manager would be Burt Shotton, who'd take over from interim skipper Clyde Sukeforth after two games of the season. He was well liked and respected, but he was shy and reticent and wore a suit and tie in the dugout à la Connie Mack just so he wouldn't be allowed to walk across the diamond to the mound in front of a crowd. His idea of a pep talk was saying, "Fellows, I saved my money and bought savings bonds—I got mine; now go out and get yours." After a loss, Shotton never yelled at his players, but just said, "There's always tomorrow." Still, his team responded with victories.

Fortunately, Durocher stuck around long enough to help Rickey and Sukeforth determine Hodges' status for 1947. It was clear that Bruce Edwards was going to be the starting catcher again with Bragan as his backup. The question was whether the team could carry three receivers. Sukeforth, a former catcher, liked how much Hodges had progressed at that position. Durocher praised Gil's power, his hustle, and his character. Rickey reminded everyone that because Hodges had been on the roster since 1943, there was a good chance he'd be claimed on waivers if he were sent back to the minors. So the decision was unanimous: Gil Hodges was going to be a Brooklyn Dodger rookie, like Duke Snider and Jackie Robinson.

Robinson's historic first game was Opening Day in Brooklyn, April 15, 1947, against the Boston Braves. He was stationed at first base instead of his familiar second base, because there would be less chance of his being spiked by aggressive baserunners, especially one from the South. Facing Johnny Sain, Robinson collected just a walk and stolen base in the Dodgers' 5–3 victory. But everyone present at Ebbets Field and listening to Red Barber and Connie Desmond on the radio—the Irish, the Italians, the Jews, *and* the African-Americans—felt a tremendous surge of pride that the first African-American in baseball in the twentieth century was playing in their ballpark and town.

During the season, Robinson was subjected to gut-wrenching abuse from fans and players on the road, particularly in Philadelphia, where manager Ben Chapman was at the forefront of the racist heckling, and St. Louis, where several players grumbled about a boycott. "In those days all rookies, especially those with reputations for being pretty good, got abused," Ralph Branca has pointed out. "But Jackie got more than a double dose. Some of the other teams rode him unmercifully." Silently, Robinson dodged bean-balls, sidestepped spikes (although the Cards' Enos Slaughter bloodied him by running up his leg on a play at first), and dealt with death threats.

Robinson received gallant support from Reese, who heard the catcalls and famously put his arm around his shoulders at Crosley Field in Cincin-nati to assure Robinson and his enemies that he wasn't alone. He received support from other Dodgers as well, including, unexpectedly, Eddie Stanky, who resented the cowards who heckled a man they knew couldn't fight back; from the Pirates' Hank Greenberg, once a target of anti-Semitism; and most of all from his wife, Rachel. "I never missed a home game, and Jackie would look for me in the stands," she recalls. "I would try to communicate with him through the airwaves mentally."

She still credits Branch Rickey for her husband getting through diffi-cult times: "Sometimes I must reinforce my belief that it was a collaboration, a pairing of two men who needed to respect and trust each other so that they could make it work. They talked sporadically, usually about something that was coming up that they had to plan together. It was frequent at certain stages, early on in particular, and it was in person. Jack would go to his of-fice. Occasionally, I would be invited to sit in and observe. I loved seeing Jackie and Branch together."

Robinson didn't just succeed but triumphed. He'd bat .297, accumulate 175 hits, 13 on bunts; swat 12 homers; rip 31 doubles and 5 triples; lay down 28 successful sacrifice bunts; steal a league-leading 29 bases; and top the league in terrorizing pitchers by threatening to steal, taking extra bases on weak-armed or napping outfielders, and escaping rundowns. On Sep-tember 12, baseball's most competitive player was selected the National League's first Rookie of the Year by the *Sporting News*, a conservative St. Louis–based publication that hadn't been welcoming to Robinson when he broke in. His first year would be chronicled by scores of writers who recog-nized the rare intertwining of baseball history and social history.

Hodges and Snider, who rented a room together on Bedford Avenue in Flatbush, within walking distance of Ebbets Field, marveled at what their fellow rookie was achieving. They both would have liked to have played more with Robinson, but Hodges was Shotton's third-string catcher and Snider his sixth outfielder. Even after Pete Reiser almost killed himself by slamming his head into a concrete wall in Pittsburgh—last rites were administered—Shotton played Walker in right, Furillo in center, and Gene Hermanski in left. Snider batted only 83 times all season, and never homered while hitting .241.

Hodges struggled in his 77 at-bats, getting only 12 hits, but did slug his first big-league homer, against the Cubs' veteran right-hander Hank Borowy, to go with 3 doubles and a triple. His microscopic .156 average resulted both from inactivity and his discomfort batting against pitchers who knew he couldn't hit breaking balls. His lone longball came after an inspirational visit he and Snider spent in Branch Rickey's office. Rickey told them that someday they would be the right- and left-handed power hitter on the Dodgers. In future years, Snider would say there was no one better than Rickey at predicting how young players would develop.

"I think the Dodgers appreciated Gil's skills," says Ralph Branca. "Gil wasn't in many games that year and spent most of his time in the bullpen, but I think they saw that he was already a hell of a catcher. He had great hands, great footwork, and a strong, accurate arm. He was a natural, just terrific."

In 1947, Brooklyn went 90–64, going 52–25 in the friendly confines of Ebbets Field, to win the pennant by 5 games over the Cardinals. By the end of June they were in first place to stay, building their lead with a 25–8 July that included a thirteen-game winning streak. They clinched on September 22, and the celebration continued on the twenty-third, when "Jackie Robinson Day" was held at Ebbets Field and he received a car and many other gifts. Among those gathering near home plate to honor him was Dixie Walker.

Other than Robinson, Walker was the biggest threat in the lineup in '47, with a .306 average and 94 RBIs. The other key figure was Reese, who played solid defense, was a dependable clutch hitter, and was the glue of the team. "We all rallied behind Pee Wee, our leader," said Jorgensen. "He kept us focused on winning, which made us a close team. We knew he was going to make the right play or say the right thing. He was always helpful, to Jackie and the other players, too."

The Dodgers had an underwhelming offense, but they played excellent defense, and their staff had the third-best ERA despite Ebbets Field's being a bandbox, and led the league with 14 shutouts (tying the Boston Braves). Their ace was the twenty-one-year-old Branca, who on September 11 became the youngest Dodger to win 20 games when he defeated St. Louis 4–3 in the first game of a showdown series with the Cardinals.

On September 26, the sidewalks on Flatbush Avenue were packed as a seventeen-car motorcade proceeded to Borough Hall. There, Hodges and twenty-six other Dodgers received watches, praise, and cheers, and a teary Jackie Robinson and Dixie Walker spoke gratefully about the support the team received from the best fans in the world. The Dodgers faithful had done their part to help their team reach the World Series.

The Dodgers' adversary would be the New York Yankees. The 1947 Fall Classic was a rematch of 1941, only this one was watched on television by 3.9 million people, including 3.5 million in bars in New York, Philadelphia, Schenectady, and Washington, D.C. The first televised Series helped popularize the new medium. Managed by Bucky Harris, the Yankees were there by virtue of running away with the American League pennant by 12 games, and the Dodgers didn't underestimate them. They still had three stars from the '41 championship team—Joe DiMaggio, Tommy Henrich, and Phil Rizzuto.

Playing before 73,365 and 69,865 fans in the first two games at Yankee Stadium, New York won 5–3 behind Spec Shea (14–5 during the season) and relief specialist Joe Page; and 10–3 as ace Allie Reynolds (19–8) went the distance. But the Dodgers were resilient. Before 33,098 fervent, sharp-tongued fans at Ebbets Field in Game 3, they broke out to a 6–0 lead and escaped with a 9–8 victory as Hugh Casey shut down the Yankees for the final 2⅓ innings.

Game 4 would be a classic. The Yankees' Bill Bevens came within one out of throwing the first no-hitter in Series history. But he walked his ninth and tenth batters, and pinch hitter Lavagetto doubled off the right-field wall to score them and give the Dodgers an improbable 3–2 victory.

With the Series even, Shea tossed a 4-hitter to win the pivotal Game 5 at Ebbets Field, silencing the cacophonous, wandering five-piece Sym-Phony Band, superfan Hilda Chester's cowbells, and the wild cheers of 34,378 other fans who realized the Dodgers had little chance of winning the next two games at Yankee Stadium.

But before a new-Series-record 74,065 fans, the Dodgers audaciously won Game 6 as their first three hitters, Stanky, Reese, and Robinson, combined for 7 hits, 5 runs, and 3 RBIs. Branca claimed the victory in relief, and Casey recorded a save with another scoreless frame. But the Dodger best remembered in that game was Al Gionfriddo. With Brooklyn clinging to a 7–6 lead in the bottom of the seventh inning, with two on and two out for the home team, DiMaggio hit a screamer to deep left field. Gionfriddo raced back toward the wall, stuck out his glove, and caught the ball just before encountering the bullpen fence. As well-known as the film clip of that marvelous catch is the image of DiMaggio, in a rare display of emotion, kicking the dirt in disgust when he realizes he was robbed.

In Game 7, Brooklyn took a 2–0 lead in the second inning off Shea, but they were frustrated the rest of the way by Bevens and Page, who yielded only 1 hit over the last 5 innings. Hodges, who had been a spectator for the first six games, made his World Series debut against Page. Batting for reliever Rex Barney in the seventh inning, he hoped to duplicate catcher Yogi Berra, who in Game 3 hit the first pinch homer in Series history.

"I didn't really know much about Gil then," says Yogi Berra sixty-four years later. But Berra made a mental note that Hodges had trouble hitting a good curveball. Page threw a wicked one and Hodges went down swinging. By that time, the Yankees were ahead 5–2, and that was the final score as they captured another world title at Brooklyn's expense.

In the spring, Durocher had promised his players that Jackie Robinson would lead them to the Series and they would receive a large sum of money as their share. So big were the Series crowds that the losers received a hefty $4,081. The grateful players voted Durocher a partial share—but Happy Chandler disallowed it and Durocher got nothing.

On October 6, as Hodges and his Dodgers teammates filed out of the locker room at Yankee Stadium, contemplating how close they had come to beating mighty New York and becoming the world champions, they heard Shotton say softly, "There's always next year."

CHAPTER EIGHT

It wasn't worry that dogged Hodges after the 1947 season, but common sense. Branch Rickey had implied he was a star of the future, but all Hodges saw in the mirror was a third-string catcher who had batted an embarrassing .156 and couldn't hit a major-league curveball. He knew better than to count on a lengthy baseball career. He again thought of a future as a basketball coach and decided that in the off-season he would go back to college for a term to work on his degree and play basketball. He enrolled at nearby Oakland City College, which was known for turning out teachers, ministers, and coaches.

Hodges moved back into the family home in Petersburg and waited for the winter term to begin in early December. Marjorie was away at nursing school in Terre Haute, but Bob was back home after a disappointing season in professional baseball. He played minor-league ball only that summer for independent Mahanoy City, Pennsylvania, in the North Atlantic League. Pitching for the Bluebirds, he compiled a 3–6 record with a high 5.35 ERA; and playing 28 games in the outfield, he batted .225 in 71 at-bats, with no home runs. "Bobby would say he would make the majors and Dad would smile, but his arm went dead when he was playing Class-D ball," Gil told reporters a few years later. "Bobby pitched too much. He kept throwing and throwing and throwing and wasn't in shape. He was just never in the proper condition to do that much pitching."

"Dad was still good enough to pitch semipro ball in Indiana," says Mike

Hodges, "but he couldn't throw as hard after he hurt his arm; good hitters took him downtown. He was okay with it and just moved on."

In early December, Gil entered Oakland City College as a junior, majoring in physical education and social studies. He proudly commuted from Petersburg each day in the Mercury the Dodgers gave him for being in the World Series—it was so new that it didn't have bumpers, just two-by-twelve-foot blocks of wood. Many of the approximately 250 students at the Baptist college were awestruck when they saw a celebrity on campus. "The first thing we thought was, 'He is a real star who plays for the Brooklyn Dodgers,'" recalls Harry Goerlitz, who became his closest friend on the basketball team. "But after that he was accepted as part of the student body and basketball team, and nobody mentioned that he was famous or asked for his autograph."

"It was a big deal to me that Gil Hodges played for Oakland City College," recalls Bill Marshall, who still lives in the town. "I was on Oakland City High School's basketball team and we shared their gym. I talked to Gil whenever I had the chance. I remember telling him I'd read that Leo Durocher said he was a good prospect. He just kind of stopped and smiled and said, 'Well, that was *last* year.' He reminded me of Lou Gehrig—quiet, strong, smart, personable, and patient with strangers who wanted to talk to him."

Like most of his teammates, Hodges was at school on the GI Bill, was older than most students on campus, and wanted to be a coach. The Oaks' coach, Delbert "Chief" Disler, who had played football at Purdue, was much better at coaching football at the high school level than coaching basketball at the college, but his players loved him. Disler was a lot of fun—particularly when they all played poker—and was sensitive to the trauma many had experienced in war.

"I didn't see any combat when I was in the service," says Goerlitz, "and I don't know how the war affected Gil, because he wouldn't talk about it, but I know some of those guys went through pure hell. Back then we didn't know about post-traumatic stress disorder, and if someone was acting strange we'd just say they were 'battle-rattled.' Disler had the knack for knowing how to treat us. If it hadn't been for him, I'm sure a lot of guys would have given up and quit the team and school."

Oakland City College went 1–3 before Hodges joined the team. In his first game, played in the school's small gym above the library, he scored 11 points as the Oaks triumphed over Fort Knox, 66–56, and the *Oakland City Journal* singled him out as "the star of the game."

Despite being the same height as the Oaks' center, Kenneth "Tot" Nelson, the six-foot-one-inch Hodges played guard for Disler. "He really played everywhere on the floor," recalls Nelson, who went on to become a very successful high school coach. "He'd be guarded by a smaller guard, so he'd go under the basket and we'd pass the ball to him. Also, he'd guard the other team's forward, so he'd end up under the basket then, too, to pull down rebounds. Gil didn't score a lot of points, because he was more of a defensive player, but he had a hook shot and made a lot of layups. He was very adept at faking an opponent out of position and at dribbling with either hand."

"He was really active and could get off the floor," remembers Arvin Roberson, who had just gotten out of the service and returned to his home in Oakland City. "He had monstrous hands, and when they'd throw a pass to him he'd reach out with one hand and grab it. He was a big attraction, and all the schools that were on the Oaks' schedule publicized he'd be playing."

The Oaks finished their year with a 9–10 record, including winning their last five games. If Disler could bring in a second star player to complement Hodges, then they figured to be much improved in 1948–1949. Goerlitz would soon marry and not play basketball the following year. His wife would give birth to twin boys—Gil and Delbert.

After the Oaks' season, Hodges continued to play in rough-and-tumble games off campus on a team with Red Robert Smith, his former rival at Winslow High. Smith and Jim Pegram had been selected over the Hodges brothers at the St. Louis Browns' baseball tryout in Princeton in 1941. But while Pegram played briefly in the low minors, Smith was never offered a contract, and stayed in the area playing semipro baseball and basketball. "One basketball game was really rough and we both hit the showers early," recalls Smith. "Gil was all bruised and battered and said, 'I'm under contract to the Dodgers. I can't break an arm or leg. I got spring training to go to tomorrow.'"

Spring training began that February in Santo Domingo. Cuba had flunked the test of being a friendly site for black ballplayers, and the baseball-crazy Dominican Republic was given an opportunity to do better. Jackie Robinson and Dan Bankhead (who had been disappointing as the majors' first black pitcher in 1947) stayed with the rest of the team at the Hotel Jaragua, and Campanella stayed with the Montreal team at a swanky hotel in San Cristobal.

Hodges arrived in camp unsure of his status. He hoped to move up to backup catcher but knew he needed to hit better to prove he should be even a third-stringer again. "I was more than a little confused about what was going to happen to me," Hodges wrote in his 1969 book. "I had no idea there were so many things happening that would change my life."

Leo Durocher had returned as manager, bringing his wife Laraine Day with him to the island. He and Robinson were surely relieved that Dixie Walker wasn't in camp, having been dealt to Pittsburgh two days after Durocher was re-signed. Rickey wanted so badly to have a harmonious clubhouse in '48 that all he asked for in return was left-hander Preacher Roe, who was coming off a 4–15 season, and slight shortstop Billy Cox, who was battling depression and hadn't regained all the weight he lost during the war after contracting malaria.

Durocher was surprised to learn that his favorite player, Eddie Stanky, was on the trading block. Without consulting his manager, Rickey had decided to move Robinson to second base, his position at Montreal, making "the Brat" expendable. Stanky was sent to the Braves on March 6. As a result, Durocher seemed to deliberately antagonize Rickey to widen their rift. He flaunted his relationships with gamblers in the Dominican Republic. He was arrogant toward the players who missed Burt Shotton (who had been given a consulting position), and those who didn't want him back under any circumstances. He kept pushing Rickey to keep the gifted Campanella on the parent club all year, possibly as the starting catcher. And when Robinson reported to camp overweight, he called him insulting names and ordered him to run off the extra pounds in a rubber suit.

Durocher had no such trouble with Hodges, who came into camp in exemplary shape. Hodges didn't think Robinson's move to second base would affect him, because he didn't consider himself a candidate for first base, along with Chuck Connors, Preston Ward, Ed Stevens, Howie

Schultz, and Pete Reiser, who put retirement on hold despite his head injuries. But he worried that he might never play, because he was fourth on the depth chart behind Edwards, Campanella, who was primed to be the first black receiver in the majors, and Bragan (who now got along with Robinson). However, he caught more than expected because Edwards was recovering slowly from an off-season arm injury, and Rickey ordered Durocher not to use Campanella much, because he planned to send him to St. Paul to integrate the American Association. Hodges was happy to be in the lineup both in the Dominican Republic and, later that spring, at the Dodgers' new training camp in Florida.

The facility at Vero Beach was constructed on a onetime naval air station, on land that Rickey leased for a dollar a year. Even for the abbreviated camp in 1948, more than six hundred major- and minor-league players were housed in the barracks. "It was very primitive," recalls Carl Erskine, who was on Fort Worth's roster that spring. "The wooden barracks were creepy, with a lot of spiders and I don't know what else running around at night, and there were a lot of cracks that let the wind blow through. There were snakes and gators and other wildlife in the ditches and underbrush. We knew better than to reach in and pick up a ball that was not in plain sight. We'd carry fungo bats in case we had to kill a snake on the way to one of the ballfields."

There was no heating or air-conditioning system. For evening entertainment, if the exhausted players could stay awake, there was a Ping-Pong table, a pool table, and a jukebox. But the players were there to work, not enjoy amenities. And for the war veterans like Gil, who had spent many hours in foxholes, the Vero Beach facility posed few problems.

From dusk till dawn, on several ballfields, in a pitching area called "the Strings" with a simulated strike zone, and in sliding pits, the players moved through their drills. "It was more or less like an army camp," Turk Lown recalls. "Every time they blew a whistle, three hundred kids would run around the field. They taught you how to play in the organization."

"Mr. Rickey functioned with clockwork precision," said Al Campanis, who would become the Dodgers' longtime scouting director. "He used the rotation system—a player would rotate from one learning session to another.

At night, the faculty would compare impressions with Mr. Rickey, who made an analysis of every boy in camp."

The players were indoctrinated by Durocher and the coaches in what Rickey formulated as the "Dodger Way." Each day during the first week of camp, Rickey himself conducted half-hour lectures. Test papers were passed out and had to be turned in by the players the next day. Rickey taught players how to bunt, slide, execute the hit-and-run, hit the cutoff man, run through bases, and position themselves in the field. They became well versed in the fundamentals and the nuances of the game.

While the "Dodger Way" was a blueprint for the correct way to play baseball, Rickey's core lessons were designed to teach the young professional ballplayer the proper way to conduct his life. For Hodges, who continued to adhere to the "right way" on and off the ball field, the Dodgers were the ideal organization. He appreciated the orderliness, organization, and narrow focus of the Dodgers; the rules, the repetitive routines, and how players were expected to work on their deficiencies until they became efficient, for as long as it took.

It took a lot of extra batting practice and work with coaches before Hodges' hitting started to come around. The more he played, the more he impressed Durocher, and when he got hold of a pitch, everyone stopped what they were doing to watch the ball take flight. At times, Durocher was effusive about Hodges. At the same time he was telling Rickey that he needed Campanella to be his catcher, he was promising reporters that "Gil Hodges will be the best catcher in America within a year."

As Hodges made inroads as a catcher and hitter, he also took on a role that he would be known for his entire career: peacemaker. During an exhibition game between the Dodgers and their Fort Worth farm team, Pee Wee Reese got into a dustup with Cats manager Les Burge. Dee Fondy, a six-foot-three, 190-pound first baseman, moved in to provide physical support to his manager. He never got there. Gil grabbed Fondy, calmly lifted him off the ground as if he were a toddler, and murmured, "I don't know where you're going, Dee, but it'd better not be near Pee Wee."

There were fewer witnesses to another incident where Hodges' prodigious strength came into play. It involved future manager Dick Williams, who played for Fort Worth in 1948 and would make the parent team in the middle of the 1951 season. One night aboard a train, Hodges finished playing cards and headed to his Pullman compartment to get some sleep. He found the young utility player occupying his lower bunk. When Williams didn't volunteer to move, Gil simply picked up the 190-pounder and tossed him onto the upper bunk.

The Dodgers made their way north to Brooklyn, and on April 11, the 1948 team debuted at the Polo Grounds to play the Giants. The Dodgers had come within 1 game of being the world champions in 1947, but their manager was different from the previous year's opener, and only two players, Robinson and Reese, were again in the lineup—though not in the same places—and only the venerable shortstop was playing the same position in the field. Right-handed Rex Barney, who threw as hard as anyone in baseball, got the start and batted last in a lineup of Jackie Robinson, 2B; Arky Vaughan, LF; Preston Ward, 1B; Carl Furillo, CF; Pee Wee Reese, SS; Dick Whitman RF; Billy Cox, 3B; and Gil Hodges, C, getting his first Opening Day start.

Durocher didn't see this as his permanent lineup. Vaughan and Whitman would make fewer appearances in the outfield than Gene Hermanski, a left-handed hitter who would bat .290 with 15 homers in 400 at-bats; minor-league hitting star George Shuba (who would be dubbed "Shotgun"); and Duke Snider, who'd hit his first 5 career homers after spending the early part of the season at Montreal. Durocher had moved Cox from short to third only as a stopgap measure, because Spider Jorgensen had damaged his shoulder when his hunting rifle recoiled in the off-season. No one expected the 150-pounder to become the best-fielding third baseman in the league and a clutch hitter.

The six-foot-three, twenty-year-old Ward had won the first-base job by default. "I kept expecting to be shipped out," he recalls, "and on Opening Day I had no idea I was in the lineup until Johnny Mize, the Giants' left-handed-hitting first baseman, warned me, 'Ward, you'd better play fifteen feet back on the grass, or I'll kill you!'" And Hodges was in the lineup because Edwards had arm troubles and a skin infection, and Campanella was still destined to be, reluctantly, a civil-rights pioneer at St. Paul once major-league rosters were trimmed in mid-May.

In the opener, Hodges went 0-for-2 and was pinch-hit for by Jorgensen as the Dodgers beat the Giants 7–6. In a loss the following day, Hodges again went 0-for-2 and was pinch-hit for by Jorgensen. Bruce Edwards was behind the plate as the Dodgers won the rubber game of the series, going 3-for-5, with 3 RBIs. Hodges was back in the lineup versus the Phillies in the fourth game of the season, and for the third time went 0-for-2. Hodges didn't reappear until the team's thirteenth game, the second half of a twin bill after Bragan caught the opener. Hodges finally got a hit, a single, going 1-for-3. Two games later, the Dodgers beat the Cubs on a snowy day at Wrigley Field. Ward drove in 4 runs for the second time, but Hodges got another hit and drove in the first 2 runs of his season.

Ward got off to an excellent start but badly strained a calf muscle legging out a triple, so Durocher temporarily moved Robinson back to first while he mended, and had Eddie Miksis come off the bench to play second base. Moving Robinson to second had been the right move, but it opened up a new set of problems for him in his sophomore season. In the 1994 oral history *We Played the Game*, the Phillies' rugged outfielder Del Ennis pointed out, "In 1948 everyone went after Robinson at second base on force plays. He had one rhythm and it was easy to time him. He took more knocks than Carter had liver pills." But, Ennis added, Robinson "was agile and strong and avoided getting hurt. He'd also retaliate, using his spikes when he came down on runners and sliding up into infielders who had slid hard into him."

"Robinson wouldn't take as much abuse as he had as a rookie," said Phillies catcher Andy Seminick. "Now he'd talk back to umpires and talk back to players, just like other players would. He was a tough cookie."

"Jackie was never told by Branch Rickey that it was a two-year trial," Rachel Robinson states. "The media had decided that, or they had heard from Rickey that it might take two years. I always felt that they had some objectives that had to be met before Jackie could be free to be himself. I thought that Jack determined that as much as Rickey did. Rickey would expect Jackie to say, 'The conditions are such that I can be myself and not do any damage to the experiment.' Jackie changed by the second year; he was no longer taking anything from other players. He'd also now argue with umpires, and I'd try to mentally tell him not to get kicked out of the game, because foremost I was a fan who wanted the Dodgers to win."

Robinson also squabbled in the clubhouse with his manager. Since their confrontation in the spring over Robinson's weight, things hadn't improved. Robinson was hitting over .320, but Durocher didn't think he was igniting the offense as he did in '47 and going all out for him. Since the team wasn't winning, Durocher looked for a scapegoat rather than blaming himself, and at times he'd bench Robinson for Eddie Miksis, displeasing Rickey.

Hodges roomed with Miksis, a light-hitting utility man who first joined the Dodgers in 1944, at home and sometimes on the road. They'd pal around with pitcher Joe Hatten and his roommate, Ralph Branca, who still at times was Hodges' road roommate. "The four of us would go to dinner, go to the movies, play cards," recalls Branca. "We'd usually play hearts, and we'd be zinging one another the whole time. We were all Catholics and never missed Mass."

Hodges enjoyed his time on the road with his friends, but he was eager to get back home. He'd met someone special, a striking, hazel-eyed, dark-haired young woman who was born right there in Brooklyn.

Joan Lombardi had graduated from Public School 235 and Girls Commercial High School. As a teenager she played softball—she was a catcher with a good arm!—and had the gumption to write Branch Rickey and ask him whether she could be the Dodgers batgirl. She wasn't amused when he wrote back and advised her to continue going to school and loving the Dodgers. She recalls:

My parents were born in Italy, and they got their citizenship and became Americans. They met in Italy, but my sister, brother, and I were all born here. We spoke only Italian at home and read *L'Espresso*, so I was speaking broken English when I went to school. My father, Frank Lombardi, was a butcher. I don't want to use the word "tough" in regard to my mother, Olga, so I'll just say she was a leader and my dad didn't have too much of a chance to say anything!

My mother, dad, and sister were not sports fans. They couldn't tell a baseball from an onion. I loved sports, always. I was always a Brooklyn Dodgers fan, and I'd listen on the radio and make my own scorecards. We used to save Hoffman ginger ale bottles and return them for five-cent deposits, and when we accumulated fifty cents, my friends and I would go to Ebbets Field and sit in the bleachers.

Peggy Chase, a lady that I was working with at A&S, lived with her husband, Ben, on Bedford Avenue between President and Sterling, and she had Gil and Eddie Miksis staying in her basement. She was having a birthday party for her son, who was eleven or twelve, and wanted to make miniature pizzas, so I went to her house and made the sauce. Then I went downstairs to go home. It was really raining, April showers, so we had to wait inside for a taxi. Gil and Eddie pulled up and got out of Gil's car, and Peggy introduced us. She said, "We're trying to see if we can get a cab; my friend has to go home." Gil asked me where I lived and said, "Come on, I'll be only too glad to take you home." And he drove me home. It was early in the season and Gil wasn't a star yet, but I knew who he was. We had only radio then, so I didn't recognize him.

I was engaged to be married, so meeting Gil didn't make that much of an impression on me. At that time, the famous singer Jane Froman was appearing at the Riviera in Jersey. I wanted to see her so badly and was supposed to go with my fiancé. But he couldn't go. Gil and Eddie were going with Peggy and Ben and a few other people, so I went with them. I didn't go with Gil—we *all* just sat together at a table. I wasn't even thinking about Gil, just Jane Froman, who was marvelous. It wasn't a date, but that's how it started.

Reporters always found it hard to get a usable quote from Hodges, because he was difficult to engage in conversation. Joan Lombardi had the same problem. "He would be with me for hours and wouldn't say a word," she told *Baseball Digest* in the early fifties. "He was so quiet and shy I never knew what to think. There were dates when all he could manage were 'hello' and 'good night.'"

The one subject Gil could talk to Joan about was baseball, and that would never change. She knew the game and always had an opinion, if he should ask, on what he was doing right or wrong. It's no coincidence that as their relationship became more serious, his play on the field improved.

Until May 26, Hodges was banished to the bullpen with an average so low that, the joke goes, it would go up if he made an out. However, Edwards' arm was still hurting, and Durocher had no better option than to put Hodges behind the plate and let him sink or swim. Hodges swam. In his next game, his homer off the Cubs' Johnny Schmitz was the team's lone run as it fell to 12–19. Two games later he drove in 2 runs. On June 1, he hit another homer and drove in 4 runs. The next game he had 2 doubles and drove in 3 runs, giving him 7 RBIs in two games.

Dodger fans were appreciating Hodges, but not to the point where they didn't get on him when he made a costly mistake. That was how every Dodger was treated. Hodges' longtime teammate Carl Erskine claims Hodges was the only Dodger he never heard booed in Ebbets Field, but a month before Erskine made his major-league debut, Hodges was targeted by displeased Dodgers fans after he took out Reds second baseman Bobby Adams while trying to break up a double play.

"I saw that Adams was going to cross the bag from second base toward third," Hodges told Arnold Hano of *Sport* in 1960. "It called for me to slide on my left side, something I do badly. Just as I was about to slide, I decided I couldn't slide that way, and it ended up with me diving headfirst into the base. I hit Adams [with] a body block, a football block, and I cracked a few ribs. The fans really booed me that day, and I deserved it. I will take out the second baseman on double plays every time, if I can. I absolutely must do it; I must break up the double play. But it has to be done properly. If you hit the man from the thighs down, it's proper."

Durocher moved him up to fifth in the lineup. Hodges got anxious now that he was expected to drive in runs, and went hitless in two games, lowering his average to .164, not much higher than he hit in '47. Durocher dropped him back in the order and again the relaxed Hodges drove in runs. Durocher began to move him around. His average crept over .200 and he hit his 3rd homer. His 4th came on June 18, his 5th on the nineteenth, and his 6th on the twenty-sixth. On June 27, he slammed his 7th home run, upped his RBI total to 27, and hiked his average to a decent .258. He caught *every* game for a month and a day and was quickly moving into the top echelon of National League catchers. So he must have been taken aback when Leo Durocher said, "Gil, how would you like to play first base tomorrow?"

Durocher encouraged his idle catching prospect to borrow a first base-man's mitt from John Griffin, the three-hundred-pound clubhouse man, and have some fun working out at that position. "The Senator" retrieved Jackie Robinson's glove from 1947, and Hodges took part in some informal infield practice. Immediately, the amazed Durocher declared Hodges was a natural at first and the best he'd seen there since Dolph Camilli. This was meant to be a huge compliment, although Camilli was a Dodger only five years before, and since then the only Dodger first baseman of note was Jackie Robinson, playing out of position.

Hodges' initial start at first base on June 29 coincided with Edwards' return to the lineup as a catcher. Robinson moved back to second base. Hodges went hitless in his first four games as a first baseman. That included July 2, when the media made a big deal of Durocher having three catchers in his lineup. Edwards played third base, Hodges played first, and Campa-nella, recalled from St. Paul, made his much-anticipated start behind the plate. Campanella banged out 3 hits in 4 at-bats in a 6–4 loss to the Giants. In the next game, a victory over the uptown rivals, he went 3-for-3. And in the final game of the series, he walloped his first 2 major-league home runs and got 3 hits for the third consecutive game as Brooklyn edged New York in a slugfest, 13–12. Hodges, who had broken out of a 0-for-16 freefall with a double off Larry Jansen in the previous game, chipped in a couple of sin-gles as the Dodgers banged out 20 hits.

Nobody worried about Campanella's hitting, because he'd been a star in the Negro Leagues. He ignited an offense that scored 43 runs in winning six straight, and quickly earned the trust of the Dodgers' all-white pitching staff. There were six different winning pitchers—Branca, Erv Palica, Willie Ramsdell, Barney, Hank Behrman, and Roe—but Durocher kept badgering Rickey to bring up Carl Erskine from Fort Worth. By the time Erskine pitched at Ebbets Field, Durocher was managing in the Polo Grounds.

Attendance for home games was way down from 1947, and Walter O'Malley and John L. Smith were blaming Durocher's poor public image and his team's lackluster performance. When the defending National League champions fell to seventh place and were 10 games out of first after losing to the Giants, Rickey recognized that Durocher's days as manager of the Dodgers were numbered. Even though Brooklyn then won eight of nine games, the decision to fire Durocher had been made, and Rickey couldn't save him. Durocher's final game as the Dodgers' manager was a 3–2 loss to the Giants. It was his final indignity that the Giants had a better record despite being managed by Mel Ott, whom he was referring to when he said his most famous line: "Nice guys finish last."

In a bizarre series of events, Rickey fired Durocher and rehired Burt Shotton, and Giants owner Horace Stoneham fired Ott and, with Rickey's blessing, hired Durocher.

"I was shocked that Durocher was fired," says Larry King. "But the biggest shock of all was Leo going to the Giants. We went from loving him to instantaneously hating him. Getting fired is one thing, but he went to the worst team he could go to. The rivalry between the Dodgers and Giants in those days was a hundred times greater than that of the Yankees and Red Sox."

Durocher's move uptown indeed signaled a drastic change in the Dodgers–Giants rivalry. It had always been intense and fierce, but for the next few years it would be a combination of theater and war, the personal and the epic, the cold-blooded and the deeply emotional. In two ballparks, twenty-two times a year, two teams would battle not only to score more runs but also to prove they had more mettle. Every brushback pitch and beaning, every takeout slide, and every vicious insult would be paid back in kind; nothing would be forgotten or forgiven. Quick fights and all-out brawls wouldn't be uncommon; and even benchwarmers finished games with dirty and dusty uniforms. The stakes were extremely high—every player's manhood was on the line—and for the fans of both teams, bragging rights never meant so much.

Hodges thought Durocher had done a good job but was unfazed by managerial changes, just as he was by the routine coming and goings of commanding officers in the Marines. He never met a manager he didn't like, and he played as hard for Shotton as for Durocher.

The Dodgers continued their hot streak after Durocher's dismissal, taking 10 of 12 games and moving into a tie with the Cardinals for second place, 5 games behind the Boston Braves. Picking up the last victory with an inning of scoreless relief against Pittsburgh on July 25 was Carl Erskine. Overall, he'd finish 6–3 relieving and as part of a revolving rotation with

Branca (14–9), Barney (15–13), Hatten (13–10), Roe (12–8), and, occasionally, Palica (6–6). Remarkably, Erskine would be the Dodgers' most consistent hurler for the next decade, despite soon suffering a career-threatening
shoulder injury in his first major-league start, a victory against the Cubs.
"The pain never went away, and I had to alter my delivery," says Erskine.
"Only my roommate Duke Snider and maybe Preacher Roe knew my arm
killed me my entire career."

Like the Dodger pitchers who had been with the team since April,
Erskine credited a lot of his success to his new receiver. "Campanella had a
sixth sense about catching and handling pitchers," he says. "He had a great
way of pacing his pitchers, even the experienced ones, under pressure. I
never saw Campy try to steal pitches—he was just so naturally smooth in
how he brought the ball in. He was a psychologist with umpires."

Erskine also benefited from the Dodgers' improved infield defense,
which was now anchored by Hodges at first base. "Defense was his forte,"
says Erskine. Reese—now the Dodgers' first captain since Camilli—
Robinson, and Cox discovered that they could throw the ball high, low, or
to the side and Hodges would haul it in. If they were late with their throws,
he had the uncanny ability to come off the base a nanosecond early without
the umpire detecting it. He was a large target with soft hands, agility, quickness, and anticipation, particularly on sacrifice bunts. He was, Larry King
states, "the best first baseman I ever saw at turning the 3-6-3 double play."
Already, he was considered the best-fielding first baseman in the league.

Hodges contributed offensively too as the Dodgers went on a 41–17 tear
between July 3 and August 30 and moved past the Braves into first place. In
August, he drove in 21 runs, of which 5 came in a 2-homer game against
Cincinnati. Campanella had cooled off, but Robinson and Reese were still
hitting, and the underrated Gene Hermanski was tearing the cover off the
ball. The pitching and defense were sound, and it looked as if the Dodgers
would pull off their greatest comeback ever. The possibility that neither they
nor the Yankees, who were battling the Indians and Red Sox for the American League flag, would appear in the World Series seemed as remote as
incumbent president Harry Truman defeating popular challenger Thomas
Dewey in the November election.

However, the Dodgers went into a tailspin, losing 3 of 4 to both the

Cubs and Durocher's Giants, and two straight to the front-running Braves' Warren Spahn and Johnny Sain and found themselves in third place, 4½ games out. But Rex Barney harnessed his wildness and threw the first no-hitter against the Giants since 1915. His 2–0 victory, in which Hodges and Furillo drove in runs, pulled the Dodgers to within 4 games of the Braves. But the Giants came back to win three hard-fought games and drop them 6½ behind Boston with only three weeks left in the season. Durocher delighted in knocking them out of the pennant race.

The Dodgers finished the season 84–70, in third place, 7½ behind Boston. The Braves would lose to Cleveland in the '48 World Series, the last time a New York team wouldn't play in the Fall Classic until 1959.

Hodges' 11 homers trailed only Hermanski's 15 and Robinson's 12 on the Dodgers; and his 70 RBIs were behind only Robinson's 85 and Reese's 75, and he was third among National League first basemen to Johnny Mize (125) and the Cardinals' Nippy Jones (81). But Hodges managed only one longball and 8 RBIs after September 1, and over the final thirty-two games his average fell from .266 to .249, tying him with Billy Cox (who had only 237 at-bats) for the worst average among regulars.

So at a year-end press conference, Shotton stated his need for a first baseman in 1949. Asked why he didn't endorse Hodges, he replied bluntly, "Sure, he can play first base well enough for anybody, but he doesn't hit enough to win a pennant for his club." Hodges had the uncomfortable realization that the Dodgers would spend the off-season trying to acquire an established first baseman, which would make him a player without a position.

While staying in constant contact with Joan Lombardi, Hodges returned to Petersburg. On October 29, Gil and his family were guests of the Jaycees at a banquet. Then they watched Petersburg High's football team—now eight men, not six—demolish Mt. Vernon 50–0 in the final home game of the season, completing the first of three consecutive undefeated seasons. At halftime, Gil was honored and presented with a shotgun and a three-piece set of luggage. The cheering fans appreciated that the famous ballplayer hadn't forgotten where he came from.

Hodges again attended Oakland City College. The basketball team got the star player they needed to play alongside him. Bob Lochmueller, who had played semipro baseball and basketball with Hodges and had worked at the Ditney Hill Mine, transferred from Western Kentucky. He would become nationally known playing for Louisville and briefly with Syracuse in the NBA, but the six-foot, five-inch center/forward first spent a year as the Oaks' top scorer and as a force in the middle, as they won 13 of their first 16 games. Realizing his scoring wasn't needed as much as the previous year, Hodges averaged just 7 points a game, fourth-best on the team, but led fast breaks, played tough man-to-man defense, and dominated the boards.

"Gil was an outstanding person and a terrific teammate because he made a lot of easy passes for me to score on," recalls Lochmueller. "He was an outstanding all-around player. He was also a leader on the team. He wasn't a rah-rah type, but if something needed to be said in the huddle, he'd speak up and tell us what we needed to do. Everyone respected what he said."

Not surprisingly, Hodges was named the captain of the Oaks. As captain he had an obligation to school tradition. In addition to placing a tiara on the head of the "basketball queen," the captain was expected to buss her on the cheek. On December 10, prior to Oakland City's easy 89–54 victory over Scott Field, everyone in the crowded gym watched Hodges place the crown on the head of pretty Babs Hayes, who had been elected basketball queen three weeks before. Says Bill Marshall, "I was there and I remember that he didn't kiss her. He shook her hand! Everyone thought it was because he had a girlfriend."

On the side, Hodges played semipro basketball. He'd also drive his married friend Red Robert Smith to his games for Enos Coals. "One game in Princeton, we played against an all-girls team, the All-American Redheads," recalls Smith. "They were pretty good and we sold out the gym. During a time-out, I told some of those girls, 'That's Gil Hodges, the baseball player. He's single and available!' They heard that and went over and covered his face with lipstick. Gil told me later, 'I'm gonna kill you!' One night Gil said, 'I won't see you for a while.' I said, 'What's the matter?' He said, 'Nothing. I'm going to get married.' I laughed and said, 'Gil, you have to have a girl to get married.' And that's when he told me that he had a girl. He never told anybody anything."

Gil had proposed to Joan Lombardi. "I don't know if you would call it a proposal," she recalled sixty-three years later. "We were talking to each other on the phone every other day. One day he said, 'I'm coming to New York on my Christmas break.' I said to him, 'Oh, how wonderful!' He asked me, 'You know why I'm coming?' And I said to him, 'Are you making an appearance or is something going on?' 'No,' he said. I didn't know what he was getting at. He asked me again. So I finally said, 'Gil, are you asking me to marry you?' And he said, 'Yes. I thought we'd get married, and then we could go to spring training in Florida for our honeymoon.'"

It was good news, but Joan had a hard time breaking it to her parents. "They were very much against her getting married to Gil," remembers Louis Lombardi, Joan's brother. "They had nothing against Gil personally, but they thought all ballplayers bummed around after hours on the road. They didn't know anything about baseball, but after they got to know Gil, it was a joy to see them become ardent fans."

"We were married December twenty-sixth in Brooklyn at St. Gregory's Church," Joan reminisces. "It was such a wonderful day. Gil's brother, Bob, was his best man and my cousin from New Haven, Josephine Perolla, was my maid of honor. Unfortunately, Gil's mother needed gallbladder surgery and his parents weren't there, but we knew we'd see them when we went to Oakland City so Gil could finish the term. We had eight ushers. Ralph Branca and Eddie Miksis were the tallest, so they were at the end. When I walked in wearing a white gown, they were the first two people I saw. They were always joking, and Ralph muttered to me, 'It's not too late for you to change your mind.' Eddie said, 'If you want me to help you out of here, I will.' It was an absolutely lovely wedding with many happy tears.

"I had never been to Indiana before and thought it was beautiful. Gil took me to Princeton and showed me the houses he grew up in. And, of course, he showed me around Petersburg. We visited my new in-laws whenever we could. Irene was a woman of few words, like Gil. My father-in-law was jovial, more like Bob. He was a man who really had gone through an awful lot, but he loved his wife and children. Bob was a true angel. I adored him. Gil and I stayed in a tiny apartment near campus in Oakland City, and Bob gave us a toaster as a wedding gift. The first time I used it I tried to grill a cheese sandwich for when Gil came home from school for lunch. Smoke started coming out, so I pulled the cord and hid the toaster and burned sandwich under the bed. But Gil found it that night because of the smell. I didn't want Gil to know I didn't even know how to grill a sandwich."

Joan Hodges remembers their time in Oakland City fondly, particularly socializing with Bob and Nancy Lochmueller at home and on the road. She became a well-known presence at Oaks' basketball games. "Oh, they always knew I was there!" she says today. "I was notorious for getting excited, because Gil would get a thousand fouls called against him before he even got on the court, because he was so big and good. My poor mother-in-law and father-in-law would say, 'Joan, please try to control yourself!' Gil never reacted negatively to a bad call and never said anything to an official, the same as in baseball. He said it wouldn't have done any good."

Hodges had given up thoughts of playing professional basketball but still expected to coach someday, although probably not in Indiana. For now he focused on a career in baseball and starting a life with his bride in Brooklyn. As they traveled to Florida for spring training and their delayed honeymoon, he may have realized that he'd never again attend college, play meaningful basketball games, or return to his home state for anything but brief visits.

CHAPTER NINE

In Florida, Joan experienced culture shock. "There were Jim Crow laws there, and I hadn't seen anything like that before," she recalls. "In one exhibition game it wasn't until the second inning that they opened the entrance in center field and let black people into the ballpark. Then they had them sit in one section and us sit in another, which was utterly ridiculous."

She and Rachel Robinson bonded in an unusual way. "The Dodgers were going on a bus trip and Jackie said, 'Rachel isn't feeling well. Would you call her and see how she's doing?' I said, 'Have no fear.' I drove over to see her. At the time, they had only one child, Jackie Jr., who I absolutely adored and would hold in my lap at ball games in Brooklyn. I took him and went to the store and got chicken soup and other groceries and brought it to her." In Roger Kahn's 2006 book *Into My Own*, Joan said, "Would you believe that some of the other Dodgers wives were critical of me? They didn't believe it was right for a white woman to look after a lady who was black."

Gil and Joan were determined to enjoy their time in Florida despite his legitimate insecurity about his job. As a married man, he had new responsibilities, so he was uneasy not knowing what the Dodgers had in store for him. He was relieved that Rickey had whiffed trying to swing a deal for an established first baseman, including the Giants' Johnny Mize, a left-handed batter who had blasted 91 homers and driven in 263 runs in the previous two years. It was never disclosed exactly what was offered for the Big Cat, but the package probably included Hodges, Miksis, and some cash.

In the 1952 book *Baseball Is Their Business*, edited by Harold Rosenthal,

Hodges wrote of "my darkest moment": "During spring training in 1949, the Dodger management took little pains to conceal the fact that they were looking for a new first baseman. I felt pretty bad, though I tried not to let my discouragement show in my playing. Through it all there was one coach who probably did more to help me than anyone else. Clyde Sukeforth, the former major-league catcher, used to try to cheer me up at every opportunity. 'Don't worry,' he'd say. 'You'll be the regular first baseman. Just don't worry.'"

Hodges diligently worked on his hitting every morning under the guidance of Sukeforth, Hall of Famer George Sisler, and scout John Carey. They taught him through repetition how to use a comfortable shorter stance and keep his stride in check. He credited Shotton for helping him correct his habit of turning his head away when he swung.

Shotton was encouraged by Hodges' quick progress and started to play him regularly. He smacked a triple and scored to break up a close game. The following day he blasted a homer that carried well over 400 feet. He kept hitting until he was, as the Indiana papers declared, "socking the apple all over Florida." Soon Shotton announced that three of his four infield positions were set for the season: Reese at short, Robinson at second, and Hodges at first. Of the other first-base candidates, Chuck Connors, who gave his annual performance of "Casey at the Bat" for all the minor leaguers in camp, would get one at-bat for the Dodgers in 1949, which was one more than either Preston Ward or Dee Fondy got. They became the first of many first-base prospects over the next decade who were sent to other organizations because of Hodges. Connors, after failing in a brief stint with the Cubs in 1951, would settle in Hollywood and become a TV star as the lead in the popular Western *The Rifleman*.

On April 19, before 34,530 boisterous fans at Ebbets Field, Branch Rickey announced the lineups. Gil Hodges, number 14, became one of the few players in history to start at first base on Opening Day after having started at catcher in his team's previous year's opener. Unlike on Opening Day in 1948, when Durocher started only three players—Robinson, Reese, and Furillo—who he believed would play regularly, all Shotton's starters would be everyday players all year, with the exception of left fielder Cal Abrams. Hodges at first, Robinson at second, Reese at short, Cox at third, Furillo in right, Snider in center, and Campanella behind the plate would be Dodger fixtures through 1954. Six of the seven starters were exceptional hitters, and the other, Cox—a peerless third baseman who would examine the ball before throwing out runners at first—was a superb clutch hitter. Year after year, it was as good a lineup as there was in baseball.

The Dodgers thrilled the home fans by crushing the Giants 10–3, behind Joe Hatten. Hodges went 2-for-4 and scored 2 runs. He didn't mind batting seventh in the strong lineup, especially since Campanella batted eighth. Campanella hit a 3-run homer off former Dodger reliever Hank Behrman, while Robinson, who would bat fourth all year, and Furillo had solo shots against Larry Jansen. The Dodgers took two of three from the Giants and then two of three from the Phillies before splitting two games with the Braves. Shotton was patient with Hodges while he hit .200 with no homers or runs batted in. He went fourteen games without either. Although expressionless, he was probably feeling the pressure build up. Finally, in game fifteen, a 5–1 victory over Cincinnati, he collected 3 hits and drove in his 1st run. The following game he smashed his 1st homer, a clutch 2-run blast in the bottom of the eighth inning as the Dodgers won 7–5. He was on his way.

The Hodges were living on Foster Avenue and East Thirty-second in Brooklyn with Reese, Cox, Clyde King, Jack Banta, and their wives. "We all became very close," recalls Joan. "In fact, the entire Dodgers team was like a family. All the players seemed like my brothers, and I was friends with Dottie Reese, Rachel Robinson, Bev Snider, and all the other wives." For his 2005 book, *Brooklyn Remembered,* she told Maury Allen, "I used to play gin rummy when the players were on the road with the wives of Clyde King, Spider Jorgensen, and Jack Banta. Once I had a big run and took everyone's money. But Gil said it wasn't good for team morale, so I had to give it all back."

On the road, Hodges and Furillo usually roomed together. Furillo had snapped and beaten up his previous roommate, his poor friend Tommy Brown, so Dodger management wasn't sure who would be a good fit for him. Hodges was as tough as Furillo and got along with everybody, so he was the logical choice. It turned out that they became such close friends that they roomed together until 1956. "I didn't know Carl was supposed to be difficult," says Joan. "He and Gil got along very well; they never had a prob-

lem. They'd go fishing together, and I was friends with Carl's wife, Fern."
In 2011, Roger Kahn reflected on a reason for their compatibility: "Gil and
Carl were both comfortable in silence."

Furillo appreciated his roommate's openness, honesty, and class; the
respectful way he dealt with everyone; and that he was no different after
hitting a big home run and striking out in a crucial situation. He admired
Hodges for never losing his cool, something he had a hard time doing. In
his defense, Furillo was subjected to heckling from the other dugout, and
being thrown at by pitchers, while opposing managers, even Durocher, left
Hodges alone. Furillo and Hodges spent a great deal of time together, but
even the fellow ex-Marine was unable to get Hodges to open up about his
war experiences: "In all the years he never said a word." If something trau-
matic happened on Okinawa, or if Hodges was experiencing survivor's guilt,
no one knew, not even his wife.

"From the very, very beginning, I felt that he kept too much inside,"
Joan Hodges says. "I knew he was that way, so I always tried to make him
relax and open up more."

"Whether it was about his family, baseball, whatever, he had an expression that would tell me if something was bothering him," says Louis Lombardi, who then was a percussionist at a French nightclub in Manhatttan
called Bal Tabarin (where he met his singer wife, Alma). "But we weren't
concerned then. It was just a characteristic of Gil's."

Neither Gil nor his roommate had much to worry about on the field.
Furillo had hit over .290 the previous two seasons, but 1949 was his break-
through year as he batted over .300 with more than 100 RBIs. The man
with two nicknames—"Skoonj" and "the Reading Rifle"—also did a fabulous job defensively after moving to right field to make room for Duke
Snider in center. He'd gun down 13 baserunners for the third consecutive
year, brilliantly field caroms off both the thirty-foot-high right-field wall
and the scoreboard in right-center with the Bulova clock on top, and make
sure no batter hit a fly ball against the park's most famous sign on the outfield fence: HIT SIGN. WIN NEW SUIT. In all the years Furillo played right
in front of the two-foot-high sign, clothing manufacturer Abe Stark never
gave away a new suit. He and the new center fielder blanketed the outfield
from left-center to the right-field seats like no twosome in the game. "I [still

picture Duke] out there in center field, racing past the ads for Van Heusen shirts and Gem Razors, while executing a brilliant running catch," Ralph Branca wrote of his teammate after his death in 2011.

Hodges also continued to impress everyone with his fielding. "Hodges was the most graceful and skillful defensive first baseman of his time," wrote eminent baseball historian Lawrence Ritter in his book *East Side, West Side*. "On close plays at first base his footwork was so hocus-pocus that opposing players who were called out often left the basepaths grumbling that 'he never touched the bag.' The hand, they say, is faster than the eye. Actually, he frequently *didn't* touch the base, but neither did he want to get run over; since he rarely argued with umpires they were inclined to give him a lot of leeway."

But it was his hitting that was a pleasant surprise to Shotton, the press, and the fans. He was batting around .300 with power. On May 14, he clubbed a grand slam in the eighth inning against the Braves. It erased a 4–1 deficit and might have received more press if the Braves didn't come back to win in extra innings—and if anyone expected Hodges to eventually become the National League's all-time career grand-slam leader.

The 7–6 twelve-inning loss to Boston dropped Brooklyn to 12–13 and 4 games out of first place. But the Dodgers turned it around the next game. The pivotal play came in the top of the eleventh with the Dodgers and Cubs deadlocked 2–2. Hodges beat out a bunt, and Robinson scored all the way from second. The floodgates opened and the Dodgers scored 5 more runs in the inning, and then held on as starter Ralph Branca (6–0) and Erv Palica, the team's top reliever after the departure of Hugh Casey, yielded 3 runs in the bottom of the inning. The next day, also at Wrigley Field, Gil and every other starter notched at least 2 hits as they won 14–5. On May 21, the Dodgers drubbed the Cardinals 15–6, thanks to Reese's scoring 5 times and Robinson's driving in 6 runs.

The following day, twenty-two-year-old Don Newcombe got his first start against the Reds. He'd been bombed two days before pitching in relief in his major league debut, but this time the menacing six-foot-four right-hander rewarded Shotton for sticking with him by shutting out the Reds 3–0. He even drove in 2 runs. Hodges, Cox, and Snider were establishing themselves as tremendous everyday players, Campanella and Erskine (though not a starter yet) were enjoying their first full seasons on the parent club, Furillo was settling into right field, and Roe was emerging as a key man in the rotation. And in early 1949, Newcombe broke onto the scene as an instant star, a pitcher as good as anyone on the Giants or Yankees. This marked the moment the postwar Brooklyn Dodgers team of history and lore was finally in place. As Erskine says, "That 1949 season set the tone for the next decade."

The Dodgers finished May tied for first place with the Braves after winning eleven of their final fifteen games. They continued their torrid play, going 18–9 in June as they outscored their opponents by an astounding 102 runs. On three consecutive days during an eight-game winning streak they scored in double digits. In the third game, a 20–7 shellacking of the Reds in Brooklyn, Hodges entered the Dodgers' record book for the first time by accumulating 8 RBIs with a 3-run homer and RBI single in a 10-run fifth inning, and his 2nd grand slam of the year in the seventh off Johnny Vander Meer, the pitcher who struck him out twice in his debut in 1943. He stole the headlines from Cox, who also hit 2 homers and drove in 6 runs.

Hodges, hitting .313, was one of five Dodgers in the lineup that day batting over .300. Hermanski, who was now getting a lot of playing time, was hitting .363, Robinson .343, Reese .311, and the supposedly light-hitting Cox .302. And everyone was hitting in the clutch, including Hodges. He did go into a brief home-run drought, but broke out of it in a titanic way on June 25, when he slammed his 10th and 11th homers and hit for the cycle. He drove in 4 runs, as did Robinson, and scored 4 runs in his 5-hit game, leading the Dodgers to a 17–10 victory at Forbes Field. He impressed Pirates slugger Ralph Kiner, who also hit two balls into "Kiner's Korner" as he moved toward a fourth consecutive National League home-run crown with 54, the highest total of the decade.

"Gil wasn't much of a talker," recalls Kiner. "Whenever I'd single or walk and stand next to him at first, I'd just say, 'How's it going?' or something boring like that, and he'd answer, 'Nice to see you,' or whatever. Fraternization was frowned on in those days, but there was nothing resembling a conversation with him. Hodges was stoic like DiMaggio, but friendlier and a better teammate. Joe wanted to eat dinner alone; Gil's teammates liked him because he was one of the guys."

As good as the Dodgers were in June, playing at a .667 clip, the Cardinals were better, going 21–9 and beating them 4 out of 6 times head-to-head. By the end of the month, as the Giants and other teams fell back, St. Louis moved to only 1 game behind Brooklyn. When things got tense for the young Dodgers, Reese was the stabilizing force on the team, according to Erskine: "Pee Wee was whom the writers would go to first. And he was deserving of that. He was a little older than the rest of us, he'd been there longer, and he handled himself extremely well with the press. He was an extension of the manager."

In early July, in the ten games leading up to the All-Star break, the Dodgers split 2 games with the Braves, won 2 of 3 from the Phillies, and split 6 games with the Giants. Perhaps Newcombe's most significant start, if only for the symbolic value, came when he faced Hank Thompson, the Giants' first African-American player. It was the first time a black pitcher had ever faced a black batter in the major leagues. The Dodgers lost to the Giants on July 9, but came away with a big victory on the 10th to enter the break a half game ahead of the Cardinals. Hodges went hitless, but he was still batting .323, behind only Robinson's .362 on the team.

Braves manager Billy Southworth named Hodges to the National League All-Star team as the backup at first base to Mize. Hodges was grateful to Clyde Sukeforth for helping him achieve this honor. In *Baseball Is Their Business*, he wrote: "When I played in the All-Star Game for the National League a few months later I think Clyde was as proud as I was that I had made the grade."

What made the sixteenth All-Star Game so special for Hodges and the other Dodgers on the team was that it was played in Brooklyn for the only time. (Red Barber announced the game on CBS-TV.) Hodges heard the cheers from the 32,577 fans when he entered the game in the third inning as a pinch runner for Mize and scored, and later when he rapped an infield single. Stan Musial, the one opponent Brooklyn fans always cheered, and Ralph Kiner each hit 2-run homers to lead the National League, but the American League prevailed 11–7 as Joe DiMaggio knocked in 3 runs. More significant was that the Dodgers' Jackie Robinson, Roy Campanella, and Don Newcombe, and the Indians' Larry Doby became the first African-Americans to participate in the Midsummer Classic.

Robinson still received death threats, but he was more concerned with baserunners trying to take him out at second. "When Pee Wee was picked for the Hall of Fame," says Erskine, "he certainly had the credentials, but there was always a tagline with him: '*And* he played alongside Jackie Robinson,' implying that was a major reason he should get in. They correctly pointed out that by playing alongside Jackie, Reese helped him in his career. Well, Gil Hodges played alongside Jackie, too, on the other side, and he helped Jackie too. In those early years I witnessed some hard slides and hard tags around second base, and each time that could have erupted into a confrontation, which Jackie and Mr. Rickey wanted to avoid at all costs. Gil prevented fights and pulled guys off the pile at second base. Nobody running between first and second challenged him, because he was big and strong and was respected. Hodges' subtle influence out there can't be found in any record book, and if you didn't play with him every day, you might not even have realized it was going on. But he helped Jackie by keeping the peace around second base."

Rachel Robinson recalls, "Jackie talked about how he admired and liked Gil. He thought that Gil was part of that core group that was intent on winning as a team, so he was part of the unity. Jackie thought he could trust him and also had confidence in him, both as a player and as someone he could relate to. As with Pee Wee, he could count on Gil to do his part and help him with his part. Jackie celebrated the power and skill of the entire infield, and working together with Gil and Pee Wee and having success at that."

Robinson continued to be an ultraintense, ferocious presence on the field sandwiched between two of baseball's calmest figures, Hodges and Reese. He was also having the best year of his career as the Dodgers tried to hold off Eddie Dyer's Cardinals. He was the team's driving force, inspiring Hodges and his other teammates with his effort, competitiveness, and achievements.

The Dodgers won 6 of 7 after the All-Star break to finally get some breathing room with a 3½-game cushion over the Cardinals. But St. Louis was a resilient and talented team with Musial, Enos Slaughter, Red Schoendienst, Marty Marion, and pitcher Howie Pollet, and took three straight from the Dodgers in Brooklyn later in the month to take over first place. Following a tie, the Cardinals then beat the Dodgers in St. Louis to extend their lead to 2½ games. In one of the biggest games of the season the next day, the Dodgers squeaked out a 4–2 victory behind Newcombe to avoid falling 3½ games back. Hodges had a 2-base hit in 4 at-bats and scored a run in the Dodgers' big win. Also making the game special were the one thousand exultant fans who had come by train from Petersburg and wore big red-and-white buttons that said, A GIL HODGES BOOSTER.

With Branca, Barney, and Hatten sputtering, Newcombe was the key to the Dodgers' title chances. How would the rookie hold up in a pressure-packed pennant drive? He won 8 more games, including throwing 3 straight shutouts in late August and early September to beat the Cardinals, Pirates, and Giants. "I had the talent and desire and I was cocky," Newcombe stated in *We Played the Game.* "There hadn't been a successful black pitcher in the National League and many were hoping I'd fail. The same applied to the Dodgers' pitchers. But as it had been with Jackie, they welcomed me once they realized I would help them win the pennant and receive World Series money."

The two contenders jockeyed for position into late September. The Dodgers saved their season by taking 2 of 3 from the Cardinals on September 21–22. On the twenty-first, Newcombe suffered a tough loss in the first game of a doubleheader, 1–0, when Joe Garagiola singled off Miksis' glove in the bottom of the ninth inning. The Dodgers were now 2½ games behind the Cards with only eight games to play, and couldn't afford to lose any more ground. Roe came through in the second game, shutting out the Cardinals on 2 hits, 5–0. The Dodgers scored all their runs in the fifth inning, beginning with Hodges' RBI single and ending with Snider's 2-run homer. It was Hodges' 104th RBI of the season.

In the huge rubber game of the series, on September 22, Brooklyn ran away with a 19–6 victory to cut the Cardinals' lead to only half a game. Proving to be a big-game player, Hodges had 5 more RBIs. Hermanski had 3 RBIs, Robinson and Campanella, who homered, had 2 RBIs each, and Snider had 4 hits and scored 4 runs. But the star of the game was Furillo, who stroked 5 hits and drove in 7 runs.

Two days later, Newcombe beat Philadelphia 8–1, as Campanella and Furillo homered and Hodges drove in his 110th run, to keep the Dodgers half a game back. But the following day, they suffered a crushing 5–3 defeat, as the Phillies scored 4 runs in the eighth inning off side-arming reliever Jack Banta. A fine performance by starter Ralph Branca and Hodges' 23rd and final homer of the season were wasted. The Dodgers were now 1½ games out of first, with only four games remaining, all on the road.

The Cardinals' final five games were also on the road. Shockingly, they lost two straight to the Pirates. When Roe and Newcombe outpitched Spahn and Sain, 9–2 and 8–0, in a doubleheader in Boston, suddenly the Dodgers were half a game in front. Then the reeling Cardinals lost again, 6–5 to the Cubs, and the Dodgers were now a full game up, with each team having two games remaining. On Saturday both teams lost. It was the first time all year that the Cardinals had lost 4 games in a row.

The Cardinals won their finale, 13–5, over the Cubs, as Pollet won his 20th decision. Now they had to await the outcome of the Dodgers–Phillies game to see whether there would be a playoff, as in 1946. With Newcombe pitching, the Dodgers jumped to a 5–0 lead and seemed to have the game well in hand, but their overworked ace yielded 4 runs in the fourth and hit the showers, leaving it to the bullpen to protect the lead. The Dodgers increased their lead to 7–4, but Barney couldn't hold it. With the scored tied 7–7, Shotton made another of his inspired moves. Instead of making the call for Erskine, who went 8–1 during the season, he brought in Banta, who had nearly eliminated the Dodgers from the race with a rough outing against Philadelphia earlier in the week.

This time Banta stymied the Phillies. In the top of tenth inning, Reese opened with a single. Miksis sacrificed him to second. Snider singled him home and moved to second on the throw to the plate. He scored on a single by utility player Luis Olmo, and the Dodgers had a 9–7 lead heading into the bottom of the tenth. Shotton stuck with Banta, and the Phillies went down quietly. The tall, young Kansan, whose career would end the next year when he woke up with a sore arm, had pitched 4⅓ innings of scoreless relief and was the unlikely star as the Dodgers won the National League pennant by a game over the Cardinals.

In his autobiography, *The Duke of Flatbush*, Snider remembered that when the train from Philadelphia pulled into Penn Station, "25,000 cheering, jumping Dodger fans were there to greet Train 229, and 75 extra police officers were on duty. The crowd went so bonkers when they saw Jackie, their new batting champion, that he became separated from his wife Rachel and the police had to rescue him from the mob."

The next day, the proud Dodgers were the stars of a victory parade in Brooklyn. The front-page headline of the following morning's *Daily News* read: "900,000 Roaring Fans Hail Bums. Hysterical Crowd Lines 2-Mi. Route."

A National League–high 1,633,747 fans had squeezed into tiny Ebbets Field during the thrilling 1949 season. The borough's love affair with their colorful (in several ways) and enormously talented Bums was at peak level. "The '49 team was *the* Dodger team," says Larry King. "They had the best infield I saw in my life. Everyone had good years. I thought it was the best Dodger team." The 1949 team certainly deserves consideration. It scored 879 runs, 113 more than the second-place Cardinals and 145 more than the Dodgers scored in 1948. Its .274 average was 13 points higher and its league-leading 152 homers were 61 more than in 1948—and 69 more than in its pennant-winning 1947 season.

Reese scored a league-leading 132 runs. Furillo hit .322 (fourth in the league), with 106 RBIs. Newcombe went 17–8 and was selected as the National League's Rookie of the Year. Roe, who artfully mixed pinpoint control and spitters, went 15–6 and had the rotation's lowest ERA at 2.79. Hodges and Snider—who played a terrific center field with speed, grace, a powerful arm, and steel springs in his legs—each belted 23 home runs to lead the team, and Hodges tied Hack Wilson's 1932 record for a right-handed Dodger. Campanella was just behind with 22.

For Hodges, who played 156 games, including two ties, 1949 would be the first of eleven straight seasons with more than 20 homers, and the first of seven straight seasons with over 100 runs batted in. His 115 RBIs were fourth-best in the league. He raised his batting average 36 points, to .285, although that statistic didn't matter to him that much, and stole a career-high 10 bases. He was proud that he led the league's first basemen in putouts, double plays, and fielding average. His .995 fielding average tied the team record for first baseman with Dolph Camilli in 1938. "I remember Pee Wee saying he was fortunate to have both my dad and Gil at first base," says Doug Camilli.

However, Brooklyn's most dangerous weapon in 1949 was Jackie Robinson. He led the league with a .342 average and 37 stolen bases. He finished second to Musial with 203 hits and Kiner with 124 RBIs; and finished third with 122 runs scored and a .528 slugging percentage. The man many insisted wasn't good enough to play in the major leagues two years before would be selected as the National League's Most Valuable Player. But the results wouldn't be announced until after the World Series.

The Yankees won a trip to the Series by slipping past the Red Sox with victories over them in the final two games of the season. For the first time since 1908, the races in both leagues were decided on the final day, and anticipation was high that it would be an electrifying subway series between two evenly matched teams. Making it even more intriguing was that the Yankees' first-year manager was Casey Stengel, who had skippered bad Dodgers teams from 1934 to 1936.

"In 1949, we had a very young team," recalls Erskine, "and we were playing a team with mystique. For the Series the Yankees moved their clubhouse at Yankee Stadium from the third-base side to the first-base side. However, there were two lockers that they didn't move. Babe Ruth's locker and Lou Gehrig's locker were in the Dodger clubhouse for us to see. We were just young guys walking into Yankee Stadium for the first time, thinking, 'We're in the World Series, man alive,' and there were Ruth and Gehrig's lockers staring at us and we felt like we were being haunted by their ghosts. I still believe the Yankees did that deliberately to intimidate us."

Erskine continues: "The first blow was losing the opening game. Newcombe was pitching a fantastic game against Allie Reynolds, and it goes to the bottom of the ninth with no score. He throws a pitch to Tommy Henrich, inside and low. You'd think it was unhittable. But Henrich pulled the ball down the right-field line for a home run to beat us 1–0. We won the second game behind Preacher Roe 1–0 too. Roe was a master of deception. I think they kept expecting him to throw a spitter, and he kept them waiting. Gil drove in the only run in the second inning off Vic Raschi. We'd scored only 1 run in two games yet got a split at Yankee Stadium, so that was pretty amazing. But at Ebbets Field, where the Yankees probably felt they were slumming, they scored 3 runs in the top of the ninth to beat Branca in Game 3, and it was downhill from there."

In Game 4, the Yankees got off to a 6–0 lead against Newcombe and

Hatten, but the Dodgers rallied for 4 runs on 7 singles in the sixth and had two runners on before Reynolds came in to douse the flames. He retired the final ten batters to preserve the win.

In Game 5, the Yankees took a 5–0 lead off Barney and coasted to a 10–6 victory. Hodges boomed a 3-run homer off Yankee starter Vic Raschi in the seventh inning, but struck out against a dominant Joe Page to end the game and the Series. He hit only .235 but had 4 RBIs in the five games, which was much better than the embarrassed Snider, who drove in no runs while going 3-for-21 with 8 strikeouts.

Everyone was stunned at the swiftness of the Dodgers' demise, considering how talented they were. Even if they lost—and it was conceded that Reynolds, Raschi, Page, and junkball artist Ed Lopat were superior to the Dodgers pitchers—it was expected to go six or seven games. The *Brooklyn Eagle* was not kind to Shotton. On October 10, there was this headline to Clarence Greenbaum's article: "Dodger Fans Stunned by Blow; Some Blame Shotton for Loss." The subhead read: "Wailing a Mournful Tune, the Faithful Second-Guess the Manager on Maneuvers." But Rickey stayed with him.

"A lot of us were not even twenty-five, and fighting to keep our jobs," explains Erskine, "so to be in a World Series was a highlight. We were intimidated and lost, but we knew our young pitching staff would mature together and we'd be ready the next time."

"Our dreams for a world championship in '49 withered and died," wrote Doris Kearns Goodwin in her memoir. "It was that October that I first understood the pain, bravado, and prayer woven into the simple slogan that served Dodger fans as a recurring anthem: 'Wait till next year.'"

Gil Hodges had no time for such sentiment. The loss to the Yankees had been painful, but what was on the horizon made him feel exceptionally happy. Joan was pregnant and he was going to be a father. He'd just have to wait until next year.

CHAPTER TEN

"When I became pregnant, from the first time I walked out of the doctor's office until the day I gave birth, I was very, very, very sick," remembers Joan Hodges. "I had a very difficult pregnancy, for nine months. We decided to move in with my parents."

Joan and Gil stayed in an extra bedroom in her parents' house on Hawthorne Street. Joan's older sister, Amy, had the apartment downstairs. All the Lombardis had already fallen in love with Gil, who would become a son to Joan's parents and a brother to Louis and Amy. "I'd get home after playing at the club at about three or four o'clock in the morning, and be up at nine, and we'd spend the whole day together," recalls Louis. "My father liked a card game named Brisk and taught it to Gil, and they'd play for pennies. Gil became the first person to beat him, and my father would get so frustrated. I'd pull Gil to the side and say, 'Gil, please let my father beat you; you're making him very upset.' And Gil would laugh. 'Nah, I like to see him get upset.'"

On a few Saturdays in late fall, Hodges and Branca picked up extra money selling televisions in Brooklyn for Hy Uchitel, a well-known photographer and entrepreneur. "Our job," recalls Branca, "was just to get people to come into the shop and a salesman would take over." Branca has fonder memories of their being on a Dodgers basketball team that winter with Rex Barney, Eddie Miksis, and Don Newcombe. The team played a number of exhibition games against local semipro teams at the Paramount Theater in Brooklyn. "They put up baskets on both sides of the stage and it was a very

short court," says Branca. "We'd play before the movie; if they had a double
feature, we'd play in between. We had a good team. I had played at NYU,
and Gil and Miksis had played in college and were very good. Newcombe
wasn't very good, but he helped us draw a crowd. The Dodgers didn't tell us
not to play."

Hodges tried to stay occupied because his wife's condition made him
extremely nervous. She was due in March, when the Dodgers were supposed
to be at Vero Beach, but he didn't want to leave her side. "I fell down the
stairs at one point," she recalls, "and in my ninth month I had pneumonia
and pleurisy. Gil asked for a leave from the team so that he could be with
me. Branch Rickey called our house and granted him permission." Rickey
told Hodges he could miss a week to ten days of spring training. That deadline passed, but Gil remained with Joan.

Finally, at 6 a.m on Sunday, March 12, "I woke up Gil," recalls Joan
Hodges. "I said, 'I think I'm going into labor.' He looked at his wristwatch
and the first words out of his mouth were: 'Oh, do you think you really are,
honey? I think I'll make seven o'clock Mass.' I went crazy! I said, 'You're
thinking about Mass? I just told you I'm starting labor!' He wasn't aware
that there wasn't as much time as he thought."

The Hodges got to the hospital on time, and that night Joan delivered a
boy. The *Petersburg Press-Dispatch* proclaimed, "Mr. and Mrs. Gil Hodges
are the beaming parents of a seven-pound son, born at 10:31 p.m. eastern
standard time, Sunday, March 12. While the boy has not been named as
yet, his uncle Bob of Petersburg said, 'He will most likely be Gil Junior, that
was pretty well decided before he was born.'"

A picture in the *New York Daily News* shows the happy new parents in
Joan's hospital room. Joan is lying in bed with the sleeping baby in her arms
and smiling at the camera. The grinning father is standing by the bed, wearing a buttoned sport jacket and a bow tie. The title of the adjoining article
was: "But Can He Hit to Right?"

"Gil was so proud of his new son," recalls Louis Lombardi. "He was a
beautiful boy, and Gil thought about all that they'd do together as he
grew up."

Even after Gil Jr.'s birth and after the doctors assured his parents that
everything was fine, Gil Sr. was reluctant to report to spring training. "I

realized he wouldn't leave until I had gone home from the hospital," Joan Hodges says, "so I got up and left after four days. Then Gil went to Florida."

When Hodges reported to Vero Beach, the *Press-Dispatch* explained that "he is in good condition from a winter's season of basketball and walking the maternity ward floor." He was so revved up that "I threw so hard the first day in camp my arm didn't get back in shape until the season was half over." He still got in a month's work and on Opening Day was ready to go.

The Dodgers opened the season in Philadelphia. In 1949, the Phillies had finished a surprising third in the National League, eight games over .500. This year they were regarded a dark horse for the pennant, as manager Eddie Sawyer had some of the finest young players in the league, including outfielders Richie Ashburn and Del Ennis, shortstop Granny Hamner, third baseman Willie "Puddin' Head" Jones, and pitchers Robin Roberts, Curt Simmons, Russ Meyer, and bespectacled, eccentric reliever Jim Konstanty, whose palm ball fooled everyone in the league but Hodges. The left fielder for "the Whiz Kids," as they'd come to be called because their average age was twenty-six, was Dick Sisler, the bespectacled twenty-nine-year-old son of Dodgers scout George Sisler, who batted .340 in a fifteen-year career.

In a showdown between the team's aces, Roberts outpitched Newcombe and the Phillies won easily, 9–1. If the outcome of this game were reversed, the whole season might have played out differently. At the very least, the stakes for the final game of the season, in which Roberts and Newcombe matched up again, would not have been the same.

The Dodgers bounced back to win the next day, 7–5, as Hodges went 4-for-4. His first homer of the season provided an important insurance run, coming in the top of the ninth against Konstanty. The Dodgers then won their home opener against the Giants, 8–1, and 6 in a row before Roberts bested Roe in Brooklyn.

Hodges got off to excellent start, hitting over .400 into May. He was now regarded as one of baseball's most dangerous hitters. He was a fearsome presence at the plate, with his body erect, his huge hands held high and gripping a 34.5-inch, 33-ounce bat, his right elbow straight out, his muscles rippling, his steely blue eyes fixed on the pitcher. He was a pull hitter who still had trouble with curves on the outside corner, but pitchers were at risk if they challenged him with an inside fastball and got too much of the plate. The kids at the ballpark had heroes like Robinson, and those with snazzy nicknames like "Duke," "Pee Wee," "Campy," "Oisk" (for Erskine), "Newk," "Preacher," and "Skoonj," but they were still drawn to the brawny ex-Marine who said little, expressed even less, but hit the ball a country mile.

Robert A. Caro, the Pulitzer Prize–winning biographer, was fourteen in 1950. He recalls: "I lived on Central Park West and 94th Street, and since the '47 season, a bunch of us went to games at Ebbets Field. Hodges was memorable to me because he wasn't dramatic like Robinson and his other teammates. To me he was a symbol of quiet strength and reliability. He said nothing and was modest, but he had self-confidence and always seemed to come through in the clutch. He exuded an almost John Wayne aura. Sometimes we would wait outside for the players. He would sign autographs and chat, and you had this feeling that he was approachable although he was reserved. There was a notable friendliness and dignity about him. He was also memorable because he could hit the ball in the upper deck. At batting practice, the ball would fly off his bat and we'd run to wherever he hit it."

A major reason that the Dodgers were so popular and considered part of the community was that Hodges and his teammates were so accessible to children. Players appeared on the live TV show *Happy Felton's Knothole Gang* and offered instruction and autographs to kids. There were many other autograph opportunities before and after games, in and outside the ballpark. "You could walk players to their cars or the subway," says Larry King. "I'd ask them questions rather than ask for autographs. It wasn't hard to see a Dodger in person, especially those who lived in Brooklyn, like Erskine, Reese, Snider, and Hodges, who was there in the winter, too."

Hodges had a special affinity for children and made sure to take part when the Dodgers arranged hospital visits. One visit that year made a lasting impact on a little girl. Carolyn Ahlers Joyce, a devoted Brooklyn fan as a child, was seven when she spent six months at St. Charles Hospital, which specialized in caring for children with polio. She recalls: "The Dodgers came to visit the hospital. The nuns had taught the kids in our ward to sing 'Take Me Out to the Ballgame.' When the rest of the kids sang, 'home team,' I screamed, 'Dodgers!' and Gil swept me up and danced with me. Sixty years later, I remember that. I needed the hug Gil gave me when we danced."

The kids who idolized the player who was called a "gentle giant" by Red Barber, Connie Desmond, and new twenty-two-year-old Dodgers broadcaster Vin Scully, probably assumed he was making top dollar for his long-ball feats. But they didn't understand the nature of the man who pulled the Dodgers' purse strings. Hodges was one of many underpaid Dodgers. Even after driving in 115 runs and tying the team record for homers by a right-handed hitter, all Branch Rickey offered was $13,000. He signed without protest. "Money never mattered to us," Joan Hodges says. "Gil was very happy with his salaries, and it was more important to him what he achieved than what he made."

Joan was like the other Dodgers' wives in that she gave her husband her full support in his career and made life easier for him by taking care of the home and children during the team's long road trips. Where she differed from the others is that she also gave her husband batting tips. During a slump in 1950, she stood him in front of a large mirror. "I said, 'I want you to do me a favor, Gil, and listen to me. This is crazy, but I'm telling you the truth—your left foot is out a little bit too much, and you're losing the leverage on your swing because of that. If you bring the foot back just a little bit, I think you'll have more of a compact swing.' He played the next day and moved his foot back and went 3-for-4. And when he hit a home run and crossed third base, he touched his lips and blew me a kiss in the stands. He'd do that for the rest of his career after he homered."

Until they noticed it on television years later, the fans never realized that Hodges was exchanging kisses with his wife in the stands after home runs, but the players always knew. "We teased Gil a little about it," says Erskine, "but not too badly, because he was such a good needler that he'd get us back."

There were kisses on June 20, when Hodges hit a grand slam off Pirates rookie Frank Smith in an 8–2 victory. (He'd hit another grand slam on September 20 off another Pirates rookie, Bill Macdonald.) For the first time since June 2, the Dodgers moved into first place by themselves. They were in first when they went to Philadelphia on June 30 but lost 3 straight.

The Dodgers limped back to New York, where the Giants' Larry Jansen and intimidating Sal Maglie outdueled Preacher Roe (who'd win 19 games in 1950) and Don Newcombe in the first two games of a three-game series. The Dodgers dropped into fourth place. At the All-Star break, their record stood at 39–32, 4 games behind the Phillies.

Hodges went into the break batting .291 with 11 homers and 49 RBIs. For the second straight year he made the All-Star team as a backup, this time to Stan Musial, who usually made the team as an outfielder. Other Dodgers All-Stars were starters Jackie Robinson and Roy Campanella, Duke Snider, Pee Wee Reese, and Don Newcombe. Although Burt Shotton was the manager of the National League team, Hodges didn't make an appearance in one of the most memorable summer games. Ralph Kiner's homer in the top of the ninth tied the score 3–3, and Red Schoendienst's blast in the fourteenth won it for the National League 4–3.

The Dodgers lost their first game after the break but then reeled off 5 victories in a row to move into second place, only half a game out. In the next game, Hodges wasn't in the lineup for the first time in 352 games. After going 3-for-3 in the first game of a doubleheader in St. Louis, he had to be taken out. While chasing down a foul ball, he bruised his leg badly when he ran into the edge of a steel cylinder that was jutting out from the lower stands. Joan Hodges had wanted him to take days off during his iron-man streak, but this wasn't what she had in mind. Harold Wendler, the Dodgers' trainer, told Shotton that Hodges needed to sit out a week. He came back after missing two games. At the end of the month his average stood at exactly .300, and he was doing well despite not hitting many home runs, but his team had again fallen to fourth place, 4 games back.

Perhaps the team was distracted by what was happening in the front office. One of the team's owners, John Smith, had passed away suddenly, and the feud between Branch Rickey and Walter O'Malley was out in the open. It was evident that O'Malley was working behind the scenes to depose Rickey, and it appeared that a successful coup was looming. "The news that Branch Rickey would be leaving the Dodgers at the end of the 1950 season hit me hard," wrote Jackie Robinson in *I Never Had It Made*. Robinson was loyal to Rickey and expected O'Malley to turn on him too. But those Dodgers who felt they were grossly underpaid thought a changing of the guard might be to their benefit. Hodges believed front-office matters weren't his concern.

The Dodgers began August with 3 straight wins, including 2 over visiting Pittsburgh. In the second game, Ralph Kiner put the Bucs up in the top of the ninth 4–2, with a two-out, 2-run homer off Branca, but the Dodgers came back to win when Jim Russell, the team's latest left-field prospect, hit a 2-run homer in the ninth and an RBI single in the tenth. Kiner, who would capture another home run title (and total 101 homers over two years), had an indirect influence on Hodges. "We saw him in the batting circle rubbing a towel on the handle of his bat, and we said, 'What's he got?'" recalls Erskine. "So one day at Ebbets Field we sent over our popular batboy, Charlie 'the Brow' DiGiovanna, to steal the rag. Dr. Wendler said, 'That's pine tar. You can buy it in a drugstore.' Really? So we started having a rag with pine tar on our side. Hodges loved pine tar and would put so much on his hands that they'd be totally black. It gave him a good grip on the bat. Also he'd come to the mound, guy on base, rub the ball, and hand it to me, and I'd go, 'Ooooh!' He knew what he was doing."

After their fast start in August, the Dodgers lost 4 in a row, including two by 1 run to the Phillies. Again Roberts prevailed in a matchup with Newcombe, whose role was even bigger than in his rookie year because the Dodgers had given up on Rex Barney. After the Giants' Sal Maglie defeated them on August 16, the Dodgers found themselves 7½ games out. Maglie was one of the most difficult pitchers for Hodges, because he was a great "mistake hitter," and the shrewd right-hander rarely made mistakes. But in that game Hodges touched him for 2 3-run homers.

Rather than fold, the Dodgers went on a 10-game winning streak. (Unfortunately, thirteen hundred Petersburg boosters were present the *next* game on August 27, when the Cards pummeled the visiting Dodgers 13–3.) Newcombe won 3 decisions during the streak, which moved them firmly into second place, again 4 games back. But the deficit increased to 6½ games by the time they played the Braves on the last day of August, with Erskine going against Spahn. Only about fourteen thousand fans were on hand that night to see the best game of Hodges' career. That included fourteen-year-old Brooklyn schoolboy Sandy Koufax. "Gil had been the guy I always rooted for, probably because he was a first baseman like me," Hodges' future teammate wrote in his 1966 autobiography, "and also, I suppose, because everybody in Brooklyn knew he was a nice guy."

Also in the stands was Joan Hodges, although she wasn't in a great mood, because it was only the second home game the Dodgers had played since August 9. Four years later, she bylined a piece in *Parade* magazine and recounted that her husband had forgotten to bring home a gift from the long road trip: "That's when the quarrel began. It was a pretty one-sided quarrel. I did all the complaining, and Gil just remained quiet, keeping everything bottled up inside him. Finally, as he went to leave for the ballpark, he kissed me good-bye and said he'd see me after the game that night. I answered angrily: 'You've been away so long, one more night won't make any difference.'"

Hodges took out his frustration on the Braves' pitchers. In the second inning he hit a 2-run homer off Warren Spahn. In the third it was a 3-run shot off Norm Roy. That was followed by another 2-run homer off Bob Hall in the sixth. Word got around quickly that Hodges had a chance to tie the major-league record of 4 homers in a game. They even knew about it in Petersburg. "The phone began ringing and just wouldn't stop," Bob Hodges told the *Saturday Evening Post*. "Someone called my father down at the mine, so he knew about it before he came home."

The first 3 homers landed in the left-field stands. Reese teased Hodges for deliberately prolonging a blowout. Hodges said, "Rex Barney needled me. He said, 'You haven't hit one real good yet. You're due.' Well, the fifth time I came up in the seventh I got a cheap single, and I didn't think I had a chance. But the boys batted around and Antonelli got behind on me and I never saw a curve that looked so good for that fourth homer." His eighth-inning blast, the only one he'd remember years later, landed in the rear of the upper deck, perhaps 450 feet from home plate. Joan Hodges had missed it because she held her hands over her eyes. "I didn't dare look because I knew how badly Gil wanted it," she explained.

He had hit 2 homers against left-handers and 2 against right-handers. In the twentieth century, only Lou Gehrig had hit 4 in a nine-inning game, on June 3, 1932, at Shibe Park in Philadelphia. "Gehrig had an advantage over me," Hodges told reporters later. "What's that?" "He was a better player." He was always modest, even though he'd achieved something even

Gehrig didn't do—a record of 17 total bases. His 9 RBIs in the 19–3 on-slaught also broke his own team record. His 23rd homer tied the team re-cord for righties that he'd shared with Hack Wilson. He also scored 5 runs. It took his 5 hits for him to end August, like July, with a .300 average.

Winning pitcher Carl Erskine, who threw his first complete game, had 4 singles. There was a lot of organ music that night. "Gil and I had a bond because we were both from Indiana," says Erskine. "When I warmed up or Gil did something else that was special, our organist Gladys Gooding would play 'Back Home in Indiana.' It was the second-most-played song during the 1950s at Ebbets Field behind the national anthem."

In Joan Hodges' *Parade* article, she reported, "After the game, a reporter asked Gil if he had been feeling particularly good before the game. Gil looked up and over at where I was sitting, and then we both laughed for the first time that day. He slept home that night."

After the game Joan was quoted about searching for a place to rent for her family. The headline above Dick Young's story in the *Daily News* was, "Hodges Hits 4 in 1 Tilt/Asks 1 Apartment for 4." The math was pretty close to being correct: Joan was pregnant with their second child. They were inundated with offers of apartments and houses to rent. They moved to East Thirty-second Street, between avenues K and L.

September 5 was "Gil Hodges Day" at Ebbets Field. Prior to a game against the hot Giants, Hodges was given some luggage, a chest of silver, and other gifts. Then he took the field and made a play that would be writ-ten about in the papers the next day. Erskine recalls:

> The more you played with Gil, the more you realized how he pro-cessed his job. He was a good sign stealer and was alert to things going on that guys on the bench weren't, such as when the sacrifice bunt was on. Against the Giants that day, the Giants' pitcher Jack Kramer was the hitter in the ninth inning against Erv Palica with the score tied. Bobby Thomson was leading off first and Eddie Stanky, the leadoff hitter, was on deck. Hodges told Palica not to throw over to first. Kramer bunted the ball toward first. Hodges was already charging and scooped the ball up on one hop. He reached out and tagged Kramer just as he stepped out of the box,

and then he turned and made a catcher's throw to second base and got Thomson sliding in for a double play. I've never even heard of anybody else doing it.

Kramer got his revenge by striking out Hodges to end the game in the tenth inning, with the Giants on top 8–5. This dropped the Dodgers to 7½ games out, and that increased to a season-high 9 games out. But the bats came alive and the pitching stiffened, and the Dodgers won 7 straight and 13 of 16 down the stretch to pull within 1 game of the Phillies with one game remaining. If the Dodgers beat the Phillies in the final game of the season, they would force a playoff.

As in the first game of the season, Newcombe faced off against Roberts on October 1, this time in Brooklyn, with each going for his 20th victory. Newcombe had outdueled the Phillies' star hurler 3–2 in their most recent confrontation on September 23 in Philadelphia. Before a season-high 35,073 fans, the two hurlers were in peak form, and the score was 1–1 as the Dodgers came to bat in the top of the ninth needing to push across a run to extend the season. Batting leadoff, Cal Abrams walked on a 3–2 pitch. After twice failing to bunt, Reese—who was credited with a freakish homer earlier when his fly ball lodged itself in a cement area between the screen and wall—lined a clean single to left center. With men on first and second and nobody out, Ashburn in center anticipated that Snider would bunt, so he charged in on the pitch in case there was a throw to second base that got past the fielder. Snider didn't bunt. Instead he hit a low laser over second base for a base hit.

"Abrams wasn't a fast runner," says Erskine, "and he may have hesitated, because you're taught not to get doubled up on a line drive. Then Abrams raced toward third. That's where he should have stopped and it would have been bases loaded with nobody out with Robinson, Furillo, and Hodges coming up. But Milt Stock, our third-base coach, must not have seen how quickly Ashburn picked up the ball and how close he was to the infield, which was important, because he had a weak arm. Stock waved Abrams around third. Ashburn made an accurate throw to Stan Lopata, and Abrams was so dead that he couldn't even slide into home. No one could rationalize why a good, experienced coach would send Abrams home with no outs."

It was a decision that would cost Stock his job and contribute to Shotton's dismissal.

The Dodgers still had men on second and third with only one out, and all that was needed for a victory was a lazy sacrifice fly. Roberts intentionally walked Robinson to load the bases for Furillo. He was having another terrific season with over 100 RBIs, but he popped up the first pitch to first baseman Eddie Waitkus. Two outs. Hodges came to the plate. Dodgers fans rose to their feet as he sent Roberts' fastball to deep right center. With one out this fly would have won the game. But there were two outs and Ennis got under it. And, unknown to anyone, he lost it in the sun. "It hit me right in the chest, left its imprint, and fell right into my glove," Ennis recalled in *We Played the Game.*

As the fans sank back into their seats, the Dodgers tried to quickly regroup as they took the field in the top of the tenth inning. It was hardest for Newcombe, who had assumed he'd finally earned a victory in a key game. Roberts singled up the middle. Waitkus dropped a fly into no-man's-land in short center. Ashburn bunted into a force play at third base. Dick Sisler, playing left field, came to the plate hoping to get his 4th hit of the game. George Sisler once hit .420 and had 257 hits in another season, but he never got into the World Series. His moderately talented son accomplished that with one powerful stroke that put the Phillies ahead 4–1.

Following Sisler's 3-run opposite-field homer, the Dodgers went down one-two-three in the bottom of the tenth. Once again they had tasted defeat on the last day they played. It was one of the most demoralizing losses in Brooklyn's history. "It was a quiet clubhouse as we cleaned out our lockers," recalls Erskine with regret. "It was tough. We had lost a tense game after a tense pennant race. You absorb the loss and shut up."

Robinson went into the Phillies clubhouse to congratulate the pennant winners and wish them luck against the Yankees (who would sweep the NL champs). Hodges sat on his stool in front of his locker. His head was down and he was being hard on himself for not driving in the winning run against Roberts in the ninth inning.

Hodges realized he'd had an outstanding season. He'd slammed a team-high 32 homers—one more than Snider and Campanella hit—to tie Hank Sauer for third-most in the league behind Ralph Kiner's 47 and Andy

Pafko's 36. Eighteen had come in the last two months. He also had a team-high 113 RBIs, which was third in the league behind Ennis' 126 and Kiner's 118. Hodges batted a solid .283, and only a dip in average in the final month when his power numbers increased kept him from joining Robinson, Snider, and Furillo in the .300 club. In addition he led the National League first basemen with a .994 fielding average and set a league record by participating in 153 double plays. Hodges would finish a career-high eighth in the MVP balloting. Jim Konstanty, who won 16 games and unofficially saved 22 in 74 relief appearances, was selected. But none of that mattered at the moment. Letting down his team was intolerable.

An hour passed before Hodges dressed and went home. "He came to the door and never saw me," Joan Hodges says. "Dinner was prepared but he didn't eat it. He went right up to bed."

A few weeks after the painful end to the Dodgers' season, the O'Malley-Rickey drama reached a crescendo. O'Malley had convinced John Smith's widow to make the Brooklyn Trust Company the executors of the estate. This gave O'Malley a controlling interest in the franchise. He would buy out Rickey. On October 26, O'Malley became the team's majority owner and president. He appointed longtime company man Buzzie Bavasi as his new general manager. He fired Shotton as the manager and hired former Dodger coach Charlie Dressen, who had skippered the Oakland Oaks in the Pacific Coast League the past two seasons. He also announced that small fines would be levied on Dodgers employees who mentioned Rickey's name.

Branch Rickey's unceremonious dismissal from the organization meant that Rickey Jr.'s tenure in Brooklyn was over too. He would accompany his father to the Pittsburgh Pirates, where Rickey's miserly ways would make a bad franchise even worse. He said, "I just don't like to think I'm leaving a club which has Hodges on it. He is everything you look for in a ballplayer, on and off the field."

After the season, Hodges picked up some extra money barnstorming with a team sponsored by tennis star Bobby Riggs and John J. Jachym, a young businessman who'd briefly be part owner of the Washington Senators. Several weeks later he, Joan, and Gil Jr. were in Petersburg to celebrate Thanksgiving. Marjorie had graduated from St. Anthony's in Terre Haute and was working as a registered nurse at the Putnam County Hospital upstate in Greencastle. Bob had worked in nearby Washington at U.S. Rubber, where he met Gladys Bales, a young secretary who watched him play ball for the factory team. Gladys was one-eighth American Indian, one of six girls born into a Missouri farming family. On April 21, 1951, Bob and Gladys would marry and start a large family in Evansville, where he'd work first at a Siemens factory and then in the sporting goods business for his friend Gussie Doerner, the town's first All-American basketball player. (Bob, Doerner, and Red Robert Smith had played on a strong Enos Coals contingent that narrowly defeated Gil's Oakland City College team in a much-publicized exhibition game after the Oaks' 1949–50 season.)

Gil's return home was big news, and little he did wasn't reported in the local newspapers. While bowling in Princeton, Gil's friend Stanley Bishop told him about a young boy named Joe Decker who was having serious health problems. The next day, Gil and Joan were at the boy's bedside. In 2011, Decker, who played briefly in the Reds chain, recalled:

When I was nine years old, Gil Hodges was my idol, and when I played I'd imagine I was him. That fall I suffered a ruptured appendix with little chance for survival. They did surgery and at one time there was no pulse. They sent me home after two weeks with drains in my abdomen for recovery. I was in bad shape. One day when I was lying on the couch the doorbell rang. My father brought the visitor to me and asked, "Do you know who this is?" I looked in amazement and said, "It's Gil Hodges!" Imagine my shock. He had the largest hands I had ever seen, and they completely engulfed my little paw. I showed him a scrapbook I had of him. Gil stayed for an hour talking baseball and encouraging me to get well so I could play baseball again. When he was leaving he gave me two baseballs, one autographed by Gil with, "Best wishes," and the other autographed by the entire Dodgers team. I stopped feeling sorry for myself and wanted to make a fast recovery. Gil Hodges saved my life with his special visit. I truly believe that.

CHAPTER ELEVEN

In 1951, Gil Hodges had a new owner, general manager, and manager, so it was in his best interests to report to spring training on time. However, for the second straight year he asked for permission to stay in Brooklyn because his wife was having difficulty during the late stages of her pregnancy. Buzzie Bavasi knew that Hodges wasn't insubordinate, so the new GM told him he could stay home until early March. Hodges promised he would be with the team for its first exhibition game, and true to his word, Hodges reported to Miami in time for the final workout prior to the first exhibition game that year.

While the team trained at Vero Beach—where O'Malley added insulation to the barracks and improved the dining facilities in his first spring in charge—it played a number of exhibition games in Miami, with the team staying at the McAllister Hotel. While Hodges went through the daily drills and played hard in exhibition games, he anxiously awaited word from Brooklyn. On March 20, he rushed back to be with Joan and their new seven-pound, twelve-ounce daughter at the Unity Hospital. They named her Irene after his mother. He could now concentrate on baseball for the month leading up to the season.

With Charlie Dressen at the helm, the Dodgers burst out of the gate by winning five of six, with heralded rookies Don Thompson playing left and leading off and Rocky Bridges starting at third base as Billy Cox worked himself back into shape after holding out in a salary dispute.

The Dodgers cooled off but still were at 7–4 as of April 29. The offense was being carried by Hodges, who already had 6 homers, and Jackie Robinson, who had 4 homers and a team-high 14 RBIs, 3 more than Hodges. Although his play wasn't affected, Robinson was going through a difficult period now that O'Malley ran the Dodgers. "[O'Malley] knew that I felt very deeply about Mr. Rickey and, consequently, I became the target of his insecurity," wrote Robinson in his autobiography. What made the transition easier was that he enjoyed playing for his new manager. "Charlie Dressen was his favorite manager," says Rachel Robinson. "He was a good manager who appreciated what Jack could do for the team, not just for himself. He always treated Jackie as someone who could produce for the team and for him, so he allowed Jackie the freedom to play as he wanted."

Dressen was the only person ever to prove that there can be an "I" in "team." In Dressen's parlance, "I" was certainly the most used pronoun, but his baseball IQ was as large as his ego, and Robinson and the other Dodgers and their fans were excited to have somebody who could strategically go head-to-head with Leo Durocher. One way for Dressen to prove himself was by leading his team to victories against the Giants. "After I beat them in late April they had lost 11 in a row," remembers Carl Erskine, "and Dressen was so delighted to beat Durocher that he wanted to open the door between the clubhouses and sing, 'The Giants Is Dead!' He asked me and Erv Palica to come sing it with him but we declined. He went along the row of lockers trying to recruit the players. Dressen sang it; I'm not sure anyone else did. Leo was so incensed that he went to the National League president, Warren Giles, and complained. Giles ordered that door bricked up, and it was that way for the rest of our years at Ebbets Field."

Hodges struck out 3 times when Maglie beat the Dodgers the next day, and also struck out against lesser pitchers as he slumped during a ten-game home stand. While he still had a calm demeanor, he couldn't hide his anxiety. He was a chain-smoker—he even did print ads for Chesterfields ("They give you the good pitch. Stick with it!" said the "sensational first baseman")—but the intensity of his smoking was elevated when he battled slumps (or played in close games). "[H]is hands were shaking so much he could hardly light a cigarette," claimed Snider in *The Duke of Flatbush*. "That told me that there was a lot more going on inside Gil than he was willing to show."

The most common way to get out of slumps is by hitting the ball up the middle, but Hodges stubbornly continued to pull the ball. "I used to give him hell because he'd not hit to right field," recalls Ralph Branca. "'Gil, you'll get 15 more hits and you'll hit .300.' But he didn't care about his average. He was a big, strong guy and thought hitting homers was his job, what people expected of him. So he waited for inside fastballs that he could pull for home runs, particularly at Ebbets Field, and let a lot of good pitches go by."

"He had a strike zone problem in that he'd think any borderline pitch on the outside corner was a ball," says Erskine. "But the umpire would call them strikes most of the time. It wasn't the curve so much to me as where the pitch was, whatever it was. I think Gil had kind of a blind spot on the outer half of the plate. In 1951 he struck out nearly 100 times, and so many times it was on called strikes."

"I don't think my father had a blind spot on the outside corner," says Hodges Jr., who played briefly in the minors. "When I was older, he would teach me how to hit to right field, and he'd hit the outside fastball between first and second eight out of ten times. If he had a blind spot, it was pretty well controlled for him to be able to hit to right field that way. It was the curveball that troubled him. I don't think anyone could throw a fastball past him."

Joan Hodges believes his problem wasn't a blind spot but his falling behind in the count and being susceptible to the two-strike curve: "Unless there was a call for a bunt or hit-and-run, Gil always took the first pitch. He knew it was going to be a strike, but that was all right with him. I'd say, 'I don't understand that; I'm sorry. Pitchers know they can throw their first pitch right down the center of the plate and you're going to take it for a strike.' He'd say, 'The pressure's on the pitcher, not on me.'"

What was remarkable about Hodges' slump in 1951 and in later years was that, Erskine points out, "he never got booed. The Brooklyn fans booed every one of us at one time or another—if we played bad, they'd let us know. But never Gil. It was partly that he married a Brooklyn girl and lived there year-round, but it was mostly because they recognized that he was so genuine."

Eight-year-old Doris Kearns of Rockville Centre was so concerned about Hodges' slump that she brought him a Saint Christopher medal that had been blessed by the pope when Hodges made a personal appearance at Wolf's Sports Shop on Long Island. In her memoir, *Wait Till Next Year*, the Pulitzer Prize–winning historian Kearns Goodwin recalled that he "accepted the medal with great solemnity. He told me that he, too, had once had a St. Christopher medal blessed by the Pope. But he had given it to his father, a coal miner in Indiana. Mining was a dangerous business, he explained, and his father needed the medal more than he did. He was thrilled, he said, to receive a medal of his own. He reached out in a gesture of gratitude, and my fingers disappeared in a palm four times the size of mine. The next day, the Dodgers left for a long road trip, and Hodges began to hit. Sportswriters attributed his miraculous resurrection to his ability to sleep soundly since leaving his infant at home. But I knew better."

Hodges connected on his 9th homer on the final day of the home stand against Cal McLish, as Newcombe beat the Cubs 6–1. He then went on a tear during the road trip. He again homered off McLish on May 15 and bashed another off Bob Rush as his average improved to .287, and his team moved alone into first place. On May 23, in the final game before the Dodgers' return to Brooklyn—in which they scored in double digits for the fourth straight game—he smashed his 14th homer, a 3-run shot in the first inning against Pittsburgh's Mel Queen, and upped his RBI total to 31. He had 2 other hits in the 11–4 victory as he moved back over .300. Having gone 7–3 on the trip, the Dodgers were now 2½ games in front.

The Dodgers continued to roll, winning 15 of their next 20 games, and Hodges continued to murder the ball. On June 14, in the Dodgers' fifty-third official game, he slammed his 20th homer and drove in his 39th and 40th runs when he got hold of a two-out 2–1 pitch in the ninth inning thrown by rookie Joe Presko to beat the Cardinals 2–1. Sportswriters began pointing out that Hodges was on pace to break Babe Ruth's single-season home-run record of 60, set in 1927. Since Hodges' 4-homer game in 1950, he had replaced Ralph Kiner as the player who was most expected to challenge Ruth's sacred mark.

After Newcombe defeated the Cubs 2–1 at Wrigley Field on June 15, the team's fourth straight victory to begin another road trip, the Dodgers had a six-game lead. For the rest of the season, the Dodgers and Giants, who were being sparked by their recent rookie call-up, phenom center fielder Willie Mays, would engage in a private war, and the other six teams in the National League were afterthoughts.

June 15 was the trading deadline, and the Dodgers made their biggest deal since acquiring Roe and Cox in 1948. "I was sitting on the john in Chicago," recalls Wayne Terwilliger, then the Cubs second baseman, "and I heard on the radio that I'd been traded with Andy Pafko, Rube Walker, and Johnny Schmitz to the Dodgers for Eddie Miksis, Gene Hermanski, Joe Hatten, and Bruce Edwards. It was a big shock, and awkward because we were in the middle of a series and had to pick up our gear in one locker room and carry it into the other locker room. Hodges, Reese, and Erskine welcomed me to the Dodgers. Gil was a great guy. On the field he was a total professional, all business, but in the locker room he talked and laughed a lot."

The key man in the transaction was Pafko, who would have his second consecutive 30-homer season and drive in 90 runs. O'Malley and Bavasi felt he was the star left fielder they'd been after for years. However, he wouldn't be the impact player or fan favorite that he'd been in Chicago. He was instead a mild disappointment in Brooklyn, batting only .249 for the rest of the '51 season.

Arguably, the Dodgers' biggest addition was Walker, who would prove to be a savvy backup catcher to Campanella and an effective left-handed pinch hitter. Campanella had raised his average from .266 on May 15 to .337, and entered the competition in the National League's MVP race, but Walker would be needed when he missed games due to injuries. In *We Played the Game*, Walker, who'd years later be a trusted pitching coach and friend of Hodges, gave his impressions of his new teammates:

I admired Campanella a great deal and we were good friends. He is remembered for his happy demeanor, but he was a serious player. Hodges, Snider, and Robinson were all leaders. We all thought Pee Wee could have been a great manager. We all felt Gil would be a manager. He'd get mad every once in a while, but I'd say he didn't really have a temper. What a hitter he had become since the mid-forties. He and Snider were the best righty-lefty power duo in the league. Snider was also our most consistent power hitter. In Ebbets Field, Snider could hit any right-hander. Robinson was a unique player, a tough competitor. . . . He had a lot of inner strength and wasn't afraid to speak his mind. Jackie and Pee Wee hit to all fields. So did Furillo, who was a great hitter. And a great fielder.

The Dodgers were a proud but humble team. We expected to win, but didn't gloat when we did. The Dodgers were known for their unity. We were all good friends. Some of the Dodgers played golf. I did; so did Hodges, who was a lot of fun to play with. Pee Wee could really play. Some Dodgers played pool, bowled. There were several card games going on all the time. Reese, Hodges, Snider, and Jackie played cards, mostly bridge. Clyde King, Billy Cox, and Carl Erskine liked bridge, too. There'd always be games going on for money on the train.

The unity of the Dodgers extended to the players' wives. "The team would get together for social events, and we would enjoy that," recalls Rachel Robinson. "We did get together for dinner with Joan and Gil in Brooklyn a few times. There was a warmth to Gil, not in an effusive way, but just him being himself. Quiet, but with a smile. You knew that he was right there with you and was a person you could relate to."

"One year I had a luncheon for the wives on East Thirty-second Street," remembers Joan Hodges. "The reason was so the other wives could socialize with Rachel Robinson and Ruth Campanella. I realized that there were wives who—because of their husbands—resented the Robinsons. I told the wives, 'Look, the boys are like brothers in the clubhouse, and we have to be like sisters outside the clubhouse. We're all here for the same reason, and I am giving this luncheon for that reason.' I think it was effective. I'm not going to say things changed the next day, but slowly they did."

The Dodgers played as a unified team as they increased their lead over New York to 8 games at the All-Star break, with a record of 50–26. Hodges' average had dipped to .273, but he went into the break with a league-leading 28 homers—8 more than five-time defending NL home-run champion Ralph Kiner—and 54 RBIs. He was one cog in a balanced attack. Snider had 18 homers and a team-high 59 RBIs to go with a .284 average. Robinson had a .356 average with 11 homers and 47 RBIs. Reese also had 47 RBIs and a .308 average. Furillo had 48 RBIs and a .303 average. And Campanella, coming on strong, was batting .326 with 10 homers and 38 RBIs. Roe (12–1) and Newcombe (12–4) led the pitching staff.

Hodges, who was still ahead of Ruth's 1927 home-run pace, was selected as the National League's starting first baseman in the All-Star Game. Robinson and Campanella were also in Eddie Sawyer's starting lineup at Briggs Stadium in Detroit. Reese, Snider, Newcombe, and Roe were on the roster. Hodges smashed a 2-run homer off Fred Hutchinson and added a single as he played all nine innings in the National League's 8–3 triumph. Stan Musial, Bob Elliott, and Ralph Kiner also homered for the senior circuit and the four of them posed for pictures during the postgame celebration.

The Dodgers won their first two games after the All-Star Game, but then lost 6 of 7 to the Cubs, Reds, and Pirates. The finale against visiting Pittsburgh, the only team that they'd have a losing record against in 1951, was a defeat that would come back to haunt them at year's end. The Dodgers overcame a 10–2 deficit to take a 12–11 lead, only to lose 13–12 when the Pirates scored twice in the eighth off Palica, on Ralph Kiner's 3rd homer of the game and former Dodgers star Pete Reiser's game-winning RBI single.

The Dodgers' positive response to the tough loss was a 10-game winning streak in which Roe and Newcombe won in back-to-back starts three times. Brooklyn was an impressive 21–7 in July to improve its record to 63–32, good for a substantial 9½-game lead over New York. Hodges' picture was no longer seen every day in the sports page next to Babe Ruth's, because he had fallen off Ruth's pace from 1927. But his average was up to .285.

An article by Joe King in the *Sporting News* speculated on the value of all the Dodgers if they were each up for sale. The most valuable Dodger, according to King, was Hodges, who could net $300,000 in a transaction. Robinson, Campanella, and Snider were worth $200,000. Furillo, Roe, and Newcombe were valued at $150,000. Finally, $100,000 was a fair price to pay for Cox, Pafko, and Erskine.

The Dodgers finished their road trip by splitting six games, but back in the friendly confines of Ebbets Field, they won 7 of 8, as Branca and Erskine proved that Newcombe and Roe had able support in the rotation. Three straight wins came against the Giants on August 8 and 9. Erskine won 7–2, and reliever Clyde King won twice, 7–6 in ten innings and 6–5. The Dodgers, however, made a tactical error when they returned to their clubhouse. They roused the sleeping Giants by taunting them at the door separating the two teams. Nobody remembers exactly what was said or who was involved, but it's likely the phrase "The Giants Is Dead!" was revived; "Roll Out the Barrel" was sung; and, recalls Terwilliger, "Newcombe was pounding on the separation between our shower rooms and saying, 'Eat your heart out, Leo!'" It's unlikely that Dressen remained quiet with Durocher within earshot. The Giants said nothing, but they now had impetus to mount a comeback for the ages.

August 13 at Ebbets Field was promoted as "Music Depreciation Night." It marked the welcome return of the Sym-Phony. The ad hoc band had been playing at home games since the 1930s, but they had been muted in July because the musicians' union objected to one of its members participating for free. The dispute was resolved, and to celebrate on this night any fan with a musical instrument was let into the ballpark for free. Adding to the loud festivities were the Dodgers' booming bats in a 7–6 win over the Braves. Hodges smashed a game-winning 3-run homer, his 33rd, to go with 71 RBIs, and Campanella added a 2-run blast, his 25th, to go with 79 RBIs.

The Dodgers moved to a season-high 13½ games ahead of the Giants. In both clubhouses it was stated: If the Dodgers played just .500 ball for the rest of the season, the Giants would have to play .800 ball to beat them. As the Dodgers thought about another World Series matchup with the Yankees, they didn't realize they were about to be ambushed by the other New York team, beginning August 14–16, when the Giants swept them 4–2, 3–1, and 2–1 in the Polo Grounds. When the teams next met for a two-game series on September 1 and 2, again in the Polo Grounds, the Giants sliced the Dodgers' lead to 5 games as Maglie outpitched Branca 8–1, Jim Hearn outpitched Newcombe 11–2, and outfielder Don Mueller slugged 5 home runs to tie a major-league record for two games. The Dodgers knew that they were fighting for their lives and, worse, their dignity.

The Dodgers came back strong, winning their next five games. Erskine beat the Braves 7–2. Recent call-up Clem Labine, who threw a wicked sinker and curveball, then beat Milwaukee by the same score. Then Branca upped his record to 13–5 with a 5–2 victory over Philadelphia. The score was

1–1 in the fifth inning when Furillo singled, Reese walked, and Robinson beat out a bunt to the mound. With the bases loaded and no outs, Ken Johnson struck out Campanella and Pafko. But Hodges brought the crowd to its feet with a line drive that cleared the left-field wall. His grand slam was his 37th longball of the year. The previous Dodgers record for a season was 35 by Babe Herman in 1930.

The Dodgers did play .500 ball after August 13, which was poor for them but was enough for them to avoid a "choker" label. Unfortunately for them, the Giants did play .800 ball, going a spectacular 37–7. It was as if eyes from heaven were looking down on them fondly and directing their miracle comeback. Actually the eyes were out in the scoreboard, where a Giants assistant with a telescope was stealing the signs of opposing catchers and alerting batters to what pitches were coming.

"Well, we now know the Giants cheated in 1951," says Branca. "We didn't know until years later how the Giants could play so well down the stretch. They wouldn't have scored so many runs unless their own hitters knew something. If they stole even one game they shouldn't have won; there shouldn't have been a playoff."

The Dodgers were fortunate even to be in a season-ending three-game playoff with the Giants. Roe kept winning, but Newcombe went eighteen days between victories, and Branca didn't win again. Labine gave the team a huge lift by winning 4 straight decisions after being brought up from Montreal. However, he gave up a grand slam after defying Dressen's orders to pitch from the stretch, and his manager spitefully stopped pitching him.

The Dodgers still led by 6 games, with only sixteen games to play on September 14. But the Dodgers' bats and arms, so dependable and consistent all year, came on strong one day and faded out the next, like a faraway radio station. The team went only 6–9 down the stretch as their lead evaporated. On September 27, Campanella and almost everyone on the Dodgers bench were ejected by umpire Frank Dascoli for arguing a blown call at the plate in a 4–3 loss to Boston. "Bobby Addis was trying to score," recalls Erskine, "but Campy had the ball and spun him around and he never reached the plate. But Dascoli called Addis safe and we lost the game. Those crazy things happened down the stretch." The loss went to Preacher Roe, who finished at 22–3.

After another frustrating 4–3 loss to the Phillies the next day, the Dodgers and Giants both had 94–58 records and were tied for first place. The Dodgers had to win their final two games to stay deadlocked with the rampaging Giants.

Again proving he could win the *big* game, Newcombe coolly disposed of Philadelphia, 5–0. In winning his 20th game of the season he defeated his frequent adversary, 21-game winner Robin Roberts.

On the final day of the regular season, the Giants edged the Braves 3–2. Then they waited out the ending of the Brooklyn game. They were feeling good as the Dodgers fell behind the Phillies 6–1 in the third inning. The Dodgers were trailing 8–5 with one man out in the eighth when Hodges and Cox singled, and Walker scored them both with a pinch double. Walker then scored the tying run when Furillo greeted Roberts in relief with a big single. Newcombe became the sixth Dodgers pitcher as the game went into extra innings. The Dodgers faithful found it hard to breathe. Many prayed. Showing his mettle once more, Newcombe held the Phillies scoreless for 5⅓ innings before giving way to Bud Podbielan.

In the twelfth inning it appeared that the Phillies would pull out the victory when they had the bases filled with two outs and Eddie Waitkus lined a sure single toward right center—except Robinson dived and stretched and somehow snared the ball, knocking the wind out of himself as he crashed to the ground. He kicked up a cloud of dust around him, and the Phillies screamed that he'd trapped the ball. But the umpire, knowing great baseball history when he saw it, signaled that Waitkus was out. With two outs in the fourteenth inning, the clutch Robinson capped off his unforgettable performance by slamming a Roberts fastball high into the upper-left-field stands. Podbielan retired Ennis and Waitkus with the tying run on second in the bottom of the inning, and the Dodgers triumphed in the classic game, 9–8. They had survived to play another day. For the only time, the Brooklyn Dodgers and New York Giants would meet in a three-game playoff to determine the National League champion.

Early in the year, Sal Maglie threw a too-close-for-comfort brushback pitch to Jackie Robinson, as he was prone to do. Robinson, as usual, took offense and laid down a bunt near the first-base line. He ran slowly out of the box, and just as Maglie leaned over to pick up the ball, Robinson sped up and knocked him on his rear, then continued to first base unchallenged. That was the signature play of the Dodgers–Giants rivalry in 1951. As the Dodgers and Giants got ready for the playoffs, everyone expected hard slides, collisions, and knockdown pitches to punctuate the thrilling baseball, because it had happened all season when the two teams met.

"There wasn't anything phony about the Dodgers–Giants rivalry," says Erskine. "Every game didn't have batters being hit on the head or brawls, but they were all heated contests. Neither team was intimidated by the other. When you played the Giants there was what I called *professional hatred*. You really didn't hate the players as individuals, but you hated them as a team. There was a great sense of pride to beat the Giants."

In the first game, there were a number of brushback pitches thrown by the Giants' Jim Hearn and the Dodgers' Ralph Branca. But there was only one hit batsman, Monte Irvin, the National League's RBI champion in 1951. Sure enough, two at-bats later Irvin homered. Bobby Thomson had touched Branca for a 2-run homer earlier in the game, so Irvin increased the lead to 3–1. That was the final score of the first baseball game ever telecast coast-to-coast. Pafko had homered for Brooklyn's lone run. In addition to losing the game, the Dodgers lost Campanella to a thigh injury, a major occurrence. Walker would catch the next two games.

Rather than go with Roe in the second game, Dressen suddenly had renewed faith in Labine. He must have regretted not pitching him more down the stretch, because the cocky rookie exhibited remarkable poise in the do-or-die game, limiting the Giants to 6 hits in a 10–0 victory. He was backed by homers from Robinson, Walker, Hodges, and Pafko. Hodges became the first Brooklyn Dodger in history to hit 40 homers in a season. His 103 RBIs, 5 behind team leader Campanella, gave him more than 100 RBIs in three straight years.

On October 3, the two rivals played their final playoff game, perhaps the most famous game in major-league history. When Gil and Joan parked their car in the lot at the Polo Grounds, Bobby Thomson stepped out of the neighboring car. "I'd say Gil Hodges was the only guy on that team universally admired and respected for the type of person he was," said Thomson in 1992. He extended his hand and said, "Gil, I'm going to say good-bye to you now, because one of us won't be playing anymore after today."

As her husband went into the Dodgers clubhouse to prepare for the game, Joan found her seat. "A guy came over to us as we were sitting down that day," she recalled to Maury Allen in *Brooklyn Remembered*, "just some fan who recognized us as Brooklyn wives and he said, 'If Bobby Thomson hits a homer, you'll lose the game.' I'm a Catholic and I'm not supposed to be superstitious. I just looked at him. I wonder to this day who he was."

The game had the ideal pitching matchup of 20-game winner Don Newcombe and 23-game winner Sal Maglie. They were their teams' aces, used intimidation as part of their arsenals, and made no attempt to hide their dislike of the other team. They would set the tone. Maglie had a shaky first inning, giving up an RBI single to Robinson after walks to Reese and Snider, but then held the Dodgers scoreless for the next 6 innings. Newcombe protected the 1–0 lead, and it looked as if he might toss his second consecutive shutout. However in the seventh, Thomson hit a long sacrifice fly that scored Irvin with the tying run. Newcombe got out of the inning on a smooth double play turned by Reese, Robinson, and Hodges, who participated in a twin killing for a league-record 171st time. In the top of the eighth, the Dodgers parlayed 4 singles and a walk into 3 runs.

The Dodgers were still ahead 4–1 in the bottom of the ninth as a dog-tired Newcombe made his way to the mound to try to get the final three outs. It wouldn't be easy. Leading off, Giants shortstop Alvin Dark hit a grounder between first and second. Hodges moved to his right and stretched, and the ball grazed off his glove and away from Robinson, who might have made the play if Hodges let it go. Durocher, coaching third as he often did against the Dodgers and other teams at opportune times, clapped his hands, heckled Newcombe, and urged Don Mueller to keep it going.

With the excellent left-handed batter up, there was no question that Hodges should play back. With a 3-run lead, all that mattered was getting an out, not whether Dark was able to take a big lead. So for the next sixty years, befuddled baseball writers and fans would ask: "Why was Hodges holding on Dark and not playing deep?" Mueller rapped a sharp grounder to the right side of the infield. If Hodges were in the correct position he would have fielded the ball and either beaten Mueller to the bag for the big out or thrown to second for a force and possible 3–6–3 double play. But Hodges couldn't reach the grounder and it squirted through for a single, putting Giants on first and third with nobody out, and the tying run at the plate.

Out in the bullpen, Branca and Erskine were throwing under the supervision of pitching coach Clyde Sukeforth. But Dressen stuck with his starter. He'd still given up only 5 hits and 1 run. The batter was Irvin, who had belted 24 homers and driven in 121 RBIs. On a 1–1 count he hit a foul pop that Hodges squeezed in his big glove. As Durocher heckled Newcombe, Whitey Lockman, another left-handed hitter, strode to the plate. He was very dangerous in this situation, because he rarely struck out and hit to all fields. He had pulled a single to right in his first at-bat. This time he took a high outside pitch the other way for a double. Dark jogged home. Mueller stopped at third. In fact, he came into the base so awkwardly that he badly sprained his ankle and had to be helped off the field, one of the inning's bizarre incidents. The towering Clint "Hondo" Hartung pinch-ran, his biggest moment in a disappointing career.

Newcombe walked slowly from the mound, his season over. His manager finally agreed with him that he was too tired to pitch effectively. The next batter was Thomson, and he'd already had a couple of hits, so Dressen figured it was a good time to go to the bullpen. Dressen had asked Sukeforth who was pitching better, Branca or Erskine? Branca had given up a homer to Thomson two games before, but Thomson took Erskine deep earlier in the season, so neither was a sure thing. Sukeforth told Dressen that Branca was throwing hard. He told him Erskine had bounced a couple of curves. That was actually an indication that the curve had good downward action, but Dressen decided to go with Branca.

"In the Polo Grounds there was a long distance between home plate and the screen," says Erskine, "so if there was a wild pitch, the catcher had a long way to run to retrieve the ball. Walker wasn't as good as Campanella at catching my curve when I buried it in the dirt like Campy wanted me to do. And he could not run. So that may have factored into the decision to go with Branca. Sukey, who was a class act, thought Ralph had the best stuff on the staff. If I'd pitched to Thomson I would have gone with my big curves rather than fastballs and kept everything away, because it was only 300 feet down the foul lines in the Polo Grounds. But it's all speculation. It was destiny—if Cy Young was pitching the result would have been the same."

Rather than throwing the ball off the plate with an empty base and a frightened Willie Mays on deck, Branca challenged Thomson with two fastballs.

Few homers were hit into the lower deck at the Polo Grounds because of the overhang from the upper deck. Thomson's "Shot Heard 'round the World" was the rare exception, a low liner that just cleared the fence. It wouldn't have been a homer at Ebbets Field, but just like that it turned the Giants' 4–2 deficit into a stunning 5–4 victory.

"I was sitting on the bench, at the far end of the dugout, toward left field," recalls Terwilliger, "thinking about how much money I'd get for being in the World Series. Then Thomson hit Branca's pitch! I knew he hit it good, but I didn't think it was going to get into the lower deck there, because it was kind of a sinking line drive. But then I saw Pafko turn around and watch it, and everything broke loose."

"Our hatred for Leo Durocher culminated in 1951," says Larry King, "when he was jumping up and down on third base after Bobby Thomson homered."

"I'd been working at the *Brooklyn Eagle* for six weeks as a clerk in the sports department," recalls Pulitzer Prize–winning sportswriter Dave Anderson, "and we were in the composing room when the final score came in. I can still see the printer picking up the headline saying the Dodgers had won—most of the hard type—and throwing it away."

"Sukeforth, Labine, and I were the first guys in the clubhouse, and I watched the guys come in," says Erskine. "Jackie threw his glove into his locker as hard as he could throw it. It was a metal locker and there was a loud *bang*! And Dressen came in and he took off his shirt by ripping off all the buttons. Then Gil came in and he walked over to his locker and folded his glove and laid it in the top shelf of his locker. He never made a sound, never made a gesture. It was such a contrast to everybody else. He had to have felt the pain of that loss, but there was no indication of what he was feeling."

"Without a doubt the biggest game I ever played in my life was the final game of the 1951 playoff against the Giants," Hodges wrote eighteen years later in *The Game of Baseball*. "It's a day none of us will ever forget who were in that game, much as some of us would like to."

Branca flopped down on the steps, facedown, and then turned and sat with his head buried in his hands. He didn't pay any more attention to Walter O'Malley's clubhouse pep talk than anyone else did. "Father Pat Rowley was my fiancée Ann's cousin," he recalls sixty years later. "They were in the car together about an hour after the game and I said to him, 'Why me? I love baseball. Why would it have to be me?' And he told me, 'God chose you because he knew your faith would be strong enough to bear this cross.' I don't think that's something the Dodgers asked itself as a team after losing all those big games. I don't want to say the team was crestfallen after the home run or astonished that the Giants could play so well down the stretch. We now have been told that the Giants stole the signs, including on the two pitches I threw Thomson."

"A few years ago Branca signed a picture for me," said Larry King in 2011. "He wrote, 'Dear Larry, the Giants stole the pennant. Ralph Branca.'"

The "Miracle at Coogan's Bluff" was the darkest moment in the history of the Brooklyn Dodgers. It's not known how many Dodgers could stomach watching the Giants play in the World Series, where they'd lose in six games to the Yankees. The Series featured Joe DiMaggio's final games in pinstripes, but would be known equally for the two rookies with amazing physical skills and unlimited potential who were making their initial appearances in baseball's biggest showcase—the Giants' Willie Mays (4-for-22), who'd be voted National League Rookie of the Year, and the Yankees' Mickey Mantle (1-for-5). Both would soon become towering figures in New York baseball in the fifties and have a major impact on the Dodgers' fortunes.

The premium was on catchers in 1951, and the two MVPs were Yogi Berra of the Yankees in the American League and Roy Campanella in the National League. Hodges might have been the MVP of the first half of the year but finished sixteenth. Campanella would twice more be selected MVP, which prevented his teammates from receiving due acknowledgment for their contributions. He'd graciously say, "I think any player on the Dodgers could have been the most valuable player then—Snider, Furillo, Hodges, Robinson, Reese—it was just an honor to play with them." Hodges joined Campanella and Robinson on *Look* magazine's postseason All-Star team, along with outfielders Ted Williams, Stan Musial, and Ralph Kiner, shortstop Chico Carrasquel, third baseman George Kell, and pitchers Bob Feller and Sal Maglie. He batted .268 and led the league only in strikeouts with 99, but he finished second in homers (40), third in total bases (307) and runs (118), fifth in slugging percentage (.527), and sixth in RBIs (103), and easily outpolled other first basemen.

Hodges, Robinson, and Campanella hoped to get past the dreadful conclusion of the 1951 season by playing more baseball. Each assembled barnstorming teams. Hodges planned a modest sixteen-game tour with such players as Cal Abrams, Gene Hermanski, Whitey Ford, Ralph Houk, Eddie Robinson, Chuck Stobbs, Billy Goodman, Gene Woodling, Sid Gordon, and Tommy Byrne. One time while touring in the South, they were scheduled to play Campanella's all-black squad that included Don Newcombe, Monte Irvin, Luke Easter, and Harry "Suitcase" Simpson. Because of the Jim Crow laws still in existence, the game was canceled. Elsewhere, though, the thirteen joint meetings of the Hodges and Campanella tours attracted 43,895 fans.

Putting away his bat and glove, Hodges spent some time back in Petersburg with his parents and grandmother Ellen. He was glad to see Bob, who was excited because Gladys was pregnant with their first child, Tony. Gil visited his friend Bob King, who was about to purchase the barbershop where both Gil and Bob Hodges would hang out whenever they were in Petersburg. Gil was saddened by the death that fall of Eldon Sisson, whom he'd known since he was a little kid and played for in 1941 on the Princeton American Legion team.

Charlie Hodges was busy that fall campaigning. He ran for city council, but on November 5 was pummeled by his Republican opponent, winning only one precinct. He'd never run for public office again. He didn't take too kindly to defeat. To this day there are those in Petersburg who say they heard through the grapevine that when Bobby Thomson hit his home run in '51, Charlie smashed his television set.

"Charlie was a nice gentleman but he could get excited," recalls Louis Lombardi. "One time he came in from Indiana and we went to Ebbets Field to watch Gil play. We were sitting in the stands, not far above the dugout, and Gil got hit by a pitch. Gil went right down on the ground. His father said, 'Oh, my God!' and took off. Before I knew it, he was standing on top of the dugout and trying to get down on the field. Two guards grabbed hold of him. They didn't know who he was. He said, 'That's my son, Gil Hodges!' They said, 'He'll be all right! Don't worry about him! It didn't hit him in the head.' Gil got up and ran to first and Charlie returned to his seat."

Back in Brooklyn, Hodges enjoyed spending time with his family and fishing with his brother-in-law. In January, the *New York Journal-American* sent writer Al Jonas to report on how baseball's strongest man handled domesticity. "Joan readily purrs that the Dodger star is a tremendous help around the house," Jonas wrote. "'He makes breakfast if I'm busy, helps with the children all the time, helps clean the house, takes out the garbage and does all the chores,' she says proudly." Jonas found Hodges "on the floor of his rented Flatbush house with blond Gil, Jr., twenty-two months, and brown-haired Irene, ten months, both blue-eyed. Gil . . . spends hours instructing Gil, Jr. on how to swing a tiny bat, and little Irene's play-pen toys include a regulation baseball. . . ." Jonas was surprised that Hodges was as quiet as his reputation, and came out of his shell that day only when he played with his kids.

The subject that he continued to be completely silent about with his wife, teammates, reporters, and everyone else was his service in the Marines during the war. He was often referred to in print as "the big Marine" and had tremendous pride in his service—he even sang "The Halls of Montezuma" with his kids—but he refused to discuss anything specific. Joan recalls a day when Roscoe McGowen called the house: "He wanted to talk to Gil about an article he was writing, but Gil wasn't there. Then he said, 'While I have you on the phone, let me ask you about when Gil was awarded a Bronze Star for when he was a Marine in Okinawa.' Imagine my surprise. I was married three years and I never knew that my husband was awarded a Bronze Star! And when I later told Gil about the call, he still wouldn't talk about it."

"I believe there was something that happened in the war that was kept private even from my mother and from me as I grew older," says Gil Hodges Jr. sixty years later. "I don't know if it was one incident, since in all the years it was never discussed. But there's no doubt in my mind that what he had suffered contributed to his anxiety."

Hodges was usually easygoing and cheerful when he wasn't on the diamond, so it was impossible to detect whether anything was bothering him. Even during the season, even after pressure-packed games, he was usually able to compartmentalize and leave his worries at the ballpark and eat dinner, play with the kids, and play cards or parlor games with Joan and their friends. Those times he was wound too tightly, Joan helped him relax, even taking him to the opera, which he grew to appreciate. Overall, Gil Hodges was living the life he always wanted.

CHAPTER TWELVE

Walter O'Malley was thinking big: He commissioned industrial designer Norman Bel Geddes to draw up a blueprint for an all-purpose 52,000-seat Brooklyn stadium that would have a retractable roof, a shopping center underneath, and a parking lot for seven thousand cars. For the first time, there was an indication that the days of the beloved but deteriorating Ebbets Field were numbered. The Dodgers had led the National League in attendance in 1951 with 1,282,628 fans, but O'Malley, who had a background in engineering, believed he needed to build a state-of-the-art stadium in order not to lose cash customers in future years, particularly the females he was courting. Meanwhile, he shored up the Dodgers' presence in Vero Beach by signing a twenty-one-year dollar-a-year lease for the land on which Dodgertown was built.

All Hodges and the other Dodgers who reported to Vero Beach cared about was rebounding from the previous year's heartbreak. For the third year in a row they had lost their final game. They were a team of stars who had no world championship rings on their fingers. Dressen, who had worked out with Hodges at the Crescent Health Club in Brooklyn in the off-season, assured the press that all his players were optimistic.

That spring Roger Kahn began a two-year stint as the beat writer for the *New York Herald-Tribune*. In Brooklyn, baseball fans devoured articles on their team by the *Eagle*'s beat writers, Howard Burr and Tommy Holmes, but Dick Young, because of his golden pen and the sheer volume of the *Daily News*' readership, was unquestionably the dominant sportswriter in the

Dodger world. Kahn, though, a lifelong Dodgers fan, had instant credibility and was viewed as a legitimate alternative to Young, particularly on stories involving Jackie Robinson. "Robinson couldn't stand Young, so I got all kinds of stuff from him," says Kahn.

Kahn had been introduced to Robinson, Hodges, Reese, and other players by the *Tribune*'s Harold Rosenthal the previous fall. Hodges was close to Rosenthal, so he was receptive to Kahn from the start. Kahn quickly learned the difficulty in interviewing the reserved player. "Gil was never very expansive," he recalls. "He was very bright and knew things; he just never told you. If he had a bad game, he wouldn't pull a Newcombe and say, 'I had a bad game; go away.' You could ask him questions. He tried to be open, but he was always civil and didn't want to stir up anything. He never talked about losing. He would never make a comment about a teammate who had made an error. He never complained that if he hadn't been in the service he would have been in the major leagues sooner and hit a hell of a lot more home runs. As Branch Rickey would say, there are three things you can't teach: power, arm, speed. Gil had enormous natural power. That first spring I went out to left field with Andy Pafko and George Shuba and played a little ball. Hodges hit a long drive, and I stopped to watch and it just kept carrying. It climbed and climbed. It was unbelievable. I never saw a ball hit that hard."

Kahn was aware that Hodges' salary wasn't commensurate with his contributions and value to the team. He may have been the first to relate the oft-told story of Hodges negotiating his salary with Buzzie Bavasi. Supposedly, Hodges asked for a small raise one year to $27,000, well below what he deserved but a figure he found satisfactory. But Bavasi said the team was determined to pay him a couple of thousand dollars less. "So," Kahn says, "Buzzie tells Hodges, 'You turn away and I'll put three numbers on slips of paper into a hat—25, 26, and 27 for $25,000, $26,000, and $27,000—and whichever number you pull out is your salary for next year.' So Gil turns around and Buzzie writes a number on each of the three pieces of paper, and Gil picks out a number and hey, it's 27, and he's happy and leaves. Later Buzzie told people that he wrote 27 on all three pieces of paper. Well, O'Malley didn't like that."

The big question in camp was how to replace Don Newcombe, who, much to his chagrin, had been drafted into the army for a two-year stint. There was no worry about the everyday lineup. The front office felt everyone—including the older Robinson and Reese—was in his prime, and the eight starters at the end of the 1951 season were set to start in 1952. Once again skilled position players in the minors stayed put, and bench-warmers who would be regulars elsewhere picked up more splinters.

The Dodgers won their opener 3–2 on April 15, the fifth anniversary of Jackie Robinson's major-league debut, against the same team, the Braves. Only 4,694 showed up at Braves Field despite a matchup of 20-game win-ners Preacher Roe and Warren Spahn. The Dodgers won a laugher the next day, 14–8. Hodges got none of Brooklyn's 20 hits, taking an 0-for-6 collar and fanning twice, the only Dodger to strike out. He was off to a rough start, and through April would hit a puny .162 with no homers and no RBIs.

The Dodgers won 8 of their first 9 games, losing only when Sal Maglie shut them out. Roe won 3 times, six-foot-six left-hander Chris Van Cuyk won twice, and Branca won his first decision. So even though Labine and twenty-nine-year-old rookie right-hander Ben Wade were roughed up in their first starts, Dressen felt good about his rotation. He didn't expect that Roe would come down with a sore arm and win only once more before June 6; Van Cuyk's next victory wouldn't come until May 21, and he'd win only 5 games total before his last major-league appearance on August 15; Labine would pitch so erratically as a starter and reliever that he'd spend time in the minors; and Branca, though wearing number 12 instead of 13, had the awful luck to hurt his back falling out of a chair in spring training and would win 4 games all year. "I just wish the Lord had let the injury happen one year later," Branca says, "because I could have proved what hap-pened in 1951 didn't affect me mentally."

Fortunately, Erskine was able to step into the ace role. Also Wade, who threw mostly fastballs but had a sharp slider and a big, slow curve, became a dependable starter (and pitched well in occasional relief). The strongest addition to the revamped rotation was Billy Loes, a flaky local schoolboy sensation featuring a fastball with movement, a sharp breaking ball, and a deceptive change. After going 3–0 in relief, he made his first start on May 15 and shut out the Cubs 2–0, to lower his ERA to 0.64. Dressen was able to move Loes from the pen because former Negro League star Joe Black had come on strong since debuting May 1 and was now the manager's go-to reliever. "He had a great fastball and a very sharp whatever-it-was," says Ralph Kiner, who shared the home-run title with Hank Sauer in 1952. "It may have been a slider, but I thought it was a spitball."

With a makeshift but solid rotation quickly in place and the offense still in high gear, the Dodgers accumulated four 4-game winning streaks in four weeks. But Hodges wasn't hitting his weight. He didn't get any of the Dodgers' 17 hits when they ran over the Reds 19–1 in support of Van Cuyk (who got 4 hits himself) on May 21. He did walk twice as the Dodgers set a modern National League record by plating fifteen runners in the first inning as nineteen consecutive batters reached base.

Hodges had 3 RBIs, including a game-winning eighth-inning sacrifice fly the next day against the Reds, but a week later, his average was .197 and he still had only 3 homers. If he was suffering because of his six-week slump, it was impossible to tell, because he didn't pout like Snider when he was going through a rough patch. Hodges' face was unreadable. Dodgers great Billy Herman worked with him to get him to hit the outside pitch the opposite way. "I remember going out early once and Gil was practicing hitting to right field," recalls Kahn. "He worked at it and could hit a line drive off the scoreboard in practice. But he never was a good right-field hitter. He was a solid hitter with a lot of power, but a pull hitter."

On May 29, Hodges was 0-for-3 when he pulled a home run to left off Braves reliever Lew Burdette. This gave him momentum, and in the Memorial Day doubleheader the following day, he exploded. In the first game, his 3-run homer off Jim Wilson in the eighth inning overcame a 3–2 deficit, leading to a 5–4 Dodgers' victory. In the nightcap, he smashed another 3-run homer off Dick Donovan when his team was trailing 3–2 in the fifth inning and drove in 5 runs total to propel the Dodgers to an 11–3 win. He ended the month batting only .227, but his 8-RBI afternoon gave him 25 RBIs in the twenty-six games Brooklyn played in May.

The Dodgers went 18–8 in May to improve their record to 26–10. They were in second place, only half a game behind the sizzling Giants, who went 20–6 for the month. On June 1, in Chicago, Hodges clouted a 2-run homer in the second inning, as the Dodgers beat the Cubs 3–2 and moved into first place, where they'd make a stand.

Dodgers fans cheered for Hodges when his offense returned in late May, but they had treated him the same when he couldn't buy a hit. This was partly because they knew his tendency was to slump at some time during every season and still drive in 100 runs. Also, they appreciated his stellar defense. "With Duke, if he was slumping, his fielding would suck, but if Gil wasn't hitting, his fielding was still great," Kahn recalls. "Hodges, Cox, Reese, Robinson—where can you find an infield like that? Robinson made only 6 errors at second one year, Reese was a wonderful shortstop, Cox was the best third baseman I ever saw, and except for that one goddamn ball Mueller hit in the '51 playoff, I don't remember Hodges making a bad play. He was the best first baseman of the era."

Dodgers fans were reminded of Hodges' special skills as a fielder on June 4 in Pittsburgh, when he turned two sure hits into double plays in successive innings. Snider and Robinson homered, and Reese and Campanella drove in big runs in the 7–4 victory, but unquestionably the star of the game was the first baseman, who had again proved that denying runs was as important as producing them.

"I planned to rest Hodges some time ago when he wasn't hitting," Dressen said to a Pittsburgh reporter, "but never again. He can win games without ever getting a hit."

In keeping with his being compared to Lou Gehrig, Hodges was referred to as an "iron man," because Dressen, like Burt Shotton, rarely gave him a day off. When it happened, it was news. Ironically, it happened in the next series, against the Reds. In his 277th consecutive game on June 7, Hodges was stepped on by Campanella as they both went after a foul pop. The catcher's spikes drove through Hodges' shoe and into his foot. It was an injury that made even his most grizzled teammates whimper, but Hodges sat out only one game.

The Dodgers won 12 of 13 games to open up a slight lead over the Giants. They moved to 5 games ahead on June 19, when Erskine no-hit the Cubs at Ebbets Field, allowing only a walk to the opposing pitcher, Willie Ramsdell, in his 5–0 victory.

In the final game before the All-Star break, on July 6, Brooklyn beat Boston 8–2, and the lead was 4½ games. Ben Wade said his career highlight wasn't defeating Warren Spahn, but hitting 2 home runs off him. Spahn was one of the few left-handers willing to pitch at Ebbets Field against the Dodgers' predominantly right-handed lineup and often struggled. Hodges hit Spahn well, but his 3-run blast in this game came off reliever Vern Bickford. Afterward, the reporters gathered around Hodges, Wade, Black, and Dressen. By going hitless, Robinson, who was leading the team with a .315 average, had the rare opportunity to shower and dress while not answering questions.

"It was an incredibly talkative locker room," Kahn recalled in 2011. "Campanella was talking all the time. Robinson was talking all the time. Pee Wee liked to talk. Snider, my God. Reese had a captain's chair and his own little area; everybody else around him had a stool, even Robinson. Hodges was quiet but was very close to the center of things and knew what was going on. If I was talking to just one player I'd get the quotes down, but if Robinson, Snider, and Reese were talking at the same time I'd listen and then go to the dugout and start writing down notes. Once when I didn't follow that routine, Gil silently came up behind me and put a hand on my shoulder. He said, 'Why are you taking your notes here instead of in the dugout?' I said, 'Well, Gil, some people on this club shut up as soon as they see a pencil moving.' And Gil said, 'That's right. And some people on this club won't start talking until they see a pencil in your hand.'"

Hodges' average stood at only .237 at the break, but his 17 homers and 57 RBIs earned him another selection on the All-Star team, backing up Whitey Lockman. He didn't appear in the rain-shortened game, won by the National League 3–2 in five innings. Durocher was the winning manager, because Jackie Robinson, his nemesis, hit a 2-run homer.

The Dodgers lost their first game back, but then reeled off 9 straight victories, as Wade won 3 times, Erskine and Loes won twice, and Black recorded 4 unofficial saves. When they won 7 of 8 in August, they increased their lead to a season-high 10½ games. Their lead was down to 8 games on August 31, when Hodges celebrated the second anniversary of his 4-homer game by belting a grand slam off the Giants' Jim Hearn and driving in 5 runs in support of Billy Loes' 13th victory, 9–1. It was a gratifying blow for Hodges, because, oddly, he had hit another grand slam against Hearn on August 5 to give the Dodgers a 4–0 lead, only to have the Giants come back and win in fifteen innings. His average had improved to .253, and he now had 28 homers and 93 RBIs. His team was 9 games in front, with its final twenty-eight games scheduled in September.

With Mays in the service, Durocher realized the only way the Giants could win the pennant was if the Dodgers got nervous that 1951 was repeating itself and choked. After the Giants sliced a few games off their deficit, Durocher slyly announced: "If we can pull this out, there will be a hundred thousand suicides in Brooklyn." He wanted the Dodgers and their fans to start sweating. From mid-August on, Dick Young, Harold Burr in the partisan *Eagle,* and other writers had been siding with Durocher, and hinting that the Dodgers were "beginning to crack up." Refusing to allow his managerial rival to one-up him, Dressen counterpunched with a ghostwritten article in the *Saturday Evening Post,* in which he vowed, "The Dodgers Won't Blow It Again."

The war between Dressen and Durocher wasn't just waged in the papers but on the field. Hodges would be front and center in the combat as the Dodgers took two games from the Giants, 4–1, as Roe bested Maglie, and 10–2, as Black pitched 8 shutout innings in relief. "Pitching aside, it was Gil Hodges' intensity and sheer power to intimidate that provided the spark," wrote Carl E. Prince in his 1996 book *Brooklyn's Dodgers: The Bums, the Borough and the Best of Baseball.* In Roe's victory, Hodges—looking "pale with tension," according to Kahn—drove a Maglie pitch (a curve, claimed Prince) into the upper deck to tie the score in the second inning. Reese, Shuba, and Cox homered later to seal the victory. Hodges was knocked down as he struck out twice against Maglie in the fourth and sixth innings. He was walked in the eighth inning by Dave Koslo and, in breaking up a double play, slid hard and flipped the Giants' slight second baseman, Davey Williams, who had to exit the game with a sore back and miss some playing time. The next day Hodges trotted to first after reliever Hoyt Wilhelm hit him with a payback pitch. Hodges said, "Bill Rigney came in to play second, and there I was on first again, and another ground ball came down to short. As I ran down the line I could see Rigney's body stretched out toward third [waiting for Dark's throw]. I tried to hook his leg with my spikes and flip him. Instead I gashed him down the thigh. The Giants had to use three second basemen [in two games]."

The Dodgers left the Polo Grounds 5 games in front and stumbled to the National League pennant. They had only 13 September victories, 7 by Erskine and Black. With a record of 96–57, Brooklyn finished 4½ games in front of New York. Although he had a major impact on the pennant race, Hodges managed only 4 homers and 9 RBIs in September. Although his .254 average was the second-lowest by a Dodger regular, ahead of only Furillo's .247, he led the team with 32 homers—behind only the 37 homers hit by Kiner and Hank Sauer in the National League—and 102 RBIs, which was fourth in the National League to MVP Sauer's 121, Thomson's 108, and Ennis' 107. His 107 walks were the second most in the league to Kiner's 110 and would be a career high.

The 1952 team that would face the Yankees in the World Series would be called by Snider and some pundits as the Dodgers' best of the era. It was far from it. In fact, Dressen should be given tremendous credit for winning the pennant with smoke and mirrors. Of his regulars, only Snider and Pafko had better batting averages than in 1951. Other than Robinson again hitting 19 round-trippers, every regular had fewer home runs and RBIs. Dressen wisely gave playing time to "Shotgun" Shuba, who had 9 homers, 40 RBIs, and a .305 average (second to Robinson's .308) in 256 at-bats. Where Dressen really excelled was coaxing a banged-up, shaky pitching staff to a .627 percentage—despite having Erskine lead the starters with only 14 victories—and 3.53 ERA, second-best in the league. Roe went 11–2 (to give him an amazing two-year record of 33–5), but his ailing arm limited him to half as many wins and 99 fewer innings than in 1951. Branca threw only 61 innings all season, and had 9 fewer victories. Labine flopped as a starter (though he went 6–1 as a reliever). Van Cuyk helped for a little while and then was gone.

To plug the holes in his rotation, Dressen daringly handed the ball to the unproven Loes and Wade and was rewarded with 24 wins and almost 340 innings pitched between them. But neither won a game in September, and Roe won only once. Down the stretch Dressen reached into his magician's hat once more and pulled out 2 wins each from rookie reliever Jim Hughes and rookie starter-reliever Johnny "Doc" Rutherford, a Canadian. Rutherford's 7th victory was the pennant clincher on September 23 versus Philadelphia, and was accomplished despite a torn ligament in his shoulder (which would result in his major-league career ending after pitching

1 inning in 1953). Another bright idea born out of desperation was to give a few September starts to Black. With 15 wins (1 as a starter), Black became the team's top winner, a good reason he'd be selected Rookie of the Year.

Black proved to be the perfect choice to face Casey Stengel's 95–59 Yankees in Game 1 of the 1952 World Series at Ebbets Field. He yielded only 6 hits, and his slider unnerved his opponents as much as the vocal fans and the Sym-Phony, which wandered through the stands and onto the dugout playing ragtime and ditties to accompany frustrated Yankee batters back to the dugout. Yankees ace Allie Reynolds gave up only 5 hits, but 2 were homers to Robinson and Snider; and Reese added a longball off Ray Scarborough, as Black became the first black to win a Series game, 4–2.

The Yankees came back to win Game 2 7–1, as Vic Raschi tossed a 3-hitter while Erskine and Loes were ineffective. Roe righted the Dodgers' ship in Game 3 with a 6-hitter, outpitching Ed Lopat 5–3. Hodges' third straight 0-for-3 was hardly noticed.

Black pitched another beauty in Game 4, giving up only 3 hits and 1 run on a homer by former Giant Johnny Mize in 7 innings. But Allie Reynolds was better, throwing a 4-hit shutout, 2–0, and striking out 10. Hodges grounded out, walked, and grounded into a double play. "He was a strong pull hitter," recalls Yogi Berra, "so we wanted to pitch him outside, mixing curves and fastballs. We'd also come in high and tight to keep him honest." He was now 0-for-11, 0-for-21 since September 21, and worried Dodgers fans were wondering when their reliable RBI man would show up.

There was no sighting in Game 5. Hodges went 0-for-3. However, he did walk twice off righty Ewell "the Whip" Blackwell, whose side-arm fastball was hands-down the scariest pitch in baseball for right-handed hitters. After walking to lead off the fifth inning, Hodges scored on Reese's sacrifice fly. Despite giving up a 3-run homer to Mize in a 5-run fifth inning, Erskine got the victory when Snider, who had homered and had a game-tying single, drove in his 4th run with a double off reliever Johnny Sain in the eleventh inning. In the bottom of the inning, Furillo's leaping catch robbed Mize of a game-tying home run.

The most controversial play of the game came in the bottom of the tenth inning, when Sain, who could swing the bat, led off by hitting a grounder to Robinson. Sain argued that he beat the throw to Hodges at first base, but umpire Art Passarella called him out. The next day the Associated Press circulated a photo that clearly showed Sain beating the throw. Moreover, Hodges' foot wasn't on the base.

The Dodgers were up three games to two and were going back to Brooklyn to finish the Series. They were optimistic despite Hodges' inopportune slump. Hodges himself acted no differently at the ballpark or at home. "Gil was a hundred percent 'this is what I'm supposed to do,' and certainly he was unhappy he wasn't able to do what was expected of him," says Joan Hodges. "But when he wasn't happy with a situation, he wouldn't let anyone else share his pain. He never brought it home or showed anything was wrong."

What made Hodges' slump bearable was that the fans he worried he was letting down were completely behind him. Throughout Brooklyn, in churches, bars, and classrooms, his plight was discussed sympathetically. Everyone had a kind word for him. Their reaction would be "my warmest memory in baseball," said Hodges years later. "What I'll never forget is the way the fans rallied around rather than dig a ditch for me." Dodgers fans prayed for him and sent him cards, letters, and telegrams with condolences, best wishes, and batting tips. They also sent presents, good-luck charms, and religious items. "We still have boxes of the rosaries and scapulas that fans sent to the house, praying for him that World Series," says Hodges Jr.

So when Hodges came back to Ebbets Field, instead of being booed, he was given an ovation every time he came to the plate. "I was one of those who cheered when he made all those outs in the World Series," recalls Larry King. "I can say with certainty that there was a standing ovation, because I was there in the center-field bleachers. That could only have happened in Brooklyn."

In Game 6, Dressen went with Loes. Before the Series, Loes famously told reporters that the Yankees would win in six games, but then said he was misquoted and predicted they'd win in seven. Loes could have proven himself wrong by securing a victory. But he hadn't won in more than a month and he was going against Raschi, who'd gone 16–6 after three consecutive 20-win seasons. Through 6 innings, Loes didn't allow a Yankee runner beyond first base. The hot Snider broke the scoreless tie in the bottom of the inning with a leadoff homer that carried over the right-field screen.

But Berra's leadoff homer in the top of the seventh inning tied the score. Gene Woodling then singled to center and advanced to second on a balk when Loes dropped the ball. During the regular season, Dressen might have brought in Black, but he was saving him to start if there was a game the next day, and stuck with Loes. Irv Noren struck out looking, and Billy Martin popped up to third, and, with the pitcher coming up, it appeared Loes would get out of the inning. But then the Series' most peculiar play took place. Raschi bounced a ball back to the box that looked like a sure out until it caromed off Loes' leg. Woodling came around to score on what was ruled a base hit and the Yankees led 2–1. Mickey Mantle's first World Series homer made it 3–1 in the eighth. Snider clubbed his record 4th Series home run in the bottom of the eighth to narrow the Yankees' lead to 3–2, but Reynolds came on to record the final five outs. In the bottom of the ninth, Dressen sent up Rocky Nelson to pinch-hit for Hodges. Hodges sat on the bench without saying a word or moping. Nelson struck out.

Loes was mocked in the press because after the game he told reporters that he'd mishandled Raschi's grounder because he "lost the ball in the sun." "That fit in with Billy's other bizarre statements, but he wasn't lying," claims Erskine. "In the afternoon, in the fall, the sun came through the upper and lower deck for just a few minutes, and hit the pitcher right in the eyes. It was just blinding. So when Raschi hit a high hopper toward the mound, Loes truly never saw it."

Hodges was 0-for-17 going into Game 7 before 33,195 fans at Ebbets Field. Dressen moved him from seventh to sixth in the order, thinking he might break out against the left-handed Lopat. "Every time he stepped to the plate," wrote the *World Telegram*'s Bill Roeder in *Sport* magazine in 1957, "the crowd broke out in applause, hand-clapping, cheering, shouts of encouragement that became louder and warmer the longer the streak of helplessness persisted."

With Black on the mound, to be followed by Roe and Erskine, Hodges hit the ball the hardest he had all Series. In the second he flied out to center. In the fourth inning, with the bases loaded and no outs against Reynolds in relief, he stroked a liner to left that Woodling caught up to near the line, turning what looked to be a bases-clearing double into a mere sacrifice fly.

Hodges' only RBI of the Series tied the game 1–1. The next inning, the Yankees went up 2–1 on a homer by Woodling, but the Dodgers quickly tied it again on an RBI single by Reese. Emerging from the retired Joe DiMaggio's shadow, Mantle homered in the top of the sixth to put the Yankees back on top, 3–2. In the bottom of the sixth, Campanella got aboard on a leadoff single, but Hodges bounced into a double play.

After the Yankees tacked on an insurance run on Mantle's RBI single, the Dodgers loaded the bases with one out in the seventh inning. Wanting a left-hander to face the left-handed-hitting Snider, Stengel brought in little-known reliever Bob Kuzava. On an outside fastball, Snider popped to third. Stengel stuck with Kuzava against the right-handed Robinson. After hitting a foul ball deep into the stands, Robinson hit a mile-high pop behind the mound. Time stood still while Martin raced in and caught the ball on his shoe top to save the day, one of the most memorable plays in World Series lore.

In Hodges' final Series at-bat in the bottom of the eighth inning, he reached on an error by Yankees third baseman Gil McDougald. He would be the last Dodgers base runner, as they lost the game 4–2, and, once again, lost the World Series to the Yankees. It happened in seven games, as Loes predicted. Black took the loss, Reynolds got the win, and Kuzava got the unofficial save with 2⅔ innings of hitless relief. He'd saved 3 games all year.

The Dodgers had experienced another wrenching defeat in the last game of the year. That the loss was to their elite crosstown rival was, of course, a major reason the players, the organization, and the fans were in such despair afterward—particularly after waiting three long years for revenge for the 1949 Series defeat. Unstated was the frustration in losing to an organization that kept winning despite refusing to sign black players.

The next day, Milton Gross of the *New York Post* stopped by the Hodges home. He was curious to see how Hodges was handling such headlines as "Hitless Hodges All Alone as Series Goat" after going 0-for-21, a record for futility that would last until the Cardinals' Dal Maxvill went 0-for-22 in 1968. He found Hodges calmly assembling a tricycle for his son. "I wish I knew what happened," Hodges told him, shaking his head. "I've had a lot of slumps, but I've finished the season strong. I've tried to figure it out, but

I can't. There were so many people pulling for me—the fans, the fellows, the writers. That's one of the things that hurts."

Hodges realized he had been the weak link in Brooklyn's chain during the World Series, but Dodgers fans throughout the city had supported him. For the rest of his baseball career, he wanted to repay them for their kindness.

CHAPTER THIRTEEN

Hodges had been the only Dodger with more than 30 homers and 100 RBIs in 1952. He was the only player in the league to have done this double feat three years in a row. Also, he was the only player in the league to have had more than 100 RBIs the last four seasons. He was the model of consistency, so everyone expected him to have another big year in 1953 despite his troubles the previous fall. It was a new year, there was even a new U.S. president, Dwight D. Eisenhower, and Hodges was cautiously optimistic when he came to Vero Beach.

Hodges understood that his career was in serious jeopardy if he didn't show he could hit the outside curve. Every hurler in the league would exploit his weakness. He again spent extra time working with Billy Herman, who still tried to get him to hit outside breaking balls to right field. During downtime, Hodges played cards with his teammates, worked on puzzles, played golf, and went fishing. Among the anglers on the team were Furillo, Erskine, Walker, and Campanella, and they'd often venture out onto coastal waters as a group. Fishing in the Sunshine State and their past barnstorming adventures cemented the relationship between Hodges and Campanella. The Dodger receiver was a smart, good-humored man who told a lot of funny stories, including about his days in the Negro Leagues, and, Roger Kahn observed, "Gil enjoyed him."

Roy Campanella II says, "My dad held Gil Hodges in high esteem, and that's not just lip service. It's truly how he felt. I think, to a certain extent, given the racial polarities of the time, my dad really respected Gil's openness. I'm sure Gil reminded my dad of his father, John Campanella, who also was a very, very open man. African-Americans develop early in life a sensitivity to prejudice, and my father recognized that Gil, like my grandfather, had that we're-all-equal attitude about people. Gil was just such a warm, friendly, humanistic man. It almost sounds silly to string together those corny words to describe him, because Gil was atypical."

Hodges had a special role on the team that he assumed naturally over the course of time because of the respect all his teammates had for him. Like Reese, he served as a unifier for the diverse personalities on the club, including the black and white players who had issues with one another, and even the team's two black stars, Campanella and Robinson. Consummate professionals, Campanella and Robinson were civil in the clubhouse and had a strong bond on the field, but their relationship was strained. Campanella was still angry at Robinson for how he divvied up the money when they barnstormed together; and Robinson had pulled away from Campanella because he wasn't as vocal as him on political issues. Hodges didn't choose sides, but remained friends with both and was a link between the two. "Gil lockered next to Jackie," recalls Kahn, "and though I didn't observe much back and forth between the two of them, I could tell Gil enjoyed him. Sometimes he just burst out laughing at something Jackie said. It was the same with Campy. Gil was just a solid guy. Conservative, certainly, but without the slightest trace of bigotry."

In what was the biggest story of the spring, Robinson was put on the defensive for being "divisive," but it had nothing to do with Campanella and, he insisted, had nothing to do with race, at least on his end. Dressen announced he was going to move Robinson to third base to make room at second for Jim "Junior" Gilliam, a multitalented African-American prospect who had done well at Montreal. That meant Billy Cox would sit, and Robinson, who knew Cox was unhappy being displaced by a black rookie, worried fans and writers would point out that he couldn't carry Cox's glove at the hot corner. He avoided being accused of making waves and not being a team player by accepting his new position. Denying reports of racial tension on the team, he was conciliatory when he finally addressed the press: "What's good for the Dodgers is good for Robinson," he commented. "If this kid [Gilliam] can hit .275, I think our club will be stronger with him at second base. He can get to balls that I can't reach anymore—maybe two or three years ago, but no more. After all, I've only got a couple years left."

Exhibition games began in Dodgertown on March 21, when the Philadelphia Athletics played the Dodgers in the inaugural game at the 5,000-seat Holman Stadium, which was named for a local official. When Hodges did not hit in the exhibition games, there was major concern that what he was experiencing wasn't transitory. Making matters even worse was that Hodges first missed games because of a finger injury and later sat when he began to feel considerable pain in his ankles and lower legs due to an inflammation in the joints of his feet. Soon the inflammation spread to his wrists.

He was frightened when doctors raised the possibility of arthritis and was told to rest indefinitely. He left the team and flew home, where he underwent tests at Long Island College. It turned out Hodges' problems were brought on by an allergic reaction to penicillin, after he'd been injected recently for an infection in his thumb. When the swelling went down, a relieved Hodges rejoined the team in Washington as it made its way north. Missing ten days near the end of spring training didn't help his situation. He was still clueless about how to overcome his curveball woes.

The Dodgers opened the year by winning 4 of their first 5 games against the Pirates and Giants, losing only to Sal Maglie. It was immediately apparent that Gilliam was the best leadoff hitter the Dodgers had had since the war. The switch-hitter from Tennessee had equal success against left-handers and right-handers. He had an exceptional eye and worked a lot of walks while rarely striking out. He had the speed and daring to take the extra base and was the stolen-base threat the team needed now that Robinson and Reese were slowing down. He was often on base, providing the batters behind him with RBI opportunities. In a 12–7 win against Pittsburgh he scored 4 runs and stole 3 bases. In his rookie year, he'd score 125 times, walk 100 times, and swipe 21 bases. Also in the lineup was Don Thompson, who got his second chance to be the Dodgers' left fielder because Andy Pafko had been traded.

With Newcombe still in the service, Branca soon to be waived, and Wade and Labine assigned to the bullpen, the Dodgers traded for a right-handed starter, the Phillies' Russ Meyer. He'd won 17 games in 1949 but was considered expendable after three losing seasons and giving Phillies managers a lot of headaches with his antics. He was known as "The Mad Monk" because of his temper, and the Dodgers took a chance adding him to a colorful but highly disciplined team. The risk paid off. He'd make thirty-two starts and win 15 games. "He was a nice guy with a good sense of humor, and always willing to do someone a favor," wrote Hodges in *The Game of Baseball*. "But when the game started, he was all business. He was a tough competitor. But when he blew his top, it was like plugging a hose into an electric socket."

"Meyer was great to be around," recalls Dave Anderson, who became the Dodgers' beat writer for the *Brooklyn Eagle* in 1953, after Howard Burr fell and broke his hip. "Roscoe McGowen used to play rummy with him on the train. And whenever they lost a hand, they'd throw the cards up in the air." On those train trips, the dapper Meyer would bring a steamer trunk with four or five snazzy suits.

The Dodgers also brought up Johnny Podres after only two years in the minors. He was ready. The twenty-one-year-old left-hander had a good fastball and curve and would develop the best circle change in baseball. He had a lot of confidence and was unfazed when, in his first two major-league starts, Dressen pitted him against two aces, the Giants' Maglie and the Phillies' Roberts. He lost both decisions, though he pitched well against the Giants, but he'd appear in thirty-one more games as a spot starter and reliever and win 9 of his final 11 decisions.

After five games, Hodges was hitting just .211, above only Thompson's .150. His 4 hits had all been singles, and he had just 1 RBI. It was too early to be certain that his grave troubles from the fall hadn't gone away, but a good indication of this was that he had already struck out 7 times, 5 times looking.

Hodges' feeble plate appearances continued into May. By then it was clear that he was mired in one of the longest slumps in baseball history. He raised his average slightly to .220 by May 4, but he had no extra-base hits and still had only 1 RBI, and he was striking out with frightening frequency. Dressen patiently kept him in the lineup, because the Dodgers were still scoring a lot of runs and his glove was still saving runs. On his one day off, Hodges practiced hitting the outside pitch under the supervision of coach Cookie Lavagetto.

The next day, he crushed a 2-run homer off the Cardinals' Joe Presko in a 7–3 victory. The drive into the upper left-field stands at Ebbets Field was Hodges' 140th career homer, eclipsing Dolph Camilli's Dodgers record. Hodges later had an RBI single to improve his average to .241, so the hope was that his big homer had ended his slump and he was ready to erupt.

Instead he fizzled. By the middle of the month his average was down to .187 and he had gone 19 at-bats without a hit. "I couldn't get any lower if I had been crawling," he said a few months later. "It was really rough."

When Joan Hodges was later asked by a reporter whether her husband was fit to live with during his ordeal, she replied, "Oh, very much so. He did nothing unusual except talk a bit less. I'm the one that's not fit to live with, especially when we play those Giants."

It wasn't so easy being Hodges' road roommate during this time. In *Bums*, Furillo remembered that Hodges slept well, but when awake he'd lie in bed, stare straight ahead, and mutter to himself, "All it takes is a couple of hits. Just a hit or two and I'll be all right."

Hodges was distraught at being in the throes of a slump, but, Erskine remembers, "He never said anything. When he wasn't hitting, he never gave an alibi or said he wasn't seeing the ball well or his timing was off. There was no crybaby stuff. He'd just go out early and work on his own, trying to get his timing back." But the players who knew him best could detect when he was agonizing over his game by gazing into his eyes and by watching his chain-smoking become even more intense. "Gil smoked a lot," wrote Snider in his autobiography. "It wasn't unusual for him to sneak a cigarette on the bench even though it's against major league rules."

"Jackie, Duke, and I didn't smoke," Erskine remembers. "But most of the guys did, and Gil was a very heavy and intense smoker. There was a little space behind the dugout on the lower level. That's where the guys would light up, because you weren't supposed to smoke in the dugout. We'd call out, 'Gil, you're on deck!' And he'd call back, 'Okay'—puff—'I'll'—puff—'be'—puff—'there.'"

After Hodges went hitless in three consecutive losses, Dressen informed him that he would sit out a few games. "I told him," Dressen told reporters, "'I'm not giving you a rest, because you're not tired. I just want to help you get back on the beam.'" In a doubleheader against the Cincinnati Redlegs—

which the first professional team would, after bowing to rampant anticommunist sentiment, call itself until after the 1958 season—Dressen used Robinson at first and Cox at third against a southpaw, and Robinson at third and Wayne Belardi at first against a right-hander. Hodges watched from the dugout. He did not protest. Dressen was the manager and he respected his decision, and there was no need to ask for an explanation or ask when he might return to the lineup. When he'd manage, Hodges would expect the same attitude from his players. "Charlie Dressen was very fair with Gil," said a diplomatic Joan Hodges. "He went about as far as he could with Gil, and it was very nice to tell him about it before he read it in the papers."

New York's sportswriters took it harder. "The lynching of Gil Hodges, a possibility for several days, became a fact today," wrote Roscoe McGowen in the *Times* on May 16.

"This is an anomaly if ever there was one," wrote Arthur Daley in his *Times* column about the biggest sports story in the city. "The best fielding and longest hitting first baseman in the league has been benched."

As during the World Series, shaken Dodger fans sent him kind words, good-luck charms, religious medals, and hitting advice. What more could they do to help their local hero? Father Herbert Redmond of the St. Francis Xavier Roman Catholic Church in Brooklyn had an idea. Addressing his congregation in late May, he delivered some of the most quoted words ever uttered by a priest: "It's too hot for a sermon today. Go home, keep the commandments, and say a prayer for Gil Hodges." And that's what they did. So did thousands of other fans as Father Redmond's genial command was repeated throughout the borough.

"That 'pray for Gil Hodges' business absolutely happened," says Roger Kahn. "People at church, in their homes, on the subway, at work, at school—they *prayed* for Gil."

"You couldn't believe how hard we all prayed for him," recalls Bob Aspromonte, who played ball with Sandy Koufax at Lafayette High before signing with the Dodgers in 1956. "There was this incredible feeling across all of Brooklyn."

"I was Jewish but I knew about the priest asking everyone to pray," Larry King remembers. "Everyone in the city prayed for him. Well, I didn't pray. I was an agnostic, so I rooted for him and crossed my fingers. We all loved Gil Hodges."

"Gil Hodges could do no wrong in Brooklyn," says Tommy Davis, who grew up playing ball in Bedford-Stuyvesant before signing with the Dodgers. "To me he was like a big teddy bear."

The Flatbush faithful were loyal to the player they dubbed "Hodgiss of Dodgiss" because he never pretended to be perfect and never acted like he was better than the other guy, whether it was a pitcher he took deep or a fan who wanted a moment of his time. He was always genuinely modest, even self-deprecating when he had success, so the fans felt empathetic when he experienced failure, especially because they knew how much he wanted to give *them* their money's worth. That Hodges did battle with a fatal flaw that threatened his livelihood—he couldn't hit a damn curveball—made him even more sympathetic and human, an Everyman. He was a wonderful role model for kids because he played the game with fairness and a sense of honor, breaking up fights rather than starting them. He even refused to take Dressen's standing offer of fifty dollars to vigorously argue with an umpire just once about a bad call. "I'm just not built that way," he said with a shrug.

The fans felt he was a Brooklyn man now, a neighbor, because he had married a Brooklyn girl; chose to reside with his family all year 'round in Flatbush; and walked the streets, shopped, went to church, played sports in Prospect Park, and even sold cars every off-season at Century Chrysler on Fourth Avenue, in the borough. "My father was visible in the community," recalls Hodges Jr. "If you wanted to run into him, all you had to do was go to our church on Sunday."

Dodgers fans also appreciated that the star first baseman was so underpaid by the notoriously tightfisted organization, yet he still turned down appearance fees when he agreed to do clinics for kids or speak at benefits at churches and synagogues. Even young fans knew that Hodges didn't make a mint from product endorsements or outside business interests. His friend and business attorney Sid Loberfeld, a pioneer radio play-by-play man and the first announcer at Ebbets Field, told Randy Harris on WFPC Petersburg in 1991, "Whenever I made some deal for him, he worried that we shouldn't take advantage of the other fellow, that maybe we'd get too much money."

"There was no dirty laundry," says Kahn, "nothing negative to write about Hodges." Here was a guy who, while his teammates waited impatiently on the bus, would stand in the hot sun, the sweat soaking through his dress shirt, until he'd accommodated the last autograph seeker. Arthur Daley contended years later that he "was such a noble character in so many respects that I long believed Gil to be one of the finest men I met in sports." Dick Young could be nasty toward players, but he admired Hodges tremendously, and repeatedly reminded his two million readers that he was an ex-Marine of exceptional character.

"Hodges was a sweetheart," recalls Dave Anderson. "I'd sit on an equipment trunk in the clubhouse listening to conversations between all the players, and Gil was one of the guys I enjoyed talking to most. He was very quiet and succinct, but he was friendly. And had a great sense of humor. There were times on planes that I couldn't find my typewriter because Hodges had snatched it, but then it would show up on the conveyor belt with the luggage."

Anderson was one of the first writers to recognize the twenty-nine-year-old's leadership skills: "Every now and then, Hodges walked over to the mound and talked to the pitcher. Whenever he said anything, people listened. They didn't want him mad at them. He had 'the Look.' It was the look your father has when you've done something wrong."

Kahn, too, saw that the quiet man could be a take-charge guy: "We were in Chicago at the end of a series against the Cubs. A charter flight, a DC-6, I imagine. They were doing some work inside the plane, so Gil and I went outside to wait. It was raining, so we stood under a wing. There was a mechanic with a screwdriver and wrench working outside on one of the engines. He was getting frustrated and then, finally, he said, 'The hell with it!' and started to walk away. Hodges took three giant steps and grabbed his shoulder and said, 'The hell with what?' That mechanic got right back to work. As far as I know, Gil never mentioned to his teammates how he looked after them."

"He was a leader," says Erskine. "I was the player rep and Reese was the captain, but he's the one who presided over all the meetings when we divided up Series money. He was like Pee Wee in that he needed only a word or two or that look of his to get his point across. He could give you a jab that would go right to your socks."

By the time Anderson started covering the Dodgers in late May, Hodges' slump was over. Hodges credited the fans for their prayers and "for sticking with me when I couldn't buy a hit"; his father for reminding him that "prayer makes all the difference"; and his own prayers: "Before each game I would ask God not to let anyone get hurt, and to remember those I love, to give us good health, and forgive us our mistakes." But most of all it was Charlie Dressen who saved Gil Hodges' career.

Hodges dutifully listened to suggestions about his hitting, but he could be very stubborn when he believed only his opinion was correct, and couldn't be swayed. So it was frustrating for anyone who tried to tell him that he needed to change his stance, swing, or style. Hodges needed proof that they were correct about what he was doing wrong. Dressen supplied it. Hodges told the AP's Frank Eck: "Charlie had Barney Stein [the *New York Post* and Dodgers photographer] take 16 millimeter movies of my swing from all sections of Ebbets Field while I was in the slump. You could see the catcher giving the pitcher a target at which to throw the ball outside the strike zone. Gosh, it was something terrible the way I was pulling away from the ball. I was turning my head, putting my foot in the bucket, taking pitches that were strikes and going after curves that were four inches to a foot outside the strike zone. I didn't want to believe the things I was doing wrong at the plate but the movies convinced me."

Dressen's remedy for Hodges' tendency to step into the bucket when a right-hander threw him a curve was for him to move his front foot up a little and his back foot farther from the plate. In that way, if he stepped back he'd actually be stepping into the proper line and be able to stride toward the ball. "It's hard to explain, but it helps me get that outside pitch I used to miss," Hodges confirmed.

Back in the lineup, he had an ideal compact swing, and his new setup allowed him to better see the outside pitch and distinguish between balls and strikes. He'd fallen into the trap of always guessing curveball, but now he could go back to looking for the fastball and adjusting to the curve, a tenet of good hitting. Hodges came back to life on May 24 and 25, when he got 5 hits and 3 RBIs as the Dodgers beat the Phillies twice. In one eleven-game stretch he went 19-for-42, a .452 clip, with power.

Furillo started hitting at the same time. Surely it was because his vision had improved after a cataract was removed, but perhaps it made a difference that his roommate was no longer muttering eerily about a need to get a hit. Except for a parade of left fielders, everyone in the lineup had produced since Opening Day, but they were in fourth place until Hodges and Furillo came around in late May. Then the team jelled, winning 10 straight and 19 of 22 games. On June 28, the Dodgers moved into sole possession of first place with a 42–25 record. On June 30, Hodges and Furillo ended the month by combining for 7 RBIs against the Phillies.

Over the first thirty-two games of the season, Hodges had 1 homer and 5 RBIs and batted .181. At the All-Star break on July 12, he was up to 17 homers, 64 RBIs, and a .306 average. Furillo, whose average was .263 on May 23, had climbed to a robust .327. With those two big bats joining an offense that already had Robinson, Snider, Cox, and Campanella batting over .300 (with Reese close behind at .283), the Dodgers led by 1½ games over the Braves. As Red Barber would say on WMGM and WOR-TV, they were "sittin' in the catbird seat."

Reese and Campanella were starters in the All-Star Game at Crosley Field in Cincinnati. Hodges, Robinson, and Snider were reserves in the National League's 5–1 victory. Furillo, on the way to a batting title, and Erskine, headed for his first 20-victory season, weren't picked for the team, although Dressen was the manager. Hodges went 0-for-1 after replacing Ted Kluszewski, who would have an impressive line in '53: 40 homers, 108 RBIs, and a .316 average.

In the first game after the break at Ebbets Field, Hodges crushed the third pitch he saw from Stu Miller for his ninth career grand slam. He added a second homer off Lefty Chambers as the Dodgers defeated the Cardinals, who were managed by Eddie Stanky, 9–2. Hodges still had momentum. His hitting exploits were accompanied by glowing articles with titles like "Gil Hodges Hero of Dodger Win," "Gil Hodges Hottest Batter in Majors," and "Life Bright Again for Dodgers' Gil Hodges." With him leading the way, the Dodgers went 21–8 in July to up their record to 65–34, 8 games ahead of the Braves.

On May 22, Hodges had trailed Campanella in RBIs 46 to 5; on July 22, exactly two months later, he knocked in 3 runs to temporarily pass Campanella, 85 to 84. In the 11–1 victory over Chicago at Ebbets Field, he and Furillo each homered and went a combined 5-for-9, with 4 runs and 5 RBIs. On July 28, in a 13–2 thrashing of the Cubs at Wrigley Field, the roommates homered again and went a combined 7-for-8, with 5 runs and 6 RBIs. Furillo was now hitting .329 and had 61 RBIs, although he was batting seventh. Hitting in the fourth, fifth, and sixth spots in Dressen's order, Hodges was batting .316, with 24 homers and 90 RBIs.

It was telling that Hodges was putting up the big numbers although he still had difficulty hitting the curveball. For decades after Hodges' playing career had ended, many sportswriters who didn't see him play (including Hall of Fame voters) would try to negate his achievements by pointing to his inability to conquer the curveball. But perhaps Hodges' greatest feat was to hit so many homers and drive in so many runs despite a weakness and a fear he had since childhood. "He had courage and strength, but was born with neither," wrote Dick Young. "He made himself do things, forced himself to stand up to the plate, overcame the common tendency to bail out, the ballplayers' expression for striding away from the pitch on a breaking ball. Sometimes his front leg, planted astride the plate, would quiver visibly. 'That's my *curve ball knee*,' he would say smiling."

"It is a measure of courage that Hodges fought his cringe reflex, year after year," wrote Kahn in *The Boys of Summer*. "To taste fear as he did, and to choke it down and make a fine career is a continuing act of bravery."

Hodges continued to pound the ball in August, when the Dodgers went 25–6 and made a shambles of the pennant race. So did Snider, who was thriving facing almost exclusively right-handed pitching but smashed the first of 2 grand slams he had in a three-game span against Reds' lefty Joe Nuxhall. On August 17, with the Dodgers down 2–0 to Pittsburgh in the bottom of the ninth, Snider tied the score with a 2-run homer, and Hodges clouted a 3-run homer in the bottom of the eleventh inning for the victory. The next day, Hodges' sacrifice fly in the thirteenth inning, his third RBI of the game, beat the Giants 4–3. They were baseball's most formidable 1–2 punch.

Clem Labine won both games in relief and also won back-to-back games against the Giants on the twelfth and thirteenth. By this time, Labine was the Dodgers' top reliever, replacing the ineffective Joe Black. He'd go 10–4 with 7 unofficial saves in 30 relief appearances in 1953. "Clem Labine was the big man in the Dodgers' bullpen," wrote Hodges in his book. "What a pitcher he was, too! Labine was strong. Labine was fearless."

The game in which Labine beat the Giants on August 13 was memorable because it confirmed that the New York teams' rivalry was still strong even without the Giants in the race. Durocher took out his frustrations on the Dodgers every chance he got, because those were the only meaningful games his team played. In this game he ordered Ruben Gomez to hit Furillo. Rubbing his wrist, Furillo jogged to first base as Durocher added insults to his injury. Suddenly Furillo veered off the baseline and charged into the dugout, a man possessed, as those Giants who stood between him and his prey parted like the Red Sea. Furillo started choking Durocher. Umpire Babe Pinelli supposedly yelled, "Kill him, Carl, kill him," but before Furillo went that far, he was pulled away by several Giants. One, Monte Irvin, stepped on Furillo's finger during the melee, perhaps intentionally. It was broken, and Furillo, who had locked up the National League batting championship, missed the rest of the regular season.

Durocher would have been overjoyed if he was responsible for an injury that cost his rivals the pennant, but even with Furillo sidelined, the Dodgers went 31–12 in the final six weeks of the season and coasted to the National League title, 13½ games in front of the Braves. They were the first team to win back-to-back National League pennants since the Cardinals did it in 1943 and 1944. For Hodges, Robinson, Snider, Reese, and Furillo, it was the fourth pennant in seven years. For the fourth time they'd be facing the Yankees in the World Series.

They had lost Series to the Yankees in 1947, 1949, and 1952, but the Brooklyn Dodgers were never better than in 1953. Their 105 wins—against only 49 losses—were the most in Brooklyn history. They scored 955 runs, which were 186 runs more than anyone else in the league. They slammed 208 homers, 32 more than second-place New York. They stole 90 bases, 41 more than the Cubs, and had four of the top five base thieves in the league. Their .285 team batting average was 14 points above St. Louis. Additionally, Brooklyn led the league in fielding percentage, and its pitchers accumulated the most strikeouts, despite Newcombe's being in the service and Branca's going to the Tigers on waivers in July.

The Dodgers had eight players who reached double figures in home runs, and four with more than 20. Furillo, who hit 21, drove in 91 runs, but because of the missed time he was deprived of being a fourth Dodger to drive in 100 runs. However, his .344 average was best in the league, and the highest by a right-handed Dodger since Oyster Burns batted .354 in 1894. Snider's .336 average was fourth-best in the league. His 42 homers surpassed Hodges' team record of 40, and was second to the 47 by the Braves' young slugging third baseman Eddie Mathews, who dethroned Ralph Kiner as homer champion after seven years; his 126 RBIs was third-best. Campanella led the league in RBIs with 142 in 144 games, finished third with 41 homers, and batted .312 in his second MVP season.

Jackie Robinson had his final exceptional season, batting .329 with 109 runs and 95 RBIs as the cleanup hitter. Because Cox hit a surprising .291 and played his usual spectacular defense, Robinson never became Dressen's full-time third baseman as planned. He made only forty-four appearances at third; for the first time in his career he played the outfield, appearing in seventy-six games in left. Gilliam, his replacement at second base, would win the Rookie of the Year award after batting .278 and leading the league with 17 triples and finishing tied for second in walks, third in stolen bases, and fourth in runs.

Over the final 122 games, Hodges belted 30 homers, drove in 117 runs, and raised his average 121 points. Despite his horrendous start, he batted .302, with 31 homers (sixth in the league) and 122 RBIs (fifth). He batted .300 for the first time, hit 30 homers for the fourth year in a row, and had his fifth consecutive 100-RBI season.

With Furillo back, the Dodgers' lineup matched up well against the Yankees, who had won 95 games in capturing their fifth consecutive American League flag under Casey Stengel. The big question was whether Carl Erskine (20–6), Russ Meyer (15–5), Billy Loes (14–8), Preacher Roe (11–3, and a three-year record of 44–8), Johnny Podres (9–4), and Clem Labine (11–6) could hold their own against Whitey Ford (18–6), Ed Lopat (16–4), Allie Reynolds (13–7), Vic Raschi (13–6), and Johnny Sain (14–7).

Yankees announcer Mel Allen and Vin Scully were the broadcasters for the 50th Anniversary World Series. Red Barber was asked by Gillette to represent the Dodgers' broadcast team, but he turned down the small fee they offered, so Scully stepped in. Barber was so incensed that O'Malley, who may have anticipated the announcer's response, didn't back him against the sponsor that he resigned, and would join Allen in the Yankee booth in 1954.

Dodgers fans thought this was finally the year their team would win it all, but their confidence disappeared after two crushing losses at Yankee Stadium. The Yankees scored first in five of the six games, including Game 1 when they lit up Erskine for 4 runs in the first inning. Gilliam, Hodges, and pinch-hitter Shuba later homered off Reynolds, and Furillo had a clutch RBI single off reliever Sain as the Dodgers fought back to tie the score 5–5. But the Yankees scored 4 times off Labine and Wade for a 9–5 victory.

In Game 2, Roe, going against Lopat, held a 2–1 lead and had given up only 2 hits when Billy Martin homered to tie the game in the bottom of the seventh. Mantle slugged a 2-run homer in the eighth to win it 4–2.

The Dodgers showed fortitude by winning the next two games in Brooklyn. Erskine, coming back on short rest, threw a 6-hitter to outduel Raschi 3–2. It was a historic outing, because he set a World Series record by fanning 14 Yankees. Campanella was the first guest on Edward R. Murrow's new television interview show, *Person to Person*. At the rehearsal, Murrow joked that the show would get a real kickoff if Campanella hit a game-winning homer that night. He did exactly that in the eighth inning off Raschi.

In Game 4, Loes gave up only 3 runs and struck out 8 in eight innings, and Snider drove in 4 runs with a homer and 2 doubles, as the Dodgers prevailed, 7–3. With the Series even, Dodgers fans got back some of the optimism. So did Yankee haters across the country who'd been waiting five years for any underdog to upset the boys in pinstripes.

Podres got the start in the pivotal fifth game, and was greeted with a leadoff homer by Gene Woodling. The Dodgers tied the game in the bottom of the second on a bad throw by Phil Rizzuto. Having an up-and-down Series, Hodges singled twice but was thrown out at the plate in the bottom of the second and made the biggest error of his career in the top of the third. "Gil Hodges boots easy ground balls as often as a lunar eclipse," wrote

Tommy Holmes in the *Brooklyn Eagle* about Hodges allowing the tying run to score when Joe Collins' two-out grounder glanced off his glove.

The young Podres was shaken and proceeded to graze Hank Bauer with an inside pitch and walk the free-swinging Yogi Berra to load the bases. Dressen brought in Russ Meyer, who promptly gave up a grand slam into the upper deck by Mantle. All 5 runs were unearned. The Yankees increased their lead to 10–2 and held off the Dodgers, 11–7, to go up 3–2. Of Mantle, Hodges raved years later: "There's never been any player like him as a switch-hitter with power. Besides that, when he hit right-handed he was the equal of any right-hander in the game, and when he swung left-handed he was the equal of any left-hander."

In Game 6, Erskine pitched more like he did in Game 1 than Game 3. "For a couple of innings," wrote Holmes, "Erskine was in more trouble than a prisoner of the Soviet secret police." The Yankees scored 2 runs in the first on an RBI double by Berra and an error by Gilliam and went up 3–0 in the second on Woodling's sacrifice fly. Then the Yankees' bats were silenced by Erskine, Bob Milliken, and Labine. The Dodgers scored a run in the sixth inning off Ford, and then tied the game on Furillo's stunning 2-run homer off Reynolds in the top of the ninth. Had that blow reversed the Dodgers' fortunes? That question was quickly answered. In the bottom of the ninth, Labine walked Bauer, Mantle beat out a high bouncer between the mound and third base, and Billy Martin delivered his 12th hit of the Series, a single to center field. Bauer beat Snider's throw to the plate, and the Dodgers had lost a heartbreaker on the last day of its season for the fifth consecutive year. The Yankees' dramatic 4–3 victory gave them a remarkable fifth world championship in a row.

"We were beginning to wonder if we were ever going to beat the Yankees," Snider said. "The Yankees weren't better than us. I'm not saying we were better, but we felt we were just as good."

"You can't call them lucky," said Erskine after the game in the Dodgers' gloomy clubhouse. "They've done it too often for that. They played fine ball and gave us nothing." Erskine was quoted by Holmes in a column he titled, "Yanks on Their Game—Our Guys Weren't." It was a title that was equally appropriate for the 1947, 1949, and 1952 World Series as well.

Even after his amazing season in which so many positive things happened on and off the field, Hodges was distressed and confounded by still another World Series loss to the Yankees. It was probably good that he had no time to replay the Series in his mind and dwell on the reasons the Dodgers weren't champions. A few days after the Series, he left on the Jackie Robinson All-Stars barnstorming tour. Beginning in Baltimore on October 9 and concluding in Houston on November 1, it was intended by Robinson to be a groundbreaking tour in which an integrated team would travel through the South and Southwest.

Four white players were on Robinson's roster: Hodges, Branca, St. Louis Browns' second baseman Bobby Young, and star Indians third baseman Al Rosen, who would hurt his back and leave the tour early. Among the black players were Robinson, Athletics pitcher Bob Trice, Indians first baseman Luke Easter, and Dodgers farmhands Charlie Neal and Maury Wills. "Jackie thought the tour would move the process of desegregation forward," recalls Branca. "He asked Gil and me because we were very close to him. We played all-black local teams and other barnstorming teams. We realized that it was a gambit for integration."

The tour went well until it arrived in Birmingham, Alabama, where there was a city ordinance forbidding mixed athletic events. If Hodges, Branca, and Young played, they would be arrested. Rather than cancel the game, Robinson and his tour's longtime promoter, Ted Worner, agreed to have the white players sit in the stands and watch. Willie Mays, home in Alabama while on leave, filled in. The same thing happened in Memphis, where the All-Stars played the Indianapolis Clowns.

Robinson was vilified and defended in the black and political press across the country for agreeing to sit the white players after bringing them into the two cities that he knew had ordinances against mixed sporting events. The *Chicago Defender* got a lot of attention when it printed an op-ed piece titled "Jackie Disgraces the Race." Its conclusion: "We think Jackie owes an apology to every white member of his squad for the embarrassment he has subjected them to. We feel that Jackie should also apologize to every real American who is fighting against racial discrimination in this country." Even Red Smith in the *New York Herald Tribune* didn't understand Robinson's decision to play the games without his white players: "From here it looks as though he blew a great chance to make a big score for tolerance."

Trail-blazing black journalist Luix V. Overbea of Chicago was one who defended Robinson, writing, "Isn't it amazing that so many swivel chair analysts can expect Jackie Robinson to go into two cities like Birmingham and Memphis and change conditions in one day when thousands of Negroes living there every day can do nothing?" When Birmingham ended its racial sports ban four months later, Robinson could have been given more credit, but over all, contends Rachel Robinson, "It was a negative experience for Jackie because his objectives weren't met. He felt he should have been more vocal about seeing that everyone played or, if they didn't, that no one played."

Hodges' participation in Robinson's tour was his most noble and visible gesture on behalf of equal opportunity for blacks in sports, but as someone who avoided publicity and tooting his own horn, he never really talked about the experience, even of nearly spending time in jail. The Birmingham police were serious about arresting Caucasian players who suited up with Robinson's All-Stars, as was demonstrated when officers charged into the dugout to arrest Hodges' replacement. They left red-faced and rednecked when they discovered Willie Mays wasn't white.

CHAPTER FOURTEEN

By the time Hodges and Robinson completed their tour, Charlie Dressen was out as the Dodgers' manager. Pushed by his wife, he had demanded a three-year contract. Walter O'Malley stated that club policy, his policy, was that managers received only one-year contracts. Dressen quit, spurning O'Malley's offer of a salary increase and ending his eventful three-year run in Brooklyn.

On November 24, O'Malley announced that Montreal manager Walter Alston was Dressen's replacement. The *Daily News* responded with the headline: "ALSTON (WHO HE?) TO MANAGE DODGERS."

Most likely, Buzzie Bavasi recommended Alston to O'Malley, since they'd worked together at Nashua and Montreal, where the forty-two-year-old culminated a fourteen-year minor-league career with two pennants in three seasons. O'Malley was glad to have a manager who would be content with one-year deals in case a better manager came along. Also, it seemed like a shrewd move to replace the popular Dressen with someone who had managed seventeen players on the 1954 team.

More than with Durocher, Shotton, or Dressen, Hodges could relate to this Midwesterner who played baseball and basketball in college, taught physical education, played a mean game of pool, hunted, became a first baseman—he struck out on three pitches in his only major-league at-bat—was as strong as an ox, and did little talking in the clubhouse. He had a colorful nickname, "Smokey," but was as reserved as Hodges and without his humor. He was so straitlaced that he once seriously asked his players what they did at nightclubs. The wildest thing he ever did was, at Bavasi's suggestion, sneak into New York using an alias prior to the press conference announcing his hiring.

"In spring training," recalls Erskine, "the writers came to me and said, 'Hey, tell us about Alston. He won't talk! We can't write yes and no!' I played for him in the minors, and said, 'He won't fabricate a story or tell you what you want to hear; he'll tell you the straight stuff. Just give him time.' The writers had to learn to ask the right questions, and listen."

"Alston had it bad, because the players had loved Dressen because he was feisty and always talking," recalls Dave Anderson. "They thought, 'Who's this guy, a minor-league manager, and what can he tell us that we don't know?'"

When Alston managed, his strategy was so conservative that it seemed to the players that he was just trying to avoid mistakes that would cost him his job. Some players questioned whether he was capable of employing strategy at all. "I learned everything from Dressen," says Don Zimmer. "He knew a lot more about baseball than Alston."

"I remember more than once, Pee Wee, Jackie, and Gil and all of them were talking about Alston," Furillo said in *Bums*, "and the boys were really down on him and Pee Wee made a remark, 'If he keeps fooling around like this, I'll take his damn job.' I wish Pee Wee would have. 'Cause Alston was not a manager."

Furillo was probably wrong to include Reese and Hodges among those who were impatient with Alston. In 1972, Alston recalled, "It was guys like Hodges, Pee Wee Reese, and Roy Campanella who made it easy for me by helping a rookie manager. Gil was that type of man. He never gave anyone any trouble; he was a great man on the field and off it."

Robinson was openly critical of his new manager. He despised O'Malley, and Alston was O'Malley's man, and Robinson challenged him for control of the clubhouse. "Whatever happened between Jack and Alston, they didn't like each other very much, right at the beginning," recalls Rachel Robinson. "Jack missed Dressen, so he might not have been receptive to Alston coming in. Then Alston was the opposite personality-wise of Dressen, quiet, withdrawn, and less expressive. And probably not a good manager. Jack was a very good judge of that. So they just didn't work together."

Their relationship became more strained when Alston cut down on Robinson's playing time and Cox's, too, in order to play Don Hoak, his third baseman at Montreal. After seven years in the minors, Hoak would make more appearances at third (75) than either Cox (58) or Robinson (50) in 1954. Robinson played mostly in the outfield, sharing left-field duties with the left-handed Sandy Amoros, who had been a fine hitter in the Negro Leagues, Cuban winter ball, and the International League.

Hailing from Roulette, Pennsylvania, Hoak was a mercurial ex-Marine who was called Tiger. He had boxed professionally, losing all his fights, and was often foolishly prodding Hodges with annoying jabs on his arms and shoulders. Hodges always laughed and walked away, but one day he picked him up and deposited him in a garbage bin. Hoak brought out the wild in Hodges. They would, according to Snider's autobiography, "race their cars on the way home from Ebbets Field, two Marines trying to beat each other, Hoak in his Packard and Gil in his big white and black Chrysler. One day some of us followed behind them to see who won. Three or four blocks from the ballpark we saw Gil run Hoak up over the curb and into Prospect Park. Hoak jumped out of his car and raised his clenched fist, but Gil just tooted his horn and kept on going, one more victory for the quiet man."

In numerous accounts, the Dodgers got off to a slow start and never were in contention for a pennant in 1954, so Alston was always expecting a pink slip. That wasn't the case. On June 13, having won 14 of 17 games, they were tied for first place with the surprising Giants with identical 34–21 records. For much of the summer there was a race between the bitter rivals. Joan Hodges reissued her decree that no one in the Hodges household could wear orange and black, the Giants' colors. ("Of course, that made things difficult around Halloween," recalls Hodges Jr.)

Hodges had picked up where he left off in 1953 and was a third of the way through his first slump-free season. "I'm through trying to hit to right," he stated. "Some fellows can do it and others can't. I'm a longball hitter and that's what I'm going to do." He had 50 RBIs in his team's first fifty-five games, with a .312 average and 14 homers. His eighth homer of the year on May 16, which beat the Reds' Herm Wehmeier, 4–2, was his 10th career grand slam, placing him only 2 behind Rogers Hornsby and Ralph Kiner in

National League annals. Hodges batted fifth or, when Robinson didn't play, in the cleanup spot.

The Giants were having a resurgent season with Mays back (as was Newcombe on the Dodgers) and on his way to being the National League's MVP. Also Don Mueller was challenging Mays and Snider for the batting title. And Johnny Antonelli, a young lefty, would win 21 games after they pried him away from the Braves. By the All-Star break on July 11, the Giants had built their lead over the Dodgers to 5½ games. In the first game of the doubleheader that day, won by the Dodgers 8–7, Hodges launched two balls out of the park to up his totals to 25 homers and 75 RBIs, which were highs on the team above Snider's 20 homers and 70 RBIs. A debilitating hand injury kept Campanella from putting up big numbers as well, and at the break he was struggling with a .215 average and only 32 runs batted in.

Nevertheless, Campanella was on the National League's All-Star Game roster, along with Hodges, Robinson, Reese, Snider, and Erskine. More than 69,000 fans were in Cleveland to watch Casey Stengel's American League squad score 3 runs in the bottom of the eighth to pull out an 11–9 victory over Walter Alston's team. Hodges, replacing Ted Kluszewski, popped out in the ninth inning in his only at-bat.

The Dodgers started slowly after the break and fell to 7 games back on July 21, but they were only 4 games out on August 8, when they rallied to score 12 unearned runs against the Reds with two outs in the eighth inning to earn a 20–7 victory. The historic inning ended when Hodges' bid for another grand slam was caught high off the center-field wall.

When the Giants visited Ebbets Field August 13–15, the Dodgers were 3½ out and needed to sweep. On Friday, Furillo's 2-run homer in the seventh inning gave the Dodgers a 3–2 win. On Saturday, the Dodgers trailed 5–0, but Furillo hit a grand slam, and Campanella drove in Hodges twice with singles for a 6–5 victory. On Sunday, Snider and Hodges hit back-to-back homers off Al Corwin as the Dodgers won easily 9–4 to narrow the gap to half a game. Hodges became the first Brooklyn Dodger in history to hit 200 homers. He also reached 30 homers for the fifth consecutive year. On August 26, in a 13–12 victory in St. Louis, he belted 2 homers and became the only active major leaguer with six consecutive 100-RBI seasons.

The Dodgers were still only 1½ games out on August 29. However, the anticipated down-to-the-wire September battle between the two teams never materialized, because the Dodgers were a disappointing 13–13 down the stretch. They wound up with 92 victories, 5 fewer than the champion Giants, who would sweep the heavily favored 111–43 Cleveland Indians in the World Series. It was the Dodgers' worst finish since 1948. However, they won the last game they played for the first time since 1945.

That victory on September 26 was achieved by Karl Spooner, who looked like the second coming of Bob Feller. The lefty phenom from Oriskany Falls, New York, made his debut on the twenty-second and threw a 3-hit shutout against the Giants, striking out 15. His follow-up was almost as dominant, a 4-hit shutout against the Pirates, fanning 12—for a record 27 strikeouts in his first two outings. The Dodgers won 1–0 on a seventh-inning homer by Hodges in his final at-bat of the year.

In his finest statistical season, Hodges had a .304 average with 106 runs, 130 RBIs, and 42 homers, which was second in the league to Kluszewski's 49. He and Snider tied for second in RBIs behind Kluszewski's 141, and became the first teammates in the National League to have 130 RBIs each since 1932. Hodges' 19 sacrifice flies set a major-league record that remains unbroken. Snider led the league in total bases and runs (tying Musial) and finished second in hits and doubles; his .341 average trailed only Mays' .345 and Mueller's .342 in a batting race that went down to the final day. Fans weren't just debating who the city's best catcher was—Campanella or Berra?—and who the best shortstop was—Reese or Rizzuto?—but were now having heated arguments over who was the best center fielder—Snider, Mays, or Mantle?

Meanwhile there was discussion about who was the National League's best first baseman—Hodges or Kluszewski? Kluszewski's hitting stats were slightly better than Hodges' for three or four years, but Hodges also put up exceptional numbers and did it for longer and during pennant races. Unquestionably, Hodges was the better fielder. They admired each other's talents and were friends rather than rivals. "One time when the Dodgers were playing a series with the Reds, Gil and I went to the movies," recalls Joan Hodges. "We sat in the balcony and on our way out we passed a big man sitting on the aisle in the last row. Gil recognized him and without saying a word pinched him real hard on his cheek. We walked into our hotel lobby and Ted Kluszewski was standing there. Gil said to him, 'What are you doing *here*? I just saw you in the theater and pinched your face!' Ted said, 'What theater? I wasn't in a theater.' Gil had pinched some stranger."

In November, O'Malley signed another left-handed pitcher who threw the ball 100 mph. O'Malley didn't think Sandy Koufax, a Brooklyn native whose parents thought he played only basketball at the University of Cincinnati, had the future of Spooner, because he was extremely wild. But he could afford to give him a $14,000 bonus after shipping aging Preacher Roe (3–4, 5.00 ERA) and Billy Cox (.235 in 226 at-bats) to the Baltimore Orioles. (Roe would retire; Cox would play one more year.) O'Malley didn't expect a lot of wins from Koufax, but as he stated at his press conference, he hoped the youngster's presence would attract more Jewish fans to Dodgers games.

At such times it appeared that O'Malley had no intention of taking his team out of Brooklyn and sincerely planned to build a new stadium there. He had his sights on the site occupied by the Long Island Rail Road Terminal and the Fort Greene Meat Market, at the intersection of Flatbush Avenue and Atlantic Avenue. The railroad was essential, because O'Malley wanted the Dodgers fans who were migrating to the suburbs in droves or already lived there to have easy access to the stadium. But he likely was weighing his options, because urban planner Robert Moses—an unelected buildings commissioner who was given carte blanche by the city's mayors—wasn't eager to let him purchase prime real estate in Brooklyn. "Moses didn't want to build a new stadium in Brooklyn," states Robert A. Caro, whose biographies include the best-selling *The Power Broker* about Moses, "because it was O'Malley's idea. O'Malley had his own strong personality, and Moses couldn't tolerate that."

On August 24, 1953, at a meeting of major-league owners, O'Malley had announced that he'd received a letter from a wealthy Los Angeles politician who promised the Dodgers a new stadium if they moved west. "Every so often the *Eagle* would mention the Dodgers' interest in Los Angeles," recalls Dave Anderson. "We believed O'Malley was in contact with the mayor there. We just knew that sooner or later O'Malley was going to move the Brooklyn Dodgers to L.A."

PART III

A Two-Time World Champion

CHAPTER FIFTEEN

At spring training in 1955 there were rumors that Walter Alston's job was in jeopardy. The source was probably the front office, as it would be every year for the twenty-three years Alston managed the Dodgers, including after seven pennant-winning and four world championship seasons. It was O'Malley's way of reminding the future Hall of Famer that he was expected to produce a winner to be offered a new one-year contract.

The scuttlebutt about Alston's imminent dismissal quickly subsided as Brooklyn got off to perhaps the greatest start in major-league history. It was unexpected, because after the '54 season many pundits believed the Dodgers were in decline, particularly since several core players were aging: Robinson and Reese were thirty-six, Campanella and Furillo were thirty-three, and even Hodges was thirty-one.

In the opener in Pittsburgh, Hodges, who walked in his first two at-bats, drove in the season's first run by lining a first-pitch single to center in the bottom of the sixth inning. Erskine threw a 7-hitter, and the Dodgers earned a 6–1 victory. The next day at the Polo Grounds, they suffered through the indignity of standing along the third-base line and watching the gloating Giants raise the 1954 National League and World Championship flags. They got a smidge of revenge by winning the game 10–8, as Don Newcombe and Campanella homered off Sal Maglie, and Furillo took knuckleballer Hoyt Wilhelm deep. Of note was that five of their nine starters were black. The Dodgers won the next game as well, 6–3, as Billy Loes tossed a 6-hitter, Furillo smashed his third and fourth homers, and Snider hit his first of the year.

In Pittsburgh, Russ Meyer 2-hit the Pirates, 6–0, and Podres became the fifth consecutive Dodger starter to notch a victory, as Brooklyn trounced the Pirates 10–3. In the nightcap of the twin bill, Clem Labine got a spot start and held the Bucs to 5 hits in 8+ innings. The only player who gave him trouble was rookie outfielder Roberto Clemente, who doubled and singled. The Dodgers had signed Clemente but tried to hide him in their system rather than give him a chance to win the left-field job. The alert Branch Rickey claimed the supremely talented Puerto Rican on waivers.

The Dodgers next beat the Phillies 5–2 and 7–6 at Connie Mack Stadium, as Erskine and Newcombe recorded victories, getting unofficial saves from rookie right-hander Ed Roebuck. Featuring a heavy sinker, Roebuck had pitched well for Alston at Montreal and would be a longtime member of the Dodgers and a good friend of Hodges. "I met Gil in Vero Beach in 1949," recalls Roebuck. "They had a movie theater on the base and he was there with Joan, and I recognized him and said hello. Six years later we were playing together on the Dodgers. He was a strong, gentle, moral, and compassionate man who commanded respect at all times. He was the role model for everybody."

The Dodgers and Phillies next played two games at Ebbets Field, with the same results. The Phillies led the first game 2–0 until the Dodgers scored 3 runs in the bottom of the seventh. Hodges' single up the middle scored the tying and winning runs. The next game was a runaway, with the Dodgers winning 14–4. Furillo and Don Zimmer had 4 hits each; Hodges had 3 hits and scored 3 times; and Zimmer, Sandy Amoros, Robinson, and Snider homered. The almost forgotten Joe Black recorded his final victory for the Dodgers. With Labine, Hughes, and Roebuck doing well out of the pen, the Dodgers' pitching sensation of 1952 would be shipped to the Reds on June 9.

Karl Spooner, projected as the Dodgers' ace of the future, hurt his shoulder in spring training and lost some speed on his fastball. It was upsetting, but the Dodgers were 10–0 out of the gate, and nobody was worrying about the team's pitching. *Sports Illustrated* wondered why the Dodgers' hurlers were doing so well and did a story on how Alston was turning them into students of their craft. He was having them, rather than pitching coach Joe Becker, chart every pitch thrown by the Dodger pitcher each day and the result. Alston wasn't known for being an innovator, but this detailed pitch-charting was ahead of its time.

The Giants came to Brooklyn and ended the winning streak by rallying from a 3–0 deficit with 5 runs in the eighth inning. The Dodgers came back the next day to win 3–1, as Erskine outdueled Maglie. They broke a 1–1 tie in the eighth when Hodges doubled, Amoros tripled, and Furillo singled. In the bottom of the fourth inning, there was another demonstration of how much the crosstown rivals despised one another. After Maglie knocked him down, Robinson bunted, hoping Maglie would be covering first base for some retribution. But Maglie stayed out of the play and Robinson instead plowed into second baseman Davey Williams covering first. The dugouts emptied and there was plenty of shoving and shouting before order was restored. Unfortunately, the well-liked Williams hurt his back and would play only eighty-two games in his sixth big-league season and retire at the age of twenty-seven.

The Giants won the rubber game 11–10 when they scored 6 runs in the top of the tenth and the Dodgers managed only 5 runs in the bottom of the inning. The Dodgers then won 11 straight games, during which Newcombe tossed a 1-hitter to improve his record to 4–0, and Erskine tossed a twelve-inning, 6-hit 2–0 shutout as his record moved to 5–0. The Dodgers were a remarkable 22–2, a .917 percentage, and were 9½ games ahead of the second-place Giants. It was only May 10, but some writers were insisting that the pennant race had been decided.

Although he had several clutch hits, Hodges got off to a slow start. He didn't hit a homer until the Dodgers' sixteenth game, a solo blast against the Cubs' Sam Jones. Alston dropped him to sixth in the batting order. Alston moved Campanella up to fourth rather than Robinson, who had manned that spot for years. Robinson was hitting around .250 and wasn't pleased with how Alston was using him.

In spring training Robinson had grown increasingly agitated with how much time he spent on the bench while Alston evaluated other players. He asked Dick Young whether he had heard anything about how much playing time he would get that season. "Word got out that I had asked Dick the question, and Walter hit the ceiling," Robinson wrote in *I Never Had It Made*. "Alston and I got into a shouting match that seemed destined to end in a physical fight. Gil Hodges kept tapping me on the arm, advising me, 'Jack, don't say anything else. Cool down, Jack.' I listened to Gil because I had a tremendous amount of respect for him."

Everyone, including Robinson, realized that he was past his peak and his career was winding down. However, he wasn't pleased giving up so much playing time to Don Hoak, Amoros, and his roommate, Junior Gilliam, who shifted to left field when Zimmer played second base and Hoak played third. Even Hodges made twenty-four appearances in left field, the first time in his career he didn't play in the infield. Unable to find his rhythm, Robinson would bat .256 with only 36 RBIs.

The Dodgers' lead dwindled to 5½ games over the Cubs at the end of May—the Giants were still 9 games out—and it appeared that there would be a pennant race after all. But Brooklyn won 12 of their next 14 games, and on June 14 they had increased their lead to 11½ games over Chicago and 14 games over New York. The fans of Brooklyn were excited, making sure not to miss any games on television or radio, or to tune in *Warm-Up Time* on WMGM, and listen to Marty Glickman, Ward Wilson, Bert Lee Jr., and Gussie Moran talk about their team.

On June 24, against the Braves in Milwaukee, nineteen-year-old Sandy Koufax made his major-league debut, doing early mop-up work for Erskine in the fifth and sixth innings of an 8–2 loss. His first inning in the majors was an adventure, as he loaded the bases with no outs. He struck out Bobby Thomson swinging. Up next was powerful Joe Adcock, who in a game against the Dodgers at Ebbets Field in 1953 had a record-tying 4 homers and a double for 18 total bases, breaking Hodges' record of 17 that he set in his 4-homer game in 1950. Koufax induced him to bounce into a double play.

In his rookie season, the bonus baby spent most of this time waiting for Alston to remember he was on the team, but he felt special being teammates with Hodges. In his eponymous 1966 autobiography, Koufax wrote whimsically about the daily interplay he observed between Hodges and Reese in the Dodgers' locker room: "Reese and Hodges will always be needling each other in a dry, deadpan sort of way. From Hodges will come innocent throwaway remarks about aging ballplayers, since Reese has been losing half a step for half a dozen years. Reese will offer asides about Hodges' saintly nature and superhuman strength, the picture of him (and a true one) that is always presented by the press."

The Dodgers still led by 11½ games at the All-Star break on July 10, only it was now the improving Braves who were in second place. The Dodgers' record stood at 58–26, a .690 percentage. Hodges had recovered from his slow start and was batting .281, with 14 homers and 59 RBIs. Snider was having another banner season, hitting .319. Again they were on the National League's All-Star roster, along with Campanella and Newcombe, whose record was a sterling 14–1. Snider started on Leo Durocher's team ahead of Willie Mays, while Hodges and Stan Musial—who was chosen by *Life* magazine as the Player of the Decade (1946–1955)—backed up Kluszewski at first base. The game was played in Milwaukee, and the National League came back from a 5–0 deficit and won in the twelfth inning 6–5 on Musial's homer off Frank Sullivan. Hodges singled as a pinch hitter against Early Wynn in the sixth inning.

After the break, the Dodgers won 7 of 10 games to build their lead to 14½ games on July 22. On his thirty-seventh birthday, 33,033 fans charged through the Ebbets Field turnstiles to celebrate "Pee Wee Reese Night" and sing "Happy Birthday" to the beloved Dodgers captain. Rising to the occasion, Reese doubled twice in the 8–4 victory over second-place Milwaukee. Hodges and Furillo homered to offset 4 solo homers yielded by the winning pitcher, rookie Roger Craig, 1 each to Aaron and Adcock, and 2 to Del Crandall.

"Gil, Pee Wee, and Jackie were real helpful after every game I pitched," recalls Craig. "They spent time teaching me what I needed to know. Gil was a complete gentleman, but he could have fun. He didn't drink much, but one night in Philadelphia he and Pee Wee went out. I was on the train waiting to leave the station when here comes Gil rushing down the platform with Pee Wee on his shoulders. Pee Wee wasn't a little guy, but Gil was strong and wasn't even sweating."

On August 3, this time in Milwaukee, Hodges had his biggest day of the year as he stroked his 19th and 20th homers in a 9–3 victory. The first, off Ray Crone, was the 11th grand slam of his career, putting him only 1

behind Rogers Hornsby and Ralph Kiner in National League history. The
second, off Dave Jolly, was a 2-run blast that gave him 6 RBIs for the game
and 80 for the year.

At this point, Snider was outpacing Hodges with 36 homers and 106
RBIs, but the Brooklyn fans weren't nearly as supportive of him. Unlike
Hodges, who went through even the most awful slumps with his head up
and mouth shut, Snider usually made things worse, as he did one night in
August. After Snider was booed for going 1-for-9 in a doubleheader, he told
the press that Dodgers fans didn't deserve a pennant. Roger Kahn, who was
writing for national magazines after leaving the *Herald Tribune*, recalls,
"Snider was saying the fans in Brooklyn were the worst fans in baseball. I
said, 'He's just talking, fellows.' But Snider said, 'I'm not just talking and I
want you to write it.'" They wrote it, and the booing got worse.

The fan who gave Snider the most trouble was Hilda Chester, who, with
her cowbells and gravelly voice, contributed to the carnival atmosphere at
Ebbets Field for years. "Duke and I usually drove in together and parked in
back of Ebbets Field at a filling station," recalls Carl Erskine. "One time
Duke had a bad game and she picked us up as we were going to the car. She's
yelling at him and insulting him and the streetlight is coming down and
accentuating all this fuzz on her face. Duke finally had enough and said,
'Hilda, why don't you go home and shave?'"

The Dodgers got two brilliant pitching efforts from both Koufax (a
2-hitter with 14 strikeouts followed by a shutout) and Spooner (a 6-hitter
with 9 strikeouts followed by a shutout) as they maintained a double-digit
lead. When they clinched the pennant with a 10-2 victory over Milwaukee
on September 8, they had a 17-game lead. They coasted to the end of the
season, allowing their lead to shrink to 13½ games. Their 98–55 record was
tops in the majors.

The pitching star for the Dodgers was Newcombe, who returned to his
1951 form and went 20–5 with 143 strikeouts and a 3.20 ERA. Labine's 13
victories—10 coming in relief—was second most on the club, ahead of Erskine's 11 wins and Loes' 10 wins. Newcombe also batted .359 and tied a
record for pitchers with 7 home runs in a season. The Dodgers offense was
led by Snider, who batted .309 with 42 homers—behind Mays' 51, Kluszewski's 47, and Ernie Banks' 44—and a league-leading 126 runs and 136

RBIs. Campanella batted a team-high .318 with 32 homers and 107 RBIs. Furillo hit .314 with 26 homers and 95 RBIs. Hodges hit .289 and overcame a slow start to hit 27 homers and drive in 102 runs. His string of five consecutive 30-homer seasons came to an end, but he managed his seventh straight year with more than 20 homers. Also he drove in more than 100 runs for the seventh straight season, only one year behind Mel Ott's National League record, set in 1936. Campanella was selected the National League MVP for the third time, while Snider was named the *Sporting News'* Player of the Year.

Having won three pennants in four years, the Dodgers were the premier team in the National League. But that wasn't a good enough legacy for one of the most talented groups of players ever assembled. They needed to win a world title before time ran out on them.

It was inevitable that there would be yet another World Series showdown between the two best teams in post-WWII baseball. But the Yankees almost didn't make it. They trailed the defending American League– champion Indians as late as September 14, but won 10 of their last 12 games to take the flag by 3 games, with a 96–58 record.

The rivalry between the Dodgers and Yankees was different from the one between the Dodgers and Giants. The hatred was strictly between the hungry Dodgers fans and the Yankees fans who had an infuriating sense of entitlement in regard to world championships. "There was no hatred between the Yankees and the Dodgers," said Bob Turley, who won 17 games for the Yankees in 1955, in *We Played the Game*. "We all liked Campanella, Hodges, Snider. There was a mutual respect between the teams."

"When we played the Giants, it was profound hatred," states Erskine. "Against the Yankees, games were played in a zone above intense competition. This was classic baseball."

The Dodgers saw the Yankees as an infernal hurdle they needed to get over to validate their own greatness and, on a deeply personal level, give every player pride and comfort. To the Yankees, the boys from Brooklyn were a colossal nuisance that wouldn't stay in its place, which was second place. The Yankees had won 6 titles in 8 years, but felt two years without a ring would be too long a wait and were eager to capture another flag. Casey Stengel didn't worry about his team being overconfident, but feared that the law of averages would catch up to them as the evenly matched teams dueled for the fourth time since he became the Yankees' skipper.

In Game 1 of the first World Series televised in color, Newcombe went against 18-game winner Whitey Ford, the Yankees' ace now that Allie Reynolds, Vic Raschi, and Ed Lopat were gone. Before 63,869 fans at Yankee Stadium, the Yankees' left-hander wasn't in top form, but he got the win because Newcombe's postseason woes continued. The weary-armed righty gave up 6 runs in 5⅔ innings. Mickey Mantle was out nursing a sore leg, but Yankee left fielder Elston Howard, who that year became the team's first black player, hit a 2-run homer in his first Series at-bat, and left-handed first-baseman Joe Collins belted 2 homers in the Yankees' 6–5 victory. In the Series' most famous play, Robinson stole home despite a 2-run deficit with two outs in the eighth inning. "He was out!" Berra still proclaims.

An even larger crowd of 64,707 fans sauntered into Yankee Stadium the next day and saw Tommy Byrne (16–5) become the first left-hander to pitch a complete game victory against the Dodgers all year. The thirty-five-year-old also drove in 2 runs in a 4-run fourth inning that knocked out Loes in a 4–2 victory.

Down 2–0, the Dodgers' only chance was to sweep the next three games in Brooklyn, but the Yankees had been swept in a 3-game road series only by Detroit in mid-July, and hadn't lost 3 games in a row since then.

Alston's choice to get the Dodgers off life support the next day at Ebbets Field was Johnny Podres. He'd gone only 9–10 during the season and almost didn't make the postseason roster because in early September a member of the field crew rolled the batting cage into him, damaging some ribs. "Sometimes when I think of how close I came to not playing in the '55 Series," he recalled in Donald Honig's 1970 book *The October Heroes*, "I break out in a cold sweat." September 30 was Podres' twenty-third birthday, and Campanella's present was a 2-run homer in the first inning off Turley, who didn't make it out of the second inning. There would be three more 2-run innings in the 8–3 victory. Podres went the distance, giving up 7 hits and 2 earned runs. He was unfazed when Mantle made his Series debut with a homer to center field in the second inning. Hodges' 0-for-5 day meant he was 1-for-12 for the Series thus far, but opportunities to produce lay ahead.

Feeling slightly more optimistic, 36,242 fans crowded into Ebbets Field for Game 4. The usually reliable Erskine left in the fourth inning with his team down 3–1, and opposing pitcher Don Larsen looked strong. But in the bottom of the fourth, the Dodgers asserted their power. Campanella led off with a solo shot into the lower seats in left. Then after Furillo's infield hit, Hodges put Brooklyn ahead 4–3 with a blast over the scoreboard. A third homer by Snider in the fifth and an RBI single by Hodges in the seventh provided the final runs in the 8–5 victory, as Don Bessent (8-1 in his rookie year) and Clem Labine held the Yankees in check. The Series was now tied, 2–2.

With Newcombe done, Alston went with another youngster, Roger Craig, in Game 5. "I was in the bullpen before the game getting my throwing in, and Walter asked how I was feeling," recalls Craig. "I said, 'I haven't pitched yet, so I'm strong as a bull.' He said, 'Well, you're pitching *now*.' I pitched the best I could and had faith in those great veterans around me, like Gil, Pee Wee, and my catcher."

Craig gave up only 2 runs in 6+ innings and outpitched Bob Grim. He was backed by 2 homers by Snider—it was the second time he hit 4 homers in a World Series—and one by Amoros as the Dodgers prevailed 5–3. They had swept the Yankees in Brooklyn to take a 3–2 lead in the Series. One more victory would give them an elusive world title.

There was no need to travel during the Subway Series, so Game 6 was played the next day. Ford was Stengel's choice in what was, amazingly, a must-win for the Yankees. Alston rolled the dice with still another youngster, Spooner, who had gone 8–6 during the season. Pitching in relief in Game 2, he had given up only 1 hit in 3 strong innings, fanning 5. If he found his old magic, the Yankees would be lucky to put their bats on the ball. But he lasted just a third of an inning in what would be his last major-league appearance. The big blow in the Yankees' 5-run inning was a 3-run opposite-field homer by right-handed first baseman Bill Skowron. Ford threw a 4-hitter and came away with a 5–1 victory.

It was fitting that the Dodgers and Yankees would play a seven-game World Series, and the outcome would go down to the final inning. The classic Game 7 was played before 62,465 fans at Yankee Stadium. Meanwhile, throughout Brooklyn, in homes, apartments, bars, and classrooms, radios and televisions were tuned to the game that would determine the team's legacy.

Stengel's pitcher in Game 7 was Byrne. Once more, Alston went with Podres. He was young and brash, two pluses. On the team bus that traveled from Brooklyn to the Bronx, he pleaded, "Get me one today; just get me one run." Everyone heard him.

Joan arrived at Yankee Stadium with Charlie and Irene Hodges. They took their seats by Fern Furillo, Dottie Reese, and Bev Snider. Joan held a rosary in her hands the entire game.

Both teams went down in order in the first inning. It was obvious that Podres had his good stuff when Gil McDougald struck out with the bat on his shoulder for the final out. McDougald, an off-season hunting buddy of Hodges', usually batted second but was moved into the third spot in the injured Mantle's absence. Missing in the lineup for the Dodgers was Jackie Robinson, as Alston chose to go with Hoak at third, Zimmer at second, and Gilliam in left. It was the only World Series game he ever missed, and, ironically, it was the most meaningful game of his career next to his debut on April 15, 1947.

In the second inning, Hodges walked to become the game's first baserunner, but the Dodgers didn't score. In the bottom of the inning, the Yankees got their first baserunner, when Skowron smacked a ground-rule double, but he was stranded at second.

The Yankees mounted the game's first real threat in the bottom of the third, when with two outs Phil Rizzuto walked and Billy Martin singled him to second. Then in a key play, McDougald sent a high bouncer toward Hoak. If it was an infield hit, the bases would have been loaded for baseball's most dangerous clutch hitter, Yogi Berra, who would win his third American League MVP award after the Series. But the ball struck Rizzuto's foot as he slid into third for an automatic out.

"I thought Rizzuto being called out like that to end that inning was a good omen," says Erskine. "Strange plays like that usually happened to us, and it contributed to our losses to the Yankees. For once, it happened to them."

The offense got Podres his run in the top of the fourth inning when Campanella doubled into the left-field corner, moved to third on Furillo's ground out, and scored on Hodges' solid two-out single to left. In the top of the sixth inning, Hodges also provided him with an insurance run. With

Reese on third and Snider on second with one out, Stengel elected to have Byrne walk Furillo to load the bases and then brought in the right-handed Bob Grim to face Hodges. Stengel was hoping for a strikeout or double-play grounder, but his maneuver backfired when Hodges—the single-season sacrifice-fly record holder—went with the outside pitch and drove it to deep right-center. Bob Cerv made a nice running catch, but Reese jogged home to make the score 2–0. Both runs had been driven in by Hodges, and an admiring Stengel would call him "the best first baseman since Lou Gehrig" after the game.

Alston chose to have Shuba pinch-hit for Zimmer in the top of the sixth inning, and a defensive shift was required. To replace Zimmer at second, Alston brought in the right-handed Gilliam from left field. He sent Amoros out to left, and that he wore his glove on his right hand would be a major factor in what was about to happen.

In the bottom of the sixth, the Yankees mounted their biggest threat. Martin drew a leadoff walk from Podres. McDougald followed with a bunt single. With the two runners on and nobody out, the left-handed-hitting Yogi Berra, a notorious pull-hitter, hit a slicing and sinking line drive down the left-field line toward the corner. The runners took off, thinking they'd both score on a double, but Amoros had taken off with the pitch, too. As he sped into the left-field corner near the 301-foot marker he stuck out his right hand and the ball dropped into his glove. Then Amoros whirled around and fired to Reese, who made the accurate relay throw to Hodges on first, doubling up McDougald. (Hodges would receive praise for having a solid offensive Series, batting .292 with 5 RBIs, including 2 in the seventh game, but he also set two defensive records for first basemen—participating in 11 double plays and starting 3 of them.) Martin was stranded on second when Bauer grounded to Reese.

Podres flirted with trouble the next two innings, but going into the bottom of the ninth, he still clung to the 2–0 lead. First up was Skowron. He grounded to the box and Podres calmly tossed the ball to Hodges. Next was Cerv, who would become an All-Star in the late fifties with Kansas City. He lifted a routine fly to Amoros in left. Two outs, still nobody on base. As Howard strode to the plate, Dodgers fans worried that everything was going too easily.

"We always sat between home plate and third base," Joan Hodges recalls, "but I was so nervous that I forgot where I was. I'm embarrassed to say it, but I stood up on my seat. Can you imagine? I was looking to heaven and talking to God, telling him, 'Please, please, just this once be *with* us, please.' I forgot I was at the ballpark and was praying out loud."

She was not alone. Dodgers fans everywhere prayed, crossed themselves, crossed their fingers, shut their eyes, held their breaths. Before they could concoct worst-case disaster scenarios, the ball was bounding across the left side of the diamond.

That night Roger Kahn and Pee Wee Reese had a few celebratory drinks at a bar in Manhattan. Kahn asked him what he was thinking with Howard up. "'I'm thinking,' said the bravest shortstop I've ever known, 'I hope he doesn't hit the ball to me.'" But Reese needn't have worried. He scooped up the easy grounder and threw to first.

"For years we needled Pee Wee about making a low throw to first base," Erskine laughs. "Pee Wee always said he made a good throw. And Hodges contended it was one of the worst throws he ever had to dig out of the dirt. A few of us were in L.A. years later for an old-timers' game. It was about 3 a.m. and I was in a bar with Pee Wee, Roebuck, Zimmer, and maybe Duke, and we got to talking about that play. Pee Wee was still insisting he made a good throw, so we called Hodges and got him out of bed to ask about that play." Hodges growled that it was low and hung up.

Hodges leaned forward and snared the throw easily, bringing glove and ball up to his belt in a flash as he made the putout that ended the World Series. As he and Campanella rushed to join the wild celebration on the mound, Snider leaped toward the clouds in center field.

At approximately 3:45 p.m. on October 4, 1955, in the World Series broadcast booth, Vin Scully said simply, "Ladies and gentlemen, the Brooklyn Dodgers are champions of the world." He was too choked up to say more.

Across Brooklyn there was instantaneous celebration as everyone stormed into the streets, hugging their neighbors and strangers alike. Paper and objects flew out windows. Bells rang out, car horns sounded, revelers screamed themselves hoarse. Scully described the scene when he came through the Battery Tunnel a few hours later: "It was like V-J Day. People were literally dancing in the streets. All of Brooklyn was a block party."

The stunned fans in Yankee Stadium watched the Dodgers swamp Podres and then disappear underground. "I walked in with the guys and we were getting beer and champagne," recalls Craig. "It caught me off guard how quiet it was. There were guys like Pee Wee and Gil just sitting by their lockers with tears in their eyes."

"Jackie, Pee Wee, Gil, the guys who had been there for so long, all needed a minute before we started pouring champagne or spoke to the press," Erskine recalled. "Besides what it meant for us, there was this feeling that we had finally won one for our fans who had supported us so well all those years we didn't win. I honestly believe we were happier for the fans in Brooklyn than we were for ourselves."

Hodges had smiled broadly as he walked past the cameras, not trying to contain his emotions at all. He was tired but mostly he was just happy. "I found him in the clubhouse," recalls Joan, "and he was smiling. I don't think he was feeling relief—the joy was so overwhelming that he couldn't feel anything else."

"It was poetic justice that Gil drove in both runs to win Brooklyn's only title," says Erskine. "I was so happy for him. I can't describe how happy we all were. I still can't describe it, and for years I wouldn't even try."

The celebration by the long-suffering kids and adults of Brooklyn literally brought traffic to a halt, so it took a long time for the bus carrying the players to make it back to Ebbets Field, where they had parked their cars. "I came back with Gil and the other players," Louis Lombardi remembers. "The men were in one bus and the women in another. Everybody was there waiting for their team to come home, and people were coming out into the middle of Flatbush Avenue and trying to stop the bus. It was an exciting time. And Gil was very, very happy. When something like that happened, he showed his emotions."

"People knew where we lived, so the police set up four blocks of barricades leading to our house, from Nostrand Avenue to East Thirty-second," recalls Joan. "It wasn't scary, just happy, with people applauding, laughing, crying, and screaming at Gil, 'Thank you! Thank you! Thank you!'"

"When I got home to change my clothes and go to the victory party, there was a tremendous crowd around my house," Hodges wrote in *The Game of Baseball*. "It was very nice because these people were more than just fans, they were also friends."

"When Dad came home after winning the championship in 1955, the whole block was going crazy," remembers Hodges Jr. "I didn't understand what was going on. I was five years old and didn't know he was a ballplayer. Duke and Pee Wee? I just thought they were my father's friends who visited our house. I wasn't a baseball fan yet and wasn't interested in talking about the game. I had just been watching *Ramar of the Jungle* on TV and wanted to talk to Dad about that."

Gil and Joan made their way to the victory party at the Bossert Hotel, where there would be dancing to big-band music and Schaefer beer would flow like champagne. The crowd on the sidewalk near the hotel was ten deep, and they were all hollering. When the Hodges pulled up they spotted a couple of dummies wearing Yankee caps, hanging from light poles. A sign on their chests read, DEAD YANKEES. Joan Hodges recalls, "It was such an emotional night. We were just so happy. What I remember most is that Gil and Johnny Podres went outside to talk to the press and wave to all the fans standing outside."

The celebration would continue the next day, when Dodger fans, some who hadn't been to sleep, picked up the *Daily News* and saw a jolly Brooklyn Bum on the front page under the headline, "WHO'S A BUM!"

Clearly, Brooklyn fans were showing their unmatched love for their baseball team. Surely, those fans believed, the city wouldn't allow a world championship team to leave for another city. Positively, city officials believed, O'Malley now had Robert Moses over a barrel and he had no choice but to let the Dodger owner build his six-million-dollar domed stadium near the Long Island Rail Road terminus in Brooklyn. Moses would now, they assumed, stop talking about building a stadium in Flushing Meadows, in Queens, that O'Malley could lease. Also, everyone believed, if O'Malley's decision in August to have the Dodgers play several home games in 1956 and 1957 in Jersey City reflected that he was considering leaving Brooklyn, now he'd scrap such plans.

A move by his team to California would have a tremendous impact on

Hodges, a year-round Brooklyn resident. But that October night, after the Dodgers' glorious victory, he wasn't thinking of anything but celebrating with his wife and teammates. "I don't have many of my father's autographs," says Hodges Jr. "But I have a framed black-and-white picture that is from early in 1956. It's him swinging his bat, and above his signature, he wrote the words, 'This IS next year.'"

CHAPTER SIXTEEN

In February 1956, for maybe the first time, a reporter asked Hodges whether he was interested in managing after his playing career was over. "Very much so," he replied. "Baseball has been extremely good to me and I would like to continue in some capacity." Hodges' bold statement received no reaction in the New York and national sports scenes, because it was said to a reporter for a tiny weekly Petersburg paper. In New York no one thought to ask him such a question, because everyone assumed he was too quiet to be in charge of twenty-five players and deal with the contentious media. In Indiana, however, the idea of his managing wasn't far-fetched, because everyone remembered that he once aspired to be a coach and work with young athletes.

For certain, Hodges never wanted to stop dedicating time to kids, with whom he had a special affinity. As a World Series winner, he frequently visited children in hospitals and made personal appearances for various child-related charities. "The Muscular Dystrophy Association was Gil's number one priority," Joan Hodges says, "because it crushed him that at the time the life expectancy of a child who was dystrophic was thirteen years. He admired Jerry Lewis a great deal for his devotion to the cause."

Additionally, Hodges spent time with youngsters learning to play baseball. "We became friendly," recalls Yogi Berra, "doing baseball clinics for kids in the off-season." In the mid-fifties Sid Loberfeld was working with the South Highway Little League, a Brooklyn sandlot organization, and asked Hodges whether it could be renamed in his honor. The proud Hodges not only gave his name to the Gil Hodges Little League, but also spent much of his free time watching the boys play and giving them instruction.

At Ebbets Field during the season, another Little Leaguer sought his tutelage. Roy Campanella II recalls, "I was sometimes assigned to play first base, and Gil gave me a really thorough introduction to the position. He took the time to demonstrate and explain everything I needed to know about covering the base, including the footwork. He answered my questions about going after balls in the dirt and other bad throws and everything else about the craft. I got to see what a beautiful position first base is. All the Dodgers were nice guys and would have helped me, but Gil in particular was able to establish a great rapport with kids."

Steve Garvey, who became a star first baseman for the Los Angeles Dodgers in the mid-seventies, was about to play Little League ball for the first time in 1956. Before that he benefited from meeting Hodges in Tampa, Florida. His father transported the Dodgers by bus to play an exhibition game against the Yankees in St. Petersburg, and Steve got to be the batboy. That first day he waited for the players to emerge from the clubhouse in their uniforms. He wrote in *My Bat Boy Days:*

> The first player to come out was Gil Hodges. He picked up a ball and motioned as if he wanted to play catch with me. Me! I pointed my finger at myself, he nodded, and I grabbed my new Rawlings mitt. His first toss was arced high and intended to test my ability. I must have impressed him with a clean catch, as the next few throws were harder. I remember feeling a sting with each one and wondering if the new gear had enough padding. More and more players came out, and finally Gil said, "One more, son!" That last toss had no spin to it and only my chest kept it from going by me. The loud thud probably scared Mr. Hodges, who came up to me to see if I was all right. Hodges was the first to teach me lessons about digging balls out of the dirt and the smooth footwork around the first-base bag that would put me years ahead of the other kids. Over the next several years, Gil always had ten minutes to share with a bat boy.

Garvey's family had relocated from Long Island to Florida. Still on Long Island, in Baldwin, was another youngster who fell under Hodges' spell. Jonathan Demme, who would win an Oscar for directing 1991's Best Picture, *The Silence of the Lambs*, recalls, "I liked Gil Hodges, and when I was in the fifth grade I taped my ears forward when I went to bed. The reason is that his ears stuck out a little and I wanted to wake up looking exactly like him."

Another young Hodges devotee who ended up in the entertainment field was Brooklyn native Gary David Goldberg, who would create the television series *Family Ties*. In the early nineties, he also created a semiautobiographical series called *Brooklyn Bridge*, about a Jewish American family in Brooklyn in 1956. In the first scene of the premiere episode, a young boy is taken by his grandparents to an autograph signing by Gil Hodges at a bank. Hodges (played by Jeffrey Nordling) catches on that the kindly grandfather (played by Jules Berger) had fibbed to his grandson about having played baseball against Hodges in Russia. Rather than humiliate him, Hodges tells the grandfather, "Good to see you *again*," in front of the awestruck boy. The grandfather says, "You should know what a *mensch* is—because that's you."

In the dictionary, a *mensch* is defined as "a person of integrity and honor," but it's something more. "I'm Jewish and we would call Gil Hodges a *mensch* when I was a kid," says family friend Dave Kaminer, who today runs a public relations firm. "He not only walks tall, but makes everybody feel better about themselves."

For the first time in their history, the Brooklyn Dodgers showed up at Vero Beach as defending world champions. They had always been a proud bunch, but they had a little more swagger this spring training than any Hodges had attended.

There were three new players in camp who were part of the Dodgers' future plans. Don Drysdale was an imposing, temperamental six-foot-five rookie right-handed pitcher from California who had the stuff and attitude to become a star once he really learned to pitch. He was only nineteen, but he had a good chance to make the team, because Podres was in the Navy, Meyer had been traded, Spooner was finished, Loes' arm was aching, and Bessent hurt his arm throwing a golf club at a snake at the Vero Beach Country Club.

Charlie Neal was expected to be the starting second baseman in 1956, with Gilliam shifting to left field. The tall and wiry Neal was coming off a big year at Montreal, where he had 29 doubles, 14 triples, and 16 homers. As they'd done with Gilliam, both Jackie Robinson and Roy Campanella looked after Neal, an African-American from Longview, Texas. Hodges, Reese, and the other veterans made Drysdale feel like part of the group in Florida.

Randy Jackson had been a two-time All-Star third baseman with the Chicago Cubs when Bavasi acquired him in December for Meyer, Don Hoak, and Walt Moryn. "Handsome Ransom" had belted 40 homers over the last two years and was expected to share third base with Jackie Robinson and take over the position when Robinson retired. "All the players knew me and welcomed me the first day of spring training," recalls Jackson. "No one resented I was going to be playing Robinson's position. I had such respect for him. Even in 1956, he was a great ballplayer. When spring training was over, Alston told me, 'I've got to start Jackie.' I said, 'I understand. I'm just glad to be here.'"

The 1956 season opened on April 17 against Philadelphia. Alston's lineup was Jim Gilliam, LF; Pee Wee Reese, SS; Duke Snider, CF; Roy Campanella, C; Gil Hodges, 1B; Jackie Robinson, 3B; Carl Furillo, RF; Charlie Neal, 2B; and Don Newcombe, P. Seven of the nine Dodgers had started in the historic game won by the Phillies on the last day of the 1950 season. Incredibly, the Phillies' lineup also had seven players who appeared in that game: Richie Ashburn, Granny Hamner, Del Ennis, Stan Lopata, Willie Jones, Andy Seminick, and Robin Roberts, yet the Dodgers were still annual contenders, and the slow-to-integrate Phillies had fallen on hard times.

Despite homers by Campanella and Gilliam, the Dodgers were beaten by the Phillies 8–6. Two days later, April 19, the two teams met again, with the Dodgers prevailing 6–5 in ten innings. Hodges' first hit of the season was a bases-clearing double in the second inning to give Brooklyn a 3–0 lead. Played before 12,214 spectators at Roosevelt Stadium, this was the first of the seven home games O'Malley scheduled away from Ebbets Field.

"I realized the Dodgers might actually move when I turned on the TV and saw a game coming from Jersey City," recalls sportswriter George Vecsey. "They'd talked about it before, but honestly I hadn't paid attention."

"When they played those seven games in Jersey City I started hearing rumors of a move," Larry King remembers. "This was nuts to me. Brooklyn was permanent—no one moves."

"I didn't think the Dodgers would move," Ed Roebuck said in *We Played the Game* in 1994. "I really thought O'Malley was bluffing to get what he wanted in Brooklyn. To me, the Brooklyn Dodgers were an institution. It was like moving the White House out of Washington, D.C."

The Dodgers went to Pittsburgh after their split with Philadelphia, and for the first time in eight years, Hodges wasn't rooming with Furillo. The front office decided to room young ballplayers with veterans who could show them the ropes. So Furillo became roommates with Koufax, and Hodges was assigned Drysdale.

"When you roomed with Gil, it felt like you were rooming with a saint," wrote Drysdale in his 1990 autobiography *Once a Bum, Always a Dodger*. "He was the most impressive person you could ever want to meet. All you had to do was watch how he carried himself, on and off the field, and you knew that his was the right way of going about being a major league ball-player."

Drysdale appreciated that Hodges treated him like an equal and never left him behind when he went out to dinner or to have a few drinks. "He knew when to call it a night and hit the sack," wrote Drysdale. "I never barged in at three in the morning, but there were times when I'd get the gleam in my eye and want to go a little longer than he did. I'd arrive a couple hours later, give a knock, and he'd come to the door, which he liked to chain from the inside. He'd let me in, and fall right back to sleep. Every once in a while, the next morning over breakfast, he'd drop a little message on me. 'What time was it that you got in last night?' he'd ask. 'Right about twelve-thirty, maybe one o'clock,' I'd say. 'Really? Geez, I thought it was a little later than that.' And you'd sit there, feeling about six inches tall."

Not surprisingly, Drysdale was awed by his roommate's strength. He would recall the time he and Hodges returned to their hotel room after a night game but couldn't get in because the bellboy had left their heavy trunk-size suitcases next to the door. "'Roomie,' Hodges said, 'let me get at that,'" wrote Drysdale. "First, he pushed the door open, which was no small task. Then he reached in and grabbed those suitcases, one at a time, and picked them up and threw them across the room. He didn't bother using the handles, either. He put his hands around them like you would put your hands around your thigh, and he just tossed them like they were nothing! I was flabbergasted."

Hodges was a man of order and routines, and Drysdale knew that every morning, he'd get up early and put on his suit and tie and go down to the hotel coffee shop and order "orange juice, bran flakes with a banana on top, eggs and sausage and toast and milk and coffee. Whenever we went to St. Louis, Gil liked to have brownie à la mode at the Chase Park-Plaza. He could eat pies and cakes and all that stuff without ever putting on an ounce."

Drysdale was given his first start on the road trip and came away with an impressive 6–1 victory over the Phillies. He gave up 9 hits, but they were all singles, and he struck out 9. However, he was hit hard against Pittsburgh, giving up 5 earned runs in 5⅔ innings, and took the loss, 10–1. One of his mop-up men was Koufax, who was also knocked around. Obviously, Koufax needed either seasoning in the minors, which he couldn't get because his "bonus-baby" status required that he stay on the parent team, or steady work, which Alston wouldn't give him because he was too wild.

Brooklyn closed April with a 7–4 record and maintained a half-game lead over Milwaukee. With the Giants in flux after Durocher was replaced as manager by Bill Rigney, the Braves seemed to be the biggest threat to the Dodgers' supremacy in the National League. They had a number of players who were impressive both offensively and defensively: catcher Del Crandall, first baseman Joe Adcock, shortstop Johnny Logan, center fielder Billy Bruton, and their two stars, right fielder Hank Aaron and third baseman Eddie Mathews. Plus they had three outstanding starting pitchers—perennial 20-game winner Warren Spahn, Lew Burdette, and Bob Buhl, who dominated the Dodgers.

The Cincinnati Redlegs were the other contender. Other than Joe Nuxhall, their pitching was suspect, but they had an excellent double-play combination in second baseman Johnny Temple and shortstop Roy McMillan, and unmatched power. They would smash 221 homers, with five players hitting more than 25 homers and three hitting 35 or more: Ted Kluszewski (35, with a team-high 102 RBIs), Wally Post (36), and Frank Robinson (a rookie-record 38), the team's first black star.

The Dodgers knew they had an outstanding lineup, but they worried about having enough starting pitching behind Newcombe and Craig. The big question mark was Erskine, who had lost 2 of his first 3 decisions and, though he kept it to himself, was battling extreme pain in his shoulder. It was hurting something fierce on May 12, yet he threw the second no-hitter of his career, dominating the Giants 3–0. However, he would lose 4 straight decisions, including on May 28, when Pirates first baseman Dale Long made national headlines by homering in his eighth consecutive game.

Two days after Erskine's no-hitter, Loes was sold to Baltimore for $20,000. He was only twenty-six, but the Dodgers wrongly believed his career was over. His spot on the roster was filled by a surprising choice—Sal Maglie, who had tripled Dodgers' batters' laundry bills all those years when he carried out Durocher's orders. After he hurt his back, the Giants had no more use for him, and Cleveland picked him up on waivers in 1955. The Indians now thought the thirty-nine-year-old was through and gladly sold him to the Giants' rivals. His arrival stunned the Dodgers fans, who hated him, and the players, who still held grudges. Bavasi got Alston's and Reese's approval before bringing in the big-game pitcher. When Maglie walked into the Dodgers clubhouse for the first time, Carl Furillo was the only player inside. For years, Furillo had vowed to pummel Maglie for all the times he literally tried to stick it in his ear. But Furillo's first words were, "Welcome to our side." "What Maglie didn't know," says George Vecsey, "is that Bavasi gave Furillo some cash to take him out for dinners and make him feel at home."

For a time the Dodgers struggled to find victories from anyone but Newcombe. On June 2, their record was 19–19 and they were in fifth place, 3½ games out. Then Koufax, with help from Labine, earned his first win of the season, 4–3, over Chicago as Hodges slammed his 8th homer and picked up his 26th RBI in twenty-eight games. The Dodgers then went to Milwaukee, where Maglie got his first win in a Dodgers uniform in spectacular fashion, shutting out the Braves on 3 hits, 3–0. Craig then tossed a 2-hitter and Newcombe a 5-hitter as the Dodgers beat the Braves twice more. Buhl salvaged the final game for Milwaukee, but the Dodgers had proven that they had what it took to ward off all challengers.

Maglie became an effective part of the rotation with Newcombe, Craig, and Erskine, who got back in the win column on June 12, but his biggest contribution to the Dodgers in the long term was having Koufax and Drysdale learn from him. Koufax said Maglie was the only pitcher who "worked from behind a batter. He would pitch exactly as if the batter had to go to Sal's pitch." Maglie taught Drysdale how to tell what a batter was thinking by the movement of his feet, and *when* it was effective to throw a knockdown pitch—which became a major part of the young pitcher's arsenal.

In mid-June, Hodges took another young player under his wing. After graduating from Lafayette High School, seventeen-year-old Bob Aspromonte joined the Dodgers for the remainder of the season. Aspromonte recalls: "A week before I was hoping to get their autographs, and now I'm sitting next to Jackie Robinson, Duke Snider, and Gil Hodges. Gil made sure I felt comfortable. He'd invite me to lunch at the hotel, and if he ordered something he'd say, 'Make that two!' We talked baseball and he worked with me in the field as well. I'd take balls at short during infield practice, using a glove Robinson gave me—which was incredible—and I'd throw over to Gil at first, where he was so smooth. There was a natural leadership to him in a very quiet, gentle way. He was as big as a statue, but all he'd need to do was look at me and I'd know I wasn't doing something right; or he'd pat me on the back and I'd know I did the right thing. Gil had a unique way of getting across the point, 'You can do this better.'"

Relegated to the Dodgers' bench, as the young Hodges had been in 1943, Aspromonte witnessed one of the most unusual endings in team history on June 29. The Dodgers trailed the Phillies 5–2 in the bottom of the ninth. Phillies starter Stu Miller walked Gilliam leading off, but then struck out Reese. Snider then hit his second homer of the game to cut the deficit to 5–4 and send Miller to the showers. Jackson greeted reliever Jack Meyer with a game-tying homer. Then Hodges smashed the Dodgers' third consecutive homer, his second of the game, and the Dodgers won 6–5. "I had never seen three consecutive homers win a game in the last of the ninth," Jackson remembers. "The fans went crazy."

Hodges played left field that game, Jackson third base, and Robinson first base. "Walt started Jackie at third base for about a month," recalls Jackson. "When he slumped he didn't play as much, and I played and batted fourth. That was the way it was until the All-Star break, when a shower knob broke off in my hand and gashed my right thumb down to the bone. From then on, Jackie started at third again and played well."

Hodges hit a 3-run homer off Roberts in the next game to finish June with 16 homers and 39 RBIs. His average was only .242, and his 100-RBI streak was in jeopardy, as was his being selected to the All-Star team every year since 1949. But with the 10–7 victory, the Dodgers improved to 37–28 and were tied with the Redlegs for second place, only 1 game behind Milwaukee.

The Dodgers and Phillies split a doubleheader the next day, with Hodges hitting a 2-run homer in the 4–1 victory in the nightcap. On July 2, the Dodgers hosted the Giants, and though they lost 5–2, it was memorable for Hodges. For the first time since mid-1948, he put on catcher's gear. He caught reliever Roebuck for two scoreless innings to finish the game. Briefly, he turned back the pages of time.

The Dodgers were 42–32 at the All-Star break, good for third place, 3 games behind the Braves. Campanella, Gilliam, Snider, and Labine made the National League squad. For the first time since 1948, Hodges didn't make the team. He had 17 homers and 46 RBIs, but the voting fans couldn't ignore his .242 average. Also missing was Don Newcombe, who was 11–5 and having his best year. He'd go 12–1 in July and August, including 3 straight shutouts as he was unscored upon in 39 straight innings. He won his 20th game in late August. His record went to 22–6 on August 31, when he beat the Giants to pull the Dodgers to within 2½ games of the Braves, and kept them 1 game in front of the Redlegs. Hodges, batting eighth because of a slump, drove in his 69th run.

Although he had a lackluster August, Hodges hit one of his most gratifying homers two weeks earlier against Phillies' left-hander Curt Simmons at Connie Mack Stadium. "I was born at noon on August 19, 1956," says Cindy Hodges. "I was told that when my mother gave birth, Daddy was playing ball. He hit a home run. He later said he hit it for his daughter, who was just born. I have a newspaper clipping of when Daddy came to the hospital to see me. My mother was holding me, and I guess someone put that in the newspaper. It's a nice memento."

"My father wanted to be at all our births, because his children super-seded everything," says Hodges Jr. "If he was at home, he would do every-thing to be there. But he had a job to do that took him to other cities, and he respected his job. He was never at our first holy communions; he was never at our graduations; he was never at anything that took place during the season. He didn't regret it. For him to miss a job where he worked only from April to October wasn't acceptable. He knew other people counted on him."

Hodges had a good September, supporting Newcombe and Maglie, who went a combined 11–2 when it counted most. Both pitched spectacu-larly down the stretch. Newcombe's lone defeat was 7–3 to Robin Roberts and the Phillies; Maglie, who went 11–3 after the break, lost 2–1 to Pitts-burgh. Otherwise, they were invincible. On September 1, Maglie beat New York 5–0 with a 1-hitter, getting sweet revenge against his old team for discarding him. On the fifth, he beat Pittsburgh 4–3, as Hodges smashed his 26th homer. On the eleventh, before more than 33,000 fans at Ebbets Field, he defeated the first-place Braves 4–2, as Hodges hit his 27th homer. The Dodgers were now tied for first for the first time since May 20. Maglie's besting Buhl was no mean task, considering the Braves right-hander had gone 8–0 against the Dodgers in '56. On the sixteenth, Maglie outdueled the Redlegs' Joe Nuxhall 3–2, to put the Dodgers alone in first place for the first time since April 29. Batting fifth, Hodges drove in the game's first run with a double off the Redlegs' left-hander.

Following his loss to Pittsburgh on the twenty-first, Maglie rebounded on the twenty-fifth by throwing a no-hitter against the Phillies and winning 5–0 in one of the most notable big-game pitching performances in baseball history. Maglie and Erskine became the first staffmates to throw no-hitters in the same season since Ernie Koob and Bob Groom did it on consecutive days for the St. Louis Browns in 1917. In Maglie's final start of the regular season, against Pittsburgh in the first of a twin bill, he put the Dodgers 1 game ahead of the Braves with a 6–2 victory. Hodges stroked his 32nd and final home run of the season. In Maglie's 6 victories in September he pitched 53⅓ out of 54 possible innings. At thirty-nine, he was pitching as well as he had in his entire career.

Newcombe was also a workhorse down the stretch. He pitched an eleven-inning 6-hitter to beat the Giants 3–1; shut out the Cubs 3–0 on 3 hits; went 7 innings and blasted 2 home runs as the Dodgers mauled the Cardinals 17–2. On the twenty-third, a tired Newcombe needed relief from Labine, but Hodges hit two longballs, and the Dodgers easily beat Pittsburgh 8–3. After losing to the Phillies in game 151, Newcombe came back to pitch game 154 following a doubleheader sweep of the Pirates the previous day by Maglie and Labine in a rare start. The Dodgers had a 1-game lead over the Braves and needed a victory over Pittsburgh to avoid a playoff, so Newcombe was eager to start despite his fatigue and having such a bad cold that he needed a shot of penicillin. He was given a 7–2 lead courtesy of a 3-run homer by Snider and solo blasts by Robinson and Amoros, but when he was replaced by Bessent after 7⅓ innings, he had given up 6 earned runs. Amoros hit another homer in the eighth to put the Dodgers up 8–6, and they should have scored another run but Hodges, who had singled, was thrown out at home plate when he made a base-running gaffe. When he took the field, "Hodges could not stop berating himself," wrote Michael Shapiro in *The Last Good Season.*

Fortunately, they didn't need that run because Bessent preserved the 8–6 lead in the ninth. The Braves won their final game, but it didn't matter. For the sixth time since Hodges joined the Dodgers in 1947, they were the National League champions.

Hodges raised his average to .265 and clouted 15 homers in the second half of the season, but he drove in only 41 more runs and failed to tie Mel Ott's league record of eight consecutive 100-RBI seasons. As Roscoe McGowen pointed out, in 1952 Hodges drove in 102 runs when he had 129 hits, including 27 doubles, 1 triple, and 32 home runs, while in 1956 he drove in only 87 runs despite accumulating 146 hits, including 29 doubles, 4 triples, and the same 32 home runs. "Apparently there weren't as many Dodgers on base ahead of him [in 1956]," McGowen surmised.

It was the fate of the Brooklyn Dodgers to play all of their six post-WWII World Series against the New York Yankees. The 1956 Yankees weren't out of first place after April 20, and their 97 wins were nine more than runner-up Cleveland's total. Their ace, Whitey Ford, had a 19–6 record and led the American League with a 2.47 ERA. Johnny Kucks went 18–9,

Tom Sturdivant 16–8, and Don Larsen 11–8. On offense, several players put up solid numbers: Yogi Berra hit .298, with 30 homers and 105 RBIs; Moose Skowron batted .308, with 23 homers and 90 RBIs; Hank Bauer clouted 26 homers and drove in 84 runs; and Mickey Mantle realized his potential by winning the American League's Triple Crown, with a .353 average, 52 home runs, and 130 RBIs.

Newcombe had perhaps the greatest year by a pitcher in the decade, going 27–7 with a 3.06 ERA. He would be selected the National League's MVP and win the inaugural Cy Young Award, covering both leagues. Maglie went 13–5, Erskine 13–11, Craig 12–11, and Labine 10–6 with 19 unofficial saves. Because Newcombe seemed to be the victim of Yankee fans practicing voodoo every time he made a World Series appearance, Alston was counting on his other pitchers to step up.

The Dodgers lineup wasn't as formidable as it had been in previous Series. Snider's 101 RBIs were good enough to lead the team. More impressive were his 43 homers, which was tops in the league. It was a career best and broke the Brooklyn Dodgers' record of 42 that he held with Hodges. It was the fourth straight year he passed the 40-homer mark. Gilliam led the team with just a .300 average, ahead of Snider's .292. Campanella had 20 homers and 75 RBIs, but batted only .219 in an injury-riddled year. Robinson hit .275 with 10 homers and 43 RBIs in limited time. Reese, Furillo, Jackson, Amoros and Neal—who played part-time—had just average seasons. The Dodgers were the defending world champions, but it made sense that they were the underdogs.

The 1956 World Series began on October 3, and President Dwight D. Eisenhower was at Ebbets Field to throw out the first pitch. It was a new month, but Maglie continued to excel, pitching a complete-game victory over Ford, 6–3. Mantle boomed a 2-run homer in the first inning for New York, but the Dodgers tied the game on Robinson's homer, Hodges' single, and Furillo's RBI double. They took the lead for good in the third inning, when Hodges muscled a 3-run homer into the left-field seats.

In Game 2, before 36,217 of the Brooklyn faithful, the Dodgers quickly fell behind 6–0. Once again Newcombe imploded in postseason competition, and Brooklyn fans weren't happy with him as he gave up a single run in the first inning and 5 runs in the second, the big blow being a grand slam by Berra, his nemesis, that ended his afternoon. "I always said Berra would swing at a horse turd and hit it," recalled Newcombe in *We Played the Game*. "Every pitch I threw him I wanted back."

Remarkably, the Dodgers came back in the bottom of the second to knock Larsen from the box. He had given up only 1 run—Hodges had a leadoff single and scored on Campanella's sacrifice fly—but left with the bases loaded. Reese's single off Kucks brought in two runners, and Snider's 3-run homer off Byrne tied the game. Bessent relieved for the Dodgers in the third inning and went the rest of the way, yielding only 2 runs. The Dodgers moved ahead 7–6 in the third inning when Hodges worked a walk from Sturdivant and scored when Furillo and Bessent singled. In the bottom of the fourth, Hodges' 2-run double off the wall broke a 7–7 tie. The Dodgers went on to win 13–8. In two games, Hodges had 5 RBIs.

For the Yankees to have a realistic chance to win the Series, they'd have to duplicate what the Dodgers did in '55, which was to sweep Games 3, 4 and 5 at home. A rainout between Games 1 and 2 allowed Stengel to come back with Ford in Game 3. Alston could have done the same with Maglie, but instead went with Craig, despite his poor second half of the season. Hodges scored a couple of runs, but the Yankees won 5–3 as Ford went the distance and onetime Cardinals great Enos Slaughter smashed a 3-run homer.

The next day, the Yankees won Game 4 6–2, as Mantle and Bauer homered and Sturdivant hurled another complete game. Roebuck remembers giving up Mantle's solo shot into the right-center-field bleachers: "Duke was in center. He didn't turn around at first, then had a second thought and turned to see how far it would go. It was a tremendous blast. I was proud to be part of it."

The team that won the final game at Yankee Stadium would tip the scales in its favor. Those who were present for Game 5, or watching on television, soon forgot the ramifications of a win or loss and got caught up in one of the most famous games in baseball history. Don Larsen learned that he would be the Yankee starter in the pivotal game of the Series after a hard night out on the town when he opened his locker and discovered that pitching coach Jim Turner had placed the game ball in his shoe. His opponent would be Maglie, so the six-foot-four-inch right-hander, who just two years before went a wretched 3–21 with the St. Louis Browns, figured he had to pitch the game of his life to beat him. He was correct.

Maglie gave up only 5 hits in eight innings. The Yankees didn't get their first hit until Mantle jacked one into the short lower right-field stands in the fourth inning. Their next 3 hits, all singles, came in the sixth inning and gave them an insurance run. The 2–0 score—the same score as the seventh game of the 1955 Series—would stand up, because Larsen was perfect, literally. Hodges, who would lead the Dodgers with 8 RBIs in the Series and tie Snider for the team lead with 7 hits, 5 runs, and a .304 average, came closest to ruining Larsen's masterpiece. With one out in the fifth inning, he drove a 2–2 pitch to deep left-center field.

"We tried to pitch Hodges inside a little bit, the hard stuff," recalls Larsen. "One mistake and that perfect game was gone."

"We didn't want to make a mistake with Hodges," says Berra. "He was too dangerous."

Larsen did make a mistake with Hodges, but got away with it. "Gil would punish a mistake, and I sure made one with him. What he hit would've been a home run in any park today. I looked out there and thought, 'Oh, Jesus.' Then I saw Mickey running after it. Mickey could run like a deer, and the stadium had wide-open spaces in those days, and I thought, 'He's going to catch this.' Mickey saved me."

Mantle's terrific backhanded catch while in full stride was disappointing to the Dodgers, but they continued to believe they'd reach Larsen. Hodges batted for his third and last time in the eighth. Umpire Babe Pinella heard him say under his breath, "I'll get to this guy." He almost did. On another 2–2 pitch, he lined out to Andy Carey at third. Amoros lifted a long fly to Mantle in center to end the inning, and Larsen needed only three more outs.

The gutsy Maglie ended his fabulous season in style, striking out the side in the bottom of the eighth. Then the Dodgers came up for their last swings in the top of the ninth. The 64,519 fans at Yankee Stadium were surprisingly quiet as they anxiously watched history unfold. Their tension increased as Furillo flied out to Bauer in right and Campanella grounded out to Martin at second. The twenty-seventh batter was Dale Mitchell, who, ironically, had begun the season in Cleveland with Maglie, for whom he was now pinch-hitting. He was a dangerous hitter with a good eye. After fouling off a 1–2 pitch, he checked his swing on a fastball that looked to the casual viewer to be high and outside. Larsen and Berra have always insisted that Pinelli got it right when he called it a strike, startling Mitchell and the rest of the Dodgers. "It was down the middle," they say, straight-faced. The final call of the retiring Pinelli's long career in blue made it official: Larsen had pitched the only perfect game in World Series history. Berra ran out and leaped into his arms, an image familiar to all baseball fans.

What can you do for an encore after a perfect game? Nothing, which is why many baseball fans think Larsen's perfect game ended the '56 Series. Others realize it just put the Yankees up 3 games to 2, but still don't remember the tremendous but anticlimactic Game 6, when Turley and Labine dueled into extra innings without giving up a run. Through nine innings, Turley had yielded only 3 hits and struck out 11; Labine had given up 7 hits and had fanned 5. In the bottom of the tenth, Gilliam walked with one out, was bunted to second by Reese, and, after an intentional walk to Snider, scored the team's first run in two games on a line drive by Robinson over the leaping Slaughter's glove in left. The 1–0 thriller evened the Series and set the stage for Game 7.

Brooklyn went with its ace, Newcombe, and New York countered with Kucks. This was the opportunity for Newcombe to silence his critics by shutting down the Yankees in the biggest game of the year. But Kucks was the one to dominate. He gave up only 2 singles to Snider and 1 to Furillo and coasted to a 9–0 win. The Dodgers, who hit .195 for the Series, scored only 1 run in their final three games.

When Kucks whiffed Jackie Robinson to end the game and the Series, no one knew it was Robinson's last major-league appearance.

Two days after the Series ended in disappointment, the Dodgers were in Los Angeles on their way to a five-week goodwill tour of Japan. Players received a tax-free $2,500 stipend on top of their $6,934.34 World Series share, but many of the players were tired of baseball and weren't eager to participate. If Hodges didn't want to go, he made the most of his trip. Unlike Furillo, who refused to take part, he harbored no animosity toward Japan because of his war experiences. He enjoyed the people, the food, and the sights. He and Reese even got to play some golf—their caddy was a little old lady who ran up the fairway after every shot with their heavy bags on her shoulders. Hodges made a lot of friends just walking through the streets, particularly the children who flocked around the gentle giant.

Where Hodges really made an impression was at the ballpark, and not just with long home runs. From out of the blue, this staid ballplayer became another Al Schacht, the "Clown Prince of Baseball." In the April 1957 issue of *Sport* magazine, Vin Scully reported on Hodges' strange transformation:

> It all started one day after the Dodgers had left Tokyo to tour northern Japan. The Dodgers were leading by a big score, and when one of the local hitters came up, Gil, who was playing left field, turned to the fans in the left-field stands and asked them in panto- mime where he should play the hitter. Of course, the fans gave him about six different suggestions and Gil began wandering around frantically, as if he were completely confused. This brought a de- lighted roar of laughter from the fans. Then Gil began imitating every move the pitcher would make. He would bend down to get the sign, rub up a new ball, pretend to be holding the runner close to first base, go into an exaggerated windup and shake his head in sorrow if he didn't get the strike on the batter. The crowd loved it.
>
> Gil soon began to elaborate on his routine. Being a former catcher, he can give an uncanny imitation of Roy Campanella. He would imitate the hitter. He would stagger around rubber-legged under fly balls and catch them with a last minute lunge. When Hodges left the game, the crowd cheered so loud and long that he had to return for a curtain call, tipping his cap and bowing from the waist in a Japanese gesture of appreciation. We thought the crowd would never stop cheering.

Hodges' most memorable comedic act came after a teammate was so incensed at a third-strike call that he slammed his helmet to the ground and it bounced on top of the Dodgers' dugout. "The Japanese had never seen an umpire held up to such humiliation," wrote Scully, "and it was an embar- rassing moment for us in the Brooklyn party. But Gil saved the day. While the crowd still sat in stunned silence, Gil suddenly appeared, jumped up on the dugout roof and approached the helmet as if it were a dangerous snake. He circled it warily, made a couple of tentative stabs at it, then quickly pounced on it, tossed it back on the field and then did a swan dive off the top of the dugout. The fans beat their palms and shouted until they were hoarse."

"We'd known Gil for years and knew he had a sense of humor, but we never saw that side of him before," says Erskine. "He was very clever and the fans over there loved him."

When Hodges returned to the States, everyone wanted to know whether he would repeat his comic antics during regular season games. "Not intentionally," he deadpanned.

O'Malley resumed his negotiations with Robert Moses about receiving land for a new stadium. In late December, he warned New York City officials that if they didn't take action on a new ballpark within six months, "I will have to make other arrangements."

Even more shocking was an announcement that came a couple of weeks earlier. On December 13, Buzzie Bavasi traded Jackie Robinson to the New York Giants for journeyman pitcher Dick Littlefield and $30,000.

Robinson had aged and wasn't the player he once was, but he was still worth a lot more than what Bavasi got in return. Besides, Bavasi knew he was the symbol of the postwar Dodgers and had no business forcing him to don a Giants uniform. Earlier in the year, Robinson did Bavasi a favor by calling Tommy Davis and convincing him to sign with the Dodgers rather than the Yankees, so he had to believe he would be around when Davis arrived and that no trade was in the works. So what went wrong?

Roy Campanella II believes that Robinson was traded because of an incident during the tour of Japan: "The players were told they were not allowed to have their wives ride with them in the same car of the train in Japan. Their wives rode in separate cars. But the top brass—O'Malley, the manager, and the coaches—had their wives with them in their car. So Jackie questioned that double standard in front of Reese, my dad, and the other players. Jackie protested and Pee Wee whispered to my dad, 'How much do you want to bet that Jackie won't be back next year?'"

"Jack had begun to sense that these were his last years," says Rachel

Robinson. "Even before Buzzie called him to say he'd been traded, Jack had submitted a story to *Look* magazine stating that it was almost time for him to retire. But the Dodgers traded him without discussing it with him, or preparing him for it. Given his status, his importance to the team, and his years of service to the team, they could have planned something ceremonial leading up to the trade. It wasn't just that they traded him but how they went about it that was disturbing. Buzzie just picked up the phone and said, 'You're traded.' And of course to be traded to the hated Giants was another part of the disrespect they showed him."

Hodges had been saddened when previous teammates were traded—he equated them with family members—but Robinson's loss probably hit him the hardest. Although Robinson was older and they entered their Dodgers careers under very different circumstances, they had been rookies together in 1947 and had played together in every campaign since. They had lockered next to each other, endured defeats of Shakespearean proportions together, won several pennants and one world championship together, barnstormed together, and even socialized a little at a time when that was a rarity among ballplayers of different races. For years they had counted on each other and had come through splendidly for each other and the team. Their friendship would continue, but their relationship as teammates was unique to both of them and would be greatly missed.

In early January, Robinson retired rather than play for the Giants, ending a ten-year career that was incredible on many levels. For many Brooklyn Dodgers fans, the era came to an end when he departed. For everyone else, there was still a year to go.

CHAPTER SEVENTEEN

When the Dodgers assembled at Vero Beach in the spring of 1957, the absence of Jackie Robinson was conspicuous. Without his fiery presence on the field and in the clubhouse, the players felt the team's foundation was cracked. It cracked a little more when Walter O'Malley announced the Dodgers had acquired the Los Angeles Angels of the Pacific Coast League and the Angels' twenty-two-thousand-seat ballpark, Wrigley Field, from Cubs owner Philip K. Wrigley in exchange for three million dollars and the Fort Worth ballclub in the Texas League. By securing territorial rights in Los Angeles, O'Malley cleared a necessary hurdle for a move to take place. "Suddenly all of us," Duke Snider wrote in *The Duke of Flatbush*, "fans, players, reporters, and everyone else—began waiting for the second shoe to drop."

In a season when thousands of worried fans would circulate petitions directed to O'Malley, Robert Moses, and politicians, and would carry banners to Ebbets Field that read, STAY TEAM STAY, the Brooklyn Dodgers had their final Opening Day in Philadelphia. The batting order was: Jim Gilliam, 2B; Gino Cimoli, LF; Duke Snider, CF; Carl Furillo, RF; Gil Hodges, 1B; Randy Jackson, 3B; Roy Campanella, C; Don Zimmer, SS; Don Newcombe, P. Hodges was the only infielder who had started 1956's opener.

Once again, Newcombe went against Robin Roberts, and both went longer than their stuff deserved. Newcombe lasted 7 innings and left trailing 6–5. Roberts went all 12 innings, giving up 12 hits, including a game-tying solo homer to Hodges in the seventh inning that got Newcombe off the hook, and a go-ahead homer in the top of the twelfth by Cimoli, a Californian with matinee idol looks. Labine pitched his fifth shutout inning, and the Dodgers came away with a very satisfying 7–6 victory.

The Dodgers won their next game 6–1 over Pittsburgh, as Maglie threw a 4-hitter and Hodges hit his 2nd home run. Maglie wouldn't win again until May 30, but during this period both Drysdale and Koufax won 3 starts, and Newcombe looked like his old self by winning 4 of 6 decisions and shutting out the Cardinals and Giants. When St. Louis came to town, Brooklyn fans reveled in getting their last glimpses of Stan Musial, their favorite visiting player. At the age of thirty-six, the great Cardinal, whom Dodgers fans had respectfully dubbed "Stan the Man," would hit .351 to capture his seventh National League batting title and propel his team to its best record in a decade.

The Dodgers took 2 of 3 from the Cardinals at Ebbets Field and later in the month swept a two-game series at Busch Stadium. Hodges went 5-for-10 in the 10–4 and 10–3 victories, as visitors from Petersburg cheered him on. Although the train excursions carrying hundreds of Petersburg residents to St. Louis to watch Hodges play had ended long ago, his family, friends, and groups of fans still made regular trips there. "We'd go by bus to St. Louis and sometimes Cincinnati," recalls Jack Pipes, who was Charlie and Irene's paper boy and as an adult would run Petersburg's Little League (including the Hodges Dodgers team). "We would arrive early, and during batting practice Gil would always come over and shake hands with everyone from Pike County."

At the end of May, the Dodgers had a record of 23–15 and were in second place, 2 games behind the Reds and half a game ahead of the Braves. But they dropped their first two games in June to the Phillies and found themselves in fourth place. They reeled off 5 straight wins, and when Podres beat the Redlegs on June 8, 9–2, as Hodges got 3 hits and his 25th RBI, Brooklyn climbed past Cincinnati in the standings.

It would be the Dodgers' only day alone in first place in 1957. The next afternoon Cincinnati beat them in a twin bill. Milwaukee then came into Ebbets Field and won the first two games behind Dodger-killer Bob Buhl and Ray Crone. The Dodgers held off a Braves rally to win the third game

11–9, leaving both teams at 29–21, half a game behind Cincinnati. Hodges had an RBI single in his only official at-bat as Braves hurlers walked him 3 times, increasing his average to .372 with nearly one-third of the season over. It was his highest ever at this point of the season.

The next day, Hodges scored twice and drove in a run but went 0-for-3 in an 8–5 defeat that included one of his signature moments as a peacemaker. Down 4–0 in the second inning, Drysdale angrily hit Johnny Logan in the back with a 95-mph fastball. Logan said a few nasty words to him as he went to first base. He took a small lead and Drysdale threw over to first, a hard throw that struck Logan. Logan charged the mound, expecting his friend Eddie Mathews to do the real fighting, as he always did when Logan had a spat with a pitcher. Sure enough Mathews—a tough ex-Marine who would go out nights with Buhl looking for bar fights—reached Drysdale at the same time as Logan and hit him in the face with a hard right cross. A pile soon formed, with Mathews and Logan wrestling Drysdale. When Hodges saw his roommate in trouble he raced to the mound.

"Gil just picked up Mathews by one leg and arm and sat him down," remembers Roger Craig. "He told Mathews, 'Just stay out if it!' And Mathews did as he was told."

"Drysdale had a high knuckle, and when it hit Logan's eyebrow it took it right off," recalls Joe Pignatano, who was a twenty-seven-year-old rookie catcher for the Dodgers in 1957. "And then Mathews had Drysdale on the ground. Gil ran over and when he got to the pile, he didn't throw any punches but just started moving heads. When he found Mathews, he grabbed him by the back of the collar and jerked him out of the pile. He just stood him up and said, 'That's enough!' And everybody went back to their dugouts."

Pignatano was signed by the Dodgers back in 1948 and had a long, circuitous minor-league career. Hodges introduced himself to Pignatano in 1955 at Vero Beach, having heard he was from Brooklyn. They became close friends, as did their wives, and the four of them socialized every off-season. "Gilly and Pee Wee were the two nicest guys I ever met in baseball," says Pignatano. "They were also the leaders of the team. Alston left it to them to tell guys what to do. Gilly had been a catcher and showed me how to get on top of the ball when I threw, how to use my hands, and the proper footwork.

He could catch balls between his legs, with his glove behind him, and off to the side. And he got me doing it! He could have been the best catcher. He had the best hands I've ever seen."

The Dodgers lost 15 of 27 games heading into the All-Star break. With a record of 41–36, they dropped into fifth place, 5 games behind St. Louis. Hodges was hitting .309 at the break, but he had a power shortage because he was playing with bruised ribs, and had a modest 10 homers and 38 RBIs. He, Labine, and Cimoli played in the All-Star Game at Sportsman's Park in St. Louis. Trailing by 4 runs in the bottom of the ninth, the National League rallied for 3 runs to make the score 6–5. But pinch-hitting with the tying run on third base and two outs, Hodges lined Bob Grim's pitch to left fielder Minnie Minoso to end the game.

In late May, O'Malley had taken a helicopter tour escorted by Los Angeles County supervisor Kenneth Hahn of the 302-acre site in Chavez Ravine that would become home to the Dodgers if they relocated to L.A. It was another indication that he and Moses weren't going to come up with a solution to the stadium crisis. Attendance at Ebbets Field dwindled as the Dodgers began the second half of the season, despite there being three big series in a row against other contenders, the Reds, Braves, and Cardinals.

The opener against Cincinnati was marred by what Vin Scully called the best baseball brawl he had ever seen. It began when rookie reliever Raul Sanchez threw a purpose pitch at Gilliam, who retaliated by flattening Sanchez when he tried to field his bunt. For fifteen minutes there were skirmishes between the two teams, including Charlie Neal nailing Redlegs third baseman Don Hoak with a hard right to the head. Finally, players were ejected, lineups were adjusted—Hodges moved to second base for the only time in his career—and order was restored. But suddenly Hoak charged into the Dodger dugout trying to get to Neal. "Hodges got up," wrote Arnold Hano, "and let Hoak run square into him, and then wrapped his arms around the third baseman, holding him in an iron embrace until he cooled off."

The Dodgers came away with a 5–4 victory, as Snider hit 2 2-run homers and Hodges chipped in with an RBI single. They also won the next game 3–1 on Cimoli's 2-run eighth-inning triple, as Newcombe tossed a 5-hitter.

Next were two games against the Braves. Maglie went against Buhl in the first game. With the Dodgers down 2–1, Cimoli walked to lead off the bottom of the ninth inning. With the Braves expecting a bunt, Hodges sent Buhl's first pitch into the left-center-field seats, between the bright red Flying A Gasoline and blue-and-orange Brooklyn Union Gas Company signs. "Not often has a more full-throated roar greeted a game-winning blow than that which swelled from the throats of the 20,871 cash customers," wrote Roscoe McGowen in the *New York Times*. "There were no defections among the Dodgers. Every one of them raced from the dugout to greet the smiling Hodges."

The Dodgers won the next game as well, clobbering the Braves 20–4. Hodges drove in a couple of runs, but didn't hit any of the team's 6 home runs. He did slam his 12th homer in the next game, a 7–5 victory over the Cardinals. Erskine got the win that pulled the Dodgers to within half a game of the Cardinals, Braves, and Phillies, who were in a virtual tie for first.

The Dodgers' winning streak ended the next day, when, in a matchup of baseball's two best black pitchers, Sam Jones bested Newcombe 7–3. In the rubber game, the Cardinals scored 7 runs in the ninth inning—including 4 unearned runs due to a rare Hodges error—to take a seemingly insurmountable 9–4 lead. But the Dodgers scored a run and Hodges came up against Vinegar Bend Mizell with the bases loaded. He got hold of a 1–1 pitch and drove it toward the stands in left center. The crowd went wild, because Hodges had tied the game 9–9 with his 12th career grand slam, matching the National League record of Ralph Kiner and Rogers Hornsby. Craig pitched 2 scoreless innings, and the Dodgers scored an unearned run in the eleventh to escape with a tremendous 10–9 victory.

"I was just trying to hit the ball deep and keep the rally going," Hodges told reporters after the game. "Mizell is too fast to pull with confidence. But darned if the darn thing didn't go into the stands. Some days a fellow doesn't know his own strength. I'll try to remember that one. I am not being coy, but I honestly don't remember the details of any grand slam I ever hit before, so this had to be the most important I ever hit."

Hodges' parents and siblings, Bob and Marjorie, witnessed his record-tying grand slam, because they had come to town a day early in anticipation of "Gil Hodges Night," when there would be a celebration between games of a Friday doubleheader with the Cubs. The event was the brainchild of Jo Ann Duffy, a fifteen-year-old schoolgirl from Hewlett, Long Island, who was president of the Gil Hodges Fan Club. She wrote letters to merchants throughout Brooklyn asking for support, and among the donations were eighty-five billboards in the borough advertising the special night.

The Dodgers and Cubs went into extra innings in the first game of the twin bill with the score deadlocked at 2–2. Lee Walls homered off Labine to give the Cubs a 3–2 lead going into the bottom of the tenth. Snider homered to tie the game. Then Hodges beat out a grounder to third and scored the winning run when rookie catcher Johnny Roseboro slammed a 3-run homer over the scoreboard off Turk Lown, Hodges' teammate at Newport News in 1946.

Then the happy fans watched Hodges be honored in a forty-five-minute ceremony. They were reminded that he hit 4 home runs in one game, drove in 100 runs in seven consecutive seasons, and led all Dodgers with 999 RBIs and 164 homers at Ebbets Field. He was showered with gifts, including a Dodge convertible, a silver serving tray that was engraved with his teammates' signatures, a trip for two to Hawaii, a set of golf clubs, and a year's supply of dill pickles. Among the telegrams he received was one from President Eisenhower: "As a distinguished player and outstanding gentleman, Gil Hodges makes a splendid contribution to the game. His quality of sportsmanship is an example to the youth of the land." Another from retired Admiral "Bull" Halsey referred to Hodges as "a member of my team in the South Pacific."

In his speech, the nervous Hodges said, "To all you friends, all I can say is I thank you from the bottom of my heart for making this wonderful evening for me and my family. May God bless you."

Charlie Hodges threw out the ceremonial first pitch of the second game to Gil. It went across the middle of the plate letter high, earning a hug from his son. Then in the first inning, against Tom Poholsky, Hodges lined a 1–0 pitch into left center field for a single that drove in Gilliam for the first run of the game. That was the 1,000th run batted in by Hodges, and when that fact was announced to the 28,724 fans, the cheering was even greater than during the between-games ceremonies.

The Dodgers prevailed 5–3, as Maglie pitched 6 strong innings and

Roebuck shut out the Cubs for the final three frames. It was the Dodgers' first doubleheader sweep of the year, and they were only 1 game out of first place, so the home folks went home happy despite its being 12:15 a.m. No game at Ebbets Field for the rest of the season would attract more fans.

Returning home after his time in New York, Charlie Hodges told the *Petersburg Press* that his visit had been "fabulous." He shook his head when talking about his son, saying, "I don't know how Gil stands the pressure. One week almost killed me and I was just standing around watching."

On August 1, Sandy Koufax gave up only 4 hits and struck out 11 as the Dodgers defeated Chicago 12–3. He got much support from Hodges, who drove in 5 runs. Four came on Hodges' 13th career grand slam, making him the first National Leaguer to accomplish this feat. "Not until I saw where the ball was hit while rounding first did I think of the record, believe me," Hodges told reporters. The victim of the fifth-inning blast was Dick Littlefield, who came to St. Louis after the Giants failed to trade him to Brooklyn for Jackie Robinson. The ball was caught by Robert Chilla, a twenty-eight-year-old North Side resident. He returned it to Hodges and received an autographed ball and a box seat for the final four innings.

The Dodgers were edged the next day by Milwaukee 1–0, and fell 3 games behind. They'd split the other two games of a three-game series that would draw 128,317 fans to County Stadium. The Dodgers returned to Ebbets Field, where they attracted only 77,938 fans for a four-game series with their archrival Giants. While Brooklyn fans were having sleepless nights waiting to find out whether the Dodgers were leaving or staying, Giants fans were going through the same misery. Horace Stoneham had initially hinted that he'd move his team to Minneapolis, but it was no secret that O'Malley had convinced him that there was more revenue in San Francisco, including from closed-circuit television.

On August 19, Giants fans received a deadly blow when the board of directors of the National Exhibition Company, the corporation operating the New York Giants, voted 8–1 to approve a move to San Francisco for the 1958 season. National League president Warren Giles had told O'Malley to get Stoneham on board, because there needed to be two teams going to California for major-league baseball to approve the franchise shifts. Once the Giants announced they were moving west, Brooklyn fans knew for certain that their beloved Dodgers would go too.

After the Giants series, the Dodgers were 5 games behind the Braves, and they wouldn't get any closer in the final two months. On September 1, realizing they were out of contention, they waived Maglie (6–6), allowing him to go to the Yankees for their pennant drive.

Only 38,000 fans showed up for a three-game series, August 30–September 1, the last time the New York Giants would ever play at Ebbets Field. A measly 7,936 saw the final game, won by the Giants 7–5. Hodges had an RBI single and scored as the Dodgers crossed the plate 3 times in the bottom of the ninth inning, but fell short.

Because O'Malley hadn't yet confirmed his team was leaving, there were no farewell festivities, and Dodger fans were left in limbo. Stoneham allowed closure for Giants fans, and more than 88,000 showed up at the Polo Grounds September 6–8, knowing it would be the final series between the two longtime rivals in New York. Podres pitched a shutout in the first game, 3–0. In relief of Danny McDevitt, Craig was the victor in the second game, 5–4. The Giants took the finale 3–2, as Curt Barclay outdueled Drysdale.

Hodges hit his 298th and final home run as a Brooklyn Dodger on September 20 against the Phillies' Warren Hacker. It was his 172nd homer at Ebbets Field. It gave the Dodgers a 2–1 lead, but they lost 3–2 when Erskine yielded 2 runs in the top of the ninth.

Drysdale won his last 3 starts to finish with a team-high 17 wins. His last victory was on September 22, 7–5 over the Phillies, as Robin Roberts lost his 22nd game. Snider hit his 39th and 40th homers to reach the 40-homer mark for the fifth consecutive year, tying a National League record. Hodges drove in a run, but more noteworthy was that he played third base for the first time since 1943 and played it for the entire game. Employing his one hundredth lineup of the season, Alston wanted to give Jim Gentile, who had been stuck in the minors for years because of Hodges, a chance to play first base, and he responded with a home run.

There were only 6,702 fans scattered around the stands at Ebbets Field for the last game ever played there on September 24, 1957. Fans chanted,

"Please don't go!" but it wasn't up to the sympathetic players. Hodges started at third base but moved to first in the fifth inning, and Reese came in to play third. Campanella came out of the game.

"Campanella started and I caught the last 5 innings," recalls Pignatano. "I was the last catcher at Ebbets Field. My roommate, Danny McDevitt, was often wild and threw pitches behind batters, but that night he pitched a hell of a game and we won 2–0. Young fans in the stands were crying because they didn't want us to go. I remember Gladys Gooding playing 'Auld Lang Syne.'" Hodges went 1-for-4 and his single in the third inning off Bucs' starter Bennie Daniels drove in Gino Cimoli from second base for the final run ever at Ebbets Field.

The Brooklyn Dodgers still had three more games to play in Philadelphia before their history concluded. They lost 3–2, then won for their final time in the second game, 8–4, as Ed Roebuck got the victory in relief of Rene Valdes. The Dodgers' big blow was a 3-run homer off Don Cardwell by Randy Jackson, who had missed most of the season with injuries.

The final game of the season and in the history of the Brooklyn Dodgers was played on Sunday, September 29. "Nobody remembers I started the last game for the Brooklyn Dodgers," says Craig. "It was cold and rainy and I hurt my arm. Nobody knew about rotator cuffs back then, but I knew it was that. I had to learn how to pitch all over again." Craig was protecting a 1–0 lead when Phillies first baseman Ed Bouchee hit a 2-run homer off him. In the eighth inning, Craig, who had given up only 4 hits, was pinch-hit for by Campanella. In what would turn out to be, tragically, the great catcher's final major-league appearance, the three-time NL MVP flied out to center field. The last Brooklyn Dodgers pitcher was Sandy Koufax, who tossed a scoreless eighth inning in the Dodgers' 2–1 loss. Their only run came in the first inning. Cimoli reached third base and Hodges drove in the final Brooklyn run in history with a sacrifice fly.

The Brooklyn Dodgers' record in their final season was 84–70, eleven games out of first place. Milwaukee finished 95–89 for manager Fred Haney and went on to beat the Yankees in seven games in the World Series, as Lew Burdette threw 3 complete-game victories.

The Dodgers' disappointing season was the result of ineffective pitching and weak hitting, a deadly combination. Hodges put up very good num-

The 1919 tombstone of Gil's grandparents in the Oak Hill Cemetery in Patoka, Indiana, provides proof that the family name was always Hodges, never Hodge, as many people in Indiana still believe.

Gil's mother, Irene (*third from right*), was a key player on Winslow High School's girls basketball team in 1921. Her family name was Horstmeyer, but she was listed as Hostmeyer in all her yearbooks.

Right: Gil's father, Charlie Hodges (*seated in front of the three miners on the coal cart*), was part of a crew that was photographed by the *Princeton Clarion* after it survived an accident at the Princeton Mine in 1922.

Left: Brothers Bob (*left*) and the one-year-younger Gil looked almost like twins when they were in elementary school.

Petersburg's Main Street circa 1931, when the Hodges moved to town. Today a huge mural of Hodges is at this intersection.

Above: The Hodges family's second house in Petersburg still stands on Main Street. Every day from spring to fall, Charlie played catch with his sons in the side yard.

Gil (*front row, second from right*) and Bob (*front row, first from left*) were the happiest members of Petersburg Central High's freshmen basketball team.

Gil proudly displays his huge hands while posing with Petersburg Central High's six-man football team.

Hodges (*middle of top row*) was discovered by Dodgers scout Stan Feezle while playing for Allison in the highly competitive Indianapolis Amateur League in the summer of 1943.

Right: Hodges' baseball career was put on hold during World War II when he enlisted in the Marines.

Far Right: Hodges was a catcher with unlimited potential at Newport News in 1946 and with Brooklyn from 1947 to mid-1948, when he was shifted to first base to make room for Roy Campanella.

Hodges with outfielder Gene Hermanski, Dodgers owner Branch Rickey, and baseball's first black player, Jackie Robinson, 1949's NL MVP.

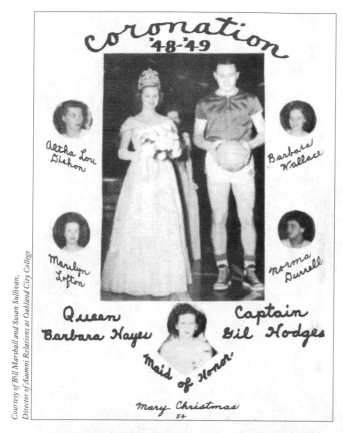

Left: Although Hodges was a professional baseball player, he still played amateur basketball in 1948 and 1949 while attending Oakland City College. As captain of the Oaks, he posed for the 1949 yearbook with the "basketball queen," Babs Hayes, at homecoming.

Below: Gil Hodges and Joan Lombardi wed at St. Gregory's Church in Brooklyn on December 26, 1948.

Baseball's strongest man and new Dodgers manager Charlie Dressen (*left*) work out with dumbbells at the Crescent Health Club in Brooklyn, after Hodges signed a new contract in February 1951.

Gil, Joan, and one-year-old Gil Jr. celebrate the birth of Irene in 1951, with Gil's parents, Charlie and Irene, and sister, Marjorie.

(*Left to right*) Bob Elliott, Hodges, Ralph Kiner, and Stan Musial celebrate clouting home runs in the National League's 8-3 victory in the 1951 All-Star Game in Detroit.

From 1949 to 1956, photographers in Brooklyn often asked the five All-Stars of the Dodgers' formidable offense to pose together. (*Left to right*) Duke Snider, Jackie Robinson, Roy Campanella, Pee Wee Reese, and Gil Hodges were considered equals at the time, yet all but Hodges would be voted into the Hall of Fame.

Hodges tags out Phil Rizzuto on a bunt play in the first inning of Game 7 of the 1952 World Series, in which the Yankees would defeat the Dodgers 4-2.

Hodges surely would have won numerous Gold Gloves before he captured the first three ever given to first basemen from 1957 to 1959, because he not only had sure hands, quickness, and remarkable anticipation, but also exceptional range.

New Dodgers manager Walter Alston (*center*) presents his Opening Day lineup in 1954: (*left to right*) Jim Gilliam, Pee Wee Reese, Duke Snider, Jackie Robinson, Roy Campanella, Gil Hodges, Carl Furillo, Billy Cox, and Carl Erskine.

(*Left to right*) Duke Snider, NL president Warren Giles, Dodgers owner Walter O'Malley, Game 7 victor Johnny Podres, and Hodges celebrate the Brooklyn Dodgers' only world championship in 1955.

Above: Pee Wee Reese (*left*) and Carl Erskine help honor Hodges on "Gil Hodges Night," one of the few cheerful days at Ebbets Field in 1957.

Left: Hodges smashes an eighth inning home run off the White Sox's Gerry Staley at the Coliseum to give the Los Angeles Dodgers a 5-4 victory and a commanding three-games-to-one lead in the 1959 World Series.

Courtesy of Gil Hodges Jr.

Hodges, Gil Jr., and Irene ride on a float with manager Casey Stengel in the "Meet the Mets" parade in New York City prior to the new National League team's inaugural 1962 season.

National Baseball Hall of Fame Library, Cooperstown, NY

Longtime Brooklyn Dodgers teammates Gil Hodges and Duke Snider were reunited briefly on the 1963 New York Mets.

Courtesy of Gil Hodges Jr.

Left: Hodges ended his playing career during the 1963 season to become the expansion Washington Senators' second manager.

Below: Senators manager Hodges and Yankees manager Yogi Berra pose with former president Dwight D. Eisenhower at Griffith Stadium in 1964.

National Baseball Hall of Fame Library, Cooperstown, NY

Above: Throughout his career, Hodges worked closely with many charities, particularly those that aided children in need. Since his death, Joan Hodges and Gil Hodges Jr. have continued his work through a foundation.

Left: Gil gives Barbara a push as (*left to right*) Cindy, Irene, Gil Jr., and Joan join in, circa 1967.

New manager Gil Hodges and his players Ed Charles (*next to Hodges*), Al Jackson, Ron Swoboda, Bud Harrelson, and the barely seen Ron Taylor stand outside "The Mets Hot Stove League Express" at Jamaica Station in Queens on a publicity tour prior to the 1968 season.

All Photos This Page Courtesy of Gil Hodges Jr.

Hodges proudly shows a cameraman his two young pitching stars, right-hander Tom Seaver and left-hander Jerry Koosman.

During his years as a manager, Gil spoke frequently by phone to his older brother, Bob, in Indiana about baseball strategy. Best friends since they were young boys, they cherished the times they were able to see each other.

In 1997, Gil Hodges Jr. traveled to Petersburg for the unveiling of a bust of his father, an event that was hosted by the mayor, Randy Harris.

One of the most feared batters of his time, Gil Hodges drove in a hundred runs in seven consecutive seasons and slugged 370 home runs to set an all-time National League record for right-handed hitters.

bers, .299, 27 homers, and 98 RBIs, but if he were the type to make goals he would have thought them just short in all three categories. He finished first on the Dodgers in RBIs, second in homers to Snider's 40, and second in average to Furillo's .306.

For the first time Hodges' fielding prowess was officially recognized. Back in January *Look* magazine contained an article with elegant photographs titled, "Gil Hodges: Ballet at First Base." Also, after nine seasons of performing magic at his position, Hodges was the recipient of the first Rawlings Gold Glove Award ever given to a first baseman, beating out the Kansas City Athletics' fancy-fielding Vic Power. Willie Mays and Roy McMillan were the only other National Leaguers to win the award.

On October 8, at the Waldorf Astoria Hotel, publicity representatives of the Dodgers and National League announced that the Dodgers had accepted Los Angeles' bid to move the team there. The second shoe had dropped. In Brooklyn there was a collective moan, with many residents instantly ceasing to be baseball fans.

The Dodgers players were divided on whether they desired to stay in Brooklyn or move to Los Angeles, where some were from. "Gil and I were from Brooklyn, so we didn't want to move," says Pignatano. "Neither did Labine, Campanella, Reese, or Erskine. Duke and Drysdale were from California, so they were mixed, as was Koufax, who was from Brooklyn but had family out there, too. The fans sure didn't want us to go and were in shock. Well, they could thank Robert Moses for that. It wasn't O'Malley. He wanted to build the new baseball stadium where the Fort Greene Meat Market was, and Moses told him that he was crazy and they couldn't get rid of the meat market. Well, two years later, the meat market business left there anyway. All the players knew it was Moses' fault from the beginning."

"When it happened I thought it was entirely O'Malley's fault that the Dodgers left for Los Angeles," says Robert A. Caro. "It was startling when I learned later that O'Malley would have kept the Dodgers in Brooklyn if he could. He even offered to pay for a new stadium. All he needed was the city to use the power of eminent domain, because there were some small-property owners who were resistant to moving. If Moses had done that, the Dodgers would have stayed."

Time has healed some wounds and clouded some memories, and

O'Malley's reputation has improved from the days angry fans in Brooklyn compared him to Hitler and Stalin. But there are still many who believe O'Malley always intended to move, particularly because he saw a gold mine in pay television, and that his negotiations with Moses were a charade. They contend that he didn't consider refurbishing Ebbets Field because he feared it would be located in the middle of an increasingly black and Latino section of Brooklyn. They point out that he was willing to lease Ebbets Field from real estate developer Marvin Kratter after selling it to him in October 1956, but never considered striking a deal in which the city would build and own a new stadium in Brooklyn that he would lease. Instead he insisted that he be given land for a private stadium; and though he claimed he had the money to build it, others estimated that the type of stadium he proposed would cost five times what he stated and the city would be forced to help out. O'Malley was boxed in by Moses, as his defenders attest, but was that exactly the position he wanted to be in to justify leaving Brooklyn? And was his not admitting that he was planning on moving, even after Stoneham did, his way of ensuring he'd get a better deal in Los Angeles?

"Somehow, the Dodgers managed to put the propaganda out, which succeeded, that it was all Moses' fault the team was leaving Brooklyn," says Dave Anderson. "But anybody who was around the team from '54 on—and I was around as a kid with the *Eagle* and I was still covering them occasionally for the *Journal American*—knew that they'd go to L.A. one way or another. Sure, O'Malley offered to build a domed stadium for six million dollars in downtown Brooklyn. But I can't believe he really thought it was going to happen. He was just making sure that Moses wouldn't give him anything. Moses did offer to lease him land in Queens where Shea Stadium was built, and he said, 'Oh, I couldn't take the Brooklyn Dodgers to Queens.' So instead he took them to L.A.!"

"In 1957, after O'Malley decided to uproot the team, Branch Rickey stated he never would have entertained such thoughts," claims Lee Lowenfish, the author of *Branch Rickey: Baseball's Ferocious Gentleman*. "And neither would have the late John L. Smith, who lived near Ebbets Field and was a pillar of Brooklyn society."

The Brooklyn Dodgers from 1947 to 1957 were the most beloved baseball team ever assembled. In hindsight, one could say that so many things were changing on the team personnel-wise that the final day of the 1957 season was the appropriate time for the story of the postwar Brooklyn Dodgers to end. "There never was an appropriate time," counters Larry King. "Baseball should have expanded to California, but with different teams going there. The story of the Brooklyn Dodgers should never have ended."

CHAPTER EIGHTEEN

Hodges was affected by the Dodgers move from Brooklyn to Los Angeles more than any other player, yet he never reflected on or contributed to the controversy surrounding it. "He respected Walter O'Malley a great deal," according to Hodges Jr., and took the news like a loyal employee and dutiful soldier. "I was sorry to see the team move," he said three years later. "Very sorry. But no more than that. No, I wasn't burned up. I'm employed by this team. If they say we'll play from now on in Hong Kong, and if they feel they need or want my services, I'll do everything I can to move with them to Hong Kong."

Hodges' main concern that fall was the health of his father. Charlie and three Ditney Hill crew members had gone into the mine to repair damage caused by falling rocks when they were caught in another rock slide. The *Princeton Clarion-Democrat* reported on October 3: "Emmet Elvis Williams, 34, Oakland City, was hit in the head by a large rock and killed. Charles Hodges, 57, Petersburg, the baseball star's father, was hospitalized in Vincennes in 'good' condition. He sustained a possible head injury according to hospital reports."

The head injury proved to be insignificant, but Charlie, who kept working at the mine long after his wife and sons urged him to retire, broke his right foot and twisted a knee when the slate fell. On October 17, he was released from the Good Samaritan Hospital, and Irene Hodges informed the local papers that he was "improving nicely." She also said that both she and her husband had spoken to Gil several times since the accident. Bob also was updating him on their father's progress.

Hodges spent time "lollying around the house, enjoying the luxury of being with Joan and our three kids, even enjoying taking Gil Jr. and Irene to school every morning," he wrote in *Guideposts* in 1960. "Every weekend I planned to go out to see my mother and father, and I kept putting it off. . . . I telephoned, of course, but it wasn't the same as being there with him."

Charlie's recovery was going fine, except his knee was bothering him. He was reluctant to have the minor surgery his doctor recommended, but Gil talked him into it. "You're already laid up and can't work," he told him. "It's probably like a trick knee some ballplayers get. After a quick operation it clears up right away. Why don't you get it over with?"

It was advice that he would regret giving. The surgery seemed to go well, and Charlie returned home to recuperate, but a blood clot formed in his leg. On Friday night, November 22, the most important man in Gil and Bob Hodges' lives keeled over in his living room from a heart seizure and died instantly.

"I remember Dad getting that call, then hanging up the phone and packing," says Hodges Jr. "It was the first time I'd seen him cry, though I'm sure he did it when his kids weren't around. As he hurried to leave, my mother was saying to him, 'What are you doing?' He said, 'I'm driving to Indiana.' She said, 'You're not thinking things through.' He said, 'This isn't a discussion. I'm driving to Indiana.' Retrospectively, I can say that driving was a great thing for him to do. When you lose someone close you need time to be alone, and he was able to get some peace of mind and clarity during his trip."

No one knows whether Hodges suffered from survivor's guilt after seeing his fellow soldiers die on Okinawa, but after the unexpected death of his father "he had tremendous guilt initially," says Hodges Jr. "To begin with, he had 'Catholic guilt,' so even if he hadn't suggested the surgery, he was going to blame himself for not having visited his father for a while. I'm not so sure one specific thing killed my grandfather. It might not have been the operation. The medicine back then might have affected him in a bad way instead of helping him. And the clot could have happened because of black lung from years of working in the coal mine."

"The doctors said it wouldn't have made any difference," conceded Hodges, "that the blood clot could have formed at any time, operation or no operation. But if I had gone home, I would at least have been there when it happened. Why wasn't I there? Why don't we give our parents everything we can while they're alive? Driving the final few miles home for the last good-bye, I made Dad a silent promise: 'We missed too many chances to be together and talk together. I'll not let any such golden moments escape me again with Mother, or with anyone or anything [I love]. It's the last lesson you taught me. I won't forget it, Dad.'"

His Petersburg friend Bob Harris took care of the funeral. Harris' wife of one year, Sondra, already knew Bob Hodges, because he'd drop in to chat with them, but this was the first time she met his younger brother. "Gil came into the funeral home," she remembers, "and I happened to be in the office upstairs. I had wanted to meet this famous man, but not under these circumstances. I expressed my condolences, and he said, 'It's nice to meet you, Sonny, and I want to congratulate you on the birth of Lisa.' I thought, 'Oh, my goodness, how does he know both of our names?' He won me over right away."

Hodges stayed in Petersburg after his father's funeral to be with his mother and visit with his brother, who would assume the burden of looking after Irene and their grandmother Ellen. Despite his grief, he also accepted an invitation to speak about being a major leaguer at the high school to the Hi-Y Club, comprised mostly of young Christian athletes. It went so well that he returned the next year.

The sudden loss of Hodges' father influenced his view of how fathers and their children should relate, and their responsibilities to one another. Determined to emulate his father, he, like his brother Bob, would teach his own children what he believed was the "right way" to lead their lives, incorporating his values into what they learned at church.

"Dad never used the expression, 'As long as you live under my roof, you do it my way,'" recalls Gil Jr. "There was no need for threats. We knew he was the judge and jury and was going to make the decisions. And once his decision was made, only the Lord could change it."

Another tragic accident during the off-season deeply affected Hodges, the entire organization, and all baseball fans. Early on the morning of Janu-

ary 28, while driving to his Glen Cove, Long Island, home, Roy Campanella lost control of his car on an icy road and hit a telephone pole. He
fractured two vertebrae in his neck and his spinal cord was compressed,
leaving him a quadriplegic and wheelchair-bound. (Although he was deprived of a couple more years of playing ball, he'd regain much use of his
hands and arms through therapy.)

Rube Walker, who had spoken to him a few hours before, recalled in
1994, "Roy Campanella's accident was one of those things you don't believe.
The loss of Campanella was a terrible psychological blow to the team. It was
eerie: Soon after, Jim Gilliam and then Duke Snider, Don Zimmer, and
Johnny Podres were in minor car accidents." (The worst off was Snider, who
reinjured a knee he'd been rehabilitating in the off-season.) Though Campanella would never play again, the Dodgers brought him to Vero Beach,
knowing his positive attitude—reflected in the title of his 1959 autobiography, *It's Good to Be Alive*—would inspire the team.

Spring training at Dodgertown in Vero Beach was the same as it had
been all through the years, except now there was an "L.A." rather than a "B"
on caps. There was a familiar face on the coaching staff, Charlie Dressen,
who had been unable to reverse the fortunes of the sorry Washington Senators in a little more than two years as their manager. Presumably, he accepted
a *one-year* contract from O'Malley.

The Los Angeles Dodgers took the field for the first time on March 8,
when they hosted an exhibition game with the Phillies at Miami Stadium.
They lost 7–4. Did their third-place finish in 1957 accurately reflect that
they were no longer serious contenders? Preseason prognosticators envi-
sioned even worse play ahead because of both aging and heroes missing from
the lineup. "Here are your Dodgers, Los Angeles," *Sports Illustrated* stated.
"Once they were magnificent, but now they are playing on memory."

Instead of heading north after the Grapefruit League season ended, the
Dodgers headed west to California. Hodges rented a house at 49 Senasac
Avenue in Long Beach, south of Los Angeles. Immediately it was apparent
that the new situation had problems. The house proved to be too small, and,
"We couldn't find a parochial school for the kids," Hodges told *Sport* two
years later. "Joan started to miss her family and friends. You can't just pick
up roots. It's not sensible."

"I'm the first to admit I didn't make it easy on my husband," Joan told Milton Gross. "For the first month in Los Angeles I cried every day about wanting to go home. It took me a while to realize I was hurting Gil, acting the way I was and carrying on."

"It was a terrible time for the Hodges," recalls Ed Roebuck. "They were unhappy, because they were such a part of Brooklyn."

"Gil probably felt stronger than anyone else about not wanting to leave Brooklyn," says Roger Craig. "But he knew it was a business."

Major League Baseball began on the West Coast on April 15 in San Francisco at the Giants' temporary home, Seals Stadium, where Pacific Coast League baseball had been played since 1931. For the first of six games scheduled between the two California teams to open the season—three in San Francisco and three in Los Angeles—a capacity crowd of 23,448 fans squeezed into the park to watch the historic game.

Bill Rigney's Opening Day pitcher was Ruben Gomez. Walter Alston gave the ball to Don Drysdale, who probably wished he had given it back after taking a shellacking. He lasted only 3⅔ innings. He received no support from the offense in the 8–0 defeat. Hodges went 0-for-4, a harbinger of a difficult season.

Second baseman Dick Gray, a heralded rookie who had a great start before faltering and returning to Triple A, stroked 2 of the team's 6 hits. The next game he'd get 3 more, including his first home run, and drive in 3 runs. Snider also homered; Gilliam, playing left and leading off, collected 2 hits and 2 RBIs; and tough John Roseboro, who would emerge as the starting catcher after Walker retired in midseason, smacked 3 hits in support of Podres' 5-hit, 11-strikeout performance. The Los Angeles Dodgers won for the first time, 13–1. Hodges went 1-for-3 and walked 3 times. The Giants won the rubber game 7–4, as Johnny Antonelli beat an ineffective Don Newcombe. Now the two teams, still rivals though 3,000 miles from New York, traveled to Los Angeles for another three-game series.

On April 18, there was a pregame parade to introduce the new team to the City of Angels. A caravan, with a waving Alston and Dressen in the lead car, rolled down Broadway in seedy downtown L.A. and made its way to the ballpark, where a record 78,672 fans were waiting. O'Malley had leased the

Los Angeles Memorial Coliseum, an enormous structure with over 100,000 seats that hosted the football games of the NFL's Rams and UCLA and USC. In three months a baseball field, with dugouts, press boxes, and 94,000 seats, was set up within the confines of the Coliseum. The home plate that was installed in a special ceremony with Cimoli, Hodges, Roebuck, and Gilliam was from Ebbets Field.

The Coliseum was perhaps the most oddly configured baseball stadium in the history of the major leagues. The majority of fans sat far from the field, and those in the most distant seats could have used telescopes. They brought transistor radios to listen to Vin Scully describe the action they couldn't see very well—and to learn baseball. Because of the angle, spectators on one side of the field had a hard time telling whether balls hit on the other side went a hundred feet foul or were home runs.

The stadium's most publicized feature was in left field. Because the fence was only 251 feet from home plate, a forty-foot-tall, 140-foot-wide screen was erected above it to prevent every fly ball hit to left by someone with Little League power from being a home run. The right-field pole was only 300 feet from home plate but jumped to 440 feet in right center, a different postal zone. Dead center was 425 feet away.

"Look where that right-field fence is, Duke," Willie Mays teased Snider before the game. "You're done, man!" Snider rarely had to face left-handed pitchers at Ebbets Field, because the Dodgers had so many right-handed power hitters in their lineup, but he was now getting his comeuppance in a park where left-handed hitters had little chance of reaching the seats. Playing in only 105 games because of his bad knee and a sore arm he got while foolishly trying to throw a ball out of the Coliseum, Snider—after five consecutive 40-homer seasons—would hit only 15 homers. Fewer than a dozen of the 193 home runs hit in the Coliseum in 1958 would be to right field.

The person who was supposed to benefit most from the odd dimensions of the ballpark was Hodges, a right-handed pull hitter. Reese told him that he might bat .400 with 61 home runs. Bavasi predicted that they'd soon have to dub the left-field wall "Hodges' Haven." Hodges had heard that even members of the press had hit balls over the screen. And when he did it several times with ease during that first batting practice while reporters clustered around, he admitted, "It made me almost ashamed, it was so easy. I had the feeling that all I had to do was hit the ball into the air." He told Dick Schaap of *Sport,* "Any time I hit the ball to the right side of second base, I should go home. This park is made for me." It turned out to not be made for anybody.

"It was weird, weird, weird playing in the Coliseum," says Randy Jackson. "It was such a big place. We may have had twice as many people as we had in Brooklyn, but we couldn't hear them. But it was nice that we were heroes to those fans, and it was fun looking in the stands for celebrities." Among those attending the first game were Groucho Marx, Burt Lancaster, Jimmy Stewart, Nat King Cole, Edward G. Robinson, Zsa Zsa Gabor, Gregory Peck, Brooklyn native Danny Kaye, and comedian Joe E. Brown, the latter of whom introduced the two managers to the crowd. The starting lineup that Alston handed to home-plate umpire Tony Venzon was: Jim Gilliam, LF; Pee Wee Reese, SS; Duke Snider, RF; Gil Hodges, 1B; Charlie Neal, 2B; Dick Gray, 3B; Gino Cimoli, CF; John Roseboro, C; Carl Erskine, P. Snider was playing a corner outfield spot because of his bum knee.

Erskine felt privileged to pitch the first game in Los Angeles, going against the Giants' Al Worthington. He didn't have his best stuff, but came away with a victory with Labine's help as the Dodgers won their first game in Los Angeles 6–5. Hodges was 0-for-4, striking out once looking and once swinging.

The Giants won the next game 11–4, but Hodges got 2 hits off Ruben Gomez, including his first homer as an L.A. Dodger. The Giants, who would beat the Dodgers 16 of 22 times in 1958, crushed them again in the finale 12–2, as Drysdale was hit hard for the second time. He had already made his feelings about the Coliseum known: "It's nothing but a sideshow. Who feels like playing baseball in this place?"

The Dodgers' record dropped to 2–4, but another number made everyone in the organization happy—167,509 fans had come to three weekend baseball games in a football city. In 1957, the Brooklyn Dodgers had attracted only 1,028,258 fans at home all year. More than 59,000 passed through the gates the next Friday to see the Dodgers play the world-champion Braves. Also encouraging was that 39,459 fans, which was more than capacity at Ebbets

Field, showed up for a Tuesday game against Chicago on April 22, and 24,368 more came on Wednesday.

"It was exciting that we drew large crowds to the Coliseum," said Ed Roebuck in 1994. "But what really surprised me is that there wasn't much media coverage when we got to Los Angeles. There wasn't much television, and reporters paid more attention to us back in Brooklyn."

Eighteen-year veteran Pee Wee Reese knew he wasn't in Brooklyn anymore when an L.A. photographer took pictures of him and then asked him to spell his name. More humbling was that on Opening Day, a security guard at the Coliseum didn't recognize him and refused to let him in because he didn't believe he was an athlete.

The game on the twenty-third against the Cubs was the 2,000th in his marvelous career. Reese, who was playing an extra year as a favor to O'Malley, hit his first homer as an L.A. Dodger against reliever Dick Drott to tie the score 4–4 in the seventh inning. Two batters later, Hodges smashed his second homer of the year and the 300th of his career. It would have been ideal if his monumental home run before the home crowd was a game winner, but not much went right for Hodges or the Dodgers in '58. In the ninth inning Erskine gave up a game-tying homer to Chuck Tanner, and Labine yielded a 2-run double to Bobby Thomson, who was still bringing misery to the franchise. The Dodgers lost 7–6.

The Dodgers continued to draw well at home and on the road, but their play was uninspired. After losing the first game of a doubleheader in St. Louis on May 18, the Dodgers were 10–21, 10 games out and in last place, which was unfamiliar to the old guard. Drysdale's record was 1–7, and Newcombe's 0–3.

Erskine gave the team a lift in the nightcap by throwing an 8-hit shutout, as Hodges slammed his fifth homer. It would be the final shutout of his outstanding career. He was even sharper in his next start, when he gave up only 2 hits while outdueling the Phillies' Robin Roberts 2–1. It would be his final complete game. Erskine's painful shoulder was no longer a secret, and he was enduring weekly cortisone injections to just hang on. He'd start only nine games all year. His fourth victory of the season on July 18 came in middle relief against the Phillies, in a game Hodges started in right field. It was Erskine's 122nd and final victory.

Eventually, Alston settled on a rotation of young pitchers: Podres, Drysdale, Koufax, and—because Craig was in St. Paul dealing with a stiff arm—rookie call-up Stan Williams. Newcombe was a casualty of the slow start: "It was more than upsetting to move to Los Angeles and not have Roy Campanella on the team. Over my entire career, he had been my steadying influence, the player I looked up to. In 1958, I started the season 0–6. My arm was bad. The doctors were shooting thirteen needles into my arm and it wasn't doing any good. So the Dodgers concluded my career was over, and despite my long history with the organization, traded me to Cincinnati."

For Newcombe, the Dodgers acquired Johnny Klippstein, who joined Labine in a bullpen depleted by injuries to Bessent and Roebuck. The veteran right-hander had no trouble fitting in with the Dodgers, but was surprised by how different the clubhouse was than in Brooklyn. "There wasn't much socializing on the team, considering that it was known for its unity," he said in *We Played the Game*. "Players didn't even hang around in the clubhouse after a game and talk baseball."

One reason was that the drive home took a long time. The players found it difficult getting used to how spread out Los Angeles was and that there was no sense of community. This disorientation certainly had an adverse effect on their play. "All the veteran Dodgers who had become so accustomed to Brooklyn were at sea in Southern California," remembered Drysdale, who was still Hodges' road roommate. Get-togethers between Dodgers couples for dinners or cards—the Hodges played bridge with Carl and Betty Erskine and Ed and Janice Roebuck, among others—were difficult to arrange because of the distances between their homes. It was also hard for Hodges and the other Brooklyn players to understand why the population was so detached from the team. Hodges was surprised that when he offered tickets to a local priest, he was rebuffed because the priest went only to football games. "Could you imagine a priest in Brooklyn turning down two tickets to a Dodger game?" asked the astonished Hodges.

Hodges was able to give tickets to one new friend, his mailman Herman Alevy, whose family attended twenty-seven games that year, sitting with the other players' families. "Gil never had an unkind word for anybody," Alevy told the *Long Beach Press-Telegram* in 1999. "When he moved here, he worried if the fans would like him. He wanted to be liked. He wanted to be accepted."

Hodges wanted to be liked and for the Dodgers to become part of its new city, and he believed that could happen only if he hit well and the Dodgers won games. Because Snider wasn't producing in the Coliseum and Campanella was inactive, he felt added pressure to hit home runs and take charge of the offense. The front office had said victories were needed to inspire people to vote yes in an upcoming referendum for the Dodgers to be allowed to build a private stadium in Chavez Ravine. "It wasn't the sort of the thing you discuss in the dugout," Hodges told Dick Schaap, "but naturally everyone was concerned with the referendum."

Celebrity baseball fans, including Jerry Lewis, Jeff Chandler, and Jack Benny, held an eight-hour telethon to persuade citizens to give up public land for O'Malley's private enterprise. On June 3, the referendum barely passed, 350,000 to 325,000.

Hodges was composed, as he knew a leader needed to be, but he was keeping a lot inside, and it was a very troublesome time for him. Adding to the pressures he felt trying to win over the fans was that he discovered that hitting balls over the left-field screen was difficult for a line-drive hitter. He also had incessant worry about Joan's unhappiness being away from Brooklyn. He was dealing with a bad back and, according to Milton Gross, hemorrhoids. So there were numerous explanations for why Hodges was having his worst season since 1948.

Hodges tinkered with his swing to loft balls over the high screen at the Coliseum, which increased his strikeouts and did havoc on his level swing in other ballparks. "I didn't have sense enough to go with the pitch," he told Gross in *Baseball Digest* after the season. "After a while the pitchers were hitting me on the fists with the ball. I couldn't even hit an inside pitch there. I just wasn't smart enough to combat and conquer it."

"Hodges had a bad batting habit of turning his head when he's swinging at the ball," wrote Gross. "Before he knew it, he had stopped watching the pitcher. He was concentrating on the fence. Things became so much worse when the fans began to get on Gil. In a sense he became the scapegoat for all their frustrations that the Dodgers were not the pennant-contending team they had been advertised as being."

Hodges did have some big moments, though usually on the road. On June 24, in the first game of a doubleheader against the Redlegs, he broke a 10–10 tie in the tenth inning with a 2-run homer off new Redlegs' pitcher Don Newcombe. In the nightcap, Hodges hit his 12th homer off Bob Purkey in the fifth inning, but a bigger blow was a 2-run double as the Dodgers rallied for 5 runs in the eleventh inning to win 7–2.

On July 26, Hodges drove in 5 runs on 4 hits, including his 14th homer, as Koufax, who'd go 11–11 despite wildness, went the distance to beat the Phillies 10–4. On August 23, against Milwaukee left-hander Juan Pizarro, Hodges slammed his 14th grand slam, adding on to his National League record. It was the first grand slam by a Los Angeles Dodger, and it came in the Coliseum so the home fans there could appreciate it. In the 10–1 victory, Drysdale hit 2 homers off Pizarro to tie Newcombe's record of 7 homers in a season by a pitcher. He, too, drove in 4 runs.

The Dodgers were playing their best ball of the season, having won 9 out of 11. Although they were 11½ games out of first place, they had pulled to within three games of .500, at 59–62, and were in fourth place. There was reason to hope that they could move up in the standings and finish well over .500. Instead they went 12–21 the rest of the way. Jackson, who was sold to Cleveland on August 4, recalls of the 1958 L.A. Dodgers: "Winning's a contagious thing, but losing is, too. If you don't have a winning attitude, you're probably not going to win, and we didn't. We were still a close team, but everything went bad."

Probably the highlight of the summer for some Dodgers was to make a cameo appearance in a scene with a sumo wrestler in Jerry Lewis' movie *The Geisha Boy*. "I was the Dodgers player representative," says Erskine, "and had Jerry pay everyone on the roster three hundred dollars and then choose the nine players he wanted." The players who appeared in the movie along with Alston and Dressen were Erskine, Hodges, Snider, Furillo, Reese, Roseboro, Neal, Gilliam, and Cimoli.

As it became clear that the Dodgers weren't a contender, Alston started giving more playing time to his younger position players. In the 152nd

game, he started seven rookies with second baseman Charlie Neal: Roseboro behind the plate, Jim Gentile at first, Bob Lillis at shortstop, Earl
Robinson at third base, Don Demeter in right field, Ron Fairly in center,
and Frank Howard in left. They came up with a 6–3 victory for twenty-
two-year-old Drysdale, whose 12th win placed him second on the team to
Podres' 13 in 1958.

Hodges made a big impression on the young players. "Gil was always
considered one of the great stars of the game, and he was one of my idols,"
recalls Stan Williams, whose record was 9–7 as a rookie. "He was easy to
like—an extremely strong, quiet guy with a pleasant smile. I'd have guessed
he was six-four like me, not six-one. He definitely was one of the best defensive players I've ever seen. Instead of grabbing at the ball, he scooped
everything toward his body. He had great hands and could stretch all the
way out and get it."

One of Hodges' ploys as a first baseman was to stretch as if he were
receiving a throw when actually the ball was rolling around in the outfield
and was a sure double if the batter raced around first. If the batter lost sight
of the ball and saw Hodges stretching he would slow down as he rounded
first and would then be thrown out if he continued to run to second. "Hodges
did that to me," recalls Chuck Essegian, who was a rookie with the Phillies
in 1958. "But after I rounded first base I stayed put. He smiled and said,
'You're too smart for me.' I said, 'You could have got me if I kept going,
'cause you made me stop for a second.' He told me, 'I get a lot of young guys
like that.'"

Frank Howard was a six-foot, seven-inch former basketball player from
Ohio, who could have snapped all his new teammates in two but was meek
and mild and just grateful that they noticed him. He recalls, "When I first
came up, I was a better basketball player, but I loved baseball, and guys like
Duke, Pee Wee, Furillo, and Hodges were there to teach me. Gil especially
went out of his way to teach a young, dumb ballplayer how to act on and off
the field in a very big-league, professional way. He was a great mentor, a
great help to a young guy who was trying to learn. He had tremendous
baseball instincts. One time I said to Pee Wee Reese, 'Tell me about Gil
Hodges.' He said, 'Frank, give Gil two weeks and he could play any position

on this ball club.' In other words, he could take anyone's position away from them in two weeks. I said, 'Does that include you at shortstop?' He replied, 'Yes.' That's how gifted he was."

Even near the end of a disappointing season, the Dodgers hadn't lost their senses of humor. Howard reluctantly played the central role in a prank on Reese. When Howard made his debut at Wrigley Field, he got a charley horse and had to come out of the game early. Reese and Hodges got on him: "This is your first time in the big leagues and you only stayed out there four innings? We don't do that in the big leagues." When Pee Wee left the dugout to bat, Hodges went over to Howard and said, "Look, we've been putting you on. When Pee Wee comes in the next inning I want you to pick him up and put him against the wall and tell him, 'If you ever open your mouth to me again, I'll put you right through that wall.'"

"It took Gil a while to get Frank to do it, because he didn't want to do it to Pee Wee," recalls Pignatano. "But he picked him up and started shaking him. Pee Wee's eyes got so big! Then he looked over Frank's shoulder and saw Gil rolling on the ground laughing, and yelled at him, 'You put him up to this, you big bastard!'"

The season mercifully came to an end, and, fittingly, a last-game loss dropped the Dodgers into seventh place, only 2 games ahead of the Phillies in the cellar. Their record of 71–83 was by far the worst by any Dodgers team Hodges had been on. They finished 21½ games behind the Braves. According to Buzzie Bavasi, O'Malley wanted to fire Alston after his second bad season. But it would have been a public relations disaster in his new town, and besides, he was in a good mood because the Dodgers had attracted 1,845,556 fans. He imagined how high it could go if the Dodgers had a *good* '59 season.

Furillo (18 homers, a team-high .290 average and 83 RBIs), Zimmer (17 homers, 60 RBIs), and Neal (22 homers and 87 runs) were arguably the only Dodgers with over 400 at-bats to hit well in 1958, although even their stats were modest. Hodges tied for the team lead with 22 home runs, his tenth consecutive year with more than 20. But it was his lowest total since he hit 11 homers in 1948, and his 64 RBIs were even lower than his total that year. His streak of 20 doubles in nine straight years was snapped. His .259 average was the third-lowest of his career and his worst since hitting .254 in 1952. A major consolation was that he won his second Gold Glove.

The move from Brooklyn to Los Angeles had, Hodges admitted, "affected us all psychologically." They never recovered and by the end were just playing out the string, mentally and physically. "It wasn't a very good feeling," he told Schaap. "We had been used to winning. Seventh place felt funny. We just wanted to get the season over and forget about it."

CHAPTER NINETEEN

A major reason Hodges had hitting troubles in 1958 was that while he waited for inside fastballs to drive, he again refused to believe that the curves he was taking on the outside corner were strikes. That inflexibility was part of his makeup on and off the field. "If Gil said that a fork was made of steel, and I thought it was silver, when the hour passed, I said it was steel," Joan Hodges says. "He didn't convince me; I just gave in because Gil would never change his mind. Gil could be so stubborn."

Hodges' obstinacy led to a *Tin Cup* episode while playing golf during spring training with Louis Lombardi, Joe Pignatano, and his friend Frank Slocum, with whom he'd write *The Game of Baseball*. "We were playing a water hole and everybody but Gil played an approach shot to the side of the water," recalls Lombardi. "Gil was determined to hit it *over* the water. He hit one ball into the water, two balls into the water, three balls into the water. He ran out of balls, so Pignatano and Slocom threw him a few more. Gil knew he could do it and wasn't going to stop, so he kept hitting balls until he finally cleared the water."

Hodges was one of only four Brooklyn Dodgers from the late forties on the active roster at Vero Beach, along with Furillo, Snider, and Erskine, and the last member of their great infield. As expected, Pee Wee Reese, the onetime marbles king who was discovered playing baseball in a church league, hung up his spikes at the age of forty and was now a Dodgers coach. O'Malley always wanted Alston to know there were coaches around him who were qualified to replace him.

The players' conversion to being L.A. Dodgers was complete, and unlike in 1958, it was no longer strange to head to California after the exhibition season. Gil and Joan had made a huge decision regarding their living situation. He went alone to Los Angeles and stayed at the Mayfair Hotel on Seventh Street in downtown L.A. Joan and the three children returned to Brooklyn. They would wait until school let out in June to join Hodges in Los Angeles, and then stay only until school resumed after Labor Day. Meanwhile, Joan could visit California on her own, because the kids had a governess, Betty Sample, a registered nurse who was hired when Cindy was born. Miss Sample, as she was called, lived in Bay Ridge and was with the Hodges family for fifteen years.

"I think it took a lot of pressure off Dad to have us stay in Brooklyn," says Hodges Jr. "Now we had a stable life and he could focus on baseball."

As bad as the Dodgers were in 1958, many pundits believed they might be worse in 1959 because the veterans were supposedly finished and the youngsters weren't ready yet. Dick Schaap in the March issue of *Sport* disagreed, saying, "They won't win the pennant, but this team has too much talent to be seventh again." For the Dodgers to have any hope of improving, he contended, "Hodges must hit. When the season begins, Hodges will be 35, which is not a particularly choice age for a comeback. But he is in good shape, he works hard and he could produce."

Writing in the same magazine, Milton Gross also believed that Hodges could help the Dodgers rebound: "Even at 35, he is too good, too hard working, too astute and too strong not to be able to come back. . . . For 1959, Hodges has reached a conclusion. He must not try to carry the team by himself. That was one of the many facets of his trouble."

Hodges was happy to take on responsibilities again as the team's right-handed power hitter, but this year he would have more faith in his teammates. Most important, he told Gross, "I'm going to forget the fence is there, which I couldn't do last season. Right from the first day of spring training it was always in my mind's eye."

The Dodgers pitchers, too, had changed their style in 1958 because of the screen, but in 1959 they were determined to come inside to right-handed hitters as often as they would in other parks. In fact, the attitude of all the players changed toward the Coliseum. No longer was it considered as much of an enemy as the opposing team, but a home-team-friendly ballpark. To take advantage of the short distance to the screen, Bavasi had traded Gino Cimoli to the Cardinals for outfielder Wally Moon, a solid left-handed batter with an inside-out swing that produced high fly balls to the opposite field. For the sake of Snider, the power alley in right center field was reduced from 440 feet to 394 feet (and would be shortened again after 1960 to 380 feet), and the distance to dead center went from 425 feet to 410 feet.

Moon was in left field, Snider in center, and Ron Fairly in right field for Opening Day against Chicago in Wrigley Field on April 11 and for the home opener on April 14 against St. Louis. John Roseboro was the starting catcher, ahead of Pignatano and Norm Sherry. Hodges was at first base, Neal at second, Don Zimmer at shortstop, and Jim Baxes, a minor leaguer since he signed in 1947, was at third until an injured Gilliam was ready.

The Dodgers lost both openers, 6–1 in Chicago and 6–2 in L.A. before 61,552 fans, as Hodges hit his first homer off Cards starter Lindy McDaniel. These were the only days all season that they would be under .500. On April 26, they moved into first place for the first time in their brief history when they drubbed the Cardinals in St. Louis 17–11, as Neal got 5 hits, Furillo 4, and Hodges 3 with 5 RBIs.

The Dodgers ended April in a virtual tie for first place with Milwaukee. They were obviously playing better than in 1958, but Drysdale (3–1) and Podres (2–2) were the only starters with victories. Sandy Koufax and Danny McDevitt's series of failures had been obscured by the successes of relievers Johnny Klippstein, Art Fowler, and Clem Labine. Fans were appreciative that the Dodgers were playing with new energy, confidence, and purpose, and that almost everyone on offense was making a contribution—including the vets Hodges, Furillo, and Snider, and newcomers Moon and Demeter, who hit 3 homers in a victory over San Francisco. The '59 Dodgers were winning games the '58 team let get away, and were entertaining. Attendance was high, particularly when the Giants and Braves came to town.

The event that really bonded the team with the baseball fans of the city was "Roy Campanella Night" on May 7. A record 93,103 people attended, and an estimated 15,000 were turned away. Surely some fans came primarily to see the Dodgers play an exhibition game against Mickey Mantle and the world-champion New York Yankees, but that so many were there to pay tribute to a baseball icon they'd never seen play in person was proof that they had adopted the Dodgers and their history. In the pregame ceremony, Campanella was wheeled onto the field by his old captain, Pee Wee Reese. After the fifth inning, the Coliseum lights were turned off and the crowd lit matches to create an amazing and emotional light show. "We all cried when everyone lit matches to honor my father and the entire Coliseum was like a huge birthday cake," Roy Campanella II wrote in 1990 in *Cult Baseball Players*. "The applause was thunderous. It was a beautiful, touching evening."

The Dodgers stayed above .500 but had their worst month of the season in May, going 14–17. It was encouraging that Koufax finally got his first victory on the thirty-first, 5–3 over the Cards, with relief help from McDevitt, who also picked up 3 wins in May. The previous game, the Dodgers were on the brink of going under .500 when the left-handed Fairly, who was in the second year of a twenty-one-year career, hit a leadoff home run in the ninth inning to tie the score 5–5. One out later Hodges ended it with a deep blast to left center, again off McDaniel. It was his seventh homer of the season and gave him 24 RBIs, 1 behind Snider. He'd also been the hero on the twenty-second against the Giants, when his two-out single in the bottom of the thirteenth inning gave the Dodgers a 2–1 victory. Los Angeles baseball fans were now seeing the reliable clutch hitter who was well-known to the fans in Brooklyn.

The Braves had threatened to run away from the pack, but instead floundered, going 14–15 in June. Meanwhile, the Dodgers went 18–12, including taking 5 of 8 against Milwaukee, as the starting pitching turned in a number of exceptional performances. On the third, Stan Williams 2-hit the Cincinnati Reds, as they were now called again, 5–1. On the fifth, Podres outpitched Warren Spahn and beat the Braves 5–1. The next day, Koufax gave up no earned runs in 7 innings in a 3–2 victory over Milwaukee. On the ninth, Williams, who pitched mostly in relief in 1959, gave up 1 earned run in 8⅓ innings, before Koufax got the final two outs, in a 3–2 win over Philadelphia. Two days later, Podres 2-hit the Phillies 11–0 as Demeter slugged 2 homers and knocked in 5 runs. On the fifteenth, Drysdale struck out 13 as he 4-hit the Braves and outpitched Buhl 4–0. Two days later McDevitt also shut out Milwaukee 4–0, yielding only 2 singles to Hank Aaron.

On the fifteenth, Carl Erskine, with a record of 0–3, voluntarily retired and took on coaching duties. He did it unselfishly to open up a spot for Roger Craig, who had been pitching well at Spokane after his arm mended. On the nineteenth, Craig got his first start and beat the Reds 6–2 with a 6-hitter, the first of his 11 big victories. "Because of the screen, I turned into a control pitcher," Craig recalls. "Batters expected the ball over the plate that I normally threw, but I threw a lot of bad pitches inside instead, because I knew they were so eager to hit the screen that they'd swing. Gil helped me a lot. Just like Alston, he'd come to the mound, wait a little bit, and then say something very positive. He helped in another way. He had pine oil all over his hands and glove, and if I got a slippery ball I'd toss it over to him and he'd twist it one time in his oily hands and throw it back. Then it was almost like a softball."

The exceptional starting pitching continued. Drysdale also 6-hit the Reds, 9–2, as Hodges blasted his ninth and tenth homers and upped his RBI total to 36. On the twenty-second, a dominant Koufax struck out 16 Phillies and Hodges drove in 3 runs in a 6–2 victory that began the Dodgers' season-best 7-game win streak. The next day McDevitt went the distance and defeated Philadelphia 4–3, as Hodges hit a 2-run homer. On the twenty-fourth, Craig gave up 1 earned run in 6 innings in a 9–6 victory over the Phillies, as Hodges—who, along with Gilliam, Moon, Snider, and Demeter, was hitting over .300—drove in 2 more runs. Two days later, Drysdale 3-hit the hapless Phillies, 5–2, as the hot Hodges and Snider smashed round-trippers. And on the twenty-seventh, Koufax shut out the Pirates on 6 hits, 3–0.

The Dodgers never were more than 5½ games out of first place in June, and on July 5, at the time of the first All-Star break, they were a respectable 47–37 and only half a game behind both the Braves and Giants. Hodges had 15 homers, 50 RBIs, and a .305 average—Brooklyn Dodgers–type numbers.

The Dodgers played back-to-back doubleheaders with the Cubs on the weekend of July 4 and July 5. They lost only the first game on Saturday, but ironically it was key to their successful season. Zimmer and Bob Lillis had failed in their attempts to replace Reese as the Dodgers' shortstop, so twenty-six-year-old, switch-hitting Maury Wills got the start. Alston didn't know how well he'd hit and put him in the eighth spot, but he had a lot of range and a good arm, and, though he wasn't an established base stealer yet, he could motor around the bases. Wills immediately added speed, swagger, and pizzazz to the team.

Podres was supposed to pitch that game, but his back was hurting, so they brought up Larry Sherry from St. Paul, where he was leading the league in strikeouts. He would be a revelation starting and relieving. "I caught him in Winter Ball in Venezuela," recalls Norm Sherry, his older brother. "He was having all kinds of trouble with his temper and getting people out. After a meltdown, he apologized for yelling at me and said, 'You know, I'm going to start throwing a slider.' I encouraged him and it got better and better. In 1959, it was unreal."

A grocery clerk the previous two winters, Sherry picked up his first major league win on July 23, going 7⅓ innings in a 5–3 win over the Cubs. Hodges' 2-run homer gave the Dodgers a 2–0 lead. But in the sixth inning, he slid into second trying to break up a double play and badly twisted his knee. For the first time since Newport News, he was carried off the field. At the time of his injury, Hodges had 19 homers and 61 RBIs and was possibly on his way to his sixth 30-homer, 100-RBI season—and an MVP award. But he'd miss a full month.

In his absence, Norm Larker did a solid job filling in. From late July to mid-August, Snider went 26-for-50, a .520 clip, and hit 6 home runs. Drysdale, Podres, and Sherry each picked up 3 wins. And another call-up, outfielder Chuck Essegian, made a solid contribution, batting .304 in twenty-four games. After Essegian was acquired from St. Louis on June 15, he was playing at Spokane until that team's manager, Bobby Bragan, recommended to Bavasi that he be brought up. "It was so fortuitous coming to a club that had a shot at getting to the World Series," recalls Essegian. "After two or three weeks Gil came up to me in the outfield before a game and started teasing me because I hadn't said anything to anybody. Somebody asked me a question and Gil said, 'I'll be darned. I didn't know if you could talk.' Gil was a needler, but I learned he didn't needle you unless he cared for you. I took it as a great compliment that he'd tease me a lot. He was just a terrific guy."

Several players stepped up while Hodges convalesced, but his bat and glove were sorely missed. The Dodgers went 14–13 without him and fell to third place, 4½ games behind the Giants and half a game behind the Braves. He returned with a vengeance in Philadelphia on August 24. With his wife and son in attendance, Hodges drilled a 2-run single off Bob Keegan in the first inning and a 3-run homer off Taylor Phillips in the second inning as the Dodgers beat the Phillies 8–2. For the eleventh straight season Hodges had hit 20 home runs, tying Mel Ott's National League record, set between 1929 and 1939. The benefactor was Koufax, who struck out 13.

The next day, Hodges and Snider hit their 21st homers off Robin Roberts to back Podres. Sherry would get the unofficial save in the 5–2 victory. On the thirtieth, Hodges slammed his 22nd homer, a 2-run shot off Johnny Antonelli that cut the deficit to 3–2 in an eventual 7–6 victory.

At the end of August, the Dodgers were only 1 game behind the Giants. They got a big victory at the Coliseum on the thirty-first over the Giants, 5–2, when Moon hit what the fans and press were calling "Moon Shots" over the screen in the bottom of the ninth inning with two men aboard. The winning pitcher was Koufax, who gave up a homer to sensational rookie Willie McCovey and an RBI double to Orlando Cepeda but was otherwise unhittable. He struck out 18 batters—14 swinging—to tie Bob Feller's single-game major-league record.

September would be the Dodgers' best month, despite their losing 4 of their first 5 games. They rebounded with 5 straight wins, beginning with a 7–1 drubbing of the Cubs as Hodges hit his 23rd homer and Podres threw a 6-hitter and fanned 14. Next, Drysdale struck out 11 and blanked the Phillies on 3 hits, 1–0, as Hodges drove in the only run with a two-out single in the bottom of the sixth inning. Craig followed with another shutout, 3-hitting the Phillies 5–0. The Dodgers trailed 4–3 in the next game against the Pirates but rallied for 2 runs in the bottom of the ninth on a single by Wills, a triple by Gilliam, and a single by Neal to hand forkballer Elroy Face his first defeat after 17 wins in relief. In the second game of the day, Sherry started and threw the Dodgers' third shutout in 4 games, beating the Bucs 4–0 with a 6-hitter. Moon hit his 3rd homer of the day.

The Dodgers split a showdown two-game series with the Braves, losing to Buhl but winning the second game 7–6 in ten innings as Wills collected

5 hits and scored the winning run on Gilliam's sacrifice fly. Then they traveled to San Francisco to play a huge series against the first-place Giants in San Francisco, while ground was broken for a stadium at Chavez Ravine in Los Angeles. The Dodgers swept the three games behind Craig, Drysdale, and Podres to give them 14 wins in 22 games against the Giants in '59. Humbled, the Giants would drop 4 of their final 5 games to the Cubs and Cardinals and leave the pennant race to the Dodgers and Braves.

The Dodgers were finally in first place, but they quickly fell behind the Braves when they suffered a tough 11–10 loss to the Cardinals, as Koufax didn't make it out of the first inning. But they tied Milwaukee for first when Craig shut out the Cardinals 3–0 the next day, the Dodgers' 14th shutout of the season.

In the next game at Wrigley Field, on the twenty-fifth, Hodges' 25th homer off lefty reliever Bill Henry in the top of the eleventh inning in the gloaming, beat the Cubs 5–4, and moved the Dodgers back into first place. It was arguably the Dodgers' biggest hit of the regular season and was one of his few homers that Hodges would remember and relish. Sherry got the win in relief.

However, after being crushed the next day by Chicago, 12–2, the Dodgers shared first place with the Braves with one game left to play.

On the final day of the regular season, Milwaukee beat Philadelphia, and L.A. beat the Cubs 7–1, behind Craig. For the first time since 1951, there would be a three-game playoff to determine the champion of the National League. The Dodgers hoped for a better result.

The first playoff game was played in Milwaukee on September 28. Lefty McDevitt went against fellow left-hander Carlton Willey. The Braves led 2–1 in the third when Hodges singled to drive in Moon. In the top of the sixth, Roseboro cracked a solo homer to give the Dodgers a 3–2 lead, and that would be the final score as Sherry pitched 7⅔ innings of brilliant shutout relief. The Dodgers needed just 1 more win to dethrone the two-time National League champions.

In the second game, played at the Coliseum, the Braves led 5–2 after 8 innings, but the '59 Dodgers were a resilient bunch. Moon, Snider, and Hodges singled to lead off the top of the ninth to load the bases and knock out Lew Burdette. Larker singled to greet Don McMahon, scoring Moon and Snider and sending Hodges to third with no outs. Spahn replaced McMahon. He gave up a game-tying sacrifice fly by pinch hitter Furillo, the only Dodger to have played in the '46, '51, and '59 playoffs.

As tension mounted, the game moved into extra innings. Williams pitched a one-two-three tenth inning, but then had to escape a bases-loaded jam in the bottom of the eleventh. Bob Rush came in for the Braves to pitch the twelfth, replacing Joey Jay. Hodges drew a two-out walk. That brought up backup catcher Pignatano. "The guy threw me two fastballs upstairs," he recalls. "Then the next pitch was a dinky little slider, and I hit it through the hole between short and third. It was the biggest hit of my career. Gil was on second now and gave me instructions if Furillo got a hit to the outfield. But Furillo hit the ball behind second base."

Shortstop Felix Mantilla made a fine play on an in-between hop, but made an off-balance throw to first that got by Frank Torre and allowed Hodges to score the winning run. "When Furillo hit the ball, I was already up and heading for the mound to pitch the next inning," recalled Williams in *We Played the Game*. "I was in disbelief that the game was suddenly over and the Dodgers won the pennant." In the broadcast booth, Vin Scully exclaimed, "Bad throw gets by Torre! We go to Chicago!"

The old guard had come through, and the Dodgers won the first National League pennant by a West Coast team and earned the right to play the American League champion White Sox in the World Series.

The Dodgers finished 1959 with a record of 88–68. They had the lowest number of wins for a pennant-winning team, but it was one of the most rewarding seasons for Hodges, Furillo, and Snider. For the Brooklyn trio, who first played together in 1947, this was their sixth National League title and the least expected. Their top winner, strikeout-king Drysdale, had only 17 victories, followed by Podres' 14, Craig's 11, McDevitt's 10, and Koufax's 8. Snider led the team with a .308 average, ahead of Moon's .302.

In his final season as a full-time player, Hodges had only 413 at-bats, his lowest total since his rookie season, as he missed thirty games entirely and played first base only 92 times and third 10 times. Still he led the team with 25 home runs, 2 more than Snider, and his 80 RBIs were third to Snider's 88 and Neal's 83. Hodges now had 345 career home runs, trailing only Mel Ott (511), Stan Musial (412, and still playing), Snider (354, and still playing), and Ralph Kiner (351) in National League history. He hit .276, just a point below his lifetime average. He had a .513 slugging percentage, his highest since 1954. He also led National League first basemen in fielding percentage and was awarded his third consecutive Gold Glove. Hodges was a drawing card on a Dodgers team that attracted 2,071,045 fans to the Coliseum.

The Dodgers had just an average offense, but they were a powerhouse in comparison to the Chicago White Sox. Whereas the Dodgers boasted six players who hit more than 10 home runs (Hodges, Snider, Neal, Moon, Demeter, and Roseboro), the Sox had only catcher Sherm Lollar, with 22, and left fielder Al Smith, with 17. Even former National League home-run king Ted Kluszewski, a midseason pickup, hit only 4 balls out of the park. Manager Al Lopez's team did have excellent pitching. Early Wynn led the league with 22 wins, Bob Shaw won 18, Billy Pierce 14, and Dick Donovan 9, and Gerry Staley and Turk Lown, Hodges' Newport News teammate, were excellent relievers. They also had a standout defense, with second baseman Nellie Fox, shortstop Luis Aparicio, and center fielder Jim Landis leading the league in most defensive categories. And they had speed. They were called the "Go-Go Sox" because they stole a major-league-high 130 bases, led by Aparicio's 56, and everyone but Lollar took the extra base. Their spark plug, Fox, who led the Sox with a .306 average, would be voted the American League's MVP.

For the first time since 1948, no New York team was in the World Series. For the first time in the postwar era, the Dodgers would not be playing the Yankees in the Series, because they had finished third in the American League behind the White Sox and Indians. The Sox had won 94 games and were considered the favorites.

Alston didn't mind his team being the underdogs, but he was more worried that his tired players weren't ready to begin the Series against well-rested Chicago. "We felt like a bunch of zombies," Alston said later. "We played like zombies too in the first game."

Los Angeles never got untracked against Wynn, while the White Sox lit into Craig in an 11–0 victory. The star was Kluszewski, who had 3 hits, including 2 homers, and 5 RBIs. "After we lost the first game," recalls Williams, "Don Zimmer came into the clubhouse and said, 'Boys, the Go-Go Sox are dead. They've got no chance.' Everybody laughed, though we'd just got bombed. We knew what he was saying was true. We had looked at them as a ball club and knew we were better."

In the second game, the White Sox scored 2 runs in the first inning off Podres, and Shaw protected a 2–0 lead until the fifth inning, when Neal broke the Dodgers' scoreless skein with a homer into the left-field stands. With two outs in the top of the seventh, Essegian, pinch-hitting for Podres, homered to tie the score. Then Gilliam walked and Neal slugged his second homer into the Sox bullpen in center field, giving the Dodgers a 4–2 lead. Lown pitched scoreless ball for the final 2⅓ innings for Chicago, but it was too late. Sherry gave up only 1 run over the final three innings, and the Dodgers evened the Series with a 4–3 victory.

Game 3 was in Los Angeles, the first time a World Series game was played west of St. Louis. The Dodgers were happy to hear the familiar "Charge! Charge! Charge" from the Series-record 93,394 home fans. Drysdale and Donovan pitched scoreless ball for 6 innings. The veteran Sox right-hander yielded only his second hit in the seventh inning, a one-out single off the screen by Neal. When Larker and Hodges walked to load the bases with two outs, Lopez brought in Staley. Pinch-hitting for Demeter, Furillo had one more clutch hit in him. He singled past Aparicio to drive in Neal and Larker to put the Dodgers up 2–0. The Sox loaded the bases against Drysdale and Sherry in the eighth, but Smith bounced into a double play and they scored only 1 run. In the bottom half of the inning, Neal doubled home Wills for an insurance run, and the Dodgers won 3–1.

The Dodgers won Game 4, too, in dramatic style, with Hodges planting the dagger into the hearts of Chicago fans. The game was so exciting that Bavasi collapsed afterward from nervous exhaustion and ended up in the hospital. The score was 4–4 in the bottom of the eighth when Hodges led off against Staley, who was relieving Wynn. Staley threw him a sinker that didn't sink and he unloaded, launching the ball into the left-field stands. He crossed home plate grinning from ear to ear. His game-winning home run "came one inning after the Sox had plunged the great gathering into a gloom deeper than night," wrote John Drebinger the next day in the *New York Times*. Sherry pitched 2 innings of hitless relief of Craig and, after the

Dodgers' 5–4 victory, posed with the delighted Hodges for photographers in the clubhouse.

"This was my biggest thrill," claimed Hodges, forgetting for a moment the seventh game of the 1955 World Series. Asked about his four previous World Series homers, he shrugged and said, "I guess they couldn't have been too important or I'd certainly remember them." He explained that the lipstick on his face was his wife's. After the homer he didn't just blow her a kiss but ran over to her in the stands. He was heard to say later to a friend, "Maybe this makes up for 1952."

The Sox won the final game in Los Angeles, a 1–0 pitcher's duel between Shaw and Koufax, with the only run scoring on a double play in the fourth inning. "Sandy Koufax stopped fighting himself this year," commented Hodges. "That World Series game should be the making of him. It proved to him that he could pitch top ball under the toughest kind of pressure."

Back in Chicago, Wynn, pitching on only two days' rest, and Podres squared off in Game 6 on October 8. The scoring began when Duke Snider hit a 2-run homer in the third inning. Then the Dodgers exploded for 6 runs in the fourth, as Wills and Podres knocked in single runs, Neal had a 2-run double, and Moon a 2-run homer. Podres was knocked out in the fourth inning, when Kluszewski boomed a long homer into the upper deck in right. It gave him a six-game Series record of 10 RBIs. But Sherry came in and threw 5⅔ scoreless innings to pick up the victory. The Dodgers scored once more, in the ninth inning, when Essegian clobbered another pinch homer. For the former Rose Bowl participant, it was only his 8th career round-tripper.

The 9–3 triumph gave the Los Angeles Dodgers their first world championship. It was the second world championship in franchise history. Even with the 6 postseason victories, the Dodgers won only 92 games. According to Bavasi, "It was the worst club to win a World Series. But it's also my favorite club. Those kids won on sheer courage and fortitude."

Sherry gave up just 1 run in 12⅓ innings en route to 2 wins and 2 unofficial saves. He deserved the MVP, but a number of Dodgers had a good Series, including Neal, who had 10 hits and 6 RBIs, and Hodges, who had 9 hits, batted a team-high .391, and hit the key home run.

As *Baseball Digest* reported, in the clubhouse after the final game, "Gil's arm was about the Duke's shoulder, and both were grinning as happily as if they were small boys who had just raided a banana peddler's cart. 'We did it again!' they seemed to be saying."

"I was at all the games," recalls Joan Hodges. "Of course, Gil realized he had only a few years left and this might be his last chance for another title, but he was just enjoying the moment. He was very, very happy."

There was celebrating into the night. "The only thing I remember about that night in Chicago," says Norm Sherry, "is I went down to the bar at our hotel and who's tending bar? Gil Hodges."

CHAPTER TWENTY

Despite being ancient in baseball years, thirty-five-year-old Gil Hodges had proven in 1959 that he was still one of the top sluggers in the game. So he was an easy choice to be one of the nineteen power hitters invited during the off-season to participate in a new television series, *Home Run Derby*, a no-frills syndicated program that pitted two famous active players against each other to see who could hit the most balls over the fence at L.A.'s Wrigley Field. The winner received $2,000 and a return visit the next week, and the loser went home with $1,000. Over nine "innings," while one player batted, the other engaged in banal banter with host Mark Scott. Hodges was the oldest participant and the final player to make his debut, appearing in the twenty-second of the twenty-six episodes. He knocked off Willie Mays, a three-week champion, 6 homers to 3 homers, and talked good-naturedly with Frost about how "lucky" he was to have hit 4 homers in a game in 1950 and how he was a catcher until Campanella came along. On the following show, he was dethroned by Ernie Banks, 11 to 7. Hodges left with $3,000, a nice supplement to his World Series check for $11,231.18 and $41,000 salary.

Most of the off-season, Hodges was back in Brooklyn, happy to be reunited with his family for a long stretch of time and not be immersed in baseball concerns. He told Charles Dexter of *Baseball Digest* that he thought he could continue playing "four or five years more."

"There is no reason why Gil can't last in the majors as long as Enos

Slaughter did," Dexter wrote in the magazine. "He is relaxed at all times, with no nerves, no backward look over his shoulder."

Dexter was one of many sportswriters who were fooled by Hodges' even temperament, unreadable face, and impressive numbers in clutch situations into believing he was always calm and fearless. Others, like Arnold Hano, who wrote an article about Hodges in *Sport* at around the same time, saw him more clearly: "There is a drawn, tight quality to Hodges, somewhat like a prizefighter the morning of a big fight. Worries appear to weigh heavily on him, and he suffers with them." According to Hano, the overly modest Hodges worried that he was playing in the major leagues despite problems at first base ("I can't catch pop flies"), on the basepaths ("I never have learned to slide on my left side, and sometimes you have to"), and in the batter's box ("I'm not a good hitter"). Not a good hitter? As someone who had denied his own talents since he was a boy, Hodges always worried that he was in over his head, even after 1,796 big-league games.

As usual, the Hodges family vacationed together in Florida during spring training. In 1960, they may have considered going there a few days early to avoid the local publicity surrounding the demolition of Ebbets Field to make way for a housing project. On February 23, a brass band played "Auld Lang Syne" as two hundred people watched a two-ton cast-iron wrecking ball, painted to resemble a baseball, knock the symbol of the golden age of America's pastime to the ground one pitiless blow at a time, leaving only the memories. Roy Campanella was present and was given an urn filled with dirt from behind home plate.

The Dodgers planned to phase in more young players in 1960, including Frank Howard, if they could find him a position. The mammoth right-handed batter was expected to play in the outfield, but Hodges spent time that spring teaching him how to handle first base. Hano asked Hodges whether he was cutting short his own career by speeding up the development of someone who could replace him. "'It never occurred to me,' Hodges said. Then he paused and added almost apologetically, with a brief touch of pride: 'I believe there would have been a place on the team for me. At third. The outfield. Someplace. Just so long as I can contribute to the ball club, there will be a place for me.'"

After spring training, Hodges' family returned to their house in Brooklyn and he checked back into the Mayfair Hotel in downtown L.A., steeling himself to spend much of another season alone. "The means by which you measure most professional ballplayers are invalid when you come up against Gil Hodges," wrote Hano. "We think of Willie Mays as a great ballplayer, who also happens to be married. We think of Gil Hodges as a warm and loving family man, who happens to play ball for a living. And so the Gil Hodges story isn't so much the story of a ballplayer who soon and perhaps suddenly may no longer be playing ball, but the story of a human being who the night before our interview had sat in his hotel room, alone, talking over the telephone to his wife, Joan, at home 3,000 miles away, and who the next morning wrote a letter to his son, Gil II, ten years old."

"It's not a healthy situation," he told Hano, "but until I have a more concrete job, one with more security, a future laid out, either in baseball or out, I will not move my family out here." He told Hano that in the next off-season he would open a forty-eight-lane bowling alley not far from his home. "It's a good feeling," he said, "to know you've got something going for you besides baseball. I've never learned anything in my life, other than sports. That's a problem with ballplayers. If they're hurt, there goes ten years down the drain. They have to begin a new profession ten years behind the other fellow. Bowling is thriving right now. It may be that I'll have that when I quit."

The Dodgers opened their season on April 12 against the Cubs before 67,550 fans at the Coliseum. Alston's lineup had the same starters who ended the 1959 season: Gilliam, 3B; Neal, 2B; Moon, LF; Snider, RF; Hodges, 1B; Roseboro, C; Demeter, CF; Wills, SS. Drysdale got the start and fanned 14 in going the distance. Hodges went 0-for-5 with strikeouts in his first 3 at-bats, and also misplayed a pop-up after moving to third base. It was off the bat of Don Zimmer, who had been dealt to Chicago four days earlier for future star reliever Ron Perranoski. But the L.A. Dodgers got the Opening Day victory, 3–2, when Essegian, picking up where he left off in the World Series, smashed a two-out homer pinch-hitting for Drysdale in the bottom of the eleventh inning.

"The first two guys to meet me at home plate were Hodges and Snider," recalls Essegian. "I have a picture of the three of us. It's one of my fondest memories. Obviously, Snider and Hodges were older, but everybody on the team admired those guys. I can't think of anyone I respected more than Gil. Not just because of his playing abilities, but because of the kind of person he was."

The Dodgers were shut out the next day by Chicago's Glen Hobbie, as Hodges went 0-for-3, but came back the day after to beat the Cardinals 3–2, by scoring 2 runs in the bottom of the ninth. Essegian singled, and Hodges drove him in by lining an 0–2 pitch to center that he legged into a triple. Hodges then scampered home on a wild pitch with the winning run. He drove in another run the next day as the Dodgers won again by the score of 3–2, and Drysdale picked up his second win.

Hodges hit his first homer of the year against St. Louis as the Dodgers improved their record to 4–1 with a 7–5 victory. On April 19, they won their fourth consecutive game when Johnny Podres and Ed Roebuck combined for a 4–0 shutout over the Giants. It was the first game ever played at windy, chilly, and mushy Candlestick Park in San Francisco, which many would call "one of the eight blunders of the world." The victory moved the Dodgers into sole possession of first place. It was the only time they'd be there all year.

The Dodgers had a run-of-the mill season, going 82–72 and finishing in fourth place, 13 games behind the eventual world-champion Pirates, 6 behind Charlie Dressen's Braves, and 4 behind the Cardinals. Other than a terrific July, in which they went 19–7, they were 2 games under .500. Every other month they were at or near .500: 8–7 in April, 12–14 in May, 13–14 in June, 15–15 in August, 14–14 in September, and 1–1 in October. Still, attendance at the Coliseum rose to 2,253,997. The three main attractions on offense were Maury Wills, who moved into the leadoff spot and batted .295 with a whopping fifty stolen bases, the most ever for a Hodges teammate; Norm Larker, who wrested the first-base job from Hodges and hit .323 with a team-high 78 RBIs; and Howard, who won the Rookie of the Year Award for hitting a team-high 23 homers and driving in 77 runs in only 117 games. One gargantuan early-season blast at Forbes Field in Pittsburgh traveled well over 500 feet.

Another rising star was twenty-one-year-old rookie outfielder Tommy Davis, who was a fan of Hodges' when growing up in Brooklyn. He batted .276 and had the makings of a tremendous hitter. Willie Davis, who was not related, batted .318 in 88 at-bats after he came up late in the season. The lanky left-handed center fielder was being called the fastest man in the majors, particularly when going from first to third. Wills, Howard, and the Davises made Dodger fans excited about 1961.

None of the Dodgers pitchers had an outstanding '60 season, although Drysdale won 15 games with a 2.84 ERA and a league-best 246 strikeouts, and Podres, Larry Sherry, and Stan Williams each had 14 victories. Koufax and Craig each won only 8 games, the same total as Roebuck had in relief. An arm injury to Williams ended his quest to be a 20-game winner and contributed to the Dodgers dropping from contention.

Hodges got off to a slow start, and then pulled a muscle in his left thigh on April 29. Instead of taking it easy and receiving proper treatment for his leg and a chronic hand fungus that was troubling him, he continued to play. He even traveled that Saturday and Sunday to speak at Little League openings in Covina and Encino that he'd promised to attend. "He spoke briefly," wrote Hano, "his voice edged with nervousness because he is embarrassed to speak in public. He thanked the boys for inviting him out, and then he said that the important thing to learn is to be a good sport, to get along with your neighbors. If you learn that, Gil said, it will be a successful season. Maybe you'll never be a big leaguer, but you'll be a better citizen."

After his thigh injury, Hodges went 1-for-16 with no RBIs. In other years, Alston might have let him play himself out of his slump, but the Dodgers had lost 4 straight games and were in fourth place, and he didn't have the luxury to be patient. So Hodges and his .209 average went to the bench, making room for Larker. For the rest of the season the thirty-six-year-old would be a spot starter and try to stay above .200, which he would have done if he didn't go 0-for-15 as a pinch hitter, an uncommon role for him.

The reason for his latest slump was familiar. As good a year as 1959 was, he would have gone over 100 strikeouts for the first time if he hadn't missed so many games, and in 1960 he was still striking out at a high rate due to the problem he had his entire career. "He'd take and he'd take," recalls Norm Sherry, "and I'd say, 'Gil, that's a strike,' and he said, 'No, that's outside.' A right-hander could throw him a ton of curves on the outside corner that were strikes, and he wasn't going to swing. If pitchers could pitch only on or just off the outside corner Gil never would have gotten a hit, but when they'd throw a fastball middle or in, he'd murder it. He was still tough."

"I heard Snider say that Gil would have hit .300 every year if he just squawked a little bit to umpires that the pitches they were calling strikes were outside," says Essegian. "But he would just walk away without arguing and they kept calling that ball a strike."

"With Gil, it was just getting to be time," says Bob Aspromonte, who returned to the Dodgers for the first time since 1956 and played a few games at shortstop and third base. "His timing was off, and the aging factor started to take over, so he couldn't play every day. However, his demeanor rarely changed."

Aspromonte was one of the players and coaches who also lived at the Mayfair. So did catcher Doug Camilli, the son of the Dodgers' pre-WWII star first baseman Dolph Camilli. "I rode to and from the park with Gil a lot of times after I came up late in 1960," remembers Camilli. "There were a few young players staying at the same hotel as Gil, and he would drive those of us who didn't have a car. He'd even take us to the airport. I'm sure we talked about my father, and hitting, and calling a game, but what I remember most about him is that if you needed help, he'd help."

Hodges always enjoyed the company of the younger players, including his road roommate, Drysdale, but more so than ever in 1960, because more of Brooklyn's players were gone. In addition to Zimmer being traded, Clem Labine and Sandy Amoros were sent to Detroit early in the year. Two of Hodges' closest friends, Carl Erskine and Pee Wee Reese, hadn't returned as coaches. Reese, who never became a manager, left to broadcast CBS' *Game of the Week* with Dizzy Dean. But the most jarring departure was Carl Furillo's.

The front office wanted to dump Furillo's still-modest salary now that he no longer held a regular spot in the outfield, and saw an opportunity when he pulled a calf muscle. "Furillo was running on the field and there was a soft spot and he pulled something," recalls Roger Kahn more than fifty years later. "The Dodgers were going to send him down, and he said, 'My contract says you can't send me down when I'm injured.' So they released him." Furillo sued the ball club, claiming that he could not be let go while injured and that the Dodgers had done so to weasel out of paying benefits to a fifteen-year veteran. Furillo was awarded $21,000, but "Carl never got another job in baseball. He was blacklisted, but he couldn't prove it," Kahn says.

In his book *Beyond the Boys of Summer*, Kahn wrote about Furillo: "Quite simply, he was a great player. Some write about his arm, the human cannon . . . The way Furillo played the wall describes an art form. Furillo gathered 1,910 hits in fifteen major-league years. . . . No one ever banged a baseball harder up the middle. If Furillo ever misjudged a fly I never saw it."

And then there were, like in an Agatha Christie yarn, only two left from the Dodgers' cast of the late forties—Hodges and Snider. Hodges was older and the team's highest-paid player (making $1,000 more than Snider's $40,000), so he wondered whether he was next on the chopping block. But the front office realized that he still had value to the team. He could play several positions, was popular with the fans, made appearances in the community, and was a strong, positive influence on the younger players.

"Gil was a born leader," says Craig, who would become a manager and pitching coach and help popularize the split-fingered fastball. "Alston was the same way, which makes me think Gil learned a lot from him. While neither of them had a whole lot to say, when they said something, they meant it."

"I liked that Hodges was quiet, because I was quiet," says Tommy Davis. "With Gil, you'd have to start the conversation, but just having him around you'd learn something every day. I'd admired him as a kid, but when I got to know him he was even better than I expected him to be. Big as he was, he had compassion."

"When Gil was at first base, I felt confident," says Williams. "He was one of our leaders, and a strong guy. We were playing St. Louis at home, and Gil had to stretch off first base for a throw and had his back to the runner, Daryl Spencer, a big guy. Spencer liked to take out infielders and he ran into Gil, blindsiding him. Spencer went down like somebody shot him. Gil didn't even budge; he just turned around and looked over his shoulder at the guy on the ground."

Hodges continued to play a stellar first base in a limited role, and also had some good days with the bat. There was a flash of his past on August 20, when his 2-run double off left-hander Curt Simmons in the ninth inning beat the Cardinals 2–0. In addition to such timely hits, Hodges, despite a .198 average, clouted 8 homers in 197 at-bats, a pace that would have resulted in his setting the National League record of twelve consecutive 20-homer seasons *if* he'd played regularly.

Perhaps the highlight of Hodges' season was an exhibition game on June 27 between the Dodgers and Yankees that was played at Yankee Stadium to benefit United Charities. It was the first time the Dodgers had played in New York City since the final game at Ebbets Field in 1957. The *New York Times'* Frank Finch wrote that the teams played in front of "a highly vocal crowd with a heavy Brooklyn accent" and that "the Yankees were greeted by ripe raspberries." As Finch reported, the majority of the 53,492 fans in the stadium rooted for the visitors during their 4–3 victory. The biggest cheers were reserved for Hodges and Snider. Finch also wrote about a rumored trade that would send Hodges to the Yankees.

That October, one could glimpse into Hodges' baseball future. On the seventeenth, four days after the Pittsburgh Pirates beat the New York Yankees in a thrilling Game 7 of the World Series, the National League's owners—in response to Branch Rickey's threat to start a third major league—voted to expand to ten teams, with new teams in New York and Houston beginning play in 1962. On the twenty-sixth, expansion in the American League was approved, with the Los Angeles Angels and a new Washington Senators becoming the junior circuit's ninth and tenth teams. The franchise in Washington that had been the Senators would move to Minnesota and become the Twins. Rosters of the new teams would be filled by drafting unprotected players from the eight existing teams in each league. The American League would begin to play with a 162-game schedule in 1961. In their first year, Gene Autry's Angels would play in small Wrigley Field and then become a tenant at Chavez Ravine, leasing from the Dodgers.

It was the new New York team, the Metropolitans, that intrigued *New York Journal-American* sportswriter Dave Anderson in regard to Hodges. "When the Dodgers put up some of their players as surplus for the two new

National League teams, Hodges would be a perfect pick for the New York club," he conjectured.

Hodges told Anderson, "I wouldn't mind coming to New York. I know my wife and the children would love it. But when you've been with a club as long as I have, it wouldn't be easy to leave the Dodgers."

Anderson talked to Hodges for a piece he was writing about the grand opening of Hodges' bowling alley. His new venture, Anderson realized, would make the possibility of his return to New York as a player in 1962 even more attractive to Hodges. Less than three weeks after John F. Kennedy, a Democrat and a Catholic, was inaugurated as U.S. president, Gil Hodges Lanes opened at Ralph Avenue and Avenue M in Brooklyn, a five-minute drive from the Hodges home.

The idea for the bowling alley came from his business associate, friend, and family doctor, Anthony Terranova. "Dr. Terranova and Gil opened the first bowling alley with forty-eight lanes on one level," recalls Joan Hodges. "It was beautifully designed and had the lanes, a lounge, a restaurant, and a party room for about eighty-five people. It was a nice-size property, taking up a four-block square. When Gil was in town, he would go there during the day and spend time in the office. On weekends, we'd bring guests to the lounge and have dinner there, and I would go there occasionally with Mrs. Terranova when Gil was away."

Hodges told Anderson that he received his contract from the Dodgers a few weeks before. "I never signed one so quickly," he said with a grin. Like Snider he was offered a $2,000 cut, accepting a $39,000 salary for 1961. The truth was that both players were relieved to be offered contracts at all, considering they had the highest salaries on the team but were no longer full-time players. "For the first time since he was a rookie," wrote the preseason prognosticator in *Sports Illustrated*, "[Hodges] reported to camp worried about sticking with the club."

Yet both *SI* and the *Sporting News* expected Hodges to stick with the team and get a lot of playing time. They pointed out that he was needed to back up singles-hitter Norm Larker at first; he could fill in at third base for Tommy Davis, who was a better outfielder; he could play the outfield if Howard was shifted to first; and now that Joe Pignatano had been sold to

Kansas City, he could be the third catcher behind John Roseboro and Norm Sherry. "Walter Alston has tried Hodges as a catcher in spring training," stated *SI*, "and Hodges, a thorough pro, looks good. His bat would be a big help, and his arm, too."

There were two others with Brooklyn Dodgers ties in camp. Shockingly, Leo Durocher had been hired in January to be Alston's bench coach. Out of work for fifteen months, he had called O'Malley to ask for employment. Never paranoid that his coaches were after his job, Alston gave the go-ahead. Don Newcombe was also in camp looking for work. But the rotation was set with Drysdale, Podres, Craig, and Koufax, so Newcombe would have to ply his trade in Japan.

Koufax finally harnessed his control that spring. His transition can be traced to one B-squad game. The regulars were playing the Tigers in Lakeland that day, and Alston sent the rest of the squad to Orlando to play the Minnesota Twins, with Hodges stepping in as the manager. Hodges' plan was for Koufax to pitch 5 innings and then let Ed Palmquist and a minor leaguer finish up, but Palmquist missed the plane. In the 2010 documentary *Jews in Baseball*, Koufax recalled Hodges poking him in the chest and saying, "You're going seven!" Ironically, Hodges wasn't around to watch him, because he was plunked on the head in batting practice and taken to the hospital for an X-ray.

Norm Sherry, Koufax's catcher that day, recalls:

Sandy starts out and we're mixing curves and changeups with his fastball, and he walks the first two batters. And now he's shaking me off and throwing the fastball higher and higher. He was frustrated, right? So I said, "Sandy, you have to pitch deep into the game. Why don't you take something off your fastball? Let them hit it. Otherwise, they're not going to swing and you'll walk them." So he says okay. And he strikes out the guy, strikes out the next two guys. Now we come off the field and I say, "I'm not blowing smoke up your rear end, but the way you just threw, not trying to overwhelm anybody, that's what you need to do." And it really registered. I think he gave up 1 hit. So next we're at camp and I put some dirt on the plate to give him a line on one side and a line on the other side. He hit my glove every time. So I go, "My God, this is it!"

"That day in Orlando was the beginning of a whole new era for me," Koufax contended. The long-fingered left-hander would become a star in 1961 and would be from 1963 until his retirement after the 1966 season the most dominant pitcher anyone could remember.

Still, Drysdale got the Opening Day assignment for the fourth straight year. For the first time since his rookie year, Hodges was not in the lineup to begin a season. In the 6–2 victory over the Phillies' Robin Roberts, Hodges was a defensive replacement for Larker. He spelled Larker in the second game, too, a 3–2 victory. After the pundits stated all spring how Hodges would play a number of positions in 1961, he would make 100 appearances in the field, all at first base. His role would be spot starter, defensive replacement, and pinch hitter. In the Dodgers' fourth and fifth games, he delivered pinch singles, eliminating the possibility he'd go through another season with zero hits coming off the bench.

Hodges got his first start in the Dodgers' tenth game, going 1-for-3 in an 11–2 loss to St. Louis. On May 4, in the Dodgers' twenty-first game, he got his 1st home run and RBI of the year. It came in the top of the tenth inning off Milwaukee's Carlton Willey to put the Dodgers ahead 6–5. But his chance to be a hero disappeared in the bottom of the tenth when Joe Adcock slugged a game-ending grand slam.

On Saturday, May 6, Hodges got another start in Pittsburgh, so he missed the twenty-year reunion of the 1941 class of Petersburg High School. His bio in the program said: "He has traveled just about every place and says his outstanding achievement is 'He's married.' He has lost some hair but weighs about the same. Bud writes he is sorry he can't make it to the reunion and wishes everyone a good time. [Baseball] prevents his getting here, but he sends his regards to all."

The bio for Bob Hodges said: "He has traveled every place money, time, and family would allow. He says he hasn't gained any weight—can't tell for sure if he's lost any hair. His outstanding achievement is he 'has been able to stay out of jail.'" In 1961, Bob, who was working at Gus Doerner Sports

Inc. in Evanston, became a birddog for the Dodgers. (In the mid-sixties, he'd scout for the Reds.)

In 1961, baseball fans were captivated by the headline-making home-run race in the American League—in which Roger Maris warded off the challenge of his Yankees teammate Mickey Mantle and broke Babe Ruth's single-season home run record with 61—and the pennant race between New York and Detroit. But there was also an exciting pennant race in the National League that went into September, involving the Dodgers and Reds.

For the Dodgers it was a season of spurts. With uncanny predictability, they'd put together modest winning streaks that would carry them into first place, only to immediately relinquish the top spot with some bad play. They won 5 of 6 April 18–23 to put them 1 ahead of the Giants and Cards. They won 6 in a row May 7–13 to tie for the lead with the Giants. They won 5 straight May 17–22 to catch the Giants again. They won 5 of 6 once more June 6–11 to tie the Reds. Koufax improved his record to 9–1 in winning the final game 6–3 over the Phillies as Hodges stroked his 4th homer of the year.

The Dodgers won 5 of 7 June 9–15, moving half a game ahead of the Reds and Giants when Tommy Davis hit a 3-run homer off knuckleballer Barney Schultz to beat the Cubs 6–3. After falling 6 games behind the Reds on July 15—by which time the Giants had plummeted out of the race—the Dodgers won 12 of 13 July 16–30, including a season-high 8 in a row, and moved half a game ahead of Cincinnati. In an 11–6 victory over Philadelphia on July 27, Hodges blasted a 3-run shot, the 350th home run of his career, to tie him with the younger and active Mantle and long-retired Johnny Mize for eleventh place on the all-time list. His 1,242nd RBI tied him for ninth place in National League history. It was the 700th extra-base hit of his career.

The Dodgers' next spurt was August 5–13, when they won 6 straight and catapulted over the Reds with a season-high 2½-game lead. But they immediately had a reverse streak, losing a season-worst 10 straight August 14–24 and dropping 3½ games back. A 4-game winning streak September 3–6 brought them back to being only 1 game behind. But the Dodgers then lost 3 straight and 5 of 7 September 8–13, and found themselves trailing the Reds by 5½ games with only sixteen games remaining.

In Podres' 5–4 home victory on the third, Hodges' 7th homer of the season was a solo shot off Giants' lefty Mike McCormick that turned out to be the winning run. His 8th homer came in Podres' 7–3 road loss on the eighth and was again hit off McCormick. It went to left center and scored Wally Moon in front of him. Hodges' only round-tripper at Candlestick Park was the 361st and final home run of his Dodgers career.

Barely alive, the Dodgers had one more surge in them, winning 7 of 9 September 14–23, to pull within 4 games of the Reds. On September 20, in the final game ever played at the Coliseum, Koufax went all 13 innings, striking out 15, and Fairly broke a 2–2 tie with a game-winning single. Hodges went 0-for-4 and was pinch-hit for by Larker.

The Dodgers were still 4 games behind when the season ended. Hodges didn't play in the final game, when the Dodgers trounced the Phillies 10–0. He played the game before, a 2-1 loss, batting fourth and driving in the Dodgers' lone run with a sacrifice fly off Dick Ellsworth in the first inning. In his second at-bat in the fourth inning, he grounded into a double play. He expected to bat again, but the game was rained out after 5½ innings. This was how his Dodgers career ended.

The Dodgers' 89–65 record was better than in 1959, and they went 33–15 in 1-run games, but they were just 27–27 after July 31 to seal their fate. Podres had the best year of the Dodgers starters with an 18–5 record, but it was Koufax who electrified baseball fans, going 18–13 and breaking Christy Mathewson's National League strikeout mark with 269. Williams went 15–12 with 205 strikeouts, but Drysdale was a disappointing 13–10 and Craig slumped to 5–6 as a spot starter and long reliever, making him a prime candidate for the Dodgers' unprotected list in the upcoming expansion draft. Sherry, Perranoski, and flame-throwing Turk Farrell, who was acquired from the Phillies because Roebuck had a season-ending injury, were mostly effective out of the bullpen.

The two stars on offense were Wills, who batted .281, scored 105 runs, and led the league with 35 base thefts, and Moon, who led the team with a .328 average and 88 RBIs and was second to Roseboro's 18 homers, with

17. Otherwise the best seasons were had by half-time players: Snider batted .296, with 16 homers and 56 RBIs in only 233 at-bats; Ron Fairly hit .322, with 10 homers and 48 RBIs in 245 at-bats; and Howard had a .296 average, with 15 homers in 267 at-bats.

Hodges' average went up by 44 points from 1960, to .242, but otherwise the two seasons were similar statistically. He had 18 more at-bats, 215, and 13 more hits, but he hit 8 homers again, had 5 fewer extra-base hits, scored only 3 more runs, 25, and had only 1 more RBI, 31. His biggest improvement was as a pinch hitter, finishing 7 for 28. Defensively, he made only 1 error in 454 chances, for a .998 fielding percentage, the best of his career, though in limited play.

Hodges was still producing, but his Dodgers career had run its course. In his autobiography, Drysdale said that when the season ended, he told his roommate of six years that he'd see him in the spring. "'I don't know about that,' Gil said. 'What do you mean?' I asked. 'Well, you know they have this expansion draft coming up,' he said. 'I'm not sure I'll be around here after that.' The thought shocked me. Gil Hodges, my roomie, not a Dodger? I couldn't really fathom the idea."

CHAPTER TWENTY-ONE

Gil Hodges' storied Dodgers career, which began in September 1943, came to a bittersweet end on October 10, 1961, when the New York Mets made him the fourteenth pick of the expansion draft. Before him, the Mets had chosen catcher Hobie Landrith of the Giants, infielder Elio Chacon of the Reds, pitcher Roger Craig—the first Dodger taken after Bob Aspromonte, the second choice of the Houston Colt .45s—outfielder Gus Bell of the Reds, outfielder Joe Christopher of the Pirates, and infielder Felix Mantilla of the Braves. Three other Dodgers were later selected by Houston—Jim Golden, Turk Farrell, and Norm Larker (as the Dodgers gave the first-base job to Ron Fairly). Former Dodger Don Zimmer of the Cubs was the Mets' next-to-last pick.

Houston's draft strategy was to select mostly young ballplayers, while the Mets stocked their team, through the draft and deals, with mostly veterans who had name recognition. It was never a concern that Hodges would be snatched quickly and end up in Texas. He was always part of the plan for putting fans in the seats at the Polo Grounds in 1962. His popularity in the city was well-known to the people who ran the Mets. The owner was Joan Whitney Payson, a former Brooklyn Dodgers fan. The chairman of the board was M. Donald Grant, who was the only member of the corporation that owned the New York Giants in 1957 to not vote in favor of the team moving to San Francisco. They hired George Weiss to be the team's president and run operations. As a farm director and, beginning in 1948, general manager of the Yankees, Weiss was the unsocial architect of the

Yankees' dynasty that began after WWII. He and Casey Stengel had been let go following the 1960 World Series loss to Pittsburgh. Weiss had hired Stengel to manage the Yankees in 1949, and now, in a public relations coup, he resurrected the popular New York icon to manage the city's new team.

Weiss believed Stengel would appeal to Yankee fans and that Hodges' presence might reawaken the enormous Brooklyn Dodgers fan base. Although he made a sport of cutting salaries, Weiss was enthusiastic enough about Hodges returning to New York that he gave him a $500 salary bump to $39,500.

"I'm very happy to be back," Hodges told reporter Bob Sales. "I wouldn't be honest if I said I did want to leave the Dodgers. But since I had to leave, I would rather be here than anyplace else. After all, I played here for a great number of years. My wife is very happy with the whole situation. Gil Jr.—he's eleven—I think he's happy about it, too, due to the fact that I'll be home more often." Sales' article also pointed out another reason Hodges was thankful to be living in New York full-time again: "Mrs. Hodges is expecting their fourth child."

Barbara Lynn Hodges was born the day after the draft, on October 11. The addition of another child prompted a move. Cindy Hodges recalls, "When Barbara was born we moved to a bigger house on Bedford Avenue. It's the house where my mother still lives. It has several levels, so there are a lot of steps. Mommy and Daddy were on the first level and we were in three bedrooms on the second level. As Gilly grew older, they converted the garage into his bedroom. They also put in an extension on a stand-up kitchen and that's where we had breakfast and dinner. The way I picture Daddy most is at that table. We always had a five-o'clock dinner. Our hands had to be washed and clean before we sat down. We had to finish our dinner or we didn't get dessert. After eating, we would talk about the day."

"At the dinner table, my father rarely talked about baseball and we could never tell if he had a good day or bad day," says Hodges Jr. "He was just a normal, everyday father, and what he usually talked about with my sisters and me was school. I went to nearby Our Lady Help of Christians on East Twenty-eighth Street. I got no special treatment because of my father. If I spoke out of turn, the nuns hit my knuckles with a ruler, too. That's where we all attended church. Like my father I was an altar boy."

"My father was a devout Catholic and we never missed church, even if we were sick," says Cindy Hodges, who was five when Barbara was born. "To this day I remember him getting me dressed in my room. I had bangs as a child, and he'd cut them so they'd be even before we left for church. He'd make them so short I'd cry all the way. Daddy was always smiling and a positive person, and almost all my memories are fun, good ones, but he was a strict father. I think the strictness came from wanting us all to be the best we could possibly be."

"Our dad loved his children equally but was very different with his son than with his daughters," says Irene Hodges, who was ten at the time. "He was very guarded toward us, even before we were teenagers. I never felt that he was *too* protective; I felt secure always. I didn't always agree with his decisions—it's normal to want certain liberties—but there was usually no discussion and it was what it was."

For the first time since 1946, Hodges did not report to a Dodgers spring training facility. Instead, he traveled to St. Petersburg, where every day Casey Stengel held court with reporters. Hodges, who had spent the last eight seasons being managed by the sedate Walter Alston, was asked whether he was looking forward to a manager who was just the opposite. "I think playing for Stengel will be *interesting*," he replied.

Stengel was pleased to have Hodges on the team for several reasons. He knew that Hodges played intelligent, fundamentally sound, mistake-free baseball. He felt Hodges had more good seasons in him as an everyday player. He admired Hodges' professional, even-keeled demeanor and thought he was a gentleman who could bridge the gap between the players who liked their manager and those who didn't. "He had a way of getting along with his teammates," said Stengel years later. "The best remark he ever made, if anybody said anything about him, was, 'My goodness, a man has a right to his opinion.' He had a terrific respect for standing up for the rights of himself and others." Stengel was also glad to have anyone on his revolving-door roster whom he recognized.

There was one more reason Stengel liked Hodges. He was strong as hell.

"I don't remember when he said it," says George Vecsey, who covered the Mets for *Newsday*, "but I was there and wrote it: 'Hodges can squeeze your earbrows off.' Of course there's no such thing as earbrows, but Casey believed Hodges was so strong he could squeeze them off."

Robert Lipsyte, who wrote for the *New York Times* from 1957 to 1971, recalled in his 1975 book *SportsWorld* Stengel's "earbrows" statement—only he used the word "tear," not "squeeze"—but he had a stronger recollection of Hodges in 1962: "I remembered him standing on the practice ballfield posing for a cigarette ad. A man from the company was explaining to me, 'We want to have our product associated with symbols of acceptance. Quality men use quality products. If Hodges smokes Viceroys, it might do something for you, too.'"

The Mets had improved since the draft by purchasing Richie Ashburn from Chicago and acquiring Frank Thomas from the Braves for a player to be named during the season (Gus Bell). Ashburn was a .300 lifetime hitter and two-time batting champion with Philadelphia. Thomas had hit more than 200 homers since breaking in with Pittsburgh in 1951, surpassing 30 homers and 100 RBIs twice. Hodges was so impressed by the group of veterans assembled that he boldly predicted the new Mets would finish fifth or sixth in the ten-team National League.

Hodges was asked by New York reporters for the first time whether he was interested in becoming a manager after he retired. He replied that he was still a player and managing wasn't on his mind. While admitting he'd probably play only a couple more years, he stated he was fit and expected to take the field in 125 or 130 games. But he suffered a freakish injury while traveling by bus from Clearwater to St. Pete. "Gil told me that he put his knees up on the seat in front of him," says Joe Pignatano, whom the Mets purchased from the Giants in July. "Somehow the circulation was affected and the left knee locked. It hurt just a little at first, so Gil kept playing—until he couldn't do it anymore."

The first game in the history of the New York Mets took place on April 11 in St. Louis. Casey Stengel's veteran lineup was: Richie Ashburn, CF; Felix Mantilla, SS; Charlie Neal, 2B; Frank Thomas, LF; Gus Bell, RF; Gil Hodges, 1B; Don Zimmer, 3B; Hobie Landrith, C; and Roger Craig, P. The

Cardinals got RBI singles in the first inning from Stan Musial and Ken Boyer to take a 2–0 lead. Bell got the Mets' first hit in the second inning off Larry Jackson, but they failed to score. Hodges popped out to Boyer at third in his first at-bat. The Mets tied the game in the third when Neal drove in Ashburn for the first run in Mets history, and Thomas added a sacrifice fly to bring in Mantilla. But the Cardinals took a 5–2 lead in the bottom half of the inning.

Leading off the fourth inning, Hodges hit the first homer ever for the Mets. It was the 362nd of his career, leaving him only 8 homers from being the all-time National League record holder for right-handed batters. It also moved him ahead of Joe DiMaggio into eleventh place on the all-time list of home-run hitters. Neal would close the gap to 5–4 with a homer in the fifth inning, but the Cards pulled away and won 9–4, ruining the Mets' debut. Clem Labine, who had been released by the Pirates, pitched the ninth inning for the Mets.

Labine and the other ex-Dodgers, Hodges, Zimmer, Neal, and Craig, did a lot of posing for group "nostalgia" pictures, not realizing that two of them would soon be gone. Labine made only two more appearances before his career ended. After batting .077 in fourteen games while experiencing vision problems, Zimmer found himself in a Cincinnati uniform.

Because of inclement weather, Hodges didn't play on Opening Day at the Polo Grounds, two days later. Only 12,447 fans showed up to see the historic game, less than one-third the number who attended the team's introductory ticker-tape parade down Broadway. Thomas hit the Mets' first round-tripper at home, and Sherman "Roadblock" Jones pitched well, but the Mets lost again. They would lose their first nine games before Jay Hook mercifully defeated the Pirates 9–1. Craig and Al Jackson were the only other winners in the Mets' first nineteen games.

Craig picked up his first win with 3 innings of 1-hit relief against Philadelphia, and the next day crafty left-hander Jackson tossed the Mets' first shutout, 8–0, over the Phillies. In Craig's victory, the Mets trailed 6–1 in the bottom of the sixth when Thomas and Neal hit back-to-back homers to knock out Phillies starter Jim Owens. Gene Mauch brought in right-hander Jack Hamilton, and Hodges made it 3 homers in a row. In doing so, he set an obscure major-league record with his 17th career homer off a reliever entering a game, breaking a tie with Duke Snider. The Mets rallied to win 8–6.

Hodges, Mantilla, Chacon, and Neal were all batting over .300, and Thomas was driving in runs, but the good hitting wasn't translating into victories. "Things began to look up when the Mets started to win a few games," recalls Ralph Kiner, who formed a longtime Mets broadcast trio with Lindsey Nelson and Bob Murphy. "People forget they won 9 of 12 games after their dreadful start."

Hodges homered 3 times during the hot streak. His first longball came in the second game of a doubleheader on May 12 against Braves reliever Hank Fischer in the bottom of the ninth inning, and won the game. His 364th career home run was the 28th ninth-inning homer in his career, to go with 5 in extra innings. Craig Anderson got victories in both games of the Mets' first doubleheader sweep that day to become the team's first 3-game winner. As one of many hard-luck Mets pitchers, he would lose his next 17 decisions in 1962 and never win another major-league game.

Hodges' 365th homer, on May 16 against the Cubs' tall left-hander Dick Ellsworth, also came in the clutch and was the only inside-the-park homer of his career. With the Mets trailing 5–4 with two outs in the eighth inning, he hit a ball into spacious center field that eluded Lou Brock and he circled the bases to tie the game. The Mets won in eleven innings, 6–5.

Hodges slammed his 366th homer on May 18, in a loss to the Braves. It was the seventh time in his career that he went deep off Warren Spahn. Thomas also homered for the Mets, but Eddie Mathews and Henry Aaron reached the seats for the Braves, and the ageless Spahn gave up only 1 other hit and bested Craig 5–2.

The Mets won their next 3 games but suffered consecutive 3–2 losses to Houston at Colt Stadium, on May 21 and 22, to former Dodgers Jim Golden and Turk Farrell. Because of his ailing knee, Hodges sat out both games. "Those losses to Houston were killers," recalls Kiner, "and it was downhill from there. We figured the Mets were going to be bad, but not that bad." "That bad" was losing 17 in a row.

After being swept in Houston, the Mets lost 3 straight games to the Dodgers, in the new Dodger Stadium, as Hodges returned to Los Angeles for the first time. "It was very strange not seeing Gil on our team after all those years," says Ed Roebuck, who went 10–2 as a Dodgers reliever in 1962. "It was like there was a hole in the team."

Hodges played only in the middle game of the series. He singled off Johnny Podres in his second at-bat, but was thrown out trying to make it to second on his gimpy leg. In the first game, Stengel played disgruntled veteran Ed Bouchee at first base and in the third game went with strikeout-prone Marv Throneberry, who was acquired from Baltimore on the ninth for Landrith and cash, leading to Bouchee's demotion.

The Mets were swept in San Francisco too, and then flew home to host the Dodgers. It's usually stated that the Mets were such lovable losers in 1962 that National League–starved fans flocked to their games, but they drew 922,530 fans, good for only sixth in the league. It was the first time a Hodges team failed to reach a million fans at home. Other than when the Dodgers and Giants, with Willie Mays, came to town, they never attracted even 20,000 fans. For the Dodgers' first appearance, however, a season-high 55,704 fans flocked to the Polo Grounds to see a Memorial Day doubleheader.

The star attraction was Duke Snider, who didn't play but was greeted with a standing ovation when he came out of the clubhouse and then again when he hit a ball out during batting practice. "The place went nuts all over again," he said in his autobiography. "It was the longest ovation of my career."

The Dodgers won the first game 13–6 as Maury Wills, who would break Ty Cobb's single-season record by stealing 104 bases in his 1962 MVP season, unexpectedly slammed 2 home runs among his 4 hits. Sandy Koufax, who would go 14–7 and earn his first of five consecutive ERA titles in 1962, won despite giving up 6 earned runs. The first time Hodges ever faced Koufax, he popped up; the second time, he smashed his 367th career home run. The Dodgers won the second game 6–5, on Willie Davis' ninth-inning homer, but Hodges boomed 2 home runs off Podres. His 368th career homer, with Mantilla aboard, went to right center field. His 369th homer, which tied the game 3–3 two innings later, went to left. "The Dodgers won both games," says Dave Kaminer, who was thirteen when he attended the historic twin bill, "but I think a lot of us who came to the park as Dodgers fans left as Mets fans."

At the end of May, Hodges was hitting .312, with 8 homers and 14 RBIs in limited playing time. He was on his way to having a solid year, but his knee got worse and he couldn't play much more. "Stengel had been disillusioned in thinking Hodges could still hit 40 homers and play 140 games," says Vecsey, "and he seemed very disappointed that he had a bad knee. I sensed Hodges realized that he wasn't going to be a factor and his time had passed."

Hodges didn't homer again until July 6, when the Mets beat the visiting Cardinals 10–3. It was off Ray Sadecki in the second inning, and nobody knew that Hodges had slammed his final home run, the 370th of his career. He was a guest on Ralph Kiner's popular postgame TV show *Kiner's Korner*. "As usual Gil was low-key, showing no emotion, other than a polite grin," recalls Kiner. "I tried to excite him a little by pointing out, 'You broke *my* record!'" Hodges had surpassed Kiner as the National League's all-time right-handed home-run king.

At season's end, the *Sporting News* published a list of the top twenty-one home-run hitters of all time, from Babe Ruth with 714 homers to Hank Aaron with 298 and counting. Fifty years later, Hodges was the *only* player on the impressive list who hadn't been voted into the Hall of Fame.

In mid-July, Hodges needed surgery to remove a painful kidney stone that was hampering him. He returned in September but was ineffective, and his average dipped to .252. He appeared in just 54 games all year, 11 times as a pinch hitter, and had 9 homers, 15 runs, and 17 RBIs, with only 3 coming after May 31.

On June 8, the Mets were 13–36 and they were already 23½ games out. It got worse. Between June 11 and September 15, their record was 19–70. In their season of unprecedented futility, they'd lose ugly with errors of commission, omission, and the indefinable, while the befuddled Stengel asked famously, "Can't anybody here play this game?" Throneberry, who was encouraged to use the moniker "Marvelous Marv" by his devilish locker mate Ashburn, became the symbol of the team's ineptitude. He struck out in key situations, couldn't field a lick, and most memorably failed to touch two bases on one legendary romp around the bases. But even the stars participated in the slapstick. One time on a pop fly to shallow left-center center fielder Ashburn yelled "It's mine!" in Spanish to call off shortstop Elio

Chacon, only to have left fielder Frank Thomas, who only understood English, run him over.

In the 1962 season, the Mets won 40 games and set a record with 120 losses. They almost came back in their final game, which they lost 5–1 to the Cubs, when they got their first two men on base in the eighth inning. But Pignatano, in his final major-league at-bat, hit into a triple play. They finished a staggering 60½ games out of first place. Craig led the league with 24 losses, while leading the Mets pitchers with only 10 victories. Jackson went 8–20, Hook 8–19, Anderson 3–17, and the best of the two Bob Millers went 1–12. As a team, they had the worst batting average, fielding percentage, and ERA in the major leagues.

Yet while in his hospital bed in November, after recovering from surgery to remove cartilage from his knee, Hodges—who admitted crying when the L.A. Dodgers blew the final game of the 1962 playoffs to the Giants—was optimistic about playing baseball in New York the following year. "If I wasn't confident I could do the job, I wouldn't go through all this," he contended. He accepted a cut in salary to $30,000, quipping to reporters, "There was nothing else I could do, because I didn't have a leg to stand on."

Following the advice of the club physician, Peter Lamatte, who did his knee surgery, Hodges reported early to St. Petersburg, on February 19, with the pitchers and catchers. Also present was Norm Sherry, whose contract the Mets had purchased from the Dodgers in October. "The first day Casey called a meeting," Sherry recalls, "I'm sitting next to Hodges, who Casey called 'a Big Swan' because of his big hands, and Casey talks nonstop for about half an hour. I said, 'Gil, I don't want to sound ignorant, but I'm not quite sure what he was trying to tell us.' He said, 'Don't ask me; I don't know either.' It was good being with him again."

When the position players arrived at camp, Hodges learned that he was one of four candidates for the first-base position, along with Throneberry, former Dodgers prospect Tim Harkness, and eighteen-year-old Ed Kranepool. According to the *Sporting News*, "Hodges, one of the all-time whizzes with the glove and the greatest right-handed home-run hitter (370) in National League history, would be a cinch to win out were he physically able. But at this point, the popular Gil is strictly a doubtful quantity. No one knows how far he can go, least of all Gil."

Early in camp, Weiss purchased Duke Snider, the last of the late-forties Brooklyn Dodgers to leave the franchise. Snider, who had opened his own bowling alley in California, was not pleased. "[B]eing sold to the New York Mets in those days seemed like the ultimate humiliation," Snider wrote in his autobiography. Weiss hoped the Snider-Hodges combination would be a gate attraction and also provide needed power.

The Mets opened the season with 8 straight losses. Hodges didn't appear until the seventh game as a pinch hitter and didn't start until the eighth game, going 0-for-3. "His knee was really hurting," remembers Joan Hodges, "and though he was still an excellent fielder, he was having trouble batting." He would have just 22 at-bats, and knock out 5 singles, score 2 runs, and drive in 3 for a team that would go 51–111 and finish in last place. "The Mets were a bad ball club, and I'm one of the reasons," Hodges wrote in *The Game of Baseball* in 1969. "You hear all the jokes about Marv Throneberry, well, remember that Throneberry played while I sat on the bench."

Hodges did start on Saturday, May 4, and got a single off Billy O'Dell in a 17–4 loss to the Giants before being replaced by Throneberry in the eighth inning. That was a special day for him, because over 1,200 spectators and 350 children showed up for the dedication of a facility on McDonald Avenue and Shell Road in Brooklyn, off the Belt Parkway. Gil wrote proudly in his book with Frank Slocum: "It has two ball fields, a concrete grandstand, a clubhouse, dressing rooms with lockers, lavatories and showers. There are water fountains in the dugouts, sprinkler and drainage systems on the field, and lights all around the park. It provides a place to play for five hundred boys who make up the South Highway Little League. I wish my father could have seen all this, and the sign that says, 'Gil Hodges Stadium.'"

Hodges started again in the second game of a doubleheader the next day. In what would be his final game as a player, he went 1-for-4. His final hit, in the fourth inning off left-hander Billy Pierce, drove in Charlie Neal to give the Mets a 3–0 lead. It would prove to be the winning run, in a 4–2 victory. He'd later be fanned by Don Larsen, who shared a history, and pop up to second off Jim Duffalo.

From May 8 on, Hodges was on the disabled list. As he disappeared from the box scores, there was something big going on behind the scenes involving Weiss and George Selkirk, general manager of the Washington Senators. "I don't know if Gil knew George Selkirk but they met at LaGuardia Airport," Joan Hodges recalls. "Then Gil came home. I remember that the children were at the dinner table and I'd already cut him a slice of well-made roast beef, but he said, 'Honey, you have to come upstairs, I need to talk to you.' I said, 'What's the matter?' He said, 'What would you think of my managing the Washington Senators?' I said, 'Who?' He said, 'The Washington Senators!' This was the first time we had ever discussed Gil managing. He was a little apprehensive and, naturally, he asked me what he should do. And I said, 'You're going to manage the Washington Senators and it will be just great. Just think—we don't have to see Willie Mays anymore!'"

Gil Hodges' playing career came to an abrupt conclusion. On May 23, he was officially traded to the Senators for the talented but eccentric outfielder Jimmy Piersall. It was ostensibly a two-*player* deal, but it was understood that Hodges would retire and become the Senators' new manager. "Gil had never said, 'I'm never going to play again,'" says Joan Hodges, "but because of his knee situation and age, he was ready for the change."

According to the record books, in eighteen seasons Hodges appeared in 2,071 games—making 1,908 appearances at first base, 1 at second, 32 at third, 79 in the outfield, and 64 behind the plate. He had 1,921 hits in 7,030 at-bats for a .273 average. He had 295 doubles, 48 triples, and 370 homers. He walked 943 times and struck out 1,137 times. He stole 63 bases in 94 attempts. He scored 1,105 runs and drove in 1,274. He was the National League's all-time home-run king for right-handed batters, and his 14 grand slams set a National League record, too. His 19 sacrifice flies in 1954 was a major-league record. He set numerous league and Dodgers records. He was awarded the first three Gold Gloves ever given to a first baseman and had led the league a few times in various defensive categories. Despite his 0-for-21 in the 1952 World Series, he batted .337 in the next four Series and .267 overall.

His statistics aside, teammates, managers, and opponents agreed that he had been an extraordinary player.

PART IV

The Miracle Manager

CHAPTER TWENTY-TWO

George Selkirk, who was best-known as the man who replaced Babe Ruth in right field when he left the Yankees in 1935, had been given freedom by the team's president, Pete Quesada, to make transactions to improve the Washington Senators, the worst team in baseball other than the Mets. Why he thought of Hodges, a player, to replace manager Mickey Vernon is unclear. Most likely he was recommended by a third party, probably George Weiss, Casey Stengel, or Weiss's assistant Johnny Murphy, who had been Selkirk's roommate for six years on the Yankees. Publicly, Weiss said only that the Mets "didn't want to stand in Hodges' way when he was presented with an opportunity which might not come again."

Many people in baseball expressed surprise at Hodges' sudden career change, but only because they assumed front offices would think him too nice and too quiet to manage, not because they thought he wasn't qualified. "I was surprised he was offered the job," says Ralph Kiner, "but even when he was a young player I thought he'd make a good manager, because he was always into the game and knew what was going on."

"In all the years, he never mentioned managing to me," says Dave Anderson. "I thought he'd just run his bowling alley and be a businessman after he stopped playing, so I was surprised."

"I didn't think he had the right kind of personality to become a manager," Carl Furillo told Marino Amoruso in 1991. "Once he took the job, though, I knew he'd be successful."

"There was never much doubt in my mind that Gil could become an outstanding manager, if he wanted to," wrote Don Drysdale in *Once a Bum, Always a Dodger*. "There were nights on the road when we'd stay up in the room and read that book *The Sporting News* used to publish—*Knotty Problems of Baseball*. It contained stories and vignettes about weird baseball happenings—situations that tested obscure rules, things like that. We'd go over them and then we'd go over the rule book and see if we could figure out answers and solutions and loopholes."

Taking the reins of a team that had just lost 10 of 11 games and was on pace to lose more than 100 times for the third consecutive season wasn't an ideal situation for a neophyte. Of Washington's original 1961 team, only seven players were around two years later, and only five got significant playing time: pitchers Bennie Daniels and Pete Burnside, second baseman Chuck Cottier, and outfielders Chuck Hinton and Jim King. Left-handed Claude Osteen was picked up from Cincinnati during the '61 season and was the ace of a weak staff, ahead of Daniels, Don Rudolph, and Tom Cheney, who struck out a major-league-record 21 in a sixteen-inning game on September 12, 1962. Hinton, who batted .310 in '62, and power-hitting outfielder Don Lock, who would hit 27 homers in his first full year in the majors, stood out in an offense that would bat an abysmal .227 for the year.

"We were in New York when they announced Vernon was fired," recalls Lock. "Mickey was a great guy, so we were sad to see him go. When we got back to Washington, they announced Hodges was our new manager. We were surprised, because he hadn't managed anywhere."

When Hodges came to Washington, he retained Vernon's coaches: George Susce, George Case, Sid Hudson, Danny O'Connell, and Eddie Yost. The Brooklyn-born Yost was known as "the Walking Man" as the lead-off hitter for the original Washington Senators from the late forties until he was dealt to the Tigers in 1959. He wound up on the expansion Angels, as a player and then a coach. "Mickey Vernon and I had been friends on the Senators, and when the Angels let me go, he hired me to coach third base for the expansion Senators in 1963," says Yost. "Mickey was a fantastic guy, but liberal with the young players. The team wasn't winning, and when he got fired I read that the team wanted to go in another direction. Being associated with Gil would be the biggest break of my career."

Selkirk held a press conference in Washington to introduce Hodges.

According to John Devaney's *Gil Hodges: Baseball Miracle Man*, Hodges candidly admitted his wariness about taking his new job. "It scares you a little. I don't even have the slightest idea of whether or not I can be a manager. I have the rest of the season and all of the next to find out. . . ." He also addressed the issue of being too nice to manage: "[M]anaging a ball club has nothing to do with being a nice guy. You have to get the most out of the twenty-five guys available, keep the players' respect, and make the right moves in a game."

Hodges made his managerial debut in a night game in Baltimore on May 23. He was nervous; his wife was emotional. Joan recalls: "I was bringing his car to Baltimore. My sister was driving with me and I started crying. She asked me, 'What's the matter?' I said, 'I just realized I'll never see Gil play first base again. I loved to watch him play first base.' I cried practically all the way."

Hodges' first batting order for the Senators was: Ed Brinkman, SS; Jim King, RF; Chuck Hinton, LF; Bobo Osborne, 1B; Don Lock, CF; Ken Retzer, C; Marv Breeding, 3B; Chuck Cottier, 2B; Claude Osteen, P. Other than the strong-armed Osteen, who was nicknamed "Gomer" because of his resemblance to Jim Nabors' television character Gomer Pyle, everyone had been in Vernon's last lineup, but no one was in the same spot in the order. Hodges hoped to shake things up, but instead got to see what Vernon had been enduring. The Senators managed only 2 hits off former Phillies ace Robin Roberts, and both were by the "good-field, no-hit" Brinkman. No one else reached base as Hodges' new team fell meekly, 6–0.

Years later, in *Sports Illustrated*, Hodges recalled his anxiety on his memorable night: "When we came to bat in the eighth I told Sid Hudson, then our pitching coach, to warm up another pitcher. Roberts gets our first man out in the eighth, and the Baltimore fans start clapping. When he gets the second man out there's more clapping, and I start to wonder what's going on. I turn to Hudson and say, 'Is that pitcher ready to go in? He's not even warming up. Get him ready.' The last man makes out, and I'm still waiting for our new pitcher to come in. Then I suddenly realize that we had just played the top of the ninth, not the eighth, and that the game is over."

The day after his disappointing debut, Hodges returned to New York City, where the Senators opened a four-game series against the Yankees. In the visiting manager's office he greeted the New York reporters who had covered him when he played for the Dodgers and Mets. "I remember think-ing how much Hodges seemed like a manager," George Vecsey remembers. "His transition seemed instantaneous to me. He entertained us New York-ers, politely talking baseball—not gabbing like Stengel did. I felt he was a more decent person than almost anybody you were going to meet in a man-ager's office."

The Yankees, who were on their way to a fourth straight pennant, won the first three games. Hodges could take pride in the Senators taking the finale 7–6, his first victory as a manager. Lock and Breeding got 3 hits each, and Breeding and Brinkman each drove in 2 runs as the Senators ended an 8-game losing streak. Jim Duckworth, pitching in long relief for ex-Yankee Jim Coates, got the victory.

But the Senators then lost 3 in a row to Minnesota and the first game of a series in Kansas City. They had dropped 18 of 20 games, 8 of 9 under Hodges, and their record stood at 15–35, putting them 16 games out of first place on May 31. Even the Mets were 18–31.

Then Hodges, having ordered extra batting practice and running drills for pitchers, enjoyed his first taste of managerial success as the Senators won 4 straight for the first time since the previous July. They beat Kansas City 9–1 as Lock slugged his 7th homer, and 6–4 as Lock homered again and Hinton hit a game-winning 2-run blast in the top of the tenth inning. Then, before a total of 11,679 fans, they triumphed in Hodges' first two games managing at D.C. Stadium, 1–0 behind Tom Cheney, as Lock hit his ninth homer, and 2–1 behind Dave Stenhouse and Ron Kline. The veteran Kline, who faced Hodges many times as a Pirate, would be his most effective re-liever through 1966, relying on a spitter, a pitch the manager regarded with disdain.

"Gil thought the game should be played fairly," says his nephew John Hodges. "Once Yankees catcher Elston Howard was shaving the inside points of his shin guards and cutting the ball for Ford and his other pitchers, so Gil went early to the ballpark and took Howard's shin guards from his locker and back to the Senators' clubhouse. Nothing was ever said."

The Senators resumed their losing ways, dropping 21 of their next 25 games. They finished June with a 23–56 record. A familiar sight was Hodges taking out his pitcher. "I still picture the way he went to the mound," says Russ White, who covered the Senators for the *Washington Daily News* and was allowed by Hodges to work out with the team because of his athleticism. "His hands would be out front as he'd walk and sometimes he'd swing them back and they'd come up to the front together." He had the look of a father walking to the edge of the surf to tell his reluctant kids that they'd been in the water too long.

"I don't think my father had expectations of having a rough time managing a bad team," says Gil Jr. "He had expectations only of what he could do to make it better. Managing the Senators became his passion. He was enjoying himself, but my mother worried about him more than when he was a player, because the frustration he felt was too much for him to get out of his system. As a player, Dad had a single person's responsibility. As a manager, he felt he should take on the responsibility of twenty-five others. He couldn't hit for them, run the bases for them, or field for them, but if players didn't do it the right way or try to do their best every game, he thought that was a reflection on the type of job he was doing. He needed the players to have enough pride to exert a maximum effort on every play. He took it very personally."

Early on Hodges had the troubling realization that for the rest of the 1963 season he wouldn't do any better than his predecessor with the personnel he inherited. "Hodges came to the Senators as an idealist who thought everything was going to work as he hoped," remembers Lock. "But he was new to managing and learned so much putting up with us. We gave him a good education."

Hodges wanted his players to perform and act like professionals. To accomplish this he had no problem both setting and enforcing rules, and doling out discipline. Playing no favorites, he levied fines when players missed curfews, showed up late for games or meetings, or made mental mistakes on the field. (What he didn't tell the players was that all fine money was donated to the Muscular Dystrophy Association.)

Don Zimmer was picked up, and Hodges was happy to have a veteran who could show the young Senators how to act professionally on and off the field. Zimmer discovered that his ex-teammate who never questioned authority had transformed into a strict disciplinarian whom several players nicknamed "D.I.," for drill instructor. Zimmer thought it was a good thing. "I saw that right away," he wrote in his autobiography, *Zim: A Baseball Life*. "Chuck Hinton, our best player, and Minnie Minoso, our oldest player and a bit of a legend by then, were late for a game one day. In front of everyone in the clubhouse, Gil really lit into them. I took that lesson with me for the rest of my life in baseball. The one thing I wouldn't stand for [as manager] was guys being late to the ballpark."

"Gil was in the learning stages of managing, and you could tell he was going to be good," says Ed Roebuck, whom Selkirk acquired from the Dodgers for Breeding in late July. "Gil saw the worst," he said in *We Played the Game*. "Some of us drank too much, some chased women too much, some of us gambled too much. He was trying to be too easy on us. Later he probably said, 'If this is the way it's going to be, I'm not going to be one of the boys.'"

Of the seasoned veterans and undeveloped youngsters who comprised the Senators, those who had the most trouble adjusting to Hodges thought he exerted too much authority. "When push came to shove, by God, it had to be his way," says Lock, whom Hodges criticized for striking out too often in clutch situations with the bat on his shoulder. "He had certain things that he thought everybody needed to adhere to, and that was his right. He was tough and could be sarcastic and too personal."

"He had an intimidating look, and you didn't question his decisions," says Daniels, "but he was a very nice guy and you had to respect him. We didn't have suitable players, but he did as good a job as a manager could."

It took about six weeks before Hodges' tough managerial style began to pay dividends. The Senators won their first 7 games in July, the longest winning streak in their brief history. Despite going 3–9 to conclude July, it would be their only month with a winning record, 14–12, and first winning month since May 1961.

Hodges couldn't convert the Senators into a good ball club overnight, but they were gaining respectability around the league. "I saw a difference in the Senators," said Harmon Killebrew, the 1963 American League home-run champion, in 2011. "People were saying that Hodges was more serious as a manager than anyone would have thought. I admired him from the Twins' dugout."

"I was on Kansas City," recalls Ed Charles, "and I could see Hodges' impact on the Senators. It was like night and day. They played with more energy and focus. I would critique opposing managers, and I was very impressed with Hodges."

By July, Hodges felt more settled as the Senators manager. A major reason was that his family had joined him in D.C. During the school year, Joan drove down most weekends when the Senators were at home, sometimes bringing the children. Then for the summer, the Hodges family lived together in a suite with a kitchen at the first-class Shoreham Hotel, at the intersection of Connecticut Avenue and Calvert Street. The entire family enjoyed the arrangement.

"I was fortunate being the only boy in the family, because I got to spend the summers traveling with my father and the Senators," Hodges Jr. remembers. "On every road trip, I would go with them. My father would get permission from the umpires for me to put on a uniform, work out with the team, and sit on the bench during games. The hardest part was on Sunday mornings, when we had to get up at seven to be at eight-o'clock Mass before going to the ballpark at nine thirty. It was like, 'Dad, can't we sleep? Saturday was a night game and we didn't get home until late!' 'No, we're going to church.' But when we talked it was father-to-son, not religious, and I remember Dad telling me that whatever career I chose, I should do it the best that I could."

While in Washington, Gil Jr. learned a little about his father's mysterious war history. "When I was growing up, I asked him a couple of times what he did with the Marine Corps. And he'd tell me, 'Nothing, just sat behind a desk.' He wouldn't talk about it, because there was something that still bothered him. Someone called and said he wanted to get some information about his career in the service. I said, 'Okay, but I don't really think there's much.' He said, 'I don't know what you mean by *not much*, but your father was awarded several medals.' I wasn't surprised my father didn't tell me about the medals but that he told me he sat behind a desk. I can only think he did that some of the time so that what he said was correct, because he taught his kids that 'The one thing that you don't do in life is lie.' We could do just about anything within the limits of reason, but if we lied the punishment was astronomical."

Hodges was also feeling more at home in Washington because he built friendships with members of the Washington press. Shirley Povich, the dean of the city's writers, and Bob Addie often hung around with Hodges at the ballpark and wrote warmly about him in the *Washington Post*. Unlike his close friend Russ White, they didn't care that he was bad copy. "I say this with respect," says White, "but he was the worst interview. He was happy to talk around the batting cage, but he was dull, reserved, and protective of his players. When I'd come home I'd gripe, 'Good grief, he just wouldn't say anything!'"

Hodges probably preferred not talking much to the press about games or his players during the last couple of months of the season, as the Senators went 19–38, and he spent a lot of time silently staring out the team bus window as frustration built inside. The Senators finished the season with a 56–106 record, 5 games better than the Mets, but last in the American League by 14 games, and 48½ games behind the champion Yankees. Under Hodges, the Senators went 42–79. There wasn't much to praise, statistically, other than Cheney's 2.71 ERA; Kline's 17 unofficial saves; Lock's 27 homers, 82 RBIs, and league-best 377 putouts in centerfield; King's 24 homers; and Brinkman's participation in a league-high 97 double plays. Osteen led the staff with only 9 victories. But the team was playing better fundamental baseball, and the environment in the Senators' clubhouse had changed for the better. Hodges anticipated improvement and enthusiastically looked forward to his first full year as manager.

During the 1964 spring training at Pompano Beach, he got to further stamp his identity on the Senators as well as teach and evaluate his players. "Hodges gathered us together at the beginning of spring training and said he wanted us to win more games and told us how we were going to do it," says Lock. "Like anyone taking over a team, he revealed certain philosophies and had us practice cutoffs and rundowns. It was the basic spring training everybody does."

It wasn't standard operating procedure that the manager threw batting practice so he could see how his hitters handled certain pitches. And the way he scrutinized pitchers wasn't business as usual either. "I had never heard of a manager going behind the plate and calling balls and strikes to see the pitches we were throwing," recalls Jim Hannan, who made forty-two appearances as a rookie in 1962 and thirteen in late 1963. "The umpire is your manager and he's going to make a decision on whether you make the club or not? Talk about pressure."

The addition of the erudite Hannan, whose master's thesis at Notre Dame was about baseball's pension fund, and the purchase of former Yankees' ace reliever Marshall Bridges made Roebuck expendable. After he was roughed up in a Grapefruit League game, he asked Hodges to trade him. He remembered in 2011, "He was my idol and I liked pitching for him, but I wasn't getting it done. I might have been trying too hard." After two appearances in April, he would be sold to Philadelphia, where he'd have a couple of good years under Gene Mauch.

One of the team's new additions in camp was switch-hitting outfielder Fred Valentine. He had played for Baltimore in 1963, but after the season ended he found out on his car radio that he'd been purchased by the last-place Senators. "I almost ran off the road," Valentine recalls. "I said, 'Oh, no!' But later I realized I'd get more playing time on Washington and get to play for Hodges. The only thing he told us at spring training was that he expected everybody to play one hundred percent all the time. Our only goal was to get out of the cellar."

Opening Day at D.C. Stadium on April 13 was extremely emotional, coming less than five months after the assassination of President John F. Kennedy. Catholics in America felt they lost a family member, and the Hodges were no exceptions. It would take a combination of a new baseball season and a social and cultural revolution ignited by the Beatles to revive spirits, particularly in Washington. Kennedy's successor, Lyndon Johnson, threw out the ceremonial first pitch, and the hope was that the Senators could play a part in bringing back a sense of optimism to the city.

Hodges' lineup was slightly different from in his first game in May 1963. Against Los Angeles Angels right-hander Ken McBride, Don Blasingame started at second base and led off. Onetime Yankees' All-Star first baseman Bill Skowron had been acquired from the Dodgers and was batting cleanup. The promising John Kennedy, a namesake of the late president, started at third. The outfield of Hinton, Lock, and King was back intact, although Valentine would get some playing time. Brinkman was still Hodges' shortstop, despite a .212 lifetime average. Retzer was again the starting catcher, although he would be demoted after batting .094 in seventeen games and lose his position to Mike Brumley.

This lineup did even worse than the one that got 2 hits and zero runs in Hodges' managerial debut. In a 4–0 defeat, their only hit was a double by Osteen, the losing pitcher. Still, the Senators split their first twelve games, the first time they'd done that in their history. By the end of May they were only 19–29, but they were in eighth place and had won their last 4 extra-inning games.

Hodges was pleased by his team's victories but he lost sleep over the tough losses. The worst was on May 31, when the Senators were up 6–5 in the ninth inning with two outs and two strikes on Cleveland's Vic Davalillo. Davalillo reached first base when Brumley missed a third strike, and the Indians rallied to score 4 runs for a 9–6 victory.

Hodges lamented what could have been if there hadn't been fielding lapses by Kennedy, Zimmer, and Blasingame that resulted in losses. "Except for those errors, we could have been pretty respectable this year," he observed. "I said at the beginning of the season that clubs like ours can't afford to give anything away. I refuse to believe this is a bad club in Washington. The players really try. Maybe they've been trying too hard."

The Senators' drive toward respectability took a detour when they went 3–16. On July 12, their record was a dismal 32–55, and they had fallen into tenth place. The pitching was decent but the team had scored more than 5 runs only 3 times, and even the veterans continued to make costly errors. Selkirk traded Skowron despite his respectable stats to the White Sox for Joe Cunningham, an excellent-fielding first baseman and contact hitter. Hodges juggled his lineup, often to the consternation of players who were benched against certain pitchers or platooned. "I never put anybody in the doghouse," Hodges contended. "I'm always trying to get a lineup which will win. I have to figure out the percentages and who's pitching. Some batters do better against certain pitchers. That's elementary. But baseball has become highly specialized and you can't overlook a single possibility which will lead to victory."

"When you were in the locker room," says Hannan, "you could tell when Gil walked in, because suddenly the guys who were looking in his direction became quiet. It's not that he wasn't well liked—he just had that presence about him. I had some little father-son confrontations with him, because he was a perfectionist and I wasn't, but I always respected him. He even taught me how to place my thumb so I could throw a better slider— how many managers do things like that?"

"He was a highly principled man," says Lock. "I have to give him credit for that. Eventually he became a good manager, but those first couple of years it was a real learning process for him, and he was stern and very tough. He wasn't harder on kids than veterans; he treated everybody equally. When Hinton caught a fly and forgot how many outs there were and a big run scored from second base, Hodges took out his fine book real quick."

"I thought he treated the ballplayers well and could have been harder on some of them, particularly the veterans who didn't think they had to follow rules anymore," says Valentine. "We weren't a good team and made plenty of mistakes, and he had to endure pretty much. I could tell that he was keeping too much in, because sometimes he'd get upset and you could see the muscles in his neck puffing up. He really needed to just let it all out, but he wasn't the type of person to do that."

Although the team was going through a down period, on July 1, James M. Johnston, the chairman of the board of the Senators and the new co-owner of the team with James H. Lemon, tore up the existing contracts for Hodges and Selkirk and gave them extensions. Hodges' job was guaranteed through 1966, making him the most secure manager in the majors. Hodges was elated with the new contract, which continued to pay him $40,000 a year, and that Joan and their four children could continue spending summers in the nation's capital. "We have the nucleus of a fine club," he said. "We need improvement at three or four positions and I'm sure we'll produce the players. Some of the problems already have diminished and I believe the future is bright."

In 1964, the Senators were shut out 22 times, including 4 times in a row in early September, while their own pitchers threw only 5 shutouts all season. They won games by more than 5 runs only seven times all season, while being blown out twenty-seven times. They had a winning record against only Kansas City. Their most sustained winning streaks lasted only 4 games, which they managed twice between July 26 and August 14. Yet they stayed within sniffing distance of ninth place because they never lost more than 8 games in a row. The Senators went only 9–19 in September and October, but they notched ninth place because Kansas City went 8–22, and they did well against the White Sox. Hodges reminded his team that during spring training, the Senators arrived in Sarasota to play Chicago, only to discover that the hotel rooms they had reserved had been taken over by their opponent. They hadn't forgotten the mistreatment and beat the Sox 4 out of 5 games late in the year, causing them to finish 1 game behind the Yankees, who took their fifth consecutive American League flag.

The Senators were jubilant to finish in ninth place, 5 games ahead of the A's. Their record was 62–100. They had two pitchers who won in double figures and had winning records: Osteen, 15–13, and Kline, who went 10–7, with 14 unofficial saves. Lock batted just .242, but led the team with 28 homers and 80 RBIs. Hinton had only 11 homers and 53 RBIs, but still led the team with a .274 average.

The Senators had met Hodges' modest goal of finishing out of the cellar for the first time. Now he decided to make several big changes so they could meet his next goal, which was to move farther up in the standings.

CHAPTER TWENTY-THREE

Changes for the Senators' 1965 season began with Hodges' coaching staff, after Hobie Landrith and Danny O'Connell unexpectedly quit in January to pursue careers in business. In what proved to be his wisest personnel move, Hodges brought in two former Dodgers teammates, both ex-catchers like himself. "In Brooklyn, Gil and I and our wives would often play poker to four or five in the morning," recalls Joe Pignatano. "One night after we finished playing, he said, 'By the way, would you like to coach for me?' I had just told my my manager in the minor leagues that I was retiring as a player because the money wasn't good enough. So I said to Gil, 'You gotta be kidding me! Damn right!'" Pignatano would coach first base. Hodges also hired Rube Walker, who had been managing in the minors, to be his pitching coach. (Sid Hudson became the organization's roving pitching instructor.) Yost, Pignatano, and Walker would be Hodges' coaches for the rest of his managerial career and be instrumental to his success.

Tinkering with the roster, Hodges had Selkirk trade Hinton to the Indians for outfielder/shortstop Woodie Held and first baseman Bob Chance. The Dodgers were so worried after Sandy Koufax was diagnosed with an arthritic condition that they were willing to give up Frank Howard for a good southpaw. In a blockbuster deal, the Senators sent their ace left-hander Claude Osteen, John Kennedy, and $100,000 to L.A. for Howard, left-handed pitcher Pete Richert, righty Phil Ortega, first baseman Dick Nen, and promising third baseman Ken McMullen.

Hodges remembered McMullen from his L.A. Dodgers days. "I

wouldn't know until years later that I wasn't a throw-in, but that Gil was excited to get me because of my defense," recalls McMullen, who was in-tially devastated by the trade. "I was from California and had never even been to Washington. The only consolation was that a bunch of us were go-ing." Hoping to beat out Don Zimmer at third, McMullen was one of sev-eral position players who arrived with the pitchers and catchers at spring training in Pompano Beach.

Howard arrived a few days later with the rest of the position players for the earliest regular camp in the majors. "Hodges impressed the heck out of me," Howard remembers. "If you want to talk about professionalism, dig-nity, aura, he was right up there. He was a very dapper ex-Marine—shoes were shined, pants were pressed, clean shaven every day. You don't have to be a Rhodes scholar to see class and have class." Hodges worked with How-ard on his hitting. He and his coaches were impressed by the extra time Howard spent every morning in the batting cage. "His problems weren't that hard to see or diagnose," Hodges wrote in his book. "He wanted to improve, and . . . I can say in all honesty that I never had a player who worked harder."

There was more optimism in camp than the previous year. "Those boys acted like a winning club," says Pignatano, who would eat breakfast at IHOP every morning with Hodges and Walker and go over the plans for the day. "There was no air of defeatism around here."

A major reason the camp ran better in 1965 was that Hodges made his coaches the liaisons to the players. "All managers say, 'My door is always open,' but you're hesitant to go in," McMullen says. "With Gil, it wasn't just that I found him scary but that there was the respect factor. It was like not wanting to disappoint your dad. So if there was a problem I'd speak to Ed-die Yost or the other coaches."

Walker, the liaison to the pitchers, began sitting with Hodges on the bench during exhibition games, a practice that continued during the season. "Gil and Rube were a good team," states Russ White, "especially in regard to bringing in and taking out relief pitchers. Ron Kline was a very good, reliable reliever, but they did a good job juggling the guys who weren't that talented."

Kline appreciated that if Hodges had him warm up, he was definitely coming into the game. Jim Hannan appreciated that pitchers in the bull pen learned to tell by the situation who was going to get up and pitch: "Rube and Gil obviously talked about who they each wanted to relieve before Gil made the final decision. There was no one better at handling a pitching staff."

Hodges relied on his coaches but there was no doubt that he was in charge, the field general. Coaches and players alike were amazed by his ability to assess game situations quickly. "Gil was a very quiet, straitlaced guy," Yost remembers, "but he knew the game as good as anybody. He sat on the bench perfectly still and concentrated like a chess player thinking many moves ahead."

"In addition to his tremendous instincts and insights," says Howard, "his depth perception and peripheral vision were unparalleled. He did not miss a beat as far as knowing what was happening out in left field and where the right fielder was positioned, while keeping his eye on the shortstop. He saw everything."

Opening Day was in Washington, as usual. A season-high 43,554 fans were on hand to see Hodges unveil his new lineup against Boston Red Sox ace right-hander Bill Monbouquette: Don Blasingame, 2B; Ken Mc-Mullen, 3B; Bob Chance, 1B; Frank Howard, LF; Don Lock, CF; Willie Kirkland, RF; Mike Brumley, C; Ed Brinkman, SS; and Phil Ortega, P. The Sox, managed by Billy Herman, won 7–2 in a game in which all 9 runs were scored on home runs—Boston hit 5 off Ortega; McMullen and Lock went deep for the home team. McMullen's power surprised and pleased his new manager.

The Senators beat the Red Sox in the next game, 6–4, with a late-inning rally against reliever Dick Radatz. Then they beat Chicago 3–1, as Bennie Daniels, McCormick, and Kline combined on a 4-hitter and Howard and Kirkland hit ninth-inning home runs. The Senators' record was 2–1, and though they'd play much better baseball than in their previous years, it would be the only time they were over .500 all season. Hodges wondered whether things would be any different as his team then went 2–11 to fall into ninth place. Daniels was the losing pitcher in the last game of the bad stretch. "I won in my first start but I had a bad elbow and had trouble winning," says Daniels about his last season. "I started losing my hair."

As his pitchers struggled and hitters sputtered—between April 15 and

May 7, the Senators scored as many as 5 runs only once—Hodges' hair remained on his head but his smoking intensified. "He chain-smoked one after another after another," says White. "Every year, when they came back from spring training, he had terrible colds and would be coughing and smoking. It was horrible. He was such a big, rugged man, but he was always trying to hide his anxieties. I remember a flight in '64 or '65 from Washington to Kansas City when there was a lot of turbulence. Players were losing it. Hodges had the window seat and was reading a paperback. I'm sitting next to him and thinking, 'How in the world is this guy so calm?' I looked over again and he's got this little grin on his face, and I could see that the book was upside down." In his position of leadership, Hodges wanted his players to have confidence that he was in control in *all* circumstances.

The Senators played better in May, winning 3 out of 4 from the Yankees and 6 of 8 overall as Kline won once and had 4 unofficial saves, and Ortega won back-to-back starts. Ortega's 5–4 victory over Whitey Ford, as Howard drove in 2 runs and McMullen got 3 hits and an RBI, put the Senators in seventh place for a day. They dropped their next 4 games, but the offense finally got into gear and they won 3 of 4. In an 8–7 win over Cleveland, Howard hit a 2-run homer and had 4 RBIs, and McMullen homered in the eleventh inning for a dramatic ending to the game.

Howard and McMullen gave the lineup an obvious lift. "Frank Howard in the batting order unquestionably changed the dynamic of the team," said Harmon Killebrew, a few months before his death in May 2011. "He was a real threat who gave everyone confidence."

McMullen also provided some power, and worked endlessly with Yost and Pignatano to become a premier third baseman. In a game against the Orioles, McMullen tied a record by starting 4 double plays. Hodges raved that he was the best in the league at picking up topped balls, better than even Brooks Robinson. "Eddie Brinkman and I were roommates and took pride in plugging up the left side of the infield," he says. "Eddie didn't hit too much, but he had a great arm and range."

Howard and McMullen provided heroics in several games, including when the Senators scorched Detroit 15–9 in their biggest output of the year. But when managing the Senators, pressure was a constant for Hodges, and frustration was around the corner. Indeed, a loss two games later, on May

20 against the Tigers, was probably the most maddening of Hodges' managerial career. Jake Wood homered leading off against Frank Kreutzer, and 3
runs and only 1 out later, Hodges was compelled to take out his starter. The
Senators cut the lead to 4–3 on homers by Held and Brinkman off Mickey
Lolich in the second inning, but the Tigers upped the lead to 6–3 in the
third after a two-out error by Brinkman. The Senators pecked away at the
Tigers' lead until Howard tied the game in the ninth inning on a home run
off Larry Sherry, the former Dodger. After a sacrifice fly by Kirkland, the
Senators finally had the lead, 7–6. In the bottom of the ninth, Steve Ridzik
retired the first two Tigers on ground outs, but he walked both former-
Dodger Don Demeter and Willie Horton. Hodges was already steamed
when Bill Freehan lofted a ball toward center. Held, a converted shortstop,
came in and then went back. The ball dropped behind him, allowing the
tying run to score. The game went into the top of the tenth inning with the
score deadlocked 7–7. Lock, hitting around .210, broke the tie with a pinch
homer. With two left-handed batters due up, Hodges brought in the lefty
Marshall Bridges to protect the 8–7 lead. Bridges walked left-handed Jim
Northrup leading off the inning. With one out, left-handed Dick McAuliffe
stroked a 2-run homer to give the Tigers a 9–8 victory.

Lock remembers Hodges "storming into the clubhouse" and berating
Held and Bridges. Hodges Jr. recalls, "I was with Rube Walker and wearing
my Senators uniform. As we got near the clubhouse, Rube says to me,
'Change out here and get in the shower, but don't go in there.' I'm fifteen; I
do what I'm told. Door's closed, forty-five minutes, an hour, everyone's on
the bus waiting for my father. Maybe an hour and fifteen minutes pass, the
door opens, and he comes out, all dressed. I wanted to know what took him
so long, so I looked back into the room. You know those four-legged stools,
round at the top, two sets of brackets? Well, he had pulled them apart. I was
glad I listened to Rube. Dad didn't want his players to see that side of him."

Those who knew Hodges best believed such outbursts were preferable
to his keeping his emotions in check all the time. "I remember writing a
piece after a tough loss to Minnesota," says White. "The Twins played out
in the country and we were taking the bus back to the city. He always sat in
the front row across the aisle from the bus driver, and if he wasn't talking to
Rube he'd be doing crossword puzzles. That day he just stared out the win-

dow the entire time, not uttering a word. He was angry. He was disappointed. He was brooding and contemplative. Everything was etched on his face."

"Gil had a lot tension when guys played poorly," says Pignatano. "It really bothered him, especially when a fielder didn't know what to do with the ball, which is what he emphasized beginning in spring training. When a fielder missed a cutoff man, smoke would come out of Gil's ears. But he wouldn't chew out anyone until he got them alone in his office. He didn't care if they liked him, he just wanted them to play better."

After Hodges' outburst, which he regretted, the Senators did an about-face and played good baseball for two weeks. They split 4 games at Yankee Stadium, took 3 of 4 from the Angels at home, and then swept back-to-back doubleheaders from Kansas City and the Angels in Los Angeles. It was a brief time when almost every move Hodges made paid off.

"I saw Gil as a manager who knew what he was going to do the next inning and probably the inning after that," says Pignatano. "He was always ahead of the game and would get guys ready to pinch-run or pinch-hit in advance. Gil knew how to play the game. He absorbed so much and forgot nothing. He had an amazing mind."

One of Hodges' main concerns was the high number of strikeouts his batters were accumulating. At the end of the year Lock would have 115, Howard 112, and McMullen 90. He felt that the strikeouts were a big reason his players' RBI totals were low.

"It would drive Hodges crazy when guys would take third strikes with men on base," Zimmer wrote in his autobiography. "I said to him, 'Do you think I never saw you take a called third strike?' 'Yeah,' he said, 'but that don't count.'"

At times Hodges would toss batting practice. He said he did it to help keep in shape—"I don't think it goes well for the fans to see a big, fat, sloppy manager in uniform"—and to dissect his batters' swings—"I can pick out flaws I can't see otherwise." On June 12, prior to a Friday-night doubleheader with the White Sox, he was throwing to Lock, who was hitting just .203 and was struggling his way to a 39-RBI season.

"He wanted to work with Lock, who he thought of as a pupil," says Yost. "He liked something about his hitting but wanted to improve him. After one pitch his head was hanging out the right of the screen and Lock lined the ball right off it. Gil never budged, never went down. I couldn't believe it."

"I didn't really think it was scary," says Lock. "Guys would get hit on the coconut all the time, so I didn't think much about it. I remember he was dizzy and sore, so they took him to the hospital as a precautionary thing. He might have considered it a good thing, because he was always giving me heck about not hitting the ball up the middle."

"George Selkirk called the house, and I drove to the hospital in Washington," recalls Joan. "Gil was nauseous, and his eyes were bloodshot and he had a bump the size of a small eggplant on the side of his head."

Hodges told reporters, "I had some buzzing in my head and couldn't sleep," as he returned to the dugout the next day, putting the incident behind him. He watched as Lock smashed a grand slam, only his third homer of the season, and Daniels 5-hit the White Sox, 7–1. It was Daniels' fifth win of the season. He'd lose his next eight decisions and be sent to Hawaii, his major league career over.

The Senators won only 3 of their next 15 games, but they remained in ninth place. Also Richert, who didn't have Ortega's changeup but threw harder, further proved that he was the steal of the December trade when he blanked the Orioles 2–0, outdueling emerging star Jim Palmer. He then held the White Sox in check, 5–1, besting Juan Pizarro. He established himself as the ace of the staff as the Senators went 42–47 the rest of the way, the best-sustained good baseball they had ever played.

There were still some losses that Hodges had trouble stomaching, such as 2–1 to the Yankees on July 15, when home-plate umpire Bob Stewart ruled that Ridzik nicked Clete Boyer with a pitch with the bases loaded in the bottom of the twelfth inning. Hodges joined Ridzik and his catcher Doug Camilli in an argument at home plate. Unlike when he was a player, Hodges would protest when he felt umpires blew a call. "He'd argue, but it wasn't ranting or raving," says McMullen. "He'd point his finger and get his points across. He didn't go out that often, but when there was a wrong on the field, he would be out there fighting for us."

"As a player, I had to protect only myself," Hodges told Bob Addie. "As a manager, the entire squad is my responsibility."

Among those he felt responsible for was onetime Yankees' relief ace Ryne Duren, who had joined the Senators early in the season from Philadelphia. The fireballing right-hander with poor eyesight and severe drinking problems had a few good outings, but on the afternoon of August 18 he was roughed up and realized it was becoming a pattern. That night, during one of his frequent blackouts from drinking, Duren ended up on a bridge on Connecticut Avenue near the Windsor Park Hotel, where the players stayed. He was threatening to jump, so the police summoned Hodges to talk him down in the middle of the night. "Gil told me I was too good a person to kill myself and I needed help," Duren recalled in his 2003 autobiography *I Can See Clearly Now.* "That was the end of my career and my first attempt at killing myself." (Duren would stop drinking and until his death in 2010 traveled across the country giving lectures to youths to discourage them from following his path.)

The Senators went 70–92 and moved up to eighth place, its best finish yet, well ahead of Boston and Kansas City. In the home-run department, Howard clouted 21, McMullen 18, and Lock and Held 16. Howard led the team with 81 RBIs, while Held, Kirkland, and McMullen tied for second place with only 54 RBIs. The staff was led by Richert, who went 15–12 with a 2.60 ERA, and Kline, who made 74 appearances and went 7–6 with a 2.63 ERA and league-best 29 unofficial saves. "I can't express how much it meant to me that Gil was willing to stick with me," Richert told *Sports Illustrated*, pointing out that he'd given up a run per inning in the Grapefruit League. "He shows greater understanding of pitchers than any manager I've worked under," said Kline.

Particularly gratifying for Hodges was that the Senators finished only 7 games behind the sixth-place Yankees, whose championship years were over because of age, injuries, and a downgrade in their farm system after George Weiss was let go. Although the Twins, who would lose to the Dodgers in the World Series, beat them out by 32 games, Washington's eighth-place finish meant they were no longer the punch line of the familiar joke: "First in war, first in peace, and last in the American League." They were a team on the rise.

During the off-season, Hodges was kept busy by public appearances, the winter meetings, and other baseball activities. When he had free time at home, he spent it at his bowling alley. "That was his other job, so he'd go there every day when he was in Brooklyn," recalls Cindy. "I went there a lot after school and bowled with Daddy and Gilly, who was left-handed. Both were awesome bowlers. Daddy wasn't competitive when he bowled; it was just a sport that he liked. He had his own ball, so his fingers fit."

Hodges continued to return to Petersburg in the off-season. Keeping a low profile, he'd visit Bob King in the barbershop, Bob Harris in the funeral parlor, and another close friend and huge baseball fan, Father Vieck at the church, among others. But mostly he spent time with his mother, grandmother Ellen, and Bob's family in Evansville. "We were crazy about Uncle Gil," says Ann Hodges, who was seven in 1966. "We would get so excited that 'Uncle Gil's coming!' He'd hit the door running and he was ready for us seven kids. He'd have two or three of us hanging on him at the same time, and he'd do whatever we wanted him to do. He was like a big pool toy! Uncle Gil and Dad were very close, and we never heard a cross word between them. They thought and acted alike."

"They were also alike in that they kept things bottled up inside," says Mike Hodges. "You'd never know if anything was wrong."

"Bob was a wonderful man who loved my dad," says Gil's daughter Irene. "We'd say, 'Hi, Uncle Bob, how are you?' 'Good.' 'How are the kids?' 'Tolerable.' You could ask him that question two thousand times and that's how he'd answer."

After Indiana, the Hodges family went to Florida for spring training. Louis Lombardi, who played at the Stork Club in New York for a few years, and his wife Alma moved to Miami in the sixties. He played in a band at the Eden Roc hotel and she sang at the Fontainebleau. "Gil would come down with the kids and rent a house close to where we were staying," recalls Lombardi. "Then we'd rent a boat and go fishing—Gil, Irene, and Gilly. We took pictures of us holding up all the fish we caught. I also played golf with Gil the week that pitchers and catchers came to camp."

Hodges' brother-in-law remembers when the two of them were at a New York nightclub, and Louis Prima led his band off the stage during a rousing "When the Saints Go Marching In" directly to where Hodges was sitting, one celebrity paying tribute to another. Something similar happened in Florida. Joan recalls:

One night we went with my cousin and her husband to see Frank Sinatra at the Fontainebleau. He's performing beautifully, and all of a sudden he turns to Nelson Riddle and says, "Cut the music. Somebody told me that Gil Hodges is in the audience. I want to put the spotlight on him." Gil nervously waved and took a bow while everybody applauded.

When the show resumed, my husband was told, "Mr. Sinatra would like you and your guests to come to his dressing room after the show, because he'd like to invite you to dinner." My cousin and I got so excited and rushed into the ladies' room to fix our makeup and hair. When the show ended Gil asked the waiter if he'd kindly bring him a paper and a pen. I said to him, "What was that for, honey?" He said, "Honey, we're not going out with Frank Sinatra. We're going back to the hotel." I said to him, "Tell me you're joking! You're going to say no to Frank Sinatra?" He said, "My team has lost five straight games, and you want me to be seen in a restaurant at two in the morning with Frank Sinatra?" I didn't talk to him for two weeks. I cried and everything else but he didn't feel at all guilty.

"I doubt if Gil would have had a good time with Sinatra because he had to be in his comfort zone to enjoy being with people," says Joan Hodges. "Robert Merrill, who later introduced me to Sinatra, once invited us to Toots Shor's. Gil didn't want to go because there was a game the next day, but I said, 'No, we have to go. I want to be with Robert Merrill, Richard Tucker, and other opera stars.' We went, and if Gil said two words that might be an exaggeration."

Hodges was back in his element in Pompano Beach in 1966. Again he was baseball's most hands-on manager, pitching batting practice, hitting fungoes, and instructing at first and third bases. But having been sent to the hospital in 1965 when Fred Valentine struck him on the head with his bat, he left the catching to Walker, Pignatano, and Susce. To make sure everyone would exercise and eat properly during the off-season, as he did himself, Hodges had initiated a new policy at the end of the 1965 season. He told his players to show up at camp at a projected weight or they would be fined. When Frank Howard arrived, Hodges told him he had to lose twenty pounds. After the first week, he had lost two pounds. "Panic set in," according to Hodges Jr., "and Howard began running back to the hotel wearing a rubber suit. At the next weigh-in my father told him, 'Frank, you've got to lose nine more pounds or you're going to be fined ten dollars a pound.' Thinking he could handle a ninety-dollar fine, Howard replied, 'Okay, Gil, no problem.' He began to walk out of the locker room, and at the last second my father added, 'That's a *day!*' Believe me, every time you tried to slip away from my father thinking you were home free, he would pause for a moment and then deliver his tag line."

As in '65, the Senators had a poor April in '66, going 3–9. The one bright spot was lefty Mike McCormick, who won twice and pitched well in the other victory. No longer in the bullpen, McCormick would go 11–14 for the season as the third starter, behind Richert, 14–14, and Ortega, 12–12.

Other than inserting McCormick into his rotation, Hodges' only other major moves were making Cuban Paul Casanova his starting catcher and giving the switch-hitting Valentine the right-field job. Casanova thrived under Hodges, who built his confidence by shaking his hand after every game. After Howard (.278, 18 homers, 71 RBIs), Valentine was the Senators' most consistent offensive player, batting .276, with 16 homers and 59 RBIs from mostly the leadoff spot, and 22 stolen bases. "I might have hit .300 but I played hurt," says Valentine. "I would have played for Hodges on one leg. He was a nice man trying to get the best out of his players, and they were making mistakes you don't make in the major leagues, and he would just absorb it. The only rules he enforced were curfews."

The curfew story that everyone still tells took place in the mid-sixties. One night, about ten minutes before curfew, Hodges was chatting with friends outside the hotel where the team was staying when he spotted four players going out. The next day he addressed his team, telling them that he knew four players broke curfew. "I know who you are," he said, "and I'm going to give you a chance to save some money. If the guilty ones leave checks for fifty dollars in a hat in my office, the case will be closed. If the money isn't in today, the fine will be a hundred dollars." Gil went out to hit fungoes. A short time later Pignatano came over grinning. Even Hodges laughed when he learned that there was already $350 in his hat.

On June 11, the *Sporting News* printed an article by Bob Addie titled

"NEXT SKIPPER GENIUS? GIL'S A GOOD BET." Hodges told Addie that he'd been influenced by all his previous managers (including Charlie Dressen, who'd pass away at sixty-seven on August 10). He said that "the hardest job a manager has is handling his men." "Apparently there is no complaint on that score," wrote Addie. "Several players including outfielder Frank Howard will tell you: 'If you can't play for Gil Hodges, you can't play for anybody.'"

Addie didn't seek a quote from Don Lock, but by 1966, even Lock was impressed by the Senators' improvement. "There were a lot of things about Gil that I thought were very tough," he says today, "but you gotta give the man credit. He was a damn good manager."

The biggest malcontent during Hodges' time with the Senators arrived on June 23 in a deal with Kansas City. Twenty-four-year-old Ken Harrelson belted 23 homers with the A's in 1965, and Hodges hoped he was the power-hitting first baseman the Senators had been looking for. Harrelson was extremely likable, but he was a free spirit with a forceful personality, and A's owner Charlie Finley was glad to get him off his hands. Harrelson was thrilled to break away from Finley, but he soon discovered, as he wrote in his 1968 autobiography, *Hawk*, "Joining the Senators was like starting a prison term. Hodges was the warden."

Hawk Harrelson got along with Hodges at the beginning. "He taught me things about playing first base that most ballplayers never know," he wrote. But Harrelson fell out of his good graces after making a costly error against Minnesota and going to Hodges' hotel room to apologize:

> I was there for maybe an hour, most of which was pleasant and re-laxed. I did the talking, telling Gil how much I wanted to help pull the club out of its misery, and he seemed to be sympathetic and grateful. Then I said, "Isn't there something I could do to help snap us out of this slump? Maybe I should start a fight. A good free-for-all might get us all pulling together." Without a word of apprecia-tion, talking like a school principal to a recalcitrant kid, he said, "I don't want to start a fight. This shows me something about the kind of person you are." Suddenly the room felt as if an icy blast had just gone through it. The whole atmosphere changed so fast that I got

up, thanked Hodges for listening, apologized for bothering him and left. And from that night on, he never spoke another civil word to me.

Asking Hodges' permission to start an on-field brawl was akin to inviting the pope to a Saturday-night poker game. Hodges preached the right way to be a professional ballplayer, and Harrelson had chosen exactly the wrong tack to win his favor. Their rift would widen but according to McMullen, "We didn't have a divisive clubhouse because of them. Nobody chose sides."

From June through August, the Senators moved up and down in the standings, from seventh to tenth place. In early June, they lost a season-high eight straight games. In July they won eight straight, the biggest winning streak for a Washington team since 1949, to move briefly into seventh place. Joan missed the first game of the streak so, being superstitious, she forced herself to stay home until the streak was over. "I hope she has to stay home all season," joked Hodges with reporters.

After a so-so August, in September the Senators had the semblance of a stretch drive as they battled Kansas City, Boston, and New York to determine who would finish highest at the back of the standings. It meant a lot to the players and their manager, who definitely felt stressed on September 6 in Detroit. For the first time in his career, Hodges was ejected from a game for arguing that Tigers' first baseman Norm Cash's foot was off the base on a play. The umpire was Al Salerno, who almost threw Hodges out of a previous game. Pignatano, who was coaching first base, recalls this sarcastic exchange that resulted in Hodges getting the thumb:

Salerno: I thought you were a nice guy.
Hodges: I thought you were a good umpire.

"Don't say we didn't warn you," wrote Bob Addie in the *Sporting News.* "For weeks we have been hinting that the boiling point of Washington manager Gil Hodges was getting lower and that his halo showed signs of slipping off."

"I get thrown out of a game and I am [called] rowdy," commented

White Sox manager Eddie Stanky. "Gil gets tossed out and everybody wants to run the umpire out of baseball."

The Senators found themselves in last place on September 10, having lost 8 of 10 games, 4 by shutouts, including back-to-back 1–0 losses to Chicago. There was now the danger of the Senators having a lost season. But Hodges' team showed grit under pressure and won 5 of its final 7 games. Hodges exploded again in a big 5–4 victory over Stanky's Sox, when he was ejected for arguing that Chicago's Bill Skowron had been picked off second base. Salerno was on the umpiring crew, but Bill Kinnamon gave Hodges his second career expulsion.

In the battle for eighth place, Boston and Washington played a doubleheader on the final day of the season. The Red Sox won the first game 5–0, but the Senators came back in the second game, when Hodges chose to start Boston-born Joe Coleman, a rookie who had a bright future but hadn't pitched all year. The tall right-hander improved his major-league record to 3–0, as McMullen hit a solo homer, and Lock, in his last at-bat as a Senator, drilled a 2-run homer for a 3–2 victory.

Washington secured eighth place ahead of Boston with a slightly improved 71–88 record. Their win total and .447 percentage were their highest ever; their loss total and number of games out of first place, 25½, were the fewest. For the first time they had a winning record at home, 42–36. Showing their mettle, they outplayed Boston and last-place New York late in the season and finished only 2½ games behind seventh-place Kansas City.

D.C.'s baseball fans, perhaps preoccupied by the escalation of the Vietnam War, didn't give the Senators the attention and appreciation they deserved. Attendance for the improved team was 576,260, the worst in the league. Only 485 people showed up for the season-ending doubleheader against Boston, although a place in the standings was at stake. But the front office knew what Hodges had done and rewarded him with a contract extension for two more years, through 1968. "My father intended to manage the Senators as long as they wanted him," says Hodges Jr.

Hodges began 1967, his fifth season as the Senators' manager, with only shortstop Eddie Brinkman still in the starting lineup from when he debuted in May of 1963. Lock had been traded in the off-season to the Phillies for lefty reliever Darold Knowles, so bench player Jim King was the only other

'63 starter on the roster—and he'd be traded June 15 to the White Sox. Ron Kline, who had 26 wins and 83 unofficial saves from 1963 to 1966, had been dealt to the Twins in the off-season for veteran pitcher Camilo Pascual and second baseman Bernie Allen, leaving Jim Hannan as the only pitcher who had appeared in 1963. Despite the turnover in personnel, the team, while waiting for Howard to reach his potential, didn't have significantly better statistics or more talent than when Hodges took over. That they played much better and were able to move up in the standings—including in 1967—was testament to his managerial ingenuity and, says Valentine, "his learning to handle players better."

Hodges' relationship with Harrelson was still problematic. There were incidents of Hodges' fining players for infractions, but the most publicized one was when Hodges sent Harrelson home with orders to get a haircut. "There was no time for him to go to a barber," recalls Russ White, "so Bob Humphreys, a relief pitcher, cut his hair. I was the only guy who stood up for Harrelson."

Gil Jr. could relate: "Around that time, I got a job as a lifeguard at a camp in Long Island. Irene told me all the lifeguards had blond hair, so she bleached my hair. My dad comes home and while we eat dinner he's looking at me, and he finally says, 'What the heck happened to you?' So I tell him the story and say, 'I thought it would be funny.' He said, 'Nah, I don't think it's funny at all.' I thought it was the end of the discussion and I was home free, because he started cutting his meat. But he was just waiting for a little time to lapse. He put another slice in his mouth and said, 'I dislike it so much that I think you should stay in your room until it grows out.' And he kept eating. I got my hair buzzed twice and it took two weeks before I was allowed to go out."

Hodges arranged for Harrelson to be returned to Kansas City. Harrelson fired a parting shot, saying, "I can tell you without reservation that every Washington player hates his guts." For years, other Senators would claim Harrelson's words weren't true. Notably, Howard said, "I resent his speaking for the twenty-four other players, including me. Sure, Gil is tough to play for. We had our differences. But he's fair. I have three sons, and if they grow to be one-half the man Hodges is, I'll be happy."

The Senators had their best April in their brief history, 8–9, and were in third place on May 12 with a 12–14 record. A month later they fell into last place. As weeks passed and the Senators remained in the cellar, Hodges' stress level increased. On June 26, in a 4–3 loss to the Angels, he was almost thrown out of another game. Five times in five innings, Hodges "stormed out of the dugout," wrote John Hall of the *Los Angeles Times*, "to argue that [Jack] Hamilton was employing the dreaded spitter." According to Hodges, "Hamilton consistently was throwing a spitter and I would not be fair to my men if I didn't protest."

The Senators had their usual strong July, going 19–12, to jump into sixth place. On August 13, their record was 58–58, and they threatened to become the first Senators team since 1953 to have a winning record. They couldn't continue to play .500 ball, and they remained in sixth place until September 17. On September 25, they were in eighth place, 1½ games behind Baltimore and half a game behind Cleveland. Their record was 72–85, which meant they had won 1 more game than their record high in 1966, but Hodges didn't want to finish eighth for a third consecutive year and he and his team wanted to catch Baltimore, the defending world champions.

Hodges was doing his finest job yet, carrying a team with the worst hitting in the majors and the second-worst ERA in the American League up in the standings. Pascual, a former 20-game winner, was past his prime, but still threw one of the best curves in baseball and finished the year with a winning record, 12–10. Ortega went 10–10. No other Senator won in double figures. Richert had been traded for first baseman Mike Epstein. They were also missing McCormick, who inexplicably had been traded in the off-season to the Giants, where he'd win 22 games and be the National League's Cy Young winner in 1967. To make up for his loss, Hodges got 8 wins from Joe Coleman, 6 from lefty Frank Bertaina, and many wins from his corps of relievers, led by Knowles (61 appearances, 14 unofficial saves, 2.70 ERA) and Dave Baldwin (58 appearances, 12 unofficial saves, 1.70 ERA).

On offense, Howard launched 36 home runs, the highest total of any player Hodges ever managed. He also led the team with 89 RBIs, the most by a Senator during Hodges' time with the team. McMullen had 16 home runs, and at one time had a nineteen-game hitting streak. But Howard led the team with only a .256 average. No one else hit .250, and Brinkman and

Bernie Allen were below .200. In fact, the team batted .223, which was four points worse than the hapless 1963 squad.

The team accumulated wins through clutch hitting and by playing fundamentally sound baseball. And because Hodges wouldn't let them give up. The Senators again showed they could handle pressure as they won their last 4 games, getting strong starting pitching from Buster Narum (who won his only game of the season), Ortega and Bertaina, who both shut out the White Sox, and Dick Bosman. With their final victory, they finished the season with a record of 76–85, identical to that of the Orioles. "There was big competition with the Orioles so tying them meant a lot to us," says Valentine, "and Hodges deserved a lot of credit." The two teams finished in sixth place, 15½ games behind Boston, and as Hodges had been saying since August, "first division is a distinct possibility for us next year."

Meanwhile in New York, Wes Westrum, who became manager of the Mets in July 1965, when Casey Stengel broke his hip, stepped down on September 19. Salty Parker took over temporarily as the team moved toward another tenth-place finish, after their first ninth-place finish in 1966 had given them false hope. There were rumors that the Mets' front office was interested in hiring Hodges away from the Senators for 1968. Hodges still had another year on his contract, so even if he wanted to go back to New York, it didn't seem possible.

Still, as the year drew to a close, it was obvious that the Mets were very serious about pursuing him. When they made initial overtures to Selkirk, he told confidants that the Mets would get Hodges "over my dead body." But following reports that Selkirk was "browbeaten" by Mets president Bing Devine and vice president Johnny Murphy, Hodges was granted permission to negotiate with the Mets. To Hodges that meant that Selkirk didn't really want him back, even when he offered him a three-year deal as incentive to stay in Washington. Hodges realized that he had a real opportunity to manage in New York. "I was agitated by all the speculation," he said. "I got to the point where a decision had to be made." He met with Devine, who offered him a salary of $50,000 a year for three years. Then he talked it over with his wife.

"Gil and I had never discussed the possibility that he would manage the Mets," says Joan Hodges. "He was very happy with the progress of the

Senators and liked being in Washington. The Mets were still considered the clowns of baseball, so he was a little nervous about that. He knew there would be a lot of work ahead of him, and he didn't know how it would turn out. He didn't want to disappoint the people of New York. I assured him that they would always love him even if the Mets didn't improve. I was very happy when he decided to do it. He was, too."

Gil Hodges' decision to become the Mets' manager on October 11 was met with elation in New York and the opposite in Washington, where the press and fans could foresee the Senators' return to the cellar in 1968. "I'd like to think we could have won a title in a couple of years with Gil," says Frank Howard, who would credit Hodges with his booming 136 homers and winning two homer crowns in the next three years under Jim Lemon and Ted Williams, who led Washington to fourth place with an 86–76 record in 1969. The *Washington Post* compared the Mets' move to "wife-stealing." But no one blamed Hodges for taking advantage of the opportunity. The *Post*'s Bob Addie wrote that Hodges had sent him a note saying "his days with the Senators, odd as it may sound, were among the happiest of his life."

"Gil told me he was going to the Mets, that *we* were going to the Mets," recalls Pignatano. "I said, 'Gil, we busted our butts in Washington. This club is getting close to becoming a team that can fight for the pennant.' He said, 'Joe, we're going *home*.'"

CHAPTER TWENTY-FOUR

The chant "Let's go, Mets!" sprang to life on May 4, 1963, at the Polo Grounds, in Gil Hodges' next-to-last game as a player, when the Mets were down by 13 runs with two outs and nobody on base in the bottom of the ninth inning against the San Francisco Giants. From then on, in the Polo Grounds and then Shea Stadium in Queens beginning in 1964, it was the familiar rallying cry for a team that was usually behind, a clarion call that almost always went unanswered. When Hodges played for the Mets and a few years after, they were lovable, bumbling losers whom the fans took to heart because they were the antithesis of the corporate, dynastic Yankees, and they were a new National League team in the city. However, in 1966, the Mets made the mistake of escaping last place for the first time. That spoiled their fans, and when they tumbled back into the cellar in 1967, attendance dropped. "It had been a team you had fun with," says Phil Pepe, who was writing for the *New York Daily News*. "But after a while, the losing got to be a drag."

Hodges was brought to New York because the fans and press were finally demanding improvement in the team. He was supposed to move the Mets up in the standings, as he had done with the Senators. He told reporters, "I think the Mets have some good ballplayers." When he was asked to name just two, he grinned and admitted, "I know very few of the Mets."

Hodges had connections with a few current Mets. He had played on the original Mets with left-hander Al Jackson and left-handed first baseman Ed Kranepool, who broke in when he was eighteen. As a Dodger he had hit against veteran right-hander Don Cardwell, a 15-game winner for the Cubs in 1961. His Senators had played against third baseman Ed Charles when he was on the Athletics, and second baseman Al Weis, catcher J. C. Martin, and center fielder Tommie Agee, the 1966 American League Rookie of the Year, when the three were on the White Sox. Surely Hodges knew about Mets ace Tom Seaver after his 16–7 National League Rookie of the Year campaign in 1967. He would have to learn about outfielders Cleon Jones, who was potentially the team's best hitter; irrepressible Ron Swoboda, who clouted 19 homers in 1965 and batted .281 in 1967; and left-handed-swinging Art Shamsky, who stroked 21 homers for Cincinnati in 1966. Also: catcher Jerry Grote, a tough Texan with a fabulous arm but a weak bat; rangy, feisty shortstop Bud Harrelson; and rookie second baseman Ken Boswell, who couldn't carry Weis's glove but had pop from the left side.

There was also an array of pitchers, including hard-throwing rookie left-hander Jerry Koosman; fearsome Nolan Ryan, a lean right-hander from Alvin, Texas, who could get up to 100 mph but had trouble with control; veteran sinkerballer Ron Taylor; and cheerful lefty Tug McGraw, whose best pitch, the screwball, defined his personality.

Hodges brought Eddie Yost, Rube Walker, and Joe Pignatano with him from the Senators. Also present in St. Petersburg was another former catcher, Yogi Berra, who had coached for Westrum since being fired as Yankees manager after the 1964 World Series. He filled in Hodges on the players. "I don't think he wanted me as a coach just because I had been a catcher," says Berra. "Gil wanted good baseball men. He was a good manager for us to work under, because he trusted us and wanted us to point out things to the players. The players who had been there when Wes was manager knew right away things would be different."

"It's like black and white to before," said Swoboda that spring, before his troubles with Hodges began. "He pays attention to everything that makes you a good ballplayer."

"Hodges was definitely a vast improvement over Wes Westrum," says Ed Charles. "Wes was very personable, but Hodges was a real leader and taught us the proper way to play the game, the fundamentals. He changed the climate that first spring training."

"He defined every player's role, so it was clear what was expected of each of us," recalls Ron Taylor, a doctor after his career ended. "He was honest with us, and few managers realize how important that is to players. He changed the whole personality of the club."

"We were expecting Gil to be really strict and he was just the opposite in his first year," contends Koosman. "He had fun with the guys. Gil was a teaching manager and he gathered together all the pitchers and said, 'I don't care what you've learned in the past, but you're going to bunt my way,'" says Koosman. "He expected us to bunt better than the position players."

Kranepool also appreciated Hodges' hands-on instruction: "Gil taught me more about first base in the first few months than anybody taught me in the next fifteen years. He wanted to build a team around good pitching and defense and playing the game the proper way. You don't let the other team score; you give your best effort; you don't give the ballgame away. He stressed that winning approach. You had to start believing in yourself or he was not going to let you perform."

"I wasn't set as a ballplayer or a person until Gil Hodges came along," said Grote. "He settled me down and encouraged me to think. . . . I don't think any of us realized at the time the effect Gil was having on us as men. I know he made me a better individual in a lot of ways. He had an impact on everybody he touched."

At the end of his first Mets spring training, Hodges conceded, "We can't look to be contenders this year. I still think we will be a better club than last year." In 1968, Hodges wanted to evaluate his players, teach them fundamentals and a winning attitude, give them on-field experience so they could develop their talents and get the mistakes out of their systems, and teach the pitchers to use their legs and bodies to pitch, not just their arms— and how to bunt. His attainable goals for the Mets were to climb out of the cellar, win 70 games—breaking the team's record of 66 wins—and build the foundation for better teams.

On April 4, civil rights leader Dr. Martin Luther King Jr., a friend of Jackie Robinson and Roy Campanella, was assassinated in Memphis. The country was shocked and grieving. The opening of the baseball season was moved back from April 8 so that it would take place after King's funeral. Hodges' managerial debut for the Mets took place in San Francisco on April 10. His first Mets lineup was: Bud Harrelson, SS; Ken Boswell, 2B; Tommie Agee, CF; Ron Swoboda, RF; Ed Kranepool, 1B; Art Shamsky, LF; J. C. Martin, C; Ed Charles, 3B; Tom Seaver, P. Seaver went against Juan Marichal in a marquee matchup and had the best of him, 4–2, going into the bottom of the ninth inning. Swoboda had knocked in all 4 runs, 3 with a homer. But Seaver gave up a one-out RBI single to Jim Ray Hart that cut the lead to 4–3, and Hodges went to his bullpen for the first time. Danny Frisella, who went 1–6 in his 1967 rookie season, was quickly 0–1 in '68. Before Hodges was settled on the bench, Frisella, who was born in the City by the Bay, gave up a single to Nate Oliver and a 2-run double to Jesus Alou that gave the Giants a startling 5–4 comeback victory. Hodges' debut had as deflating an outcome as any he had experienced in Washington. But when his players looked at him, he was poker-faced. "We'll win tomorrow," he assured them.

The Mets played the next day in Los Angeles. Hodges boldly made a rookie, Koosman, his number-two starter and was rewarded with his first victory, 4–0. "When I shut out the Dodgers on 4 singles, he was one happy guy," recalls Koosman. "Hodges admired Walter Alston, but he loved returning to Los Angeles for the first time as a manager and beating his old manager."

The Mets suffered another tough defeat the next day, 1–0, as Cardwell was outpitched by Drysdale. But then Ryan and Frisella combined on a 5-hitter and blanked Houston 4–0. The following day, New York lost 1–0 in 24 innings, with the winning run scoring after six hours and six minutes when Al Weis, playing shortstop, let Bob Aspromonte's grounder go through his legs. Hodges had to be delighted with the starting pitching, but for the opening road trip the Mets' record stood at 2 shutout victories and 3 wrenching defeats.

The Mets flew to New York, and before 52,079 fans at their April 17 home opener defeated the Giants 3–0. Koosman threw his second shutout in two starts. "I'm not sure if Gil cared that I was a left-hander," Koosman says, "but he loved that I threw inside, which I needed to do to get anybody out. He wanted the pitchers to own the inside part of the plate, not the hitters. Gil didn't pat me on the back. He expected me to pitch well, because that was my job."

Cardwell and Ryan lost close games in their next starts, but Seaver picked up his 1st win, defeating the Dodgers 3–2. Swoboda's 3-run homer was one of only 2 hits off Bill Singer.

With two stoppers, Seaver and Koosman, the Mets' longest losing streak all year would be only 5 games, and for a time they hovered around .500. The Mets went 7–9 in April and 13–15 in May and 16-14 in June.

On June 8, the players bonded with their manager in a unique way. Robert Kennedy, the U.S. senator from New York and the brother of the former president, was assassinated in California while campaigning for the Democratic presidential nomination, following Lyndon Johnson's decision not to run. His funeral was scheduled for that Saturday, and baseball commissioner William Eckert canceled games in New York and Washington, but not elsewhere. Out of respect for their state's senator, the Mets players, led by Kranepool, voted not to play that day in San Francisco, despite a scheduled Bat Day promotion by the Giants organization. Hodges and the Mets' front office went along with their decision. Hodges never discussed politics with his own family, much less his ballplayers, but as a Catholic and a Democrat he was greatly saddened by the assassination of another Kennedy. Bobby Kennedy had even spent time chatting with Bob Hodges at Gus Doerner Sports Inc., while campaigning in Evansville, Indiana.

"Hodges suggested that he would probably go to church that morning," wrote George Vecsey in his 1970 book *Joy in Mudville*. "He also suggested that the players avoid carousing in public places, having gone on record with their brave and respectful stand. The manager reinforced their feelings that they had made a meaningful gesture; there was a closeness between the Mets that had never been present before."

At the end of June, when Seaver beat Houston's Mike Cuellar 1–0, the Mets were a surprising 36–38 and in seventh place, 9 games behind St. Louis, and had outscored their opponents 232 to a league-low 206 runs. The previous June they were 25–44 and 18 games out, and had given up 311 runs.

"You could see the difference in the Mets," recalls former catcher Tim McCarver, whose Cardinals would capture their second consecutive National League title in 1968. "You could also *feel* that they were a changed team. Everybody had a lot of respect for Hodges and what a great leader he was. What I remember most was how impressively he carried himself."

"Gil was the same if we won or lost," recalls Kranepool. "He just sat on the damn seat in the dugout. He wasn't a cheerleader. He never changed expression, so you didn't know if he was rattled or not."

"Gil sat next to Rube, same spot every game," says Koosman, "and you couldn't tell if he was mad, happy, or whatever as he watched you. He didn't want to show the other team what his emotions were."

"I thought Gil was a manager who was way ahead of his time for psychology and dealing with players," Bud Harrelson told Jack Curry of the *New York Times* when he was the Mets manager in 1990. "He was friendly, but I was scared to death of him in the beginning. Then he would bring me into his office and we'd talk about this and that and why you did this. He really got my brain working."

"Gil was easygoing and very soft-spoken," Charles remembers, "but when he was hot, boy, you could see those veins in his neck start bulging and that voice sounded like thunder roars."

"He rarely lost his temper, but on the few occasions he did, you can bet he got our attention," wrote Harrelson in his 2012 autobiography, *Turning Two*. "[One] time we lost a game on the road and Gil didn't like something that happened on the field. After the game we came into the dressing room, and as usual the clubhouse guys had set up this postgame buffet. Gil was so angry he took the table and turned over the spread."

"As it was in Washington, it really bothered Gil when anyone played poorly, and every time somebody made a mistake, he wrote it down on a piece of paper," says Pignatano. "He always kept his office door open, and the next day when he'd spot the guy walking past on his way to the field, Gil just whistled. With his finger he'd motion for him to come in and close the door. And he'd tell him what he did wrong. And that's how they learned how to play."

"With Hodges, you couldn't keep making the same mistakes over and over," Kranepool says. "He was a strong disciplinarian. You played by his rules or you didn't play at all."

Hodges' instruction to his players continued into the season. He was able to keep Grote in the lineup by turning him into a decent hitter with a shorter, quicker swing, which was paramount, because he handled pitchers so well and had a powerful, accurate arm.

"Gil helped me when I needed him," said Agee, who would struggle badly all year at the plate but still play an excellent center field. "I was zero for two months, and he played me. I should have been in the minors. He had gone through it himself. He knew what I felt. He always said, 'Hang in there. How do you feel? How's the family?'"

"I was still trying to establish myself as a big-league pitcher," Seaver recalled. "He made me think differently and look ahead as I went through the batting order. I didn't really understand the degree to which he was an analytical manager. Gil was the first manager I'd been around who in the sixth inning knew what he'd do in the eighth inning."

"If you watched Gil Hodges play cribbage with the other coaches, you could see what kind of thinking manager he was," says Swoboda. "He played the fastest game you ever saw. His mind was so agile and he made his decisions quickly. That was the same way he managed. Gil studied the complexity of a situation and then resolved it with simplicity. I felt Hodges never tried to outsmart the game and never overmanaged."

As Seaver and Swoboda discovered, Hodges' instruction wasn't just about execution but also about being a professional. On June 20, Seaver, who would go 5–0 for the month, led the Astros 5–1 after eight innings and then lost his concentration in the ninth, giving up a single, hitting a batter, yielding consecutive RBI singles, and then issuing a walk. Hodges lifted him one out away from a complete game and then summoned him to his office. "You didn't want to go into his office," Seaver said on *The Tim McCarver Show*, "because you didn't know if you'd come out alive or with broken bones. I can joke about it now, but I was thinking, 'My God, I hope he doesn't break my neck.' I got the win, but Gil said, 'Your approach today was very unprofessional.' He gave me a piece of advice that I never forgot: 'It doesn't matter if there are five thousand people in the stands or fifty thousand people, or if you're leading by 1 run or 6 runs, or if we're 2 games ahead or 18 games behind. Your approach to your business is the same all the time. You must stay focused and professional.'"

Swoboda, who along with his roommate, Kranepool, had trouble adjusting to being platooned, was the player Hodges had the most trouble reaching. "We got on the bus taking us to the airport on a road trip," Joan Hodges recalls. "I'm sitting with Gil in the first two seats. The last one to get on the bus was Ron Swoboda. In those days, the players wore leisure suits, but Ron was casually dressed and wearing a strand of beads. My husband gets up from his seat and motions him to come up front. He gets off the bus with Swoboda. We wait a good half hour. Gil briefly gets back on the bus so he can get Ron's suitcase. He made Ron put on a suit, shirt, and tie before getting back on the bus."

"I don't remember that," says Swoboda, "but I remember coming down an elevator one night with no shoes on and he was standing there. And he wasn't thrilled the time in Houston when he saw me walk back to the hotel loaded. Also I had a way of talking with undigested thought. I didn't make anything easy for him. There wasn't anything he expected us to do other than listen and, if you were in his lineup, play. When you weren't in the lineup, you get in your workout and just behave yourself, but I didn't. Maybe it was just a clash of personalities. I had trouble with authority."

Joan had no problem with her husband trying to bring healthy doses of professionalism to his players, but she was concerned that he was focusing more on the young Mets than on their kids: Gil Jr., eighteen, was graduating from Midwood High School and would travel with the Mets in the summer; Irene, seventeen, was attending St. Edmonds High; and Cynthia, eleven, and Barbara, six, were going to Our Lady Help of Christians School. She recalls: "I said, 'You have to remember, Gil, that these *boys* on your team are grown men. They are not your children; they are your players.' And he said, 'No, honey, when they walk out on that field, they represent me. They are my children.' So he and his players developed that kind of relationship where to this day, they talk about him as if they're talking about their own father."

"Hodges was only in his mid-forties," says Kranepool, "but he was still almost twice our age. Most of our guys were under twenty-five years of age, so he was a father figure."

"Hodges was a father figure to me," wrote Harrelson in his autobiography. "He said all the right things even when I did something wrong. . . . I truly loved him as a person."

"Gil was home two weeks and gone two weeks," recalls Joan Hodges, "so I always had the major responsibility of the children. One day I was talking to him about something that happened with Cynthia at school, and he seemed to be a thousand miles away, thinking about his players. I said, 'Honey, you know you're not listening to what I'm telling you, so I'm going to get our children Mets uniforms and put Astroturf in the house, so when I want to tell you something about one of them, I'll mention the uniform number and you'll listen to me.' He turned around and called, 'Cynthia!' She said she didn't know whether to come downstairs or jump out the window."

Hodges tried to keep abreast of what was happening to his own kids as well as those of his brother, Bob, to whom he spoke by phone at length every other week. When Bob's daughter Ann was in the hospital in Evansville in 1968 to get her appendix out, he made sure to call her. "The phone next to my bed rang," she recalls. "I picked it up and someone said, 'This is Dr. Hodges, wanting to speak to the patient." I said, 'I'm sorry, you have the wrong room,' and hung up. The phone rang again, and this person says again, 'This is Dr. Hodges, wanting to speak to the patient,' and I said, 'I'm sorry, you've got the wrong room,' and hung up again. The third time the phone rang, I said, 'Hello?' And he said, 'Elizabeth Ann, this is your Uncle Gil, and don't you dare hang up on me again!' A half hour later, Dad comes walking in the room and asked, 'Did your uncle call you?' I said, 'Yes, I hung up on him twice.' And he said, 'That's what he gets for trying to be a smart-ass.'"

The Mets reached the All-Star break with a record of 39–43, which was better than their previous best for 82 games, 35–47, set in 1966. For the first time three Mets were All-Stars. In the National League's 1–0 victory, Seaver pitched 2 innings, striking out 5; Koosman picked up an unofficial save by striking out Carl Yastrzemski to end the game; and Grote went 0-for-2, starting ahead of the Dodgers' Tom Haller and Cincinnati rookie Johnny Bench.

Leading up to the All-Star break, Grote at .291, almost 100 points higher than in 1967, and Jones at .272 were the only Mets hitting above .250. As a result, the pitchers were having a hard time picking up wins. Koosman was 11–4 with a 1.94 ERA but hadn't won since June 19; and despite a 1.98 ERA, Seaver was just 7–6. Hodges was glad to get a couple of well-pitched victories from Don Cardwell, after a 1–8 start. It took him a few games to adapt after Hodges ordered him to stop throwing a spitter. "Gil thought it was cheating to throw them," says Koosman. "By telling Cardwell not to throw them, it was his chance to teach our young Mets team that we were going to play by the rules."

Hodges was smoking up to three packs of cigarettes a day, but he seemed to be keeping his stress level under control. He came within one inning of making it through half a season without experiencing his first National League ejection. It happened in the bottom of the ninth inning of the second game of a twin bill versus the Phillies on July 7. Hodges was already aggravated because the Phillies snatched the opener, 4–3, on Richie Allen's 3-run homer off Taylor in the bottom of the ninth inning. The Mets led 4–2 in the nightcap, and Hodges brought in Koosman to face left-handed Tony Gonzalez. On a 1–0 pitch, home-plate umpire Ken Burkhart was struck in the mask. He ruled it a foul tip, making the count 1–1. Then, after a brief discussion with Gonzalez, Burkhart changed the call to a ball, making the count 2–0.

Hodges charged out of the dugout. Burkhart gave him an automatic rejection for arguing balls and strikes, although Hodges was actually arguing about Burkhart's action. "You just don't change your call like that," Hodges said afterward. "Ridiculous. I've got to lose my temper on something like that." A provoked Koosman hit Gonzalez, bringing the potential tying run to the plate. But Rube Walker brought in Seaver, who got three straight outs to nail down the victory and record the only (unofficial) save of his twenty-year career. The Mets' road record improved to 21–20, by far their best showing in their brief history.

Back in the National League, Hodges often had rendezvous with acquaintances at the various ballparks. Petersburg High classmate Pauline Wilson-Orbin, his passenger when he had car accidents on consecutive nights while on military leave in 1945, lived with her family in Houston and came to the Astrodrome at Hodges' invitation. "Gil would take my son into the dugout and afterward we'd go to dinner," she recalls. "To this day, my son is attached to him. He was a very, very nice man, and we all loved him."

Folks from Indiana traveled to St. Louis to watch Hodges' team and chat with him over the railing. Many had been kids themselves when Hodges played with the Dodgers, and now they introduced him to their children. Hodges always scanned the stands for familiar faces. One day he spotted someone he hadn't seen since they played ball at St. Joseph's College and the Indianapolis Amateur League. "I was in St. Louis on business for General Motors," says Jim Beane. "The Mets were in town, so I went to the ballpark to see him that night. He spotted me and came over to where I sat and said, 'There's the old left-hander!'"

The Mets continued to play .500 ball on the road in the second half of the season. Unfortunately, they had difficulty winning at home. The pitching, led by Seaver and Koosman—what Maury Allen called "The Tom and Jerry Show"—continued to be excellent, but everyone had lengthy victory droughts. The staff finished second in strikeouts (1,014), second in shutouts (25), and fourth in ERA (2.72). However, it was 26–37 in 1-run games and 2–13 in extra innings, because they got little timely hitting. Even in the "Year of the Pitcher," when averages and production were way down on all teams, the Mets were particularly bad, posting a National League–worst .228 batting average. Jones finished the season with a .297 average, Grote hit .282, and Charles .276; but Charles' 15 homers and Swoboda's 59 RBIs were team highs. The Mets never scored more than 11 runs, and only twice did they score in double figures. In one six-game stretch in September, they lost 3–0 and 8–1, won 1–0 and 2–0, and lost 6–0 and 3–0.

After the 8–1 loss on September 10th, the Mets fell into last place. But Jim McAndrew, with relief help from Cal Koonce, and Koosman threw back-to-back shutouts. Koosman's victory was worth celebrating because it gave the Mets 67 victories, their all-time high. With his 3-hitter, he became the first rookie since Grover Cleveland Alexander in 1911 to throw 7 shutouts. He'd go 19–12 with a 2.08 ERA for the season, yet finish second to Johnny Bench in the Rookie of the Year vote.

The Mets had such a good first half of the season that without anyone really noticing, they nearly played themselves into last place by having the worst record in the league in the second half. Although Hodges' demeanor didn't change, he experienced tremendous anxiety as his team fought to stay out of tenth place down the stretch. "Most of us blow up," Pignatano told Maury Allen of the *Post*. "Gil just sits there and lets it grind away at him."

"Hodges, disappointed by the team's showing, became more and more restless," wrote Allen in *The Incredible Mets*. "He would smoke a cigarette down to its very end and start another one. He was coughing and rasping."

On September 20, the Mets began a six-game road trip to Philadelphia and Atlanta, home of the Braves since 1966. Around this time Hodges began having "sharp pains in the chest, along with other discomforts that I had never experienced before in my life." He kept his condition secret as the Mets won 3 of 4 from Philadelphia and headed to Atlanta 1 game up on Houston.

"I'm not surprised Gil didn't tell anyone when he wasn't feeling well," says Louis Lombardi. "Gil never wanted to impose on anybody. There was a night at Toots Shor's when he was on a dais. He had a kidney stone attack and was in terrible pain, but he was too polite to interrupt the speaker. Gil was about to collapse and they had to take him to the hospital."

On September 24, the Mets played the first of two games against the Braves. "About 4 o'clock," wrote Hodges in *The Game of Baseball*, "the pains started again. They were dull pains, rather than sharp. About like a toothache, except that they felt like they were going into my chest and coming out my back."

He tried to soldier through it, and even pitched fifteen minutes of batting practice. "He seemed fine," recalls Swoboda. "Phil Niekro was pitching for the Braves, so Gil wanted to get us ready for him by throwing us his knuckler."

Around the second inning, Hodges told Walker he needed to lie down and asked him to take over the team. He went back into the clubhouse with trainer Gus Mauch and stretched out on the trainer's table and listened to several innings of the Mets' 7–4 loss on the radio.

"Rube took me out of the game after the sixth inning," recalls Koosman. "I went into the clubhouse and Gil was lying on the trainer's table, blotched red in the face. I just asked him how he was. He said, 'I'll be all right.'"

"I saw him in the clubhouse," Swoboda says, "and it was scary, because he was struggling."

Mauch, who had suffered a heart attack in 1960 while working with the Yankees, called the Braves' team physician, Dr. Harry Rogers, and they agreed to take Hodges to the hospital. Dr. Linton Bishop, a heart specialist at Crawford W. Long Hospital, ordered an electrocardiogram. "I was examined and the doctor got rid of the pains for me immediately," Hodges recollected. "No pills, no injections, just one simple sentence did it. He said, 'Mr.

Hodges, you've had a heart attack.' Just that quickly, the pain was gone. I guess I was so shocked, I didn't feel anything."

Everyone was shocked. Family, friends, coaches, players. In Brooklyn, in Queens, in Indiana, around the country. "His heart attack was scary, because we felt nothing could happen to him," says Cindy Hodges. "It didn't matter that he smoked—my mother smoked, too—but he was so strong and in excellent condition."

"Anytime you don't express your emotions and keep them inside, it's like adding straw to a camel's back," says Hodges Jr., who had entered C. W. Post in Brookville, New York, that month. "The more you hold things in, the higher it piles up, and at some point that camel falls. I think that's what happened to my father."

Hodges was given medication and placed in the intensive-care unit. Joan immediately flew to Atlanta. "The heart attack was a surprise," she says. "His pressures were normal. There were no financial pressures—he never worried about money, because he always felt he could do whatever he had to do to take care of his family. There was no conflict in his life; there wasn't anything that was major that I could point to. After his heart attack was the only time that I saw Gil be concerned and shaken. It was something that he really, truly did not expect at all. But he adjusted beautifully."

"From the next morning on, she was with me constantly," Hodges wrote. "[S]he'd just sit by the bed, and our conversations were almost in whispers so that we wouldn't disturb the people around us. From early morning until late at night, she was with me. In order that she might have company at the hotel, our oldest daughter, Irene, came down to stay with her. Irene was there one day, when she came down with mononucleosis. So there was Joan, hundreds of miles from home, spending the day with a sick husband in the hospital, and the rest of the time with a sick daughter at the hotel."

Meanwhile, Walker managed the Mets through their final four games. Seaver tossed a 3-hitter to beat Atlanta for his 16th and final victory of the season, keeping the Mets 1 game ahead of the Astros. Back at Shea, the Mets suffered a crushing 3–2 defeat in eleven innings to the Phillies. Fortunately, in St. Louis, Cardinals ace Bob Gibson, completing an astonishing season, threw his 13th shutout to beat Houston 1–0. In earning his 22nd victory, Gibson, who would be the National League Cy Young Award winner, lowered his ERA to a modern-day record, 1.12.

Koosman won his 19th game, throwing a 3-hitter to beat the Phillies 3–1. On the season's final day, Seaver held the Phillies scoreless for 5 innings and led 2–0, but over the next four innings Dick Allen crushed 3 homers and drove in 7 runs, and the Phillies pulled away 10–3. But Houston had the same kind of day against the Cardinals, losing 11–1, allowing the Mets to hold on to ninth place.

The Mets' final record was 73–89, placing them 24 games behind the Cards, 1 game ahead of Houston, and just 3 behind L.A. and Philadelphia, who tied for seventh place. Their 73 wins were a Mets record by 7 games, a good reason that attendance at Shea Stadium increased by 216,155 to 1,781,657 fans in 1968.

Hodges spent twenty-six days in the Atlanta hospital, mostly resting and reading get-well cards and letters from friends and fans. He particularly appreciated reading those from people who said they were keeping him in their prayers, because, "I couldn't even go to church on Sundays, so I had to depend especially on the prayers of others to bolster my own." A Jewish-American soldier stationed in Vietnam sent his Chai, his symbol of life, to his Catholic hero. Hodges sent it back, telling the soldier he was worthier of wearing it.

When Hodges checked out of the hospital and into a local Marriott hotel, he was given the usual advice for victims of a heart attack: eat better, lose weight, don't drink, walk and walk some more, quit smoking. Do all that, the doctor said, and there was no reason Hodges couldn't manage again. That was what he wanted to hear. He needed to know for his family's sake that he wasn't putting himself in jeopardy by returning to the consuming profession. He even consulted former Pirates manager Danny Murtaugh, who had retired after a heart attack. He told Joseph Durso of the *New York Times*: "If I felt for one minute that I couldn't do my job as well as before, or if I felt it might hurt me, I wouldn't attempt it."

Because Hodges wasn't in any condition to climb steps, he and Joan didn't return to their split-level house in Brooklyn but went to St. Petersburg, where he could exercise properly and relax in the sun. He walked every day, kept to a low-calorie diet—"which is kind of tough when you've got a

wife who cooks as well as mine does," he said—and quit smoking cold tur-
key. "I didn't miss the cigarettes at first, particularly in the hospital," he told
George Vecsey, "but I do miss them now after a meal."

After about a month, the Gil and Joan came back to Brooklyn. He had
slimmed down by twenty pounds to around two hundred and had much of
his strength back. At his first press conference, he told reporters, "I got
a very encouraging report yesterday. In fact, the doctor told me to start getting more exercise. He told me I should start by walking about two blocks,
then increase it until I'm walking ten blocks. In fact, he told me I should
start playing golf in a couple more months. If the doctor gave me a bad di-
agnosis, I'd change doctors." He hadn't lost his sense of humor.

CHAPTER TWENTY-FIVE

The National League expanded to twelve teams in 1969, with the addition of the Montreal Expos and the San Diego Padres, and placed six teams in each of two divisions. At the end of the year, the two division leaders were to play each other in a best-of-five National League Championship Series to determine who would play the winner of the ALCS in the World Series. (The Kansas City Royals and Seattle Pilots joined the American League.) The Mets were placed in the National League East with the Cubs, Phillies, Pirates, Cardinals, and Expos.

After their ninth-place finish, the Mets were designated hundred-to-one long shots to win the pennant in 1969. Hodges was realistic about his team's chances for a title, telling reporters at St. Petersburg that he thought the Mets would win 85 games. They scoffed, thinking the Mets weren't even a .500 team. But Hodges gathered his players and pointed out that the team had lost 37 1-run games in '68. "If you win half of those, you are a contending ball club," he pointed out.

There was one player, though, who believed the Mets could go even further. "At spring training in 1969, Jerry Grote said we were going to win it all," Tom Seaver said in *Tim McCarver's Diamond Gems.* "And we looked at him as if he were nuts, because we'd only gotten out of the cellar. But being our catcher, Jerry knew what kind of pitching we were going to have on a day-to-day basis. There would be Jerry Koosman, who had a great year in '68, Nolan Ryan, me, and Gary Gentry, who was coming along."

Gentry was the only significant addition to the rotation, which would also include at various times Don Cardwell, Jim McAndrew, and Nolan Ryan. Joining Ron Taylor and Cal Koonce in the bullpen was Tug McGraw, who had spent 1968 in the minors. Hodges wisely convinced him to switch from starter to late-inning reliever, and it turned out his loosey-goosey demeanor made him ideal for pitching out of jams in key situations. Hodges also liked how McGraw brightened the clubhouse.

There were only two new position players who made notable contributions to the Mets in 1969, and both were part-timers. Wayne Garrett, a left-handed batter, would platoon with Ed Charles at third base and play some shortstop and second base. Rod Gaspar, a speedy, excellent-fielding switch-hitter, would make 91 appearances in the outfield and be an occasional pinch hitter. He'd bat just .228 and Garrett .218, but Hodges saw value in everyone on his roster and played them at opportune times, including as late-inning defensive replacements.

Hodges was without peer among baseball managers at instilling confidence in his players, from top to bottom on the roster. Even platooned and bench players realized that he recognized their value and would give them repeated chances to produce when the chips were down. It also gave them confidence to have a manager who could outthink any other manager, including Leo Durocher, who was now the skipper of the talented Chicago Cubs. Seaver, who thought Hodges was someone he'd want in a foxhole with him, called the Mets' manager "one of our strongest weapons." The young Mets needed him, so it wasn't surprising that they took one quick look at him at spring training and decided he was back to his old self.

"We might have been worried about him a little at first," recalls Ed Kranepool, "but I think at that stage of our lives, we thought everyone was immortal. He came to spring training with a clean bill of health from the doctors. He seemed to be in good health. He was in good shape. And he looked fine."

Some reporters took a closer look and were skeptical about his health, but didn't question him, even about the cigarettes he was bumming. "I thought about his health all the time," says George Vescey, "but it didn't seem right to ask him about it."

The reporters in Florida didn't treat Hodges with kid gloves, but pestered him at the daily press briefings about his handling of his club. Hodges ably gave it back to them in kind. "One morning," recalled Robert Lipsyte, "after two Mets had been sidelined with flu, a newspaperman asked, 'Do you think the fellas got sick because you had them run in the rain?' Hodges replied, 'I don't know, but if you think so, write it. I couldn't care less.' His steady gaze then pushed the reporter across the room. Late that afternoon, he announced the next day's schedule to the press and a different reporter asked, 'What happens if it rains again?' Hodges' gaze flicked to the morning interviewer and he casually said, 'Oh, I guess we'll just have two more men out sick.'"

For the ninth consecutive year the Mets lost on Opening Day, and this time it was to a team playing its initial opener, Montreal. The mound had been lowered from fifteen to ten inches to try to boost offense throughout the majors after the 1968 season, and the new Expos won a slugfest, 11–10, on a windy day at Shea. A bright spot for the Mets was Tommie Agee, who got 2 hits and drove in 3 runs leading off. He had 17 RBIs in all of 1968, so this was a promising start. The Mets beat the Expos the next day, 9–5, as Boswell homered; Cleon Jones, Kranepool, and Grote each drove in 2 runs; and McGraw picked up a victory by giving up only 1 run in 6⅓ innings of long relief. The Mets' record went to 2–1 for the second time in history when Gentry beat the Expos 4–2 with 8⅔ strong innings in his major-league debut. He got support from the revived Agee, who reached the seats twice.

Gentry picked up his second victory in his next start against Philadelphia, but it was the Mets' lone triumph as they lost 6 of 7 and fell into fifth place. Seaver then outdueled Bob Gibson 2–1; Ryan, pitching middle relief, also picked up a victory over St. Louis; and Koosman 5-hit Pittsburgh, 2–0. But the Mets struggled in April until their pitching dominated in the final three games. In a victory over Montreal, however, something popped in Koosman's left shoulder and he'd miss more than three weeks and lose his chance to win 20 games. The Mets finished April in third place, 5½ games behind the front-running Cubs.

After going 9–11 in April, the Mets without Koosman were stuck in neutral in May, going 12–12 and both scoring and giving up 98 runs. After his team's halfhearted effort in a 6–5 loss to Atlanta, Hodges called a meeting and chewed out everyone to make sure it wouldn't become a habit. "We needed it," Seaver said. Seaver held down the fort, going 5–1 in May. His

5–0 victory over Atlanta on May 21 lifted the Mets to 18–18, the farthest into a season they'd ever been at .500.

On the thirty-first, Gentry became the only other starter to win 2 games in May, with a 4–2 victory over the Giants. The Mets had a new hero every time they won, and in this game it was Charles, whose 3-run homer off Gaylord Perry overcame the Giants' 2–0 lead. McGraw pitched 2 innings of scoreless relief to record the second save of his career. The first, in 1965, hadn't counted because it wasn't until 1969 that *saves* finally became an official statistic.

The Mets' momentum carried over into June. In one 5-game stretch, they won 4 1-run games, including Koosman's 2–1 triumph over L.A. On June 3, Seaver, backed by 2 Kranepool blasts, struck out 14 and defeated the Dodgers 5–2. The victory gave the Mets a 24–23 record, the latest they had been above .500 in their history. It also moved them into second place in the National League East, 8½ games behind Chicago.

The Mets won again the next day, 1–0, in fifteen innings, when Garrett singled to center and Agee came around to score from first base on an error. "At different times during the season, players jumped on the bandwagon," Seaver told McCarver. "For me, it was [the] game we were playing the Dodgers at Shea Stadium. Willie Davis had a clear shot at the runner at home plate, but the ball went under his glove, and he couldn't make a throw. We had won another 1-run ball game, and at that juncture, I said, 'We're going to win this thing.'"

The Mets then swept the Padres in their first trip to San Diego Stadium, as Gentry, Koosman, and Seaver picked up victories. The Mets' team-record winning streak hit 11 games when Cardwell outpitched Mike McCormick in San Francisco, 9–4. Jones, batting .351, hit a 3-run homer, and Agee stroked 2 homers and drove in 3 runs as he returned to 1966 form.

Gaylord Perry ended the streak the next day, besting Gentry 7–2. "He didn't throw as many greaseballs as he did last time," commented Hodges. He would say the 11-game streak from May 28 to June 10 was the turning point in the Mets' season, although they picked up only 2 games on the Cubs. The streak, with many heroes, exceptional starting and relief pitching, luck, and 6 1-run victories, had shown what a dangerous team they were.

The question was whether they could compete with the Cubs, who were off to a tremendous start under Durocher, who was as irascible and bombastic as ever as he turned sixty-four. The pitching staff had three formidable starters: Ferguson Jenkins, who was on his way to his third consecutive 20-win season; Bill Hands, who would have his only 20-win season; and Ken Holtzman, who'd rack up 17 wins and become the first Cubs lefty to throw a no-hitter at Wrigley Field. Phil Regan, who in 1966 was 14–1 with the Dodgers, would win 12 games and save 17 as the Cubs' closer.

The offense had three stars: third baseman Ron Santo, who'd hit 29 homers and drive in a career-high 123 runs; smooth-swinging left fielder Billy Williams, who'd slam 20 homers for the ninth consecutive season; and first baseman Ernie Banks, who'd drive in 106 runs and slam 23 homers as he approached 500 career round-trippers. "The Cubs are going to shine in 'sixty-nine," the "Mayor of Chicago" had declared, and there were legions of fans around the country who hoped the genial thirty-nine-year-old would finally play in a World Series, which the Cubs hadn't done since 1945.

While the Mets were less experienced, they were extremely intelligent. "It was a smart team, but also there wasn't any arrogance, because Gil made sure of that," says Koosman. "There were no stars, and everybody got fined if they broke his rules, no exceptions. Late one night Gil and Rube got the management of the hotel in Chicago to let them into a closed-off bar area so they could observe the elevators. The next day Gil called a meeting and read off the names of sixteen players he was fining a hundred dollars for missing curfew. Everybody was wondering how the hell he found out without doing a room check. Gil had been around and knew the tricks."

In June, the Mets went 19–9, their best month in history, but moved only from 9 games back to 7½ back because the Cubs played well too, going 18–11. What impressed Chicago was that the Mets beat the two-time defending National League champion Cardinals, 3 of 4 in New York in June and 3 of 5 in St. Louis in early July.

"I wasn't really surprised by the Mets because of their pitching," says Tim McCarver, then the Cardinals' catcher. "Seaver was already great, and Koosman, Ryan, Gentry, and McGraw were an amazing group with a lot of promise. And Jerry Grote, the guy catching them, was the best defensive catcher I ever saw, better than Bench." (Johnny Bench himself once said, "If Grote and I were on the same team, I'd have to play third base.")

On June 15, Johnny Murphy, who had replaced Bing Devine as GM, did something no Mets team executive ever needed to do before: He pulled off a midseason trade to help in the pennant race. In an inspired deal, he acquired six-foot-four right-handed-hitting first baseman Donn Clendenon from Montreal for four prospects. Clendenon had batted .299, with 28 homers and 98 RBIs for Pittsburgh in 1966, and had driven in 87 runs in '67, despite striking out a league-high 163 times. He hadn't shown much in his first year with the Expos, so the Mets were able to acquire him and become legitimate contenders. Instantly, he provide much-needed power and strong clubhouse leadership. In early July he was blazing hot, driving in key runs in almost every victory.

Heading into a three-game series with Chicago, the Mets trailed the Cubs by only 5½ games. In the first game, Jenkins held the Mets to 1 hit through 8 innings, a Kranepool homer in the fifth, and the Cubs led 3–1 going into the bottom of the ninth. Jenkins then gave up doubles to Boswell, pinch-hitter Clendenon, and Jones, and Kranepool's single brought in Jones for a startling come-from-behind victory 4–3. Koosman went the distance to pick up the win. Afterward, the tension on the Cubs was evident when Santo, who always clicked his heels after a victory, lit into Don Young for misplaying two flies in center in the fatal ninth inning.

In the second game, Seaver went against Holtzman. For 8⅓ innings he was perfect, setting down the first twenty-five batters, 11 on strikes, as the Mets mounted a 4–0 lead. That brought up weak-hitting rookie Jimmy Qualls, batting .243. "I decided to throw Qualls a sinker," wrote Seaver in his book, "but the ball didn't sink. It came in fast, too high, almost waist-high, over the heart of the plate. Qualls swung and hit the ball to left-center field. Cleon Jones broke over from left field. Tommie Agee raced over from center, two of the fastest men on our club, and neither of them could reach the ball. It fell in, a clean single. Never in any aspect of my life, in baseball or outside, had I experienced such a disappointment."

Seaver settled for a 1-hitter and the Mets moved to 3½ games behind the Cubs. However, the Cubs would salvage the finale, 6–2, as Hands beat Gentry.

The next day, Hodges, Gentry, Seaver, Koosman, Cardwell, and Cal Koonce filmed a commercial. Hodges tells his pitchers never to throw a greaseball. Then he notices the guilty look on Gentry's face. Hodges checks his hair. "Grease!" he exclaims. "Gentry, you're the first pitcher ever sent to the showers without throwing a ball." As the embarrassed Gentry heads for the showers, Hodges tosses him a bottle of the nongreasy Vitalis. Hodges knew best, even in commercials.

After the surprising Mets took 2 of 3 from Montreal, they played another three-game series against the Cubs, and again won twice. "Hodges got a special kick out of managing against Durocher and beating him," recalls Swoboda. "Durocher was all ego, someone who was overrated in his own mind. Those games against the Cubs was the most compelling baseball we played all year long. One time we played in Chicago and there was some technical person in our dugout with Hodges, who had on a headset with a towel draped over him and he was talking to someone. He wanted Leo to think he was talking to somebody about getting the Cubs' signs. He remembered when Durocher had stolen signals against the Brooklyn Dodgers."

"Gil and Leo used to yell back and forth to one another," says Pignatano. "Gil never said he enjoyed managing against Leo, but he didn't have to. He also never said he didn't like him, but he knew Leo was a piece of crap."

In the midst of the pennant race, Ken Harrelson's autobiography, *Hawk*, was published, resulting in some major distraction for Hodges and his players. Harrelson, who was now with the Indians, wrote that Hodges was "unfair, unreasonable, unfeeling, incapable of handling men, stubborn, holier-than-thou and ice cold." Several indignant Mets weighed in on the book in the papers.

"That doesn't seem like the manager I know," said Seaver. "Mr. Hodges treats his ballplayers with an attitude of professionalism. Maybe Mr. Harrelson in his immaturity couldn't tell the difference between professional treatment and someone picking on him."

"Gil Hodges is a gentleman's gentleman," said Koosman. "He's a wonderful person. I'm proud to play under him and know him. I'd like to be like him. I don't know Ken Harrelson personally but he probably never had any respect for anybody." Even Ron Swoboda said he thought Harrelson "was really unfair." Hodges himself, wanting the controversy to go away, never commented on what Harrelson wrote. If he was going to call attention to a book it would be his own modest tome, *The Game of Baseball*, which, too, was published in 1969.

After the Mets beat the Cubs 9–5 on July 16, they trailed them by only 4 games. Durocher was going with four starters and not utilizing his bench, and the Cubs were wilting in the hot sun and were ready to be passed. On July 20, the talk around the world was of how American astronauts Neil Armstrong, Buzz Aldrin, and Michael Collins flew to the moon. It would be said that what the Mets accomplished in 1969 was an even greater miracle.

But not yet. They split four games with both the Expos and the Reds. Then on July 30, they played a doubleheader against Houston at Shea Stadium. In the first game, Koosman left after seven innings, trailing 5–3. In the top of the ninth, the Astros scored 11 runs. Koonce gave up a grand slam to Jimmy Wynn, and Taylor gave up a grand slam to Denis Menke. It was the first time in National League history that two grand slams had been hit in one inning. After suffering through the 16–3 defeat, Hodges couldn't imagine that the nightcap would be even worse.

Gentry held the Astros scoreless for 2 innings, but in the disastrous third inning, seven Astros crossed the plate against him with two outs. Hodges finally replaced Gentry with Ryan. Batting for the second time in the inning, Johnny Edwards stroked a double that rattled around in the corner in deep left field. As Jones retrieved the ball in slow motion and lobbed the ball back to the infield, Doug Rader came around from first base to score the eighth Astros run.

Suddenly Hodges emerged from the dugout as if he were on a mission. He had kept his emotions in check all year and had never even been thrown out of a game. But he was not happy. At first it was assumed he was heading to the mound to get Ryan, but he walked past it. Harrelson became terrified that Hodges was coming out to see him. But Hodges kept going into left field. When he reached Jones, they exchanged a few words and then Hodges turned around and headed back to the dugout. "Jones followed about ten paces back," wrote Jack Lang in the *Long Island Press,* "contritely and with head bowed like a little boy being sent to his room for punishment." The next batter, pitcher Larry Dierker, smashed a 2-run homer off Ryan to complete a 10-run inning for Houston.

Afterward, Hodges told reporters that he removed Jones from the game because he had seen him grab his leg and thought he may have aggravated it on the sloshy turf. But nobody doubted that Hodges had yanked Jones because he looked like he'd given up on the game when he went after Edwards' ball. Jones admitted he was embarrassed by the way he was removed and told newsmen, "It looked like what you thought it was."

Hodges would long be praised for showing exemplary leadership by pulling a star player who hadn't hustled. This incident would be a defining moment in Hodges' managerial career, and pointed to for decades as the one that inspired the Mets to play better baseball and get back into the pennant race. Even though the Mets didn't start playing better immediately, the players certainly were reminded of the effort Hodges expected of them, and that kind of thinking would come into play as the season progressed.

But had this been Hodges' noble intention? Joan Hodges recalls:

I was watching the game on TV when he removed Cleon Jones for dogging it going after that ball. I knew what was coming, because they had the camera on Gil in the dugout. I knew just by looking at him that he was in a *zone*. I said to myself, "Oh, my God, he's gone." I called Rube Walker and I said, "I can't understand why you didn't try and stop him from leaving the dugout!" Rube said, "Joan, you want to know the truth? He was too far gone when he stood up and it was too late to try to do something about it."

Gil came home, and I had his sandwich and coffee ready as I always did. He said to me almost sheepishly, "Get it off your chest." I said, "Okay. Why? I want to know why! A .340 hitter and you walk out of the dugout and go after him in left field, with all that press sitting up there? I don't care if you killed him when you got him in your office after the game—he deserved it—but why would you do that, Gil? My God, it was completely out of character." He said to me, "You know, honey, I didn't realize I was walking out there until I was at the mound, and by then it was too late to turn around." Gil knew he lost it and had done something that he shouldn't have done. But he never regretted it. He knew nothing was wrong with Cleon's ankle, but he asked him about it and that justified what Gil did in his mind.

"I'm not sure if it was like when I took the harmonica away from Phil Linz in 1964," says Yogi Berra, "but I know he surprised a lot of guys and let them know he was serious about doing things his way."

"No one felt safe not giving a hundred percent anymore," says Hodges Jr. "They knew he'd come and take them off the field."

"When I did illustrations of Gil, the characteristic I portrayed the most was strength," said Bill Gallo of the *New York Daily News* shortly before his death in 2010. "The strength in his face and the stern look. You knew the sternness didn't come from meanness; it came from a direction of leadership. Not every one of those Mets ballplayers adored him, but there was never a doubt who was in charge and who was to follow. He led those kids in 1969 like no one else could have done."

The Mets finished July with a 55–44 record, 6½ games behind Chicago. Their play didn't improve. After being swept in a three-game series with Houston, they were 10 games behind Chicago and were in need of a miracle run like the New York Giants had in 1951 to get back in the race with the Dodgers.

CHAPTER TWENTY-SIX

The New York Mets had a history that was hard to ignore, so when August began many fans gave them up for dead and expected the Cubs to run away with the division title. Instead, they won their next five games despite scoring only 11 runs. They won the fifth game 1–0 when Agee hit his 21st homer off Juan Marichal in the fourteenth inning. The next day, the Mets won 6–0 to move within seven games of the Cubs as McAndrew tossed a 2-hitter, and Shamsky hit his 10th homer and knocked in 4 runs. They lost the final game of the Giants series, but then won six straight against the Dodgers and Padres. The Mets went 21–10 in August, 14–3 over their last 17 games, and ended the month with a record of 76–53, just 4½ games back.

As it became clear that the Mets really were in a pennant race, there was a greater press presence at Shea and on the road. Hodges was constantly hounded before and after games. "I noticed that Hodges wasn't an easy guy to interview in a group setting that year," recalls Phil Pepe. "Postgame interviews were difficult. There were times he'd be asked, 'Why did you do such and such?' and he'd answer, 'Because I wanted to,' or, 'Because I'm the manager.' He was intimidating to some reporters because he'd cut them down to size and let them know he wasn't going to answer questions like that. He was different with Dick Young, Jack Lang, Jack Mann, Stan Isaacs, and others who had been around since he was a player."

The Mets lost 2 of 3 in L.A. to open September. But they returned to New York and things turned around. Seaver became the Mets' first 20-game winner, beating the Phillies 5–1 with a 5-hitter on September 5. The Mets dropped the second game that day, but came back to beat the Phillies the next two games.

The Cubs came into Shea Stadium for a vital two-game series, still clinging to a 2½-game lead and thinking that sweeping the Mets would put them to bed. Koosman went against Hands before 43,274 fans on September 8. Hands tried to put fear into the young Mets by throwing a fastball at the head of their first batter. Agee barely got out of the way. Hands' mistake was that he was going against the Mets pitcher who was known for protecting his hitters. When Santo led off the top of the second, Koosman struck him in the arm with a fastball. "He really drilled him," says Pignatano. "We thought he broke his arm." Koosman then struck out the three shaky batters who followed. Message answered.

"I wasn't thinking it was a big moment for the Mets, when we showed the Cubs nobody could push us around," says Koosman. "But looking back on it, maybe it was. Gil said early on that it was our job to protect our players, but he didn't tell me to hit Santo. I'm not sure how he reacted, because you didn't look at him while you were pitching, because he might take you out."

The Mets took a 2–0 lead in the third inning when Agee slugged a 2-run homer. The Cubs tied the game in the sixth when Koosman gave up 3 singles and a sacrifice fly. But Agee doubled leading off the bottom half of the inning and scored the winning run on a single by Garrett. Koosman shut down the Cubs the rest of the way, striking out 13, for a 3–2 victory, as the Mets inched to 1½ games of first place.

The next day, 51,448 fans and one black cat showed up at Shea Stadium. No one knew where the cat came from, but during the game it walked behind the Cubs' on-deck circle and stared into their dugout before disappearing. There was no longer any question that the reeling Cubs were cursed and that the Mets were charmed. "The general feeling was that someone was watching out for us," said Harrelson. "We started to think that we were moving through history and we were destined to win."

The Cubs' bats were feeble, managing only 5 hits and 1 run against Seaver. Clendenon and Shamsky homered in the 7–1 victory that moved the team to half a game out of first place. With their 82nd victory, the Mets assured themselves of their first season above .500. It wasn't good enough. "I came home to my wife and said, 'You know, Joan, it's just possible we might do it,'" wrote Hodges in *Guideposts* the following spring. "Even then I wasn't thinking much beyond winning the division championship."

The following day, September 10, the humbled Cubs lost 6–2 to the Phillies. When Boswell drove in Jones in the bottom of the twelfth inning for a 3–2 victory in the first game of a twin bill with Montreal, the Mets were in first place for the first time ever. In relief, Ron Taylor was credited with the historic victory. In the second game, Ryan threw a 3-hitter and struck out 11 in a 7–1 victory. The Mets completed the sweep of the Expos, 4–0, as Gentry tossed a 6-hitter and fanned 9. The Mets scoreboard had a message to the fans: LOOK WHO'S NO. 1.

Then on the twelfth, Koosman and Cardwell made it 3 shutouts in a row, setting down the Pirates 1–0 and 1–0, in the first double shutout in the team's history. Oddly, the pitchers drove in the lone runs in each game. The Mets now led the Cubs by 2½ games. They increased their lead the next day when the reeling Cubs lost and they won their 10th consecutive game, 5–2, as Seaver notched his 22nd victory and Swoboda belted a grand slam.

The Mets won in memorable fashion on the fifteenth. Cardinals left-hander Steve Carlton set a major-league record by striking out 19 Mets, including rookie Amos Otis 4 times, but Swoboda touched him for 2 2-run homers to give the Mets an unlikely 4–3 victory. Koosman and Seaver then threw shutouts against the Expos, 5–0 and 2–0, to increase the Mets' lead to 5 games as Chicago continued its downward spiral. The whole country had taken to this renegade, magical ball club that had come out of the blue to take on the baseball establishment. "Seaver, Koosman, Jones, and Agee were superior players, and Grote was a great catcher, but really most of us were just young *guys*," says Swoboda. "Dumb kids just good enough to be in the majors. And Hodges was the maestro."

"We were managed by an infallible genius for the final six weeks of the season," wrote Seaver in his book about the season, *Tom Seaver and the Mets*. "Every move Gil made worked. If he lifted a starter, the relief pitcher was brilliant. If he decided to stick with a starter who seemed to be tiring, the man revived. If he let a weak hitter bat in a critical situation, the man came through with a hit; if he called on a pinch hitter, the man delivered. He could do no wrong. If he had decided one day to have me pinch-hit for Cleon Jones, I would have hit a home run."

The Mets had a tiny hiccup on their march to a division title, losing a doubleheader to the Pirates and then being no-hit by the Bucs' Bob Moose on the twentieth. That day attendance for the season passed two million for the first time in team history. Then the Mets continued to amaze, winning 9 straight games, 4 with shutouts, to leave the Cubs in the dust.

On September 24, the Mets scored 5 runs off Carlton in the first inning on home runs by Charles and Clendenon, who'd later hit a second homer. Gentry blanked the Cardinals 6–0 on 4 hits. One year after Hodges' heart attack, the New York Mets clinched the National League East title.

"It ended when Joe Torre hit into a double play," recalls McCarver. "I was on deck. Lefty had said the Mets weren't going to clinch it against him, but they did. The fans at Shea Stadium went berserk and came onto the field and we wanted to get to the locker room as quick as we could. It surprised me. I thought the security would be better. It was nuts. Believe me; it was dangerous, not fun."

A wild clubhouse celebration followed, during which Seaver poured champagne on his happy manager's head, deciding it wise to stop after a few drops.

"I'm very, very happy," Irene Hodges told reporters back in Petersburg, saying that she was expecting her "wonderful son" to "phone me today. He calls every week, and of course, today it will be a special call." A Cleon Jones fan, she was one of many thrilled fans in town who had listened to Mets games on the radio throughout the season. Fans in Princeton were delighted, too, and its City Council passed a resolution honoring their "favorite son who brought fame to the Mets."

Hodges was later visited by Johnny Murphy, who claimed he had done the best job of managing he'd ever seen. He tore up Hodges' old contract and gave him a new three-year deal worth $70,000 a season.

The Mets didn't let up in Philadelphia as they played a meaningless weekend series against the Phillies. Koosman improved his record to 17–9 with a 2.28 ERA with a 4-hit, 5–0 victory, his sixth shutout. Seaver then picked up his 10th consecutive victory and 25th of the season against 7 defeats, 1–0, on a 3-hitter. His fifth shutout of the season lowered his ERA to 2.21. Then Gentry pitched 5 scoreless innings before giving way to Ryan and Taylor in a 6–0 victory. The 3 consecutive shutouts gave the Mets staff a major-league-best 28 for the year.

The Mets won one more time on October 1, picking up their 100th victory at Wrigley Field against the Cubs. They won 6–5 when Shamsky drove in Harrelson in the twelfth inning. For the season, the Mets went 10–6 in extra-inning games, a big improvement on their 2–13 record in 1968. Their record in 1-run games was an exceptional 41–23, a 29-game swing from the previous year. The Mets went 38–11 down the stretch, including 23–7 in September. The Cubs, who finished 8 games out, were only 21–29 in their final fifty games and 8–17 in September. Durocher, who sent Hodges a congratulatory telegram, was blamed for not using his bench and a fifth starter despite all the day games in hot Chicago.

Nobody on the Mets believed their division title had just been a fluke, although the Cubs had been a mismanaged team that tanked when pressed. But they would have to prove it to a country full of skeptics in the postseason against stronger teams. Hodges thought anything was possible. Even the Brooklyn Little League team that used his name finally reached the playoffs in 1969 and won their first title. He was on a roll.

Next the Mets went to Atlanta to play in the first-ever National League Division Championship series. Lum Harris' Braves won 93 games during the regular season to capture the National League West by 3 games over the San Francisco Giants. They had a decent pitching staff, led by knuckleballer Phil Niekro, who won 23 games, but it was the formidable offense featuring Hank Aaron (.300, 44 homers, 97 RBIs), Rico Carty (.342, 16 homers), and Orlando Cepeda (22 homers, 88 RBIs) that convinced many pundits that Atlanta would overwhelm the Mets.

But the Mets didn't feel overmatched. They had beaten the Braves 8 out of 12 times during the season and outscored them. They believed Seaver, Koosman, and Gentry were as good as any three starters in baseball, and no one had a swingman like Nolan Ryan. Plus they had two standout relievers: the right-handed Taylor (9–4, 13 saves, 2.72 ERA) and the left-handed McGraw (9–3, 12 saves, 2.24 ERA). Jones batted .340, which was third in the league to Pete Rose and Roberto Clemente and a Mets record. Agee had slugged 26 homers and driven in 76 runs while mostly batting leadoff.

The team's two first basemen, Clendenon and Kranepool, combined for 23 homers and 88 RBIs; and the two right fielders, Shamsky and Swoboda, combined for 23 homers and 97 RBIs.

The first game was played in Atlanta on October 4. Seaver and Niekro took their 48 victories to the mound and looked like journeymen, taking turns squandering leads. Then in the bottom of seventh inning, Aaron, Seaver's childhood idol, deposited one of his pitches over the fence to put the Braves in front, 5–4. Aaron tipped his cap and raised his arms over his head when he went out to right field in the eighth inning. "I thought it was all over," he said later.

But the Mets came back again, scoring 5 runs in the top of the eighth and knocking out Niekro. Jones got the game-tying RBI single and scored the go-ahead run on an infield out, but he shared the hero role with J. C. Martin, who, pinch-hitting for Seaver, smoked a liner to center field. When it got by Tony Gonzalez, all three runners scored to give the Mets a 9–5 lead. It was the biggest hit of his career. Taylor, who had pitched for the Cardinals in the 1964 World Series, held the Braves scoreless in the final 2 innings, and the Mets had won Game 1.

After Chief Noc-A-Homa led the Braves onto the field, Coretta Scott King, the widow of Martin Luther King Jr., threw out the ceremonial first pitch to begin Game 2. The Mets knocked out 18-game winner Ron Reed in the second inning, when Agee hit a 2-run homer, and built an 8–0 lead. But the Braves came back against Koosman with 1 run in the fourth inning and 5 in the fifth, 3 coming on an Aaron homer. Still needing one out to be credited with a victory, Koosman was lifted for Taylor. "I had no idea if Hodges was disappointed in me," says Koosman. "But Gil liked going lefty-righty, fastball–breaking ball. I was a hard-throwing left-hander and Ron was a right-hander with a sinker and was a veteran who knew how to pitch."

Koosman's roommate pitched through the sixth inning to pick up the victory; the save went to McGraw, who threw 3 innings of scoreless relief. Jones' 2-run homer in the seventh inning made the final score 11–6. The Mets led 2–0 and needed only one more victory to be the National League champions.

Game 3 was played in New York. Gentry went against Pat Jarvis, a 13-game winner, and quickly fell behind when Aaron smashed his third homer of the series, a 2-run shot. In the third inning, Gentry got into quick trouble, giving up a single to Gonzalez and a double to Aaron (who batted .357 for the series with 7 RBIs). He got two strikes on Carty, but the deadly fastball hitter lined a ball just foul into the stands. Hodges shot out of the dugout and pulled the mystified Gentry in midbatter. It must have been instinct for Hodges to bring in Ryan, because if he was as wild as usual, the Mets were in trouble.

He wasn't wild. He struck out Carty with the "Ryan Express," as Bob Murphy had dubbed his fastball, and held the Braves at bay for the next 2 innings. Agee and Boswell homered to put the Mets ahead 3–2. Cepeda's 2-run homer in the fifth gave the Braves a 4–3 lead, but Ryan was virtually untouchable otherwise as he threw 7 innings of 3-hit ball, striking out 7. "To bring me in in that situation, I was as dumbfounded as the fans were," Ryan said in 2011. "But that was a big moment in my career. It had an impact on my career." He was in line for the victory as the Mets came back to take the lead in the fifth inning on Wayne Garrett's 2-run homer off Stone. They'd tack on 2 insurance runs.

In the top of the ninth inning, Ryan induced pinch hitter Bob Aspromonte, the former Dodger and Astro, to fly out, and Felix Millan to ground out. Then Gonzalez hit a tricky grounder to Garrett. In *The Incredible Mets*, Maury Allen wrote: "He surrounds it. He picks it up cleanly. He throws. Kranepool catches the ball at first for the final out. Kranepool leaps into the air like some wild astronaut testing the surface of the moon. He floats. He lands with a shock. The crowd is on the field. The bases are going. The noise is deafening. The people are everywhere . . . the joy was unbounding. At 3:24 o'clock in New York City, New York, United States of America, a miracle came to pass and a dream was over. It was now real. The Possible Dream was reality."

The Mets' 7–4 victory gave them an unexpected sweep of the Braves. They had outscored them 27–15, outhit them 37–27, and even outhomered them 6–5. "We were supposed to dominate that series!" says Aspromonte. "I'm still in shock about what happened. Our whole team felt the same. We had an outstanding ball club. But sure enough, they dominated us. Unbelievable."

In their ninth season, two years after being in last place, the New York

Mets were the National League Champions. They were the first expansion team to win a pennant. In the clubhouse, while his players drank champagne from the bottle, Hodges kissed his wife. They looked at each other with amazement. For the first time since 1956, when Hodges wore a Brooklyn Dodgers uniform, a New York team from the National League was going to the World Series.

CHAPTER TWENTY-SEVEN

The Mets' World Series opponents were the Baltimore Orioles, whose fiery, diminutive manager, Earl Weaver, argued with umpires as much as Durocher did. After replacing Hank Bauer in the middle of the 1968 season, he guided the Orioles to a second-place finish. In 1969, his first full year in charge, they accumulated a whopping 109 victories and won the American League East by 19 games. Then they swept a strong Minnesota Twins team in the ALCS. Beating the upstart Mets in the World Series was considered a mere formality for this dynasty in the making.

Baltimore's offense was led by right-fielder Frank Robinson, who was the MVP for the Reds in 1961 and Orioles in '66; third baseman Brooks Robinson, the MVP in 1964; and imposing left-handed-hitting first baseman John "Boog" Powell, whose MVP award would come in 1970. In 1969, Frank Robinson batted .308, with 32 homers and 100 RBIs; Brooks Robinson hit only .234 but had 23 homers and 84 RBIs and was a Gold Glover; and Powell batted .304, with 37 homers and 121 RBIs. Paul Blair, the league's best defensive center fielder, had Tommie Agee–like offensive numbers: .285, 26 homers, 76 RBIs. Leadoff hitter Don Buford, the left fielder, batted .291, with 11 homers and 64 RBIs. Steady second sacker Davey Johnson hit .280, with 34 doubles, 7 homers, and 57 runs batted in; Gold Glove shortstop Mark Belanger had his best year with the bat, hitting .287, with 50 RBIs. And catchers Elrod Hendricks and Andy Etchebarren combined for 15 homers and 64 RBIs.

The Orioles also had outstanding pitching. Left-handed screwball specialist Mike Cuellar came over from Houston and went 23–11 with a 2.38 ERA. He and Denny McLain would share the American League's Cy Young Award. Another southpaw, Dave McNally, won his first 15 decisions and finished with a 20–7 record and a 3.22 ERA. Jim Palmer went 16–4 with a 2.34 ERA, and Tom Phoebus 14–7 with a 3.52 ERA. The bullpen was led by right-handers Eddie Watt (5–2, 16 saves, 1.65 ERA) and Dick Hall (5–2, 6 saves, 1.92 ERA), and left-hander Pete Richert (7–4, 12 saves, 2.20 ERA). Quizzed by reporters about Ken Harrelson's book, Richert expressed gratitude and respect for his former Senators manager and said, "I'm delighted that he's in the Series."

The World Series began in Baltimore on October 11, exactly two years since Hodges agreed to manage the Mets. Former Maryland governor Spiro T. Agnew, Richard Nixon's ill-fated vice president, threw out the first pitch at Memorial Stadium. After the Mets failed to score in the top of the first inning, Tom Seaver took the mound and faced Buford, two USC alums. Buford took him deep to right field, an auspicious beginning for the vaunted Orioles offense.

"That ball shouldn't have gotten over the fence," Swoboda claims. "I was so nervous. The first time you play in the World Series, the nine-year-old kid you once were suddenly is out there on the field, not the twenty-five-year-old. I looked like a mechanical man getting back on that ball, but I still should have caught it. I needed to calm my ass down. In the dugout, Kranepool told me to get over it."

Seaver had trouble relaxing too, and gave up 3 more runs in the fourth inning. Hodges lifted him after five innings. Cardwell and Taylor pitched hitless ball the rest of the way, but Cueller stymied the Mets on 6 hits, allowing only a single run in the seventh on a sacrifice fly by Al Weis.

The national media assumed the Mets' remarkable run was over after their meager performance in losing 4-1, and that a sweep was a possibility. But the Mets took their cues from their manager, who still believed they could split in Baltimore. The Mets knew they had to win Game 2 or they'd have to beat the powerful Orioles in 4 of 5 games.

Fortunately, Koosman was back in top form. He needed to be as he went against McNally, who'd give up only 6 hits on the day. Donn Clendenon hit an opposite field homer off the Orioles' left-hander to lead off the fourth inning, and the score stayed 1–0 Mets until the bottom of the seventh. Blair led off with a single to left, the first hit off Koosman. With two outs, Blair stole second and scored on Brooks Robinson's single to center. It was the Orioles' final hit. The score remained tied until the top of the ninth inning. With two outs, Ed Charles singled to left, his second hit of the game. Grote followed with a single to left, and "the Glider," as Koosman had nicknamed him, took third. Everyone expected Hodges to pinch-hit for Weis, but he'd singled earlier and Hodges left him in. He singled again, scoring Charles with the go-ahead run.

In the bottom of the ninth, Koosman got two quick outs, but then walked Frank Robinson and Boog Powell. Merv Rettenmund pinch-ran for Robinson. With Brooks Robinson due up, Hodges replaced Koosman with Taylor. Koosman didn't try to talk him out of it. In a newspaper column carrying his byline the next day, Hodges explained: "Koosman still had his stuff but his control was off and I'd rather have Taylor pitch to a right-hander like Brooks Robinson at this point. Taylor was just great the day before."

Taylor, who didn't give up a hit in seven innings of World Series play during his career, threw a 3–2 sinker, and Robinson hit a high chopper toward Charles at third base. "A lot of people make a big fuss about that play, but it wasn't anything special," says Charles. "With Taylor pitching, I moved toward the line just a little bit, and Robinson hit the ball to me. The proper play might have been to tag third base, but Rettenmund was probably going to beat me to the bag, and in that crucial situation, I wanted to make the sure out. The computer in my head said, 'Brooks Robinson is a slow runner,' and I knew I had time to actually stop before making the overhand throw to first base to get Robinson and end the game."

The Mets evened the Series 1–1 with their nail-biting 2–1 victory, and with Gentry, Seaver, and Koosman scheduled to pitch, their confidence was sky-high. It was the Orioles that were starting to feel vulnerable after being 2-hit.

In a matchup of two of baseball's best young right-handers, Gentry faced Palmer in Game 3. On his signature high fastball, Palmer gave up a leadoff home run to Agee. He'd give up only one other leadoff homer in his entire career. More shocking was a 2-run double by Gentry over Blair's head in the second inning that increased the Mets' lead to 3–0. During the season, Gentry had hit .081 with 1 double and 1 RBI in 74 at-bats, striking out 52 times. This Mets team had karma. And it wasn't just at the plate.

In the top of the fourth inning, Frank Robinson and Powell singled with two outs. Then Hendricks muscled a pitch into the gap in deep left center. A gazelle-like Agee caught up to it and snared the ball backhanded on the warning track, a snow cone, to end the threat. Agee got a deserved ovation at Shea, and across the country the number of Mets fans rose dramatically. Years before, Willie Mays had made a spectacular grab against the Dodgers, and Charlie Dressen had facetiously said, "Well, let's see him do that again." Agee would give a repeat performance.

In the top of the seventh, with the Mets now leading 4–0, Gentry walked the bases loaded. In the postseason, Hodges had quickly developed a pattern of bringing in Ryan for Gentry, with Taylor relieving Seaver and Koosman. At the risk of being second-guessed, he called for Ryan again, although he had control issues and there was nowhere to put a baserunner. Ryan's only World Series appearance in a twenty-seven-year career was memorable, thanks in part to Agee. Determined to throw strikes, Ryan got ahead of Blair 0–2. But instead of delivering a waste pitch, Ryan nipped the outside corner, and Blair reached out and hit it on the end of the bat. Agee moved over for it and seemed ready to catch it, but the wind got hold of it and he had to dive to reach it. He caught it three inches off the ground. He received his second standing ovation. Afterward, Hodges told reporters that Agee's second play "was the greatest World Series catch I've ever seen."

The bewildered Orioles went down in order in the eighth inning. They got two men on in the ninth, but Ryan zipped his fastball past Blair to end the game with the Mets on top, 4–0. The Orioles had been shut out only 8 times all season.

That night, the Hodges dined at a small Italian restaurant in Brooklyn with Gil's siblings Bob Hodges and Marjorie Hodges Maysent and their spouses. "Gil was bubbling with enthusiasm," said Marjorie, then the executive director of Landrum Hospital in Lower Merion, Pennsylvania. "He was confident New York would go all the way."

Game 4, on October 15, was played on Vietnam War Moratorium Day before 225 wounded servicemen. Around New York City flags were being

flown at half-staff, but at Shea, because of a directive by Baseball Commissioner Bowie Kuhn, it was at full staff. Seaver took the mound for the Mets,
and Hodges was relieved that he was sharp right from the beginning. Seaver
not only shrugged off his bad outing in Game 1 but also focused on the
game despite what was going on outside the stadium. He had expressed his
anti-war sentiments publicly, but he was angry that a group of protesters
were circulating their leaflets with his picture on it without his permission.
After Clendenon homered off Cuellar in the second inning, Seaver made
the 1–0 lead hold up through eight innings.

But Seaver felt he was tiring, and in the ninth Frank Robinson and
Powell singled. Brooks Robinson came to the plate with men on first and
third and one out. Rather than bring in Taylor or McGraw and hoping
for the double play, Hodges stuck with his ace. It seemed like the wrong
decision when Robinson laced Seaver's first pitch to shallow right center.
"I figured that the ball would go in between, past the outfielders to the
fence," wrote Seaver. "But then I turned and saw where Swoboda was playing in right and saw him already sprinting toward the ball." Seaver should
have been backing up home, but he was transfixed on the mound, watching
Swoboda race in and dive for the ball—and making a miraculous backhanded catch an inch above the ground. The tying run scored but a rally was
prevented.

Swoboda then made a long running catch on a fly by Hendricks, his
third putout of the inning. For the belly-sliding catch, the Baltimore native
received the same pats on the back in the dugout that Agee got in Game 3.
"I was an underrated outfielder," Swoboda says today. "I worked hard on my
fielding."

Seaver felt he had another inning in him, and without gazing at Hodges
he went to the mound in the tenth inning. Two men got on, but he struck
out Blair to end his day, thoroughly spent. The Mets came up in the bottom
of the tenth, needing a run to give Seaver his first World Series victory.
Grote doubled to short left field off Dick Hall, and Gaspar pinch-ran. Weis,
who had another 2-hit day, was given a rare intentional walk. Hodges sent
up Martin to bat for Seaver. Richert came in to pitch to the left-handed
batter. Martin laid down a bunt on the first pitch, and Richert picked up the
ball and threw to first—only it ended up rolling around in right field. The

ball had struck Martin on the wrist. Although Weaver didn't protest, Martin should have been called out for interference for being in fair territory when he was clipped. But everything was going the Mets' way. Gaspar scored the winning run without a throw, and somehow the Mets were up 3 games to 1.

Koosman told Seaver that he'd wrap up the Series the next afternoon, October 16. He didn't want the Mets to go back to Baltimore leading only 3–2 with neither of them available. But in the third inning, he threw McNally a high fastball when he expected him to bunt, and the Orioles pitcher tomahawked it into the left-field bullpen. Two batters later, Frank Robinson homered to give the Orioles a 3–0 lead. An irritated Koosman pledged to his teammates that Baltimore wouldn't score again, and he made good on his word. Meanwhile, the Mets were looking for something to change the momentum. What did the trick was one of the most bizarre plays in World Series history.

Leading off the bottom of the sixth inning, Jones claimed he was hit by a 1–1 curveball on his left foot. The ball bounced into the Mets dugout. Umpire Lou DiMuro—who in the top half of the inning called a strike on a Koosman pitch that had actually drilled Frank Robinson on the leg—didn't believe Jones any more than he had Robinson. Suddenly Hodges emerged from the dugout carrying the ball in question. He marched toward home plate exhibiting an imposing combination of authority and conviction and showed DiMuro shoe polish on the ball. DiMuro signaled Jones to first base. Weaver raced out to argue that there had been some shenanigans in the Mets dugout with the ball and that it was Hodges' reputation for honesty rather than a smudge on the ball that influenced the umpire.

Jones would always contend that he was struck on the foot by McNally. According to Kranepool, who was in the Mets' dugout, Hodges "took a ball out of a discard bucket and gave it to the umpire, who saw scuffmarks. If he would have picked out any one of the dozen balls in there, the ball would have had marks on it."

According to Hodges, the ball he handed DiMuro was indeed the ball that struck Jones. In *Guideposts*, he wrote, "I took a look at the ball—and there it was, a beautiful smudge of black Shinola. When I showed it to the umpire, we got our man on base."

Since 1993, Koosman has said that when the ball rolled into the dugout, he picked it up and Hodges told him to rub it on his shoe to get polish on it. "I didn't say anything for years because I was mixed up about it," he says today. "Is that cheating or just heads-up baseball? Gil was smart, and for him to tell me to do that was very fast thinking. I wasn't even thinking about what he was going to do with the ball. Afterward, I concluded that the ball didn't really hit Jones and that's why Hodges wanted my shoe polish on the ball."

"You've got to know the type of individual Gil Hodges was," Jones has said many times since. "There was no way Gil Hodges would ever do anything dishonest. He wasn't a cheater."

If Hodges did tell Koosman to put polish on the ball, then it's likely that he did so firmly believing it had struck Jones' foot and that he just wanted the umpire to make the right call.

"That could be," says Koosman. "Maybe there was already some polish from Jones' shoe on the ball and all I did was *add* my polish to his. We didn't have time to discuss it. Hodges took the ball from me right away and showed it to the umpire."

Weaver's protest fell on deaf ears. After Jones was awarded first base, Clendenon, the MVP of the Series, followed with a 2-run homer, his third in the five games. The Mets had cut the lead to 3–2, and momentum was back on their side. In the seventh inning, Weis, who hit 2 homers in 247 at-bats during the season, and none at Shea Stadium, somehow found the left-field stands to tie the score 3–3. (He hit .455 for the Series.) Watt replaced McNally in the eighth inning, and Jones greeted him with a double off the left center-field fence. With one out, Swoboda doubled down the left-field line to knock in the go-ahead run. Shoddy fielding allowed Swoboda to score a huge insurance run.

Koosman went to the mound in the ninth inning leading 5–3. Joan Hodges sat with Gil Jr. and Robert and Marion Merrill behind the Mets dugout surrounded by security guards. "The Merrills had been to the previous game," she says, "and I wouldn't let her change her dress." Joan prayed; she held her breath. Her brother Louis and daughter Irene sat nearby, also protected by security guards.

Koosman walked Frank Robinson to lead off the ninth. Powell forced

Robinson at second. Chico Salmon pinch-ran for Powell. Brooks Robinson flied to right for the second out. Davey Johnson strode to the plate. Would Hodges lift Koosman as he had in Game 2 for Ron Taylor, who was warming up in the bullpen? "I never looked at Hodges," Koosman says. "In that situation, I didn't want his attention because I didn't want him to think I wanted to come out."

Koosman looked only at Grote. "I felt strong. I didn't ease up at all. I was just trying to throw strikes. Hard strikes, not easy." He threw the last pitch of the game. "It was a fastball down the middle, about belt high. You don't want to throw pitches like that in that situation."

Johnson jumped at the pitch and connected. "The noise was so deafening in the ballpark," recalls Koosman, "that when Johnson hit the ball, I couldn't tell that it cracked the bat, and I didn't know if it was out of the park or not. My heart sank because it looked like maybe he did have a good hit off it. I judged according to Cleon's movements where the ball was hit. I knew then that it wasn't going out."

Johnson left the batter's box thinking *home run*. The ball made it only to medium left field. Jones, playing deep, took one step back. He made the catch, going down on one knee and looking up to the heavens.

The fans in the stadium erupted. Fans throughout New York City erupted. An entire country of Mets fans erupted.

The New York Mets were the world champions of baseball.

"I leaped into the air with a big wide grin on my face," recalls Charles. "What went through my mind was that this was the culmination of a dream I had when I was a little boy and idolized Jackie Robinson and wanted to play major-league baseball and be in the World Series like he did. Jackie opened the door and I got the opportunity in New York with that team and that manager and his coaches. I was very fortunate."

"I watched Jones make the catch," recalls Swoboda, "and took off. I saw fans coming on the field, so I was going to get into the dugout as fast as I could. It was wonderful and a little scary, because people's eyes were as big as saucers. I remember seeing Clendenon coming off the field, just whacking guys who were trying to grab his hat and glove. The best was the postgame—we hung around for a long time and just tried to soak it in. I was happy for Casey Stengel because he was alive and he saw it."

"Somebody took a picture of me jumping on Grote," recalls Koosman. "And then the fans were rushing onto the field, so I grabbed my hat and glove and I ran into the dugout. Then I had time to think that we'd won the World Series. I was happy for Hodges. We were all happy *first* for him."

Never before or after has a team won a world championship *primarily* because of its manager. The players told the press that they had just been buttons Hodges pushed all year, and that he was the one responsible for the title. Naturally the modest Hodges praised the players: "The reason for the New York Mets' success in 1969 certainly has been a great team effort. I think this is the best team effort of any team I've ever seen. Everyone on the ball club contributed a great deal to the success of the Mets."

For a few minutes after Koosman's final pitch, Hodges couldn't speak to anyone. He was contemplating that his entire career as a player and manager had gone into this victory. "Gil was overcome with emotion and started shaking," recalls Pignatano. "Rube and I took him into another room until he calmed down. He realized what he had done. He had taught these guys how to play. We were one hundred to one to win the pennant, and we won the whole ball of wax."

"This was bigger for him than 1955," says Lombardi. "He was a player then—this time he was a leader."

When Joan Hodges finally got to spend a few private moments with her husband in his office, he was calm and smiling. "It was the greatest baseball moment of his life," she says. "More than anything it was for the people of Brooklyn who gave him standing ovations when he went 0-for-21 in the 1952 World Series. He said to me, 'I'm so happy, honey, that I was able to give back to the people of Brooklyn. I was able to bring the championship back to the greatest fans in the world.' That was his goal, always, always, because of how wonderfully they treated him."

"I watched that game on TV," says Cindy Hodges. "Oh, my gosh, what the fans did to our house and the lawn! People stopped their cars in the street in front of our house and went crazy. I have friends that I've made over the years who have grass from our lawn in 1969! There's no fan like a Brooklyn fan—they're all nuts! It was bedlam, so Miss Sample took me and Barbara to her house. Afterward, my father was very happy. He worked hard to get those boys where they were, and he was proud of himself, rightly so. He smiled a lot."

However, Hodges wasn't smiling when he learned about the cover of the inaugural, October issue of *Jock* magazine. He objected vociferously to having Mets players planting the World Championship flag on the mound at Shea Stadium in the exact pose of the Marines raising the American flag at Mount Suribachi on Iwo Jima in Joe Rosenthal's famous 1945 photograph. "Nobody is prouder of my players than I am," he stated, "but they just won a baseball championship. The boys they are mocking in this picture [nearly] died for their country." *Jock* ended up using models in the uniforms of Seaver, Koosman, Grote, and Jones.

New York City was united by the Mets' victory, as when the Jets and Knicks captured world titles during this period. On "Mets Day," October 20, there was the biggest ticker-tape parade in New York since V-J Day in 1945, followed by a gathering at City Hall. Mayor John Lindsay told the fans that Hodges' street in Brooklyn was now Gil Hodges Place, forcing the worried Hodges to tell them to not take their celebration there. Hodges, a Democrat, refused to endorse the Republican Lindsay (who was running as the Liberal Party candidate after losing in his party's primary), but would inadvertently help the underdog get reelected in November by appearing often with him in public. In 1969, everything Hodges touched turned to gold—especially the Miracle Mets.

CHAPTER TWENTY-EIGHT

Hodges went through the 1969 season and postseason without experiencing any obvious health issues. That may have made him less aware of signs that he was dealing with stress, such as his need to smoke. "I saw him, a couple of times, sneaking cigarettes," recalls Cindy Hodges. "He didn't buy any, but he 'borrowed' them. That made me a little nervous, not knowing much about heart disease."

Hodges tried to relax with his family in the off-season, but the demands on the manager of a championship team in the city where he lived made that impossible. If anyone needed a speaker, Hodges was the first person they'd call, and he never said no. Sid Loberfeld told writer Rob Edelman, "A Mets ballplayer was scheduled to appear at a temple in Brooklyn for a fee. But at the last minute, he called up to cancel. Hy Schwartz, a local philanthropist, went to Gil's house on Bedford Avenue and told him of the situation. That night, Gil showed up at the temple with Joan. He refused to accept the fee and insisted the money go to charity."

One of Hodges' main beliefs, which he shared with his brother Bob, was that whoever was in charge, in the clubhouse or at home, was responsible for making everyone else do things the *right way*. Hodges believed it was the responsibility of a baseball manager to set the rules and make all the decisions, and he expected his players to never question authority. As a player, he never did. He felt they should be secure in knowing that he was leading them on the right path. It was an old-fashioned, pretty unrealistic way to manage at a time when young people in general were bucking authority, so it wasn't surprising that at times he had disgruntled players. It was pretty much the same at Hodges' house, his separate domain. The Hodges children, like some players, had a hard time conceding that their father *always* knew what was best for them. But as adults with hindsight, they would agree that the great majority of time, he did.

"My father loved his family and was very much a family man," says Barbara Hodges, the youngest daughter. "He was very involved with all of his children and wanted all of us included in everything. While he treated us similarly to his players in some ways, I don't think 'managed' is the right word to describe how he was with us. I would just say that my father demanded a level of respect from us as well as his players."

"There was a lot of warmth," says Cindy Hodges. "Daddy always had that smile and was happy. But I don't know how he would have done in this day and age. Even in the fifties, he was conservative, and it was worse in the sixties. It was tough for me, because the kids I went to school with did a lot that I wasn't permitted to do. My dad didn't own a pair of jeans. We didn't wear jeans. And it wasn't okay to wear short skirts. We didn't wear nail polish; we didn't wear makeup. Mommy only wore a very faint, silvery white nail polish. He didn't even let us sleep out of the house, and once he trudged through a snowstorm to bring me home from my best friend's house. He was just very protective of all of us."

"I was eighteen and it was New Year's Eve, 1970," recalls Irene Hodges, the oldest daughter. "My parents were playing gin rummy in our kitchen with our neighbors and I kissed everyone good night. My father said to me, 'Go upstairs and get changed.' At that time, girls wore miniskirts, and my skirt was very short. I said to him, 'No, Daddy, I am dressed. I have nothing else to wear tonight.' I was very thickheaded also. He said to me, 'No, you get changed or you're not going out.' I looked at my mother, who was always the interceder between us and him. She said, 'Gil, it's New Year's Eve. She's all dressed.' He said, 'Joan.' And that was it, no discussion. My mother had to explain to the guy that I wasn't going out with him."

Another time Irene was fixed up on a blind date by her mother's cousin with a young soldier on leave. He drank some and drove her to New Jersey over her objections, and when he brought her home very late her father was outside in his pajamas looking for them. She recalls:

My father said to the boy, "Do I smell liquor on your breath?" He wasn't close enough to him that he could smell it, but he knew just by looking at him. The boy said, "Yes, sir, and I apologize." My father said, "Son, do you see the name on that street sign—Bedford Avenue?" He said, "Yes, sir." My father said, "Don't ever look at it again. I don't want you to ever see Bedford Avenue again. Don't ever come down this block again looking for my daughter." He got in his car and I never heard from him again. I never wanted to hear from him, because I was embarrassed. My father never said another word to me about it. He said what he had to say and was done. With my mother you could tell a whole story and explain things, and she would be understanding. With my father, that never happened.

"My sisters and my brother have such a different outlook regarding my dad, due to our ages," says Barbara. "I was Daddy's baby, so I got away with more than the rest. Among my fondest memories of my dad were when he taught me to ride a bicycle and to horseback ride. We rode horses together every opportunity that we had. This was in Bergen Beach, in Brooklyn, about fifteen minutes from the house. He knew I loved horses, and I guess he did too, so we rode and he videoed me. This was just for me and him. I didn't really view my dad as strict; I just believe he had a set of rules and that's what we lived by. I don't believe that my dad did any wrong in raising any of us. I try to raise my son with the exact same morals that my dad instilled in me, and I have a great kid."

Hodges went back to Indiana in November 1969, but it wasn't for a visit. His maternal grandmother, Ellen Horstmeyer, to whom he was very devoted, passed away in November at the age of ninety-three. She was buried in Walnut Hills Cemetery beside her husband, Arnold W. Horstmeyer. While in Indiana, Hodges saw the billboards that had been erected at four entrances to Princeton and on top of the Prince Building on the north corner of Main and Broadway. They said, WELCOME TO PRINCETON, THE BIRTHPLACE OF GIL HODGES, and featured a large picture of the Mets manager. Princeton was going all out for the championship manager—in June they would rename the ballpark in Lafayette Park, where "Bud" Hodges had played Legion ball, Gil Hodges Field.

There was also a death in the Mets family during the off-season. Sixty-one-year-old Johnny Murphy suffered a heart attack and passed away in January. M. Donald Grant appointed Bob Scheffing, the director of player personnel, as his replacement, with the understanding that the former Cubs and Tigers manager would consult with Hodges on all personnel moves. Murphy had pulled off the Mets' biggest off-season deal in early December, during the winter meetings in Florida. Ed Charles had retired, so, with Hodges' consent, Murphy acquired Joe Foy, who had driven in a career-high 71 runs from Kansas City in 1969, for Amos Otis and hard-throwing pitcher Bob Johnson. It was a huge blunder. Otis would become a five-tool All-Star and drive in over 1,000 runs for the Royals through 1983.

Las Vegas picked the Mets to finish third in the Eastern Division, behind the Cubs and Cardinals, in 1970. Although Hodges contended "there could never be a repeat of last year as a whole," he felt the 1970 team could be stronger and was a good bet to repeat as National League champions, because he didn't expect his players to be complacent. He didn't object to the cover illustration of *Jock* magazine's April baseball issue showing him as George Washington in the famous painting, taking his men by boat across the Delaware. He was serious about leading his team to another championship.

The new season started out well. For the first time in their history, the Mets won on Opening Day, beating the Pirates 5–3 on an eleventh-inning pinch single by Donn Clendenon. It was a good day for Hodges, marred only by a confrontation with Swoboda in the clubhouse.

"We opened up in Pittsburgh and had a meeting about deciding when curfew was going to be," recalls Swoboda. "And he made a statement: 'You guys decide what time curfew's going to be, because you're going to have to live with it.' And somebody said that our curfew should be three and a half hours after the game. Well, that was way out of line and Hodges said so. And naturally, I was a dumb ass and said, 'Well, why don't you just tell us what time you want curfew to be and we'll get this bullshit meeting over with?'"

The Mets went 25–23 through May, 3 games better than in 1969, and the best record they ever had through the first two months. But they weren't playing nearly as well as they did the last fifty games of 1969. Agee was batting .232 and Jones .219, and Koosman had only 2 wins. "After you win you're on the banquet circuit all winter long," Koosman says. "You don't get a chance to rest or work out; all you do is put on excess weight. And because the players see each other all winter, when you arrive in spring training, it's like you just saw each other the day before. It was a busy winter, and maybe we weren't in good shape or didn't have the same hunger as the year before."

One player who was struggling was Tug McGraw, and not just in baseball. His parents had gone through a messy divorce and he was also having difficulty dealing with the May 4 tragedy at Kent State University, when Ohio National Guardsmen shot and killed four student protesters. McGraw went to his manager for counsel, to tell him he was having trouble functioning. Hodges was usually closed-minded when it came to changing the status quo—in 1970, he'd spoken out against Curt Flood's challenge of baseball's reserve clause and Jim Bouton's behind-the-scenes book *Ball Four*—but he was surprisingly open-minded with McGraw and expounded on his basic philosophy. In Peter Golenbock's *Amazin': The Miraculous History of New York's Most Beloved Baseball Team*, McGraw recalled: "'Listen,' he said, 'I was in the service, too. I was younger and it was a different situation, a hell of a lot more clear-cut. Now the only thing I can tell you, or tell myself, is that life can be bitter, the way it is today. Adversity comes and goes; bitterness comes and goes. But the thing that stays is your commitment to what's right. Think of where it all starts—your family and your sense of right and wrong, even your job, if it's good. If you let the worst in us ruin the best in us, you'll never find the answer.' There was never a time when he meant more to me."

June was the Mets' best month. They went 15–10 and moved into first place on the twenty-fourth, as Seaver and Ryan got victories in a doubleheader with the Cubs. Hodges was ejected for the first time since 1968 on June 28, when they lost to the Expos 3–2 and fell into a tie for first with Pittsburgh. Foy was robbed of a base hit on a diving catch by left fielder Don Hahn, but Art Shamsky came home on the play. However, Shamsky was ruled out for leaving third base early, and Hodges argued the call too strenuously.

The Mets spent two weeks in first place but were in second by the All-Star break. They were 47–39, 1½ games behind the surprising Pirates and 3½ games in front of Chicago. Hodges got to manage the National League at the forty-first All-Star Game in brand-new Riverfront Stadium in Cincinnati. The only two Mets on the squad were Seaver, the starting pitcher, and Harrelson, a reserve shortstop. Hodges' coaches were Leo Durocher and Lum Harris. The game would be remembered for the final play, when Pete Rose scored by barreling into young catcher Ray Fosse, who was taking a throw at the plate from former Met Amos Otis. The collision caused Fosse to drop the ball, giving the National League a 5-4 victory in the twelfth inning. Fosse, who suffered a separated right shoulder, would never be the same player.

Dave Johnson, the future sports editor of the *Evansville Courier & Press*, had known Hodges since he covered Mets–Cardinals games for a local paper while he attended Western Illinois University. "After the game I was talking to Gil while he was standing in front of his locker smoking a cigarette," he says. "I didn't smoke, but my parents smoked five packs a day between them, and my grandfather had just died from emphysema, so I was sensitive about smoking. I said to him as if I were talking to my own dad, 'Those aren't good for you.' Gil gave me a shrug like, 'What am I going to do? I can't beat it.'"

The Mets played just .500 ball for the rest of July but still ended the month back in first place. On the twenty-sixth Hodges was ejected for the final time in his career. He argued that first-base umpire Frank Dezelan had no business reversing home-plate umpire Doug Harvey's call on a bunt attempt, because Harvey hadn't asked for his help. August was the Mets' worst month of the season, as the team went 13–18 and landed in third place. But Agee, Jones, Shamsky, and Clendenon were hitting well, and the Mets were only 1½ games out heading into the stretch. Their experience from the year before made them the logical choice to grab the flag.

But unlike the previous year, discontent among players was pretty much out in the open, and winning another title wasn't what a lot of players were focused on. Maury Allen of the *New York Post* was gathering quotes from players for a 1971 magazine article that would be titled "Hodges Is a Tyrant." "Everybody on this team respects him," said an anonymous Met, "but Gil is a tyrant. He is stubborn, strong-willed and very overpowering." Pitcher Ray Sadecki complained that Hodges wasn't using him enough. Nolan Ryan complained that Hodges wasn't giving him a chance to pitch in the rotation. "He says I'll pitch in turn when my control improves," said Ryan, "but I say my control will improve when I pitch in turn." Gentry complained about getting the quick hook. "No matter what happens, Gil never takes Seaver out," he said. "Why doesn't he give me the same chance to work my way out of early jams?" Swoboda complained that Hodges wouldn't tell him why he wasn't playing. "Gil is an impossible person to talk to," he said. "You just can't communicate with him." "Ronnie is immature," countered Hodges. "When he gains maturity, he will probably be a better ballplayer."

Allen said Hodges' major managerial mistake was to recall switch-hitting outfielder Ken Singleton from Tidewater. That resulted in Kranepool being demoted to the minors, Shamsky being shifted to first, Swoboda going to the bench, and "caused an undercurrent of player unrest when Singleton failed to produce in a big way."

Ironically, it could be argued that Hodges did an even better job of managing in 1970 than 1969, because nothing was in his favor. Clendenon (22 homers, 97 RBIs, .288) and Agee (24 homers, 75 RBIs, .286) hit well, but almost everyone else had a worse season than in 1969, and even Agee faltered down the stretch. Jones batted 63 points lower, Swoboda hit just 9 homers, and Foy played himself out of New York by hitting .236 with 6 homers and 37 RBIs.

Seaver, Koosman, and Gentry all won fewer games. Seaver (18–12) didn't win after September 2; Gentry (9–9) didn't win after August 18; Koosman (12–7) won 4 times in September but only 8 times before. Ryan pitched a 1-hitter against the Phillies on April 18, striking out 15, to show his great promise, but he won only 6 more games while losing 11. Don Cardwell, who had given the Mets quality starts and a veteran presence, went 0–2 before he was shipped to Atlanta. The 1970 Mets went just 24–27 in 1-run games and 9–11 in extra innings.

Despite all that, the Mets were tied for first as late as September 14. If they had a late-season winning streak comparable to those the Mets had in '69, they might have captured the flag. But they finished the season without style, going 5–10, and wound up in third place, 6 games behind Pittsburgh and 1 game behind the Cubs. They would have finished in second, but the Cubs beat them 2–0 and 4–1 in the final two games of the season. It was a frustrating year for Hodges, but his team's 83–79 record was the second-best in Mets history. And the attendance at Shea Stadium was 2,697,479, the best in the league.

"Gil was disappointed they didn't win again and got a bit frustrated," says Louis Lombardi. "But he realized how hard it was to win back-to-back pennants. Obviously he never gave up, but he accepted the fact that they weren't going to get the breaks they needed to make it to the top again."

As the manager of the Senators and the Mets in 1968 and 1969, Hodges' forte was helping teams improve from year to year. But did Hodges change as a manager in 1970 because the 1969 team had won 100 games and a championship and there was no room for improvement? "Definitely not," says Seaver. "Hodges was the same manager in the years after 1969. His objective always was for us to play the game *correctly*. That never changed."

"Hodges was still the same manager," says Ron Taylor. "We just didn't play as well. To expect another year like 1969, especially so soon, was too much."

"I think we overachieved in '69," says Swoboda, "and the next year we were competitive but we were not magical. Everything felt forced. Agee and Jones were not the same players, and I wasn't of any use. That was the hardest baseball I ever played in my life. We couldn't sneak up on anyone again; we were in everybody's sights. The year before we were surfing up on the wave, and that year we were running in waist-deep water."

Swoboda did not challenge Hodges' curfew time when the 1971 season began, because on March 31, Bob Scheffing shipped the fan favorite to Montreal for outfielder Don Hahn. "I might not have been traded if I had shut up," says Swoboda. "I bristled because I wouldn't be playing every day, and I couldn't accept that. I made them think they would be better off getting the disruptive force out of the way. Asking to be traded was the stupidest thing."

On that same day, Hodges wrote a letter to his friend Dave Kaminer, the first PR director for the New York Cosmos. It was Kaminer who had done the publicity for the ceremony naming the Gil Hodges School (P.S. 193) in Brooklyn, which Barbara would attend. The previous November, Kaminer, who idolized Hodges since he was a boy, had named his newborn son Gil after him. Hodges had wished the young man luck when he was drafted into the military but was visibly thrilled when he was rejected because of an ankle problem. Now it was Kaminer who was worried about Hodges because he was smoking again. He sent him a letter suggesting that he switch from cigarettes to a pipe. Hodges replied, "Many thanks for the tobacco tip. I should stop altogether."

The 1971 season began on April 6 at Shea Stadium. The Mets won for the second consecutive time on Opening Day, 4–2, in a game that ended after 5 innings because of rain. Seaver got the victory as Agee, Clendenon, Grote, and Bob Aspromonte drove in runs. Aspromonte had been acquired during the off-season from the Braves to replace the departed Foy at third base. He'd always worn number 14 in honor of Hodges, but now he settled for number 2.

The Mets got off to a decent start, going 12–7 in April, as Seaver recorded 4 wins, and 15–11 in May. However, on May 31, they suffered a crushing blow. Koosman pitched 11 innings in San Francisco in forty-degree temperatures and tore the rhomboid muscles in his back. He would be on the disabled list for six weeks and go 6–11 in '71, and not have a winning record again until 1974.

On June 9, the Mets rallied for 4 runs in the eighth inning and beat San Diego 4–2. Seaver's record improved to 8–2 as the Mets moved into a first-place tie with Pittsburgh. It was a wonderful day for Hodges. Three months after his twenty-first birthday, Gil Jr. was selected by the Mets in the annual baseball draft. He had just finished the season playing first base at C. W. Post College on Long Island. His professional career would be cut short because of an injury, but he made his father proud.

June 9 was the thirty-second day the '71 Mets were tied for or alone in first place. It would be their last. Ryan lost the next day, and from June 10 to July 11 the Mets remained in second place. However, they went a dreadful 9–20 in July and 12–17 in August and spent the rest of the year in third and fourth places. If they hadn't done well in 1-run games, going 31–27, and extra-inning games, going 13–9, they would have had trouble staying above .500.

The strain of another frustrating season was evident on Hodges, exacerbated by more friction with some players. Aspromonte recalls, "It was hard for me to watch some of the players' reactions. When we started to fall back, Gil made moves and wouldn't tell you why. He didn't feel like he had to tell you. His thinking was, 'If I don't want to put you in the lineup today, that's my decision.' He'd get very quiet. He'd look at someone and listen, but he wouldn't react. It was an unhealthy time for Gil. I'd tell him to stop smoking."

Hodges did less platooning than in the past, and most of his regulars had solid years. Jones rebounded to bat .319, and Agee hit .285 with 28 stolen bases. Kranepool, up from the minors and playing steadily, batted .280. Boswell hit .273 and Grote .270. Harrelson batted .252 with 28 stolen bases and again played sterling defense. But the team scored only 588 runs, second-worst in the league, and there was a dearth of power. Jones' 69 RBIs was the team high, and he tied for the lead in homers with Kranepool and Agee with only 14. As a team, the Mets swatted only 98 homers. At the Mets' annual Old-Timers' Game, Hodges' players were humbled when he took an easy swing and drove the ball to the warning track.

Seaver finished second to Cy Young winner Ferguson Jenkins, with 20 wins and 21 complete games, and led the league with 289 strikeouts and a 1.76 ERA. Gentry tossed 203 innings and went 12–11 with a 3.24 ERA. McGraw went 11–4 with 8 saves and a 1.70 ERA. The staff led the National League with a 3.00 ERA.

Seaver's 20th victory, a 7-hit 6–1 triumph with 13 strikeouts against the Cardinals, came on the last day of the season and allowed the Mets to share third place with Chicago. The Mets finished with the identical record they had in 1970, 83–79. But this time they were 14 games behind the improved Pirates, who would dethrone the Baltimore Orioles as world champions.

Hodges believed that the Mets were just a player or two away from competing for Eastern Division supremacy in 1972. In a huge trade on December 10, they shipped Ryan and three other players to the California Angels for twenty-nine-year-old Jim Fregosi, a six-time All-Star. Fregosi was a shortstop, but Hodges believed he could play third and provide punch. In 1970, he had hit 22 homers and knocked in 82 runs. However, they should have looked closer at his 1971 stats, when he'd batted .232, with 5 homers and 33 RBIs, because that was the type of hitter he was at this point in his career.

In 1972, Ryan, who was just 10–14 with the Mets in '71, would go 19–16 with a 2.28 ERA and a league-leading 9 shutouts and 329 strikeouts, as he captured the first of 11 strikeout titles. He'd retire in 1993 with 324 wins, and two unbreakable major-league records: 5,714 strikeouts and 7 no-hitters. It was a disastrous trade that would affect the Mets for years to come. The only defense for the decision to get rid of Ryan was that the National League was a lowball league, and the Mets believed he would never get strike calls on his high fastball.

Hodges didn't mention that there was another big trade in the works that he hoped would be completed before Opening Day in 1972. Scheffing was negotiating with the Expos to acquire their All-Star first baseman/outfielder Rusty Staub for Ken Singleton, first baseman Mike Jorgensen, and shortstop prospect Tim Foli. The deal would be completed on April 5 and announced the next day.

When Milt Richman of UPI asked Hodges about his health, he replied, "Don't worry; I'm not doing anything foolish, although"—and he looked around furtively to make sure nobody was listening—"I do sneak a cigarette once in a while."

"The pressures of winning, and not winning, got to Gil Hodges as much as they get to all big league managers," wrote Dick Young in early April. "He has gone back to smoking cigarettes."

Hodges was pleased with his own physical condition but not that of Fregosi, who reported to training camp out of shape. Hodges made him his personal project. Every day, he hit hundreds of ground balls to Fregosi at third. "I never saw anybody hit harder ground balls than Hodges," wrote Bud Harrelson. "I warned Fregosi, 'If Gil picks up a fungo bat, walk away. Get out of there, man. He'll kill you.'" Fregosi's reflexes weren't sharp, and, sure enough, on March 5, he was slow responding to a hard-hit ball from Hodges and dislocated his thumb. Fregosi needed to wear a cast and wouldn't be ready for Opening Day, whenever that would be.

As March ended, a dispute between the baseball players' union, led by Marvin Miller, and the team owners over increasing payments to the players' pension and medical benefit fund was intensifying. The first players' strike in baseball history was moving closer to reality. Seaver and Ray Sadecki flew to Dallas to meet with Miller and other player representatives. Players in all major-league camps waited for instructions to walk out.

Meanwhile, Hodges spent the last few days of spring with Joan, Cindy, and Barbara. "We were having the best time in Florida that year," recalls Cindy. "I remember very well that Mommy and Daddy were kind of like kids again."

"That was Easter weekend, and on Good Friday, we were having dinner in the room," recalls Joan Hodges, "and all of a sudden Gil went into the bathroom and was sick. When he came out, he told me, 'I've got a terrible, terrible headache and I can't finish dinner.' His eyes were so bloodshot and he had a terrible pain on the side of his head where he had been hit by Don Lock a few years earlier. Since then he'd never experienced bad headaches until that night. I said, 'Let me call the doctor.' But he didn't let me. And soon after he was back to normal."

Their vacation over, Joan, fifteen-year-old Cindy, and ten-year-old Barbara, and their white poodle, Slugger, climbed aboard an Eastern Airlines jet at the Tampa Bay airport, destination New York. Hodges kissed Joan and his two daughters and headed out of the terminal. "Watch the cigarettes," Joan called after him.

On April 1, the major-league players went on strike, a walkout that would last thirteen days and delay the start of the season. Hodges, Walker, Yost, and Pignatano went to West Palm Beach to await further developments. On Easter Sunday, Hodges attended morning Mass, and then took out his golf clubs. The Ramada Inn was attached to the Palm Beach Lakes Golf Course, where the club pro was former pitcher Jack Sanford, who won 24 games for the Giants in 1962.

"There was Gil, Joe, Rube, and me," says Yost. "I think we played eighteen holes and then nine more, and then we walked back to our motel with our clubs. I asked Gil what time we were all going to eat dinner together."

As Hodges put his key into his door, he said, "Seven thirty."

"He was walking with me when he fell," remembers Pignatano.

"I heard his clubs hit the ground," remembers Yost.

"His head hit the sidewalk and it was bleeding something awful," remembers Pignatano. "I was screaming to Rube and Eddie, who ran to the front desk to call for help. I put my hand under Gil's head, but before you knew it, the blood stopped. I knew he was dead. Rube did, too. He said, 'Joe, he's turned blue.' He died in my arms."

"A policeman arrived and worked on him about five minutes, trying to revive him," remembers Yost.

"We got him to the hospital and the doctors worked on him for two hours," remembers Pignatano. "They finally came out and said, 'We did all we could.'"

Gil Hodges died on April 2, 1972, two days short of his forty-eighth birthday. The official time of death was five forty-five p.m.

Joan received a phone call and sensed he was dead before she was told. Hodges Jr. learned of his father's death at spring training for Pompano in the Florida State League. Louis Lombardi found out when he stopped in to visit his parents: "I opened the door and my father was on the second floor shaking so much that his teeth were almost coming out of his mouth, and my oldest sister was screaming, 'Gil died! Gil died!' I was shocked; I couldn't believe it. I'd just spoken to Gil on the phone that morning."

Gil's friends and relatives in Indiana were devastated, especially his mother and brother. "It was the only time I saw Dad cry," says Ann Hodges.

Grant, Scheffing, Payson, and everyone in the Mets organization expressed shock and grief. So did those who knew him going back to his Brooklyn Dodgers years.

Jackie Robinson said that he was "the core of the Brooklyn Dodgers. It's a saddening experience, losing a great man like Gil."

"Gil was a great player, but an even greater man," Duke Snider stated. "I can't believe he's gone at such an early age."

"I'm sick," said Johnny Podres. "I've never known a finer man."

"Gil's death is like a bolt out of the blue," said a crushed Carl Erskine.

"I am so stunned by this," said Buzzie Bavasi, who was then president of the San Diego Padres. "I consider Hodges one of the finest men who ever wore a major-league uniform."

"Gil's death was one of the lowest points of my life," says Aspromonte, the last of the Brooklyn Dodgers to retire as a player. "I'm still in shock."

"The news of Gil Hodges' death absolutely shattered me," Don Drysdale wrote in his 1990 autobiography (three years before his own surprising death from a heart attack at the age of fifty-six). "I just flew apart. I didn't leave my apartment in Texas for three days. I didn't want to see anybody or talk to anybody. I couldn't get myself to go to the funeral. I couldn't get myself to call his widow. I couldn't do anything. It was like I'd lost part of my family and I was devastated."

"He was someone you thought would be around forever, and without any warning he was gone," says Swoboda. "His body was flown to New York from Florida on a Yankees charter. I was on that Yankee team after playing for Montreal, and I got off and watched them load his casket. I was pretty moved by the whole thing."

On April 4, his birthday, a wake was held. "Quietly they formed behind the barricades set up by the patrolmen of the 63rd Precinct early yesterday morning," the *New York Daily News* reported. "They were Gil Hodges' neighbors and fellow parishioners, waiting outside Our Lady Help of Christians Church on East 28th St., in Brooklyn. When the casket arrived at 1 p.m., the crowd had grown to 2,500." It was later estimated that ten thousand mourners passed before the casket "and at least that many were expected during the evening."

Joan, Gil Jr., Irene, and Barbara arrived by limousine thirty-five minutes after the casket did and were escorted by one of the church's assistant pastors. "Everything happened so fast that I didn't have time to grieve," says Gil Jr. "I had to care for my mother and sisters, because everyone was in shock."

"At fifteen, when Daddy died, I chose not to go to the wake and see the open casket," Cindy says. "It was a choice I made because I wanted to remember him exactly the way I knew him, and that's the memory I have."

When Joan approached the open casket, which had been placed in front of the altar, she said softly, "My angel, my darling, and my love." According to the *Daily News*, "Hodges' mother cried briefly when she saw the body, then quickly regained her composure."

At that night's viewing, Joan lamented, "Only forty-eight years. Today was his birthday. Would you believe the children and I never had a birthday party with him? Oh, my God, if I could have him back for just one of those road trips."

The funeral was on the sixth. It was also supposed to be Opening Day of the 1972 season. Seaver and Agee were among those Mets who said that even if the strike suddenly ended, they would remain in Brooklyn for the funeral. According to Joan, "Tom came to my home with a bag full of Gil's things, and he just wept and wept. Buddy Harrelson fell down, put his head on my lap, and said, 'Why? Why? Why?' They loved him like a father."

"Father Vieck and I went to New York for Gil's funeral," Bob Harris remembers. "We went into the church for the visitation. His mother was there, and just by our looks she could tell how sorry we were. Yogi Berra drove us down to the house on Bedford Avenue. Jackie Robinson and other Dodgers were there chitchatting. The next day, Father Vieck spoke at the funeral. It was very emotional at the church."

The Mass of the Resurrection held at eleven a.m. at Our Lady Help of Christians was filled to capacity, seven hundred people, and people lined the street outside. Mayor Lindsay and other New York City officials and dignitaries attended. Sitting near one another in pews were Robinson, Erskine, Carl Furillo, Joe Black, Don Newcombe, Pee Wee Reese, Snider, and Sandy Koufax. Among the former players were Joe DiMaggio, Ralph Kiner, Phil Rizzuto, and Joe Garagiola. Joan Payson and Mets officials were there, as were Gil's coaches. Also present, with Sid Loberfeld, were the kids, in uniform, from the Gil Hodges Little League.

Most of the current Mets players were present, too. Even ex-Met Ron Swoboda was there to pay his respects. He says, "I said to Joan Hodges at the funeral: 'Look, I know Gil and I had problems, but it had nothing to do with my respect for him as a man.' She's always made me feel that that was enough. I wish I had made the attempt to know him better. He was a good man."

At one point Father Curley, who had been Gil's pastor in Brooklyn and a friend, made a reference to Hodges' slump in 1953 and what another priest had asked his congregation to do. "I repeat that suggestion of long ago," Father Curley said. "Let's all say a prayer for Gil Hodges."

Erskine was one of the honorary pallbearers: "At the conclusion of the service, we followed the closed casket as it was wheeled up the aisle and outside. At that moment the organist played 'Back Home Again in Indiana.' That really hit me hard."

"When the doors to the church opened and we came out," Dave Kaminer remembers, "there were thousands and thousands of people in the streets. It was surreal. I get the shivers thinking about it. People as far as you could see, all over the neighborhood. He was that beloved. He was a symbol of the borough. I saw Howard Cosell doing an interview with Robinson in a car, and it ran on TV. That was the last time I ever saw Robinson alive."

"Cosell grabbed me," recalls Hodges Jr., "and he brought me to a car and put me in the backseat. Jackie was sitting there, crying hysterically. He held me and said, 'Next to my son's death, this is the worst day of my life.'"

"Jackie was very upset by Gil's death," says Rachel Robinson. "It was a shock. Jackie was quoted as saying he thought he'd be the one to go first, but he died a few months later, in October. At the time of Gil's funeral, he was feeling very fragile, because we lost our son in 1971. Both of us were devastated by that."

There was a private burial at Holy Cross Cemetery in Brooklyn. They dug up a tree where they buried him. The limousines passed thousands of people standing on the sidewalks bidding farewell to the borough's beloved adopted son, Gil Hodges. Four priests, including Father Vieck, conducted graveside rites.

In the media, the assumption was that Hodges had suffered his second heart attack, and that would be the story told in newspapers, magazines, and books ever since. However, there may have been a rush to judgment, because no journalist was aware that Hodges experienced stroke-like symptoms less than forty-eight hours before. "I spoke to so many doctors afterward," Joan Hodges says, "and they said it could very well have been an embolism."

Although Hodges was vigilant about his heart after his attack in 1968 and took precautions with diet and exercise, that he still was unable to vent his frustrations likely jeopardized his health. Cindy Hodges reflects, "I would definitely say that my father taking care of a family, running the bowling alley, running a major-league ball club, and smoking and feeling stress was really not a good combination, no matter how you cut it."

Despite feeling pressure and anxiety throughout his adult life, Hodges never shirked responsibility or left an obligation unfulfilled. "I don't think my father saw anything as a burden," says Hodges Jr. "I think he took it as part of life and understood that taking on responsibilities is what becoming a man is. Raising a family and teaching Seaver, Koosman, Jones, Kranepool, Swoboda, and the others to win were responsibilities but by no means burdens."

If not a *burden*, then it may simply have been the constant *weight* of responsibilities that built up pressure in Hodges. From the time he joined the Marines, he was driven by the need to meet the expectations of himself and others, including those that were unrealistic.

"That makes perfect sense," says Louis Lombardi. "You see, there was nothing worse for Gil Hodges than letting anyone down."

"Gil was truly an exceptional person," says Joan. "He was somebody who you just can't talk about and do him justice. He never changed. We had wonderful, wonderful years together. I was blessed, and I mean that very sincerely."

CHAPTER TWENTY-NINE

On Opening Day, the American flag flew at half-staff at Shea Stadium as the New York Mets lined up on the first-base line and the visiting Pittsburgh Pirates lined up along the third-base line. They doffed their caps as a lone Marine played taps at home plate. If Hodges had been alive he would have recited a "Hail Mary" and an "Our Father," as he always did during the national anthem. The Mets wore black armbands on their left arms and would do so during the entire 1972 season. Yogi Berra was manager now, having been promoted on the day of the funeral.

"The big change came when Hodges died," Koosman said in Peter Golenbock's oral history *Amazin'*. "Oh, man, it was a huge void. [But] you had to go on. Everybody went through the motions, trying to do what we thought Gil wanted us to do; every player was trying to live up to what Gil expected of him. It didn't make any difference who the manager was, whether Yogi or anyone else. Those shoes would have been impossible to fill."

To uplift the spirits of the Mets fans, Joan Payson fulfilled her dream by bringing forty-one-year-old Willie Mays back to New York in a deal with San Francisco on May 11. The Mets promptly beat the Giants in three straight games by 1 run. In the third game, Mays made his Mets debut batting leadoff and playing first base. His dramatic home run in the bottom of the fifth inning stunned his old team 5–4.

For the third consecutive season, the Mets did not make the postseason, but it was a good year nevertheless. They went 83–73, their second-best record, 13½ games behind Pittsburgh. For a time they looked like strong pennant contenders, with a .700 winning percentage in June, and good pitching from Seaver, who would have 21 victories, rookie Jon Matlack, Koosman, George Stone, and McGraw. But injuries to Rusty Staub, Bud Harrelson, Jerry Grote, Gary Gentry, and Cleon Jones slowed down the Mets, and Fregosi was a major disappointment, batting just .232, with 5 homers and 32 RBIs.

In 1973, with Berra still the manager, and Roy McMillan, Eddie Yost, Rube Walker, and Joe Pignatano as his coaches, the Hodges-schooled Mets would win their division. They would have an amazing stretch drive that took them from last to first as McGraw shouted their battle cry, "You gotta believe!" The Mets would upset the Cincinnati Reds for the National League pennant before losing the World Series in seven games to the Oakland Athletics. It was part of Hodges' legacy.

Even before Hodges' death, he was honored many times for both his career and his character. Schools, ballfields, bridges, and babies were named after him; he was welcomed into numerous halls of fame. Five months after he died, on September 18, Petersburg mayor Jack Kinman and other officials and residents of southern Indiana turned out for the dedication of the Gil Hodges Memorial Bridge over the White River, about four miles north of town, on State Road 57. Carl Erskine and Hall of Famer Edd Roush were there to witness Governor Edgar Whitcomb and the Hodges family cut the ribbon. His many achievements were etched into a monument by the bridge, along with the words: ABOVE ALL, HE WAS DEDICATED TO GOD, FAMILY, COUNTRY, AND THE GAME OF BASEBALL. A space was left at the very bottom so it could soon be added that he had been inducted into the Baseball Hall of Fame.

The Mets honored Hodges at Shea Stadium on June 9, 1973, at the annual Old-Timers' Day, by retiring his uniform number, 14. Only Casey Stengel's number 37 had been retired before. Some fifteen hundred boys from Gil Hodges' Little League attended the tribute to their benefactor, courtesy of his business manager, Sid Loberfeld. Also present, some to participate in the two-inning Old-Timers' Game, were Dodgers teammates Carl Furillo, Pee Wee Reese, Erskine, Clem Labine, Joe Black, Eddie Miksis, Al Jackson, and Bob Aspromonte. Roy Campanella, who was in the hospital, sent a telegram that was read by Vin Scully: "Gil Hodges was the greatest guy I ever had the pleasure to play with."

On April 4, 1978, on what would have been Hodges' fifty-fourth birthday, the Marine Parkway Gil Hodges Memorial Bridge between Brooklyn and the Rockaways was dedicated at a ceremony that included a healthier Campanella. In July 1979, Hodges was one of sixteen charter members to the Indiana Baseball Hall of Fame. Erskine and Bob Friend were also inducted. Seven Hoosier inductees were in the Baseball Hall of Fame: Three Finger Brown, Max Carey, Billy Herman, Ed Rice, Edd Roush, Amos Rusie, and Sam Thompson. The expectation was that Hodges would soon make eight.

More than five hundred local people were in attendance at the Indiana Baseball Hall of Fame ceremony, but not Bob Hodges. He had continued working at Gus Doerner Sports Inc., while also coaching baseball at the University of Evansville. As compassionate and as much of a disciplinarian as his brother had been, he was the Indiana Collegiate Conference Coach of the Year in 1975 and 1976 as he guided UE to postseason tournaments in both years, but he had retired after the 1977 season because of poor health. On October 5, 1978, "he was sitting in a recliner," recalls his daughter Ann, "and nobody even knew he was feeling bad. Dad looked at my mom and said, 'You'd better take me to the hospital.' He was having a heart attack but never complained about anything."

Bob died following open-heart surgery that day, leaving behind his wife, Gladys, sons Tony, Mike, John, Andy, and Tom, and daughters Ann and Krista. "When Dad passed away we were sure it was because of *genetics,* just as with his father and brother," says John Hodges. "They all died young but we didn't attribute any of their deaths to smoking."

The loss of her other son left Irene Hodges devastated. "After Charlie and her two sons had died," remembers Bill Bahr, who had attended Petersburg High with the Hodges brothers, "she continued to live all alone in that house on Main Street. I went up there one evening to knock on her door and say hello and pay my respects to her. I could see her inside but she wouldn't even come to the door."

"In the 1960s, Grandma and I would play cards, shop at the five and dime, and go to the park and have a picnic lunch and feed the ducks," recalls

Ann Hodges, who stayed with her every summer while growing up. "She was active back then. But she wasn't the same, especially after Dad died. I think losing both her boys was more than she could handle."

Irene Hodges would outlast her oldest son by ten years, passing away in 1988 at the age of eighty-three. She would be buried at Walnut Hill Cemetery next to her husband, Charlie, who had died thirty-one years earlier. Bob Harris, who as a boy during WWII, sat with her every day on her porch, handled her funeral.

In 1981, the Mets established a Hall of Fame. Its first two inductees were Joan Whitney Payson and Casey Stengel, who both passed away in 1975. The following year Hodges and George Weiss, who also died in 1972, were inducted. The selection committee was comprised of Mets broadcasters Ralph Kiner and Bob Murphy, and sportswriters Dick Young, Maury Allen, Joseph Durso, Jack Lang, and Milt Richman. Arthur Richman, the executive director, stated, "George Weiss and Gil Hodges were as much a part of New York as the Statue of Liberty and the Empire State Building."

In September 1994, the Gil Hodges Memorial Field was dedicated at St. Joseph's College in Rensselaer. Gil Hodges Jr. made the special trip to be there. He loved the state where his father was born and raised. When his two children were younger, he would take them to Indiana, because, "I wanted them to know where their grandfather came from."

Hodges Jr. and his aunt Marjorie Hodges Maysent were present in 1997 when a bronze bust of Hodges was unveiled in the rotunda of the Pike County Courthouse on Main Street. Gil and Bob's younger sister said their parents were looking down from heaven as their son was honored. Gil Jr. thanked the people of Indiana for their continued affection for his father and assured them that he never forgot them or Indiana.

The bust was the brainchild of the mayor, Randy Harris, whose fascination for Gil Hodges dated back to when he was ten years old. In a box of junk his father gave him, he came upon a 1954 Gil Hodges baseball card and discovered he was from southern Indiana. Harris approached Evansville artist Don Ingle, whose family had owned the Ditney Hill Mine where Charlie Hodges had worked for twenty-five years, about doing the bust. Petersburg had economic problems and hadn't fully recovered from a tornado on June 2, 1990, that destroyed much of the town. But Harris and members of the Gil

Hodges Memorial Fund Committee, most notably Wayne Malotte, solicited donations and raised $12,000. It took Ingle three months to complete the bust. "I met Gil out at the mines and admired the hell out of him," says Ingle. "I worked off pictures of him when I did the bust, and thought of his calm demeanor as well as his physical strength."

There was a special ceremony at Shea Stadium on June 20, 2004. Thanks to the efforts of a retired Marine sergeant, Chris Randazzo, and Representative Vito Fossella of Brooklyn, Joan was presented with a Combat Action Ribbon that her husband earned during World War II but never received. "Gil was so proud to be an American, and he was so proud to be a Marine," Joan Hodges said. "*Semper fidelis*, 'always faithful,' is what the Marines are all about," said Randazzo. "Gil Hodges was a good man, a good Marine who should not be forgotten."

In 2009, a spectacular fifty-two-foot-long, sixteen-foot-high mural was unveiled in Petersburg, on the side of a building at Ninth and Main, at SR 57, across from the courthouse and facing north. It included large illustrations of Hodges as a Brooklyn Dodger, as the manager of the Mets, and as a batter at Ebbets Field. Faces in the crowd were sold for $100 at a fund-raiser, so local residents could be seen cheering for Hodges. The mural was the idea of former mayor Jack Kinman, and the artist was Randy Hedden, who lived in Arizona but had mowed Irene Hodges' lawn when he grew up in Petersburg. The Kiwanis Club, which made a sizable donation, and especially member Wayne Malotte helped bring this ambitious project to fruition.

In 2010, Shea Stadium, the Mets' home since 1964, was replaced by Citi Field. Two VIP entrances were dedicated to Hodges and Tom Seaver. At the ceremony attended by Joan Hodges, Seaver shared a story from 1968, about how his favorite manager came to the mound after it appeared he had intentionally pitched around a batter and walked him. Seaver struck out the next batter on three pitches. When Seaver returned to the dugout Hodges said, "I wouldn't have wasted time walking to the mound if I knew you'd strike him out."

Because Hodges has received so many honors since his death, he has remained in the public eye. "I miss him physically because I can't touch him, but I still see him everywhere I go," says Cindy Hodges, who like Barbara is now a Florida resident. "At the ballpark here, they announce when I'm in

the stands; and even five minutes from my home, at the Brooklyn Bagel
Water Company, I see my dad's pictures on the walls and watch him talking
about the Ebbets Field years in videos they show on big-screen televisions.
It gives me chills."

"Many people speak to me about my father like they just saw him, like
they just had dinner with him," says Hodges Jr. "It's hard to fathom that he
has been gone so long and that I'm fourteen years older than he was when
he died. This is somebody who didn't spend even forty-eight years on this
earth but touched so many people. I meet young people who were named
after him. I have proclamations from mayors, congressmen, and senators
about getting him into the Hall of Fame, not just because of his statistics
but because of who he was."

Hodges is in plenty of halls of fame. Among them are the Petersburg
High School Alumni Hall of Fame, the Tri-State Sports Hall of Fame, the
Marines Sports Hall of Fame, and Brooklyn Dodgers Hall of Fame.
But oddly he has been denied entrance into the Baseball Hall of Fame
in Cooperstown, New York. It is an omission that his family, friends, and
legions of fans have wanted rectified for more than forty years.

In 1959, when Hodges competed against Willie Mays on *Home Run
Derby*, host Mark Scott said to Mays, "Baseball's Hall of Fame has got a
spot reserved for both you and Gil." What Frost said raised no eyebrows,
because from the mid-1950s until his retirement as a player in 1963, it was
a *given* that Gil Hodges was destined for Cooperstown. He was one of the
great bigger-than-life stars of the era, one of its most revered players.

A Hall of Famer is supposed to be the dominant person at his position
during his era. Hodges not only was the major league's premier first baseman, making eight All-Star teams, but also was one of the most dominant
of all players. From 1949 to 1959, he averaged 30 homers and 101 runs batted in. In his time, he was the only player to drive in 100 runs in seven
straight seasons. He had five straight seasons with more than 30 homers,
and eleven straight with 20 homers, tying the all-time National League
record. For the fifties, he ranked second in the majors in homers and RBIs
behind Duke Snider, and third in total bases behind Snider and Stan Musial. He ranked in the top ten in runs, hits, and walks. He also received the
first three Gold Glove awards given to a first baseman and deserved eight

more as he set numerous fielding records. Moreover, he played a huge part as the Dodgers captured seven pennants and two world titles.

Hodges' 370 home runs put him above Mize, DiMaggio, Berra, and Kiner, whom he passed to become the National League's right-handed home-run king in 1962—not just for his era, but for the eighty-six-year history of the National League. Hodges also tied the all-time major league record with 4 home runs in a game, broke the record for total bases in a game, hit for the cycle, and was the only Dodger to drive in 9 runs in a game until James Loney did it in 2006. It was a big deal at the time when he alone in baseball had seven consecutive 100-RBI seasons and when he established a new National League record with 14 grand slams. His 19 sacrifice flies in 1954 remains a major-league record.

A Hall of Famer is also supposed to have impeccable character. No one was more beloved than Hodges, no one had more integrity and decency on and off the field, and nobody ever had such a profound positive effect on the people he met. As Erskine always points out, Reese was selected to Cooperstown partly because he was helpful to Jackie Robinson, but Robinson was equally appreciative of what Hodges did for him. Reese famously said that if he had a son, he'd want him to be like Hodges. Others saw Hodges as a buddy, a brother, a father figure, a mentor, even a confessor. Arthur Daley said he "had all the attributes of an Eagle Scout. This was quite a man."

"I appeal to fellow-voters who have not yet mailed in their ballot," wrote Dick Young in the *Daily News* in 1980. "Take a hard look at Rule 4 which accompanied your ballot: 'Candidates shall be chosen on the basis of playing ability, integrity, sportsmanship, character, their contribution to the team on which they played and to baseball in general.' No man more qualifies on all counts than Gil Hodges." Hodges was the recipient of the Lou Gehrig Memorial Award in 1959, the perfect credential for a Hall of Fame member. It is surprising that he didn't win it every year.

The members of the Baseball Writers Association of America seemed to have collective amnesia in regard to Hodges' playing career. Hadn't they been watching? Or did the voters include a new generation of writers who saw him only after he'd passed his prime and didn't bother doing any research? "I don't know how many columns I've written supporting Hodges' induction into the Hall of Fame," says Dave Anderson of the *New York*

Times. "If you saw him every day, you knew he was a great player and a Hall of Famer."

All his Dodgers teammates considered him a marvelous hitter, an incomparable fielder, and a calm leader, as did all the writers who covered the team. Erskine, Reese, Snider, Roe, Labine, Campanella, and the others would shake their heads when they became aware of the cockeyed revisionist history that was taking place, and asked repeatedly, "Why *isn't* Gil Hodges in the Hall of Fame?" It didn't seem possible that Hodges' extraordinary career had been forgotten just like that.

In 1969, his first year of eligibility, he received only 82 yes votes of the 340 ballots cast, for only 24.1 percent of the needed 75 percent of votes cast required for election. Two nominees got in, Stan Musial with 317 votes, for 93.2 percent, and Roy Campanella with 270 votes, for 79.4 percent. The twenty-three writers who didn't think Musial was worthy of being a Hall of Famer and the seventy who said no to Campanella were not thrown off the voting committee for being inept, but were kept around to vote again in future years, qualified "experts" who would help determine Hodges' fate. Of the other eleven players in front of Hodges in the voting in '69, eight would eventually be enshrined at Cooperstown. More telling—since none of these retired nominees could ever do one thing to improve their careers—is that the next six players plus number thirty-one, Richie Ashburn, who received just 10 votes for 3.7 percent, would eventually be chosen.

In the next fourteen years, as he finished third to seventh in the balloting, every player who received more votes than Hodges would be voted in that year or in a future year. In every one those years, between five and twelve future Hall of Famers received fewer votes than Hodges; in both 1976 and 1977, the next nine players behind Hodges in the voting were future inductees. "Wait until next year" had a new meaning. Hodges would receive 50 percent of the vote eleven of fifteen years he was on the ballot, establishing himself as the only player ever to receive that high a percentage (prior to 2011) and not eventually reach 75 percent and induction. The most Hodges received was 63.4 percent in his last year of eligibility, when he got 237 of the 374 ballots cast and fell 54 votes short of the necessary 281. Overall, Hodges received 3,010 votes, the most of any candidate in history who wasn't eventually enshrined.

It was disappointing that when Hodges' name was submitted in 1984 to the Veterans Committee, which included some of his peers, he couldn't get the necessary number of votes from them either. Because the voting was done by secret ballot, the committee members could not be questioned about whether they had voted for Hodges. He continued to be denied even though over the years he has had such staunch supporters as Kiner, Seaver, Mays, Aaron, and Joe Morgan, who said in 1992, "Gil Hodges should have been in the Hall of Fame a long time ago."

"Gil was a heck of a ballplayer," says Yogi Berra. "I always voted for him for the Hall of Fame; what does that tell you?"

Supposedly, one year Hodges was on the verge of being elected, but Campanella wasn't well enough to deliver his decisive vote for Hodges in person. He asked that he be allowed to vote over the phone, but was denied. The word was that Ted Williams didn't let Campanella cast that vote. In his book *Brooklyn Remembered*, Maury Allen wrote, "Ted Williams, a force on the Baseball Hall of Fame Veterans Committee throughout his lifetime, decided that Hodges was not a Hall of Famer and often talked him down at committee meetings. It was not so much Hodges' lack of Hall of Fame credentials as it was Williams' jealousy of Hodges, who had been a popular Washington manager while Williams had been unpopular [when he managed in Washington]." Russ White, Williams' friend and biographer, insists, "Williams never put down Hodges," but agrees he was primarily interested in getting his own candidates inducted, such as Bobby Doerr, Phil Rizzuto, and other American Leaguers.

Many baseball writers who hadn't covered the Brooklyn Dodgers had little sympathy for the players on that team. Robinson was voted in the year he was first eligible, 1962, but Campanella's career ended in 1957 and he wasn't voted in until 1969; Reese played through 1958 and wasn't selected until 1984; and Snider retired after 1964 and didn't make Cooperstown until 1980. After these four players got in, some voters decided that they couldn't vote in the whole team and made the cutoff. "I voted for Hodges when I was on the Veterans Committee," says Jim Palmer. "I sensed that the reason he didn't get in was that some voters felt that five players from the same team was too much." That two others with Brooklyn Dodgers roots, Koufax in 1972 and Drysdale in 1984, got in made it even harder for Hodges.

While it's true that many of his records have been surpassed, his power numbers still compare favorably to inductees whose careers began after his, including Orlando Cepeda, Tony Perez, and Johnny Bench. His slumps are looked upon derisively, but he still drove in 1,274 runs. Significantly, Hodges' troubles at the plate never affected his fielding. Hall of Fame voters hold back votes from designated hitters, emphasizing how important fielding is, yet with few exceptions they ignore a player's fielding prowess when they cast their ballots. Hodges won countless games with his glove and revolutionized the first-base position.

If the writers and veterans have an excuse for their faulty voting over the years in regard to Hodges, it is that the Los Angeles Dodgers have never retired his number. The Mets did so, but not the organization he belonged to for twenty years. The Dodgers' backward policy, even during the years Walter O'Malley and then his son Peter O'Malley ran the team, was to retire uniform numbers only *after* a player has been voted into Cooperstown. Essentially, they continue to outsource the Hodges vote to younger sportswriters who never saw him play. The Dodgers did break their policy once and retired Jim Gilliam's number. Their choosing Gilliam, who was popular for years as a player and coach in Los Angeles, and not Hodges deserves an explanation that has never been given. Meanwhile Hall of Fame voters have been able to say: *If the Dodgers don't even consider Hodges for their Hall of Fame, there's no reason I should consider him for ours.*

The rules for induction into the Hall of Fame were changed prior to the December 2011 election for the veterans class of 2012. A sixteen-member Veterans Committee voted on ten finalists who played during "The Golden Era," 1947–1972. Hodges appeared to have the best chance for induction because for the first time his playing career and managerial career could be combined. Leading up to the vote, he received much support from former Dodgers teammates and Mets he managed, including Nolan Ryan. On the eve of the vote, Hall of Fame manager Tommy Lasorda, Hodges' teammate in Brooklyn, called Gil Jr. and Joan Hodges and told them he'd made a twenty-minute speech to the other members of the committee on Hodges' behalf and he was certain he would receive the necessary twelve votes for induction. So it was heartbreaking the next day, when it was announced that only Ron Santo had been elected, and that Hodges had managed just nine votes, tying him for third place with Minnie Minoso, behind 283-game winner Jim Kaat. That Santo had been chosen over Hodges and had received fifteen of sixteen votes raised eyebrows.

Unlike Hodges and the former Chicago Cubs teammates and Hall members who pushed for his election—Ernie Banks, Billy Williams, and Ferguson Jenkins—Santo was never considered a Hall of Famer during his career. In fact, he received less than 4 percent of the vote in his first year of eligibility and was temporarily removed from the writers' ballot. But there had been serious politicking among committee members and baseball history was revised to justify the election of the former Cubs third baseman, who had become a popular Cubs broadcaster and fought a gallant fight against diabetes (having both legs amputated) before his death in 2010. His well-known wish to be recognized as a Hall of Famer was granted, albeit posthumously. Santo too was a perennial All-Star and a Gold Glove winner and had career stats that were similar to Hodges'—he, too, finished second in the NL in RBIs over a decade—but his achievements weren't comparable, particularly since he never played on a champion and never made the post-season. So that Hodges, who set all-time league and major league records and won World Series games that led to titles, didn't at very least go into Cooperstown with Santo was incomprehensible.

Joan Hodges still waits for the day her husband will become a Hall of Famer, perhaps in 2014, following the next Golden Era election. "Gil never mentioned the Hall of Fame to me," she says. "He was not that type of person. He would say, 'Honey, please, what difference does it make?'" The difference is that she wants baseball history and Gil Hodges' place in it to be corrected for posterity. She doesn't want her husband to be known for being just another *very good* player when he was far better than that. She witnessed his putting his body and soul into the game and wants his vital contributions to be remembered and appreciated.

When he finally becomes a Hall of Famer, she realizes, countless fans will learn about the man who remains, with Lou Gehrig and Jackie Robinson, baseball's ultimate role model. Then they surely will benefit from discovering the *right way* he played, managed, and lived his life.

ACKNOWLEDGMENTS

We spent two eventful years researching and writing this biography of one of baseball's greatest players and most admirable people, and it surely would have taken twice that time and been half as enjoyable if not for a roster of exceptional individuals who also believe it is time for Gil Hodges to receive his due.

Foremost, we thank Joan Hodges and Gil Hodges Jr., who were with us from the beginning. When reminiscing about her husband, Joan could not have been more gracious, generous, and candid. Their bond is as strong as ever. Gil Jr., who was always available to us and facilitated numerous interviews with family and friends, made us think at times that we were speaking directly to his father. He, too, is a class act.

We were also fortunate to speak to Gil and Joan's daughters, Irene, Cindy, and Barbara, and Joan's brother, Louis Lombardi. It is a special family, indeed.

We have deep gratitude for Ann Hodges, the daughter of Gil's brother, Bob. She was extraordinarily helpful, answering an endless litany of questions and providing wonderful stories. We also thank her brothers, Tony, Mike, and John, who still reside in Indiana. The tremendous pride they have in their father and uncle is tangible.

We could not have done this book without the help of Randy Harris, the popular former mayor of Petersburg, Indiana, and a real baseball fan and writer. He was a marvelous host, and that he was able to get so many special people who knew Gil Hodges in his native state to contribute their memories to this book is a testament to how everyone feels about him. He is a true friend. We also thank Denise, Jayla, and Jenna Harris.

Also providing vital contributions above the call of duty were Gil's longtime teammate and friend Carl Erskine; Tim Nonte; Bonnie Johnson of the Princeton, Indiana, Public Library; Bill Marshall; Susan Sullivan, the director for alumni relations at Oakland City University; and Dan O'Brien. Dan, a sports historian, ex-broadcaster and screenwriter (his colorful subject is Rube Waddell), is a researcher extraordinaire.

We are indebted to Indiana sports historian Pete Cava, who granted access to the "Gil Hodges File, Indiana-Born Major League Baseball Players, Pete Cava Collection, Indianapolis, Indiana." We also must single out transcriber-researcher Elina Mishuris and transcriber Valerie Hanley.

We were grateful to get a rare interview with Roger Kahn, the author most associated with the Brooklyn Dodgers, and to speak with four other New York newspaper legends: George Vecsey (who aided us in numerous ways), Dave Anderson, Phil Pepe, and the late Bill Gallo, the famed illustrator and writer who gave us his last interview. We also pay tribute to Russ White, Dave Kaminer, and Dave Johnson, who all wrote about Hodges and became his friends. Special thanks to authors Robert A. Caro, Lew Paper, Lee Lowenfish, Rob Edelman, and Mort Zachter.

Thank you, Rachel Robinson and Roy Campanella II.

And Larry King and Michael Griffith, one of our first boosters.

Hodges was very proud of his time in the Marines, so we salute contributors Richard Koenig, Riley Marietta, Nick Romagnoli, and Bob Stark.

We were fortunate to speak to players and coaches who knew Hodges during his baseball career as a player and manager: Bob Aspromonte, Jim Beane, Ralph Branca, Rocky Bridges, Doug Camilli, Ed Charles, Roger Craig, Bennie Daniels, Tommy Davis, Chuck Essegian, Jim Hannan, Bill Hardy, Bud Harrelson, Bob Hildebrand, Frank Howard, Randy Jackson, the late Harmon Killebrew, Ralph Kiner, Jerry Koosman, Ed Kranepool, Don Larsen, Don Lock, Turk Lown, Tim McCarver, Ken McMullen, Norman Ozark, Jim Palmer, Joe Pignatano, Ed Roebuck, Norm Sherry, Tom Seaver, Roy Sievers, Frank Staucet, Ron Swoboda, Ron Taylor,

Wayne Terwilliger, Fred Valentine, Preston Ward, Stan Williams, Eddie Yost, and Don Zimmer. Additionally, we drew from conversations conducted for the 1994 book *We Played the Game* with Johnny Antonelli, Ed Bouchee, Ryne Duren, Del Ennis, Spider Jorgensen, Johnny Klippstein, Don Newcombe, Bill Rigney, Andy Seminick, Frank Thomas, Rube Walker, and Gene Woodling.

We are indebted to others whose lives were touched by Gil Hodges, including: Charley Anderson, Bill Bahr, Arthur Beck, the late Midge Hisgen Benjamin, Howard Briscoe, Patty Manhart Culley, Joe Decker, Jonathan Demme, Roger Emmert, Monica Enspermann, Harry Goerlitz, Bill Harris, Bob and Sondra Harris, George Harris, Vance Hays, Randy Hedden, Bud Howe, Donald Ingle, Carolyn Ahlers Joyce, Teri Kennedy, Bob Lochmueller, June King, the late Wayne and Charlotte Malotte, Mary Malotte-Markham, Betty McDonald, Kenneth "Tot" Nelson, Pauline Wilson-Orbin, Tim O'Rourke, Jack Pipes, Martha Pipes, Wyatt Rauch, Arvin Roberson, the late Richard Sharp, "Red" Robert Smith, Norma and the late Bill Thomas, Ralph Thompson, Bill Tislow, Steve Voyles, Rosemary Franklin-Weathers, and Joe Wilson. Thank you for sharing your stories.

Most appreciated were Mark Langill of the Los Angeles Dodgers; Ethan Wilson of the New York Mets; Tim Wiles, Pat Kelly, and Gabriel Schecter of the Baseball Hall of Fame; Dave Kaplan of the Yogi Berra Museum and Learning Center; Mirielle Stephen of the Jackie Robinson Foundation; Bettie Ahlemann of the Princeton, Indiana, Public Library; Sharon Woods, Marty Byrd, and Shirley Behme of the Pike County Library; the staff of the East Hampton Library; the staff of the Brooklyn Public Library; the Petersburg Kiwanis Club; and Jason Rovow of CNN. Thank you, Rob Wilson, Marty Appel, Gary Schueller, Sandra Boynton, Gregg Inkpen, Robert Kramer, and Melissa Lucier.

We wish to express gratitude to Robert L. Rosen and everyone at RLR Associates, Ltd., especially our agent, Scott Gould, who found our book a home. We also thank all the people at that home, NAL/Penguin, especially our stalwart editor, Brent Howard. His assistant, Rosalind Perry, helped with the photo insert and numerous other vital tasks.

Finally we acknowledge family and friends who supported us every step of the way. Tom would like to thank Leslie Reingold, Michael Gambino, Bob Drury, Bob Schaeffer, Lynne Scanlon, and his children, Kathryn and Brendan Clavin. Danny thanks his daughter Zoë Weaver Ohler, son-in-law Gene Ohler, granddaughter Julianna Ohler, brother Gerald Peary, sister-in-law Amy Geller, and especially his wife, Suzanne.

SELECTED BIBLIOGRAPHY

Allen, Maury. *After the Miracle.* New York: Franklin Watts, 1989.

———. *Brooklyn Remembered: The 1955 Days of the Dodgers.* Champaign, Illinois: Sports Publishing L.L.C., 2005.

———. *The Incredible Mets.* New York: Paperback Library, 1969.

Alston, Walter, with Jack Tobin. *A Year at a Time.* Waco, Texas: Word Inc., 1976.

Amoruso, Marino. *Gil Hodges: The Quiet Man.* Middlebury, Vermont: Paul S. Eriksson Publisher, 1991.

Barber, Red and Robert Creamer. *Rhubarb in the Catbird Seat.* Garden City, New York: Doubleday, 1968.

Barthel, Thomas. *Baseball Barnstorming and Exhibition Games 1901–1962.* Jefferson, North Carolina: McFarland & Company, Inc., 2007.

Bavasi, Buzzie, with John Strege. *Off the Record.* Chicago: Contemporary Books, 1987.

Bragan, Bobby, as told to Jeff Guinn. *You Can't Hit the Ball with the Bat on Your Shoulder.* Fort Worth, Texas: The Summit Group, 1992.

Breslin, Jimmy. *Can't Anybody Here Play This Game?* New York: Viking, 1963.

Cairns, Bob. *Pen Men.* New York: St. Martin's Press, 1992.

Campanella, Roy. *It's Good to Be Alive.* Boston: Little, Brown & Company, 1959.

Caro, Robert A. *The Power Broker: Robert Moses and the Fall of New York.* New York: Knopf, 1974.

Cohen, Stanley. *A Magic Summer: The '69 Mets.* Orlando, Florida: Harcourt Brace Jovanovich, Publishers, 1988.

Daley, Arthur. *Kings of the Home Run.* New York: G. P. Putnam's Sons, 1962.

Delsohn, Steve. *True Blue: The Dramatic Story of the Los Angeles Dodgers Told by the Men Who Lived It.* New York: William Morrow, 2001.

Devaney, John. *Gil Hodges: Baseball's Miracle Man.* New York: G. P. Putnam's Sons, 1973.

Drysdale, Don, with Bob Verdi. *Once a Bum, Always a Dodger: My Life in Baseball from Brooklyn to Los Angeles.* New York: St. Martin's Press, 1990.

Duren, Ryne, with Bob Drury. *The Comeback.* Dayton, Ohio: Lorenz Press, 1978.

Duren, Ryne, with Tom Sabellico. *I Can See Clearly Now.* Aventine Press, 2003.

Durocher, Leo, with Ed Linn. *Nice Guys Finish Last.* New York: Simon & Schuster, 1975.

Erskine, Carl. *Tales from the Dodger Dugout.* Champaign, Illinois: Sports Publishing Inc., 2000.

Garvey, Steve. *My Bat Boy Days: Lessons I Learned from the Boys of Summer.* New York: Scribner, 2008.

Golenbock, Peter. *Amazin': The Miraculous History of New York's Most Beloved Baseball Team.* New York: St. Martin's Press, 2002.

——. *Bums: An Oral History of the Brooklyn Dodgers.* New York: Putnam, 1984.

Goodwin, Doris Kearns. *Wait Till Next Year.* New York: Simon & Schuster, 1997.

Gossett, Lou Jr., and Phyllis Karas. *An Actor and a Gentleman.* New York: Wiley & Sons, 2010.

Harrelson, Bud, with Phil Pepe. *Turning Two: My Journey to the Top of the World and Back with the New York Mets.* New York: Thomas Dunne Books, 2012.

Hirsch, James S. *Willie Mays: The Life, the Legend.* New York: Scribner, 2010.

Hodges, Gil, with Frank Slocum. *The Game of Baseball.* New York: Crown Publishers, Inc., 1969.

Honig, Donald, ed. *The Man in the Dugout.* Chicago: Follet Publishing Company, 1977.

——. *The October Heroes: Great World Series Games Remembered by the Men Who Played Them.* New York: Simon & Schuster, 1979.

Kahn, Roger. *Beyond the Boys of Summer.* New York: McGraw-Hill, 2005.

——. *The Boys of Summer.* New York: Harper & Row, 1971.

——. *The Era.* New York: Ticknor & Fields, 1993.

——. *Into My Own: The Remarkable People and Events That Shaped My Life.* New York: Thomas Dunne Books, 2006.

——. *Memories of Summer: When Baseball Was an Art, and Writing About It a Game.* Lincoln, Nebraska: University of Nebraska Press, 2004.

Koufax, Sandy, with Ed Linn. *Koufax.* New York: The Viking Press, Inc., 1966.

Lipsyte, Robert. *SportsWorld.* New York: Quadrangle/The New York Times Book Co., 1975.

Lowenfish, Lee. *Branch Rickey: Baseball's Ferocious Gentleman.* Lincoln, Nebraska: University of Nebraska Press, 2007.

McCarver, Tim, with Jim Moskovitz and Danny Peary, eds. *Tim McCarver's Diamond Gems: Favorite Baseball Stories from the Legends of the Game.* New York: McGraw-Hill, 2008.

Nordell, John Jr. *Brooklyn Dodgers: The Last Great Pennant Drive, 1957.* Archbald, Pennsylvania: Tribute Books, 2007.

Oliphant, Thomas. *Praying for Gil Hodges: A Memoir of the 1955 World Series and One Family's Love of the Brooklyn Dodgers.* New York: Thomas Dunne Books, 2005.

Paper, Lew. *Perfect: Don Larsen's Miraculous World Series Game and the Men Who Made It Happen.* New York: New American Library, 2009.

Peary, Danny, ed. *Cult Baseball Players: The Greats, the Flakes, the Weird, and the Wonderful.* New York: Fireside, 1990.

——, ed. *We Played the Game: 65 Players Remember Baseball's Greatest Era, 1947–1964.* New York: Hyperion, 1994.

Prager, Joshua. *The Echoing Green: The Untold Story of Bobby Thomson, Ralph Branca, and the Shot Heard Round the World.* New York: Pantheon, 2006.

Prince, Carl E. *Brooklyn's Dodgers: The Bums, the Borough, and the Best of Baseball.* New York: Oxford University Press, Inc., 1996.

Robinson, Jackie, as told to Alfred Duckett. *I Never Had It Made.* New York: Putnam Publishing Group, 1972.

Robinson, Rachel, with Lee Daniels. *Jackie Robinson: An Intimate Portrait.* New York: Harry N. Abrams, Inc., 1996.

Rosenthal, Harold, ed. *Baseball Is Their Business.* New York: Random House, Inc., 1952.

Seaver, Tom, with Dick Schaap. *The Perfect Game: Tom Seaver and the Mets.* New York: E. P. Dutton & Company, Inc., 1970.

Shamsky, Art, with Barry Zeman. *The Magnificent Seasons*. New York: Thomas Dunne Books, 2004.

Shapiro, Michael. *The Last Good Season: Brooklyn, the Dodgers, and Their Final Pennant Race Together*. New York: Doubleday, 2003.

Shapiro, Milton J. *The Gil Hodges Story*. New York: Julian Messner, Inc. 1960.

Smith, Red. *Red Smith on Baseball: The Game's Greatest Writer on the Game's Greatest Years*. Chicago: Ivan R. Dee, Publisher, 2000.

Snider, Duke, with Bill Gilbert. *The Duke of Flatbush*. New York: Zebra Books, 1988.

Snyder, John. *Dodgers Journal*. Cincinnati, Ohio: Clerisy Press, 2009.

Thompson, Fresco, with Cy Rice. *Every Diamond Doesn't Sparkle*. New York: David McKay Company, Inc., 1964.

Vecsey, George, *Joy in Mudville*. New York: The McCall Publishing Company, 1970.

Vincent, Fay. *We Would Have Played for Nothing: Baseball Stars of the 1950s and 1960s Talk About the Game They Loved*. New York: Simon & Schuster, 2008.

Williams, Peter, ed. *The Joe Williams Baseball Reader*. Chapel Hill, North Carolina: Algonquin Books of Chapel Hill, 1989.

Zimmer, Don, with Bill Madden. *Zim: A Baseball Life*. Kingston, New York: Total Sports Publishing, 2001.

INDEX

ABOUT THE AUTHORS

❖

Tom Clavin and **Danny Peary** are the national bestselling coauthors of *Roger Maris: Baseball's Reluctant Hero*. Tom has also written or cowritten ten other books and is a former reporter for the *New York Times*. He lives in East Hampton, New York. Danny is a writer/research for *The Tim McCarver Show* and the author of numerous books and articles. He lives in New York City.